THE
WITCH
of
LIME STREET
Séance, Seduction, and
Houdini
in the Spirit World

DAVID JAHER

CROWN PUBLISHERS
NEW YORK

Library of Congress Cataloging-in-Publication Data
Jaher, David.
    The witch of lime street : séance, seduction, and Houdini in the spirit world / David
Jaher. — First Edition.
1. Margery, 1888–1941. 2. Women mediums—United States—Biography.
3. Spiritualists—United States—Biography. 4. Spiritualism—United States—History—
20th century. 5. Houdini, Harry, 1874–1926. 6. Doyle, Arthur Conan, 1859–1930. I. Title.
    BF1283.C85J34 2015
    133.9'1092—dc23
    [B]   2105009392

ISBN 978-0-307-45106-4
eBook ISBN 978-0-307-45108-8

PRINTED IN THE UNITED STATES OF AMERICA

Jacket design by Elena Giavaldi
Jacket photographs: (Harry Houdini) *Corbis;* (Mina Stinson) *Mary Evans
Picture Library/Everett Collection*

10 9 8 7 6 5 4 3 2 1

First Edition

For my grandmother,

Henrietta Jaher,

and the memory of her son, my father,

Frederic Cople Jaher

Contents

Magick . . . is the most perfect and chief science.

—MARCUS AGRIPPA

Part I

THE DEAD BOYS

⁜

Behold, a ram caught in a thicket by its horns;
Offer the Ram of Pride instead of him.
But the old man would not so, but slew his son.
And half the seed of Europe, one by one.

—WILFRED OWEN

The Borderland

A woman in a black velvet coat pushed through the revolving doors of the Grosvenor Hotel and, waving a miniature Union Jack in each hand, waltzed slowly around the marble hall. The gentlemen loitering there watched her dance past the sitting room that had been as subdued as a séance circle moments before. Almost as one they put aside their newspapers and rose from their armchairs. Such a spectacle at eleven in the morning—in the staid Grosvenor of all places—could only mean one thing: *the boys had done it at last!* Sir Arthur Conan Doyle was among the first to cheer. For four years the famous detective writer had displayed unwavering support for the Cause. He felt strongly that the War was worth the grievous cost.

Like many parents throughout the country, Sir Arthur's thoughts turned at once to his son. Here was the sort of boy to whom the nation owed its gratitude! Capt. Kingsley Doyle of the First Hampshires had fought with distinction at Arras and been wounded at the Somme. To his father's relief, he had recently been transferred to London. Sir Arthur had seen him less than a fortnight previous, "looking his brave steadfast self." Now, for all of them, the long struggle was over. A raucous cheer was heard from the street. The woman in black departed without saying a word. Following her lead, Sir Arthur rushed out to witness the great celebration of November 11, 1918.

He didn't know how so many flags could immediately appear, but they seemed to be waving from every window along Buckingham Palace Road. An old fellow was shaking a rattle as though it were New Year's Eve. Motors were tooting. The maroons were crashing. It sounded like all of London was banging away. Jostled by a rush out of Victoria, Sir Arthur lost his bowler. Picking up another man's hat, he joined the march to the palace. Toward the Mall boisterous soldiers converged with munitions girls in overalls. A young girl, hoisted onto the top of an omnibus, led a crowd in singing "Tipperary." But then something spoiled the moment for Doyle. A motorcar pulled up with officers in staff uniforms and a "hard-faced" civilian. The man in plainclothes wrenched open a bottle and crudely poured whiskey into his mouth. Sir Arthur half hoped the crowd would lynch him. The British Empire had lost a million men. He felt no need to mourn them—mourning was, so to speak, against his religion. The Armistice was for him a day of communion and prayer.

When Sir Arthur reached the palace, he didn't attempt to penetrate the cheering throng in the courtyard. Taller than most, he could see the balcony over the main entrance festooned with scarlet and gold. It had started to drizzle. A crowd of soldiers chanted, "We want King George!" Moments later he heard a single mighty cheer. The King in his naval uniform and the Queen in a fur coat emerged from a window and stood on the balcony waving to the crowd. A sudden hush took hold as the Guards presented arms. Officers stood at attention. Men removed their hats. The band struck up and twenty thousand voices began to sing. Sir Arthur had never heard a more rousing rendition of "God Save the King."

◆

Four years earlier, under a bright August sky, Londoners then too sang the hymn and called for their Regent. War had just been declared and Sir Arthur had rushed to enlist. Despite being fifty-five at that time, he was a man with prodigious energy and verve. He still played a respectable game of cricket, broke a hundred at billiards, skied the Alpine passes, raced motorcars, and was a crack shot with both a Lee Enfield and sidearm. Respectfully, the War Board turned him down. He resigned himself to training the old chaps in the Home Guard. Few civilians, however, were as informed of the Great War's progress as he—officially a mere deputy lieutenant in the Civilian Reserve of Surrey—for Sir Arthur had performed special service for the Crown. Asked in 1914 to lend his influential pen to the war effort, he wrote an effective piece of recruitment propaganda: *To Arms!* The call of duty had also inspired him to undertake an epic account of the War—*The*

British Campaign in France and Flanders—for which the generals supplied
the material. It was the younger men in his family who did the fighting. *To
Arms!* he had urged, and to the trenches they'd gone.

♦

From the beginning it had been a ghostly war. Something otherworldly
had reportedly appeared in the sky over Mons, Belgium—where in their
first action the British Expeditionary Force was overwhelmed by the Huns.
Clouds in the shapes of celestial warriors were rumored to have protected
the small army in their retreat. Firsthand witnesses to the vision seemed
as elusive as the shades. Still, it became widely accepted in England that a
miracle had occurred. Sir Arthur was not so sure. The German waves had
met the best riflemen in Europe firing fifteen rounds a minute. Had the
British really needed ghost archers from Agincourt to save them that day in
Flanders? The battle had affected Sir Arthur in a more personal way. His
brother-in-law Malcolm Leckie had served valiantly as a medical officer at
Mons, and had died there.

When a soldier died at the front, the Tommies would say that he'd
"gone west." Sir Arthur was fond of that expression; it suggested to him
that the boy had taken a distant journey but was not lost to his comrades
and family. He might in fact still be reached via some unusual mode of
long-distance communication—such as trance mediumship or automatic
writing. As it happened, there was an eccentric young woman in his home
at Crowborough in East Sussex who believed that she was a channel to the
borderland where the dead and living might mingle.

This clairvoyant—his wife Jean's best friend, Lily Loder-Symonds—
had originally been taken in by the Doyles as a nanny. Unfortunately, she
soon developed a chest ailment and began forsaking her worldly duties.
When three of her brothers were killed at the Battle of Ypres, her condition worsened. On warm days Sir Arthur often read to her in the garden,
where one could hear the dull thunder of the great guns across the Channel. Later, in the evenings, in a room fragrant with flowers and medicine,
Lily might take up a pen and practice spirit communication. One night

Malcolm Leckie's spirit supposedly possessed Lily's hand and came through in words Arthur and Jean recognized as his own. This was how the Doyles came to believe that the dead could be reached.

Generally, Kingsley did not question Sir Arthur's views. Deferential and eager to please, he had studied medicine in accordance with his father's wishes, and when the war broke out he abandoned those studies at his behest. Religion was the only subject on which they disagreed. Kingsley was devoutly Christian like his deceased mother, Sir Arthur's first wife, and viewed Spiritualism as an occult faith. The growing sect had only a single tenet as far as Kingsley understood it—belief in survival beyond the grave—and only one established ritual: the séance. The worship of ghosts, as Kingsley saw it, was blasphemous and absurd. It dismayed him to see his father attempting to communicate with the spirits of dead soldiers and publicly encouraging the macabre practice. But he had no idea how large a role he himself would play in stoking his father's controversial faith.

When the Foreign Office had approached Sir Arthur in the summer of 1916 to observe and report on the fighting, he eagerly agreed. For a gentleman with a military assignment this first involved the traditional visit to Savile Row. "Feeling a mighty impostor," he was outfitted for the front in a "wondrous khaki garb" his tailor threw together. A caricature, in his mind, of an officer, he watched as silver flowers instead of pips were attached to his epaulettes. Before setting off for Europe he had pinned to his breast medals he had received sixteen years earlier as a field doctor in the Boer War. Yet Sir Arthur, rugged and adaptive, was to be no mere parade warrior at the front. Accepted without ceremony, he soon found himself gripping a gas mask and crouched in a forward observation trench. Men leaned beneath the parapets smoking and watching him curiously. "Holmes," one Tommy explained to another. A gaunt corporal sat on the fire-step tending a wound to his leg. Spectral faces peered out from the dugouts and mineshafts. A shell hissed overhead. Sir Arthur saw the red flash by the German line as the earth shuddered. In front of him was No-Man's-Land—a misty stretch of craters, tree stumps, rusty wire, and rotting dead, which he smelled but could not see. This was the borderland. For him, "the most wonderful spot in the world."

Two days later, Sir Arthur had the chance to see Kingsley at Mailly. The

boy had greeted him with his usual "jolly grin" and spoke of the preparations for a grand offensive in France. "Don't worry about me, Daddy," he
had said, and then went off to fight at the Somme—where 20,000 British
troops died on the first day. Something shifted for Sir Arthur after his
son was almost killed there. Back in England, where Kingsley spent two
months recuperating from shrapnel wounds to his neck, Sir Arthur began
to advocate the spiritist balm—the séance—for those whose sons hadn't
survived. Lily had succumbed to influenza by then, however, and the spirits
were temporarily silent at Crowborough.

Now it was Sir Arthur who spoke. Throughout the grieving country he
gave emphatic lectures on the "miracles" Lily had produced. No one could
doubt his own sacrifices. At a time when the life expectancy for a fighting
officer was two or three months, the roll call for soldiers from Sir Arthur's
family was answered for the most part in the next world. His sister Con-
nie's son, Second Lt. Oscar Hornung of the Essex Regiment—a simple and
religious boy—had been killed by a bomb. Another sister, Lottie, lost her
husband, Maj. Leslie Oldham of the Royal Engineers, to a sniper his first
days in the trenches. A nephew of Jean's had fallen, and so on and so on.
Through Lily, Sir Arthur had heard from all of these dead boys. He published a popular book describing his odyssey into the spirit world, *The New
Revelation.* His message to the bereaved was simple and direct: their sons
were not lost! He claimed in a letter to his mother that he no longer worried that Kingsley might fall. "I do not fear death for the boy," he said, "for
since I became a convinced Spiritualist death became rather an unnecessary thing, but I fear pain or mutilation very greatly." When Kingsley, who
had recovered from his injuries and been sent once more to the front, was
recalled to resume his medical training, that fear too was assuaged.

So it was that two weeks before the Armistice Sir Arthur was preparing to give a speech on "Death and the Hereafter" in Nottingham. By this
point all was satisfactory on both fronts: his spiritist message was spreading and the Hindenburg Line smashed. Before his talk, a telegram arrived
that he anticipated would contain more glorious news on the final push. It
was no longer a time in the War when he feared the unexpected dispatch;
Kingsley was no longer in France going over the top. But upon opening the
message, sent by his daughter Mary in London, Sir Arthur could not have

been more startled. And if, as he claimed, we are all encompassed by a band of etheric light, then his must have darkened as never before. His first coherent thought was to cancel the lecture, but he decided against it. Instead he rushed to London and the next day, at the Grosvenor, wrote the following to his mother: "I saw [Kingsley] today, looking his brave steadfast self, in the mortuary. He will be buried on Friday at Hindhead. No flowers."

As for the talk, it had not been a difficult decision to carry on. He was shaken, of course, but how would it look if he had canceled? That his faith had not transformed him as he had claimed. He would have felt as counterfeit as when he was dressed as a martial dignitary for the front. Nevertheless, that night was hard for him. Twice at the lectern he faltered. When he read aloud the message Mary had sent, there was a horrified gasp from the crowd. They had come for a salutary speech, and were not expecting such devastating news. "Not to worry," he promptly replied. For a moment he seemed to withdraw deeply inside himself and then sought out the first pair of crestfallen eyes he could lock on to. "Not to worry," he repeated. "My son survives!"

Occult Fever

Since the Great War, the peoples of the world have turned with a
quickened interest and an almost insatiable curiosity to the unsolved
problem of the ages—after Death, what?
—*Baltimore Sun,* AUGUST 24, 1919

*K*ingsley had been killed by a bug, not a bullet. Shortly after the Armistice, the Spanish influenza virus also felled Sir Arthur's only brother, Brig. Gen. Innes Doyle. An apocalyptic war had led to a medieval plague, which took more lives than the fighting that had already devastated a generation in England, France, and Germany. The world appeared to be teetering on the brink of a new dark age. Yet, like many in his movement, Sir Arthur saw the calamity as an opportunity for spiritual renewal. The unprecedented losses would turn the bereaved away from decrepit religions, he hoped, and toward spirit communion.

"All the world is asking, Where are our dead boys?" he observed. During this time of scientific breakthroughs and growing secularization his Spiritualist testament, *The New Revelation,* addressed the pressing question: What is the outcome of death? The answers from both science and religion were "unsatisfactory." The revolutionary work of Rutherford and Bohr, though few understood it, appeared to suggest a soulless return to our atomic source. As for the Church, it seemed to Doyle to offer no practical insight regarding the mystery. He considered the Bible a ceremonial relic—like the cavalry sword Kingsley had carried into a conflict that would be fought with machine guns and airplanes.

"A downright conflict between the old religion and the new" was reported in England. A reverend complained that "Sir Arthur Conan Doyle is moving from city to city ministering to a popular craze. I challenge Sir Arthur to deny that Spiritualism is perilous to the mental, moral and physical health. Every second or third young lady one meets now imagines herself a modern St. Teresa!" Such zealous resistance only spurred Doyle's campaign. Like a military commander, he kept a map of England and marked with pins those places where he had spoken of the New Revelation. "We must attack in the same bulldog spirit with which Foch faced the German lines," he wrote his friend Sir Oliver Lodge.

In Lodge he had a formidable ally. One of England's most honored scientists, Sir Oliver had spent a lifetime attempting to harness invisible forces. He had sent radio signals before Marconi; helped perfect X-ray tubes; done groundbreaking work on the discharge of electricity. And for some thirty years he had been experimenting with psychic phenomena. Where were the dead boys? Sir Oliver believed he had some insight into the answer. It had caused a great stir during the War when he claimed to be in touch with the spirit of his dead son, Raymond, who had fallen in Flanders. Lodge wrote a book chronicling their communications and explaining the science behind it. *Raymond* went through twelve printings in three years and was hugely popular at the front and at home in England. It was Sir Oliver who had incited the first wartime wave of Spiritualism. "The British soldier has certainly got religion," bemoaned one chaplain; "I am not so sure, however, that he has got Christianity."

While Doyle spoke to the heart, Lodge appealed more to reason. He was the president of the most respected group of ghost hunters in the world, the British Society for Psychical Research. During the Mons craze these investigators showed skepticism—their finding regarding the supposed miracle of the ghost archers was "negative." Sir Oliver Lodge was known in America, however, for some remarkable descriptions of the spirit world that Raymond had purportedly provided from beyond the grave. The boy told his father that he lived in a place known as Summerland. There were laboratories there that produced, not material things but "essences, ethers, and gases." All earthly things could be duplicated. It seemed there was even a celestial strain of whiskey available. And astral cigars. Raymond had seen a discarnate man smoke one.

Other eminent scientists, who weren't Spiritualists, were also linking hands in the séance. In France, Charles Richet, a Nobel laureate in physiology, experimented with the matter from which ghostly apparitions were said to form. He called the stuff *ectoplasm:* an ethereal yet viscous substance that entranced mediums secreted from their orifices. Germany too was "gripped by an occult fever." It was there that Baron von Schrenck-Notzing, a neurologist, was conducting tests involving intimate scrutiny of Richet's prized subject, the famed medium Eva C, who was thought to issue ectoplasm, the "miracle fluid," from between her legs. In the meanwhile, Lodge, a devout physicist, was focused more on interdimensional experiments than a medium's anatomy. If some quality of the human mind could be proven to transcend space and time, then it might, many psychic researchers felt, transcend death. Doyle maintained that Spiritualism was the only religion validated by science. And he, the movement's de facto leader, believed the battle for mainstream acceptance would be won or lost in America. To America! he urged; and there Sir Oliver went to make his uncanny claims.

Madame Ouija

The Lecture tour of Sir Oliver Lodge in this country has undoubtedly
aroused a new and large interest, not only in the question of
immortality and survival of consciousness after death, but also
in the more specific question as to whether it is really possible
to communicate, or receive communications
from the known dead.
—*Boston Globe*, JANUARY 25, 1920

Sir Oliver arrived in New York in January 1920—as if to inaugurate the
decade of the saxophone and spirit trumpet. At the time, the country was
mad for the Ouija board, a crass version of the séance. If you had a question
for the dead, the board would offer something! Songs were written about
Madame Ouija. Moving pictures were made. Norman Rockwell painted a
young couple experimenting with the Ouija for the cover of the *Saturday
Evening Post*. Soon some of the most acclaimed American writers—Upton
Sinclair, Hamlin Garland, and Theodore Dreiser—were caught in the psychic maze.

At Dreiser's Greenwich Village apartment, the author of *An American
Tragedy* and the arch-skeptic H. L. Mencken tried the Ouija together. Dreiser, the pioneering realist, was nevertheless an ardent believer in all things
supernatural. He was sure that the spirits of his three dead siblings had
guided him since childhood. He sat regularly with palm readers, crystal-
gazers, and spirit mediums. Mencken, by contrast, disdained the occult.
He particularly derided spiritism as the stuff of dingy back parlors. The
pursuit of immortality bored him. Mencken could imagine living happily
for a century or two—but ten million years would be dreadful, he complained. All that night, at Dreiser's place, he scoffed at Sir Oliver's notion
of the hereafter. As a rule he never trusted physicists. They spent too much
time gazing into space, he said, and were far too eager to solve mysteries.

The Greenwich Village Ouija experiment was a farce for Mencken. He kept pushing the planchette to spell out his favorite obscenities.

Soon after Sir Oliver disembarked in New York for his lecture tour, a new play called *Smilin' Through* opened on Broadway. The *Times* called it "a fair-to-middling spiritualistic fantasy." But it was the smash of the season. "Such wonderful things are happening in the world now that you can't shut your eyes to them, can you?" the star of the show, Jane Cowl, gushed. "And when men like Sir Oliver Lodge and Conan Doyle declare that something is true you must at least pay some attention to it."

Sir Oliver himself disliked the theater. It was a new kind of science he preached; he had no miracles to deliver. Intrigued by his work, even a skeptical Thomas Edison joined the quest to establish proof of survival. Edison, no friend to the Spiritualists, would announce work on a mechanism to register the messages of those who had crossed over. "I can make an apparatus better than ouija for talking with the dead—if they want to talk," Edison claimed. "He knows that many will quarrel with him, many will misunderstand him," the *Times* reported. "But he knows too, that ten million men and women who have lost dear ones in the war are hungering for word or knowledge as to the existence of life after the life we know."

The two most inventive minds of their respective nations, Edison and Lodge, were both now working on some means to contact the departed. Marvels like the telephone and wireless made access to any plane or across any distance seem possible. There was a sense in the New World of a new frontier opening.

The Ether of Space

Such was the buzz surrounding Lodge's American tour that a distinguished surgeon felt compelled to attend *Evidence for Survival* at Boston's Symphony Hall and indulge superstition one frigid January evening. Sir Oliver Lodge was the inventor of the coherer, a kind of radio detector that could receive electric waves. And fittingly, the doctor had never seen Symphony Hall so densely packed and charged with energy. Spectators were even seated onstage, right next to the podium. "It was a wonderful audience," reported the *Globe*, "composed largely of the intellectuals of Boston, with probably a few more women than men."

It was mentioned in the program that Sir Oliver Lodge had twelve children. One of them had famously died in the war. That loss had inspired him to make his first trip across the pond to speak in more than fifty North American cites. Because the doctor recoiled from anything pious, he was comforted in knowing that the clergy had spoken against Lodge's tour. Priests warned that Christians were not permitted to seek knowledge from the dead. A prominent rabbi had called mediumship and the Ouija as nefarious an addiction as drugs. Both skeptical and curious, the doctor wondered if Sir Oliver might hold a public séance that very evening and summon before the stage lights that burning cross—the ghost of his son Raymond!

The doctor's expectations were quickly dispelled. Sir Oliver had an august presence as he strode onto the platform. The Englishman had a massive domed head and a well-coiffed white beard. At six feet four inches, he towered over his listeners, appearing as stalwart as a Connecticut farmer. "He looks as Lincoln might have looked—had he lived," wrote the *Globe* reporter. Sir Oliver began by saying that he could remember when the telephone was roundly jeered. Years earlier he had seen one of the first English demonstrations of Mr. Bell's invention. The London crowd had dismissed it as a magician's hoax. Sir Oliver asked the Boston audience to maintain a more open mind. For science, he declared, "has brought us close to the mystery of life."

Lodge then spoke of the atom. An ounce of atomic matter had the force, he asserted, to raise the German fleet sunk at Scapa Flow and deposit it atop the mountains of Scotland. When the crowd murmured its disbelief, he assured them that few scientists would disagree with his statement. Was the possibility of spirit contact so much more outrageous? He prophesied a day when homes would be powered by atomic energy and each family would speak daily to loved ones in the other world.

He mentioned nothing that night about séances with his dead son but instead compared the human body to a kind of telegraph. Mind could act on mind; this he called telepathy. He and his colleagues at the Society for Psychical Research had studied the phenomenon for decades. He said that some psychics were able to communicate with discarnate minds. Such transmissions came through the Ether of Space: the supreme field that he knew to exist. We all have "etheric bodies," he explained, which psychics see as bands of variegated light. When a soldier was cut down, he abandoned his physical body—like a shriveled cocoon—for his "perfect and permanent form." Some called it the soul. But since we cannot dissect the soul—and here the surgeon felt that Lodge was speaking directly to him—we deny its existence. "Do not be afraid of death," Lodge urged. "Death" was a barbarous word! It meant extinction. He preferred to see death as emigration. The boys going west.

After the presentation, Lodge met the doctor, who was handsome in a blue-blooded way—five foot eight, slightly stooped, and slender—naturally curious and well mannered. He told Sir Oliver that his fascinating oration had given at least one naysayer deep pause for thought. Could Lodge recommend how one might pursue further inquiry? It must be said that Sir Oliver had little respect for the intellectual depth of most Americans, but the doctor asked reasonably good questions. He was direct yet deferential. Cards were exchanged. He was Dr. Le Roi Goddard Crandon, who lived in Beacon Hill with his wife, Mina, who had not attended the lecture.

Remembering that evening, Dr. Crandon later said, "I couldn't understand it. It did not fit into any pattern I had previously known about scientists. So I asked to meet him after his lectures. We talked for some time that first night."

"Sir Oliver Lodge has put the whole question of spiritism and survival after death in a somewhat new light—a light that appeals to many intellectual people," the *Globe* reported. The inventor of the electric ignition had sparked interest in spirit contact in the naturally skeptical city of Boston. However, Dr. Crandon had not found the Ether of Space to be such an eccentric theory. Einstein had once entertained it. And so, he had much to consider during his cab ride to Lime Street.

Waiting for the Sunrise

*I*n September of 1918, Dr. Crandon had married a lovely and spirited bride—he in his white naval uniform with black epaulettes; she in an ivory satin gown with organdy bows on her shoulders. The minister, linking their matrimony to the coming peace, spoke of renewal. Very few attended the simple bayside service near New London, Connecticut. The War was still on, and the newlyweds had both been previously married. For their honeymoon the doctor took his bride to the same resort in the Bahamas where he had taken the previous two Mrs. Crandons. Unfortunately, the couple returned from their jaunt just as New England was erupting in fever. As a lieutenant commander at the New London Naval Hospital, Dr. Crandon was in the very eye of the pandemic. Where were the dead boys? He had seen them stacked in the morgue ceiling high. For reasons no one understood, the illness afflicted young men and women. Thousands a week were dying in American cities. Many of Dr. Crandon's patients drowned in their own blood and mucus. His attempts to provide them with liquid oxygen were futile. New London soon ran out of coffins.

Mina Crandon raised her husband's spirits during those traumatic first months of their marriage. Friends said she lightened his "lonely at the top" disposition. So effectively did the doctor command that he was slated to take charge of Wards Island in New York—one of the largest naval hospitals in the country. As it happened, by 1919, the emergency had ended and Dr. Crandon was discharged with honors. He was then forty-six and married to a woman still in her twenties, and there was no denying the aphrodisiacal effect of a mortal crisis, or that his position must have appealed to Mrs. Crandon. The doctor owned two fine schooners and an elegant home in Beacon Hill. He had three degrees from Harvard, including his MD and a graduate diploma in philosophy. His work ethic was extraordinary. Earlier in his career he had endured twelve-hour shifts at Boston City Hospital, then read the deep thinkers well into the morning. He became instructor of surgery at Harvard, and in that position made extensive use of cadavers. He liked to point this out to strangers at parties, for some reason. Mrs. Crandon was an animated contrast to her wry husband. In Boston society they were a much talked-about couple, known for throwing splendid cocktail parties at their home in Beacon Hill.

There were gatherings with endless rounds of martinis and "The World Is Waiting for the Sunrise" playing on the Victrola. Guests nattered on about the possibility of speakeasies on the Hill and Prohibition agents raiding their homes. They would all be lawbreakers soon, they vowed. Once, when the discussion turned from the Red Scare—the recent citywide police strike—to spooks, someone had suggested a Ouija party. But dancing and charades were Mina's preferred entertainment. A fetching blonde, she had a youthful figure and, it was often remarked, sparkling blue eyes. Yet she did not seem vain, like the doctor's second wife, or callow. She had seen something of life and had brought a young son to Beacon Hill from her previous marriage. She was also a practicing Christian, Roy told his secular Harvard friends, and played the cello with the Union Congregational Church Orchestra. He had once gone to see her perform there. She was in a white cotton dress and had an Egyptian band on her bob that made her look half priestess, half flapper. He wore his tweeds—the lone unbeliever in the church, he assumed—watching her play like some jazz sister in rapture. Dr. Crandon thought then of the new beginning the minister at their wedding had promised. Where was his sunrise?

Surprisingly, his outlook would change through the influence of a Spiritualist. Sir Oliver Lodge had presented as pioneering research what Dr. Crandon had always associated with superstitions of the horse-and-buggy days: that old black magic. "We met again," the doctor said of their encounter. "We became friends. Sir Oliver suggested some reading for me, and I began, feeling somewhat foolish, but certainly intrigued."

Dr. Crandon soon realized that the séance was the one place where science and the pursuit of a hereafter merged. Darwin had solved the mystery of the origin of man, but what of his postmortem fate? The answer might be revolutionary, for biology and classical physics would become as outmoded as orthodox religion if Lodge were right about Spiritualism and the Ether of Space.

Thus, as the 1920s started, a new horizon beckoned to Dr. Crandon. This had as much to do with his family life as the Spiritualist revival. One of the preeminent surgeons in Boston, Dr. Crandon was a gynecologist and obstetrician. He knew that he would not be delivering his own baby—as he was no longer able to reproduce—so the Crandons decided to take in an orphan. Roy's father, who had been president of the Ethical Society of Boston, encouraged such humanitarian impulses. But oddly—as if Roy thought forsaken children were more an English tradition—the child he desired was searched for and found through intermediaries in London.

Roy had always wanted a son; if his name were to die, that was no kind of immortality. To his consternation, though, the London orphan did not adjust to his new home in Beacon Hill. Both the new child and Mina's son called their patriarch Dr. Crandon rather than Father. Whatever issues developed in their home beyond that is a matter of privacy.

But we do hear about these boys through the Boston newspapers in the summer of 1921. They had been playing off Point Shirley on a raft that tore loose from its mooring. Caught in a current, they were carried toward dangerous waters. Hundreds watched while two strong swimmers rescued them. The newspapers identified the distressed children as "two small boys, six and eight years respectively." The younger child was John, Mrs. Crandon's son. The older was the English boy who remains nameless and unknown; saved from the sea but lost in the ether.

Part II

THE RIVER OF DOUBT

⁂

There is an underworld—a world of cheat and crime—a world whose highest good is successful evasion of the laws of the land. You who live your life in placid respectability know but little of the real life of the denizens of this world . . . you know but little.
—HARRY HOUDINI, *The Right Way to Do Wrong*

Sir Arthur Conan Doyle and Harry Houdini, London, 1920

The Wand of Youth

*T*he first stop for the magician was the cemetery. Upon returning to New York from one of his movie productions or magic tours, it was his ritual to visit the Queens grave site of Cecilia Weiss. At the height of his fame he told a movie magazine that his greatest ambition was to prove himself worthy of the mother who raised him. The umbilical was the one bond he had never slipped in his career as an escape artist. Even when touring abroad, as long as Cecilia lived he would try to return home for her birthday. When anxious he would rest his head on her chest—just like when she calmed him as a child. He had always wanted to be the center of his mother's life, but this was rarely possible growing up. She had six other needy children vying for her affections and a defeated husband whom she cherished. Her third son, Ehrich, hoped to do something extraordinary to win her attention. When he grew up to jump from bridges, his mother was his imagined audience.

Before winning acclaim as an escape artist, he had been a trickster on the dingy circuit—a medicine-show mountebank, even a fraud medium. Yet when it came to judging right from wrong he had a venerable model in his father. Rabbi Mayer Samuel Weiss had always abided by the strictures of the Talmud and had also earned a law degree in Budapest to bolster his authority. Many evenings he recited moral fables to his sons and daughter. But despite his scholarly air, he was in worldly ways a failure. There was no magic in Mayer Samuel's life except for his young and devoted second wife, Cecilia. His efforts lacked the relentless drive that would become their third son's trademark.

In 1878, four years after Ehrich's birth, Mayer Samuel found a rabbinical position in the town of Appleton, Wisconsin, and brought his family from Hungary to join him in the New Wilderness. In the magician's memory, his parents sit together under pine trees in an Appleton park, drinking coffee, speaking intimately—a moment of connubial bliss during an unusually stable period for the family. It was not that life was easy in Appleton; Mayer Samuel earned a mere $750 yearly as a rabbi—barely enough for the frugal Weisses to scrape by. In light of all that followed, though, Ehrich idealized an early childhood that included surrey rides, winter sledding, and steamer excursions on the Fox River. Most exciting of all was when the traveling circuses—Barnum's and Forepaugh's—pitched their tents outside of town. Sneaking under canvases, the boy encountered firewalkers, Arabian jugglers, and magicians—with names like "Peerless Mysteriarch of Three Continents" or "The Wonder Working Wizard of the World"—who claimed to be from mysterious places like Venice, Persia, and Hindustan. No itinerant trickster ever claimed wholesome roots, but Ehrich Weiss would one day declare himself a clergyman's son, a boy brought up with small-town values. Nevertheless, he owed his inspiration to diabolists like the Englishman Dr. Lynn, who dismembered his patients onstage with a surgeon's saw then magically reassembled them.

There was greater magic beyond the circus canvas. Appleton was where the world's first hydroelectric plant went into operation. Mysterious forces were harnessed in its operation. And this was somehow related to the work of Thomas Edison, the Wizard of Menlo Park, who lit homes in New York City without a gas lamp or a candle. But unfortunately for the Weisses, Mayer Samuel could not keep up with the march of progress. The Jewish community soon dismissed him as rabbi of the Zion Congregation. His inability to adapt, to learn a new language, had cost him his position. He was fifty-four and had no other opportunities in Wisconsin. A dark period for the family began. Relocating to Milwaukee, they lived off Jewish charity—often switching residences to elude persistent creditors. Of this time Ehrich later recalled, "the less said the better."

His parents sent him back to Appleton to apprentice as a locksmith—invaluable training for a future escape artist. By the age of twelve, however, he already felt confined. His father's hopes dashed, Ehrich decided that it was only through finding work in a traveling circus—he'd once performed rudimentary rope tricks as "Prince of the Air"—that he could earn enough to help the family. With confidence in his repertoire of street-fair magic, he hopped a side-door Pullman bound for Kansas.

◆

The magician rarely spoke publicly of his trek across the Midwest as a child—the locomotive whistle would never be his siren. But traveling many years later in the comfort of a parlor car he would remember the exhilaration of the boxcar hop and feel again the bite of steam and cinder. By the 1920s he would practically require a circus train to convey his ensemble and magic apparatus. And it would give him satisfaction to know that he, a former freight tramp, could now command a Pullman.

For over a year after running away, Ehrich Weiss sought a magical fix for his family's troubles. Hoping to become his mother's provider, he sent her little more than postcards from places like Kansas City and Hannibal. In his recollections, he hooks on with a circus but more likely survived as a street performer, beggar, and shiner. He then tramped back to the place where his family had originally arrived in the United States—in 1887 he returned to New York City and reunited with his father.

Having failed to hold a congregation in Wisconsin, Mayer Samuel was shopping his rabbinical skills in the ghetto. One year later, Ehrich's income as a messenger and newsboy, combined with his father's as a Hebrew tutor, was enough to send for the rest of the family. Cecilia and Ehrich's siblings joined them in a tenement on East Seventy-fifth Street that shook with the passage of the Third Avenue El train. Nothing could be further from pastoral Appleton. There were fewer buildings, though, on the West Side of Central Park and farther north were shrub and swampland. Through this morass Ehrich Weiss ran ten miles regularly. He would set a record for racing the loop around Central Park. Running and athletics were his escape from the indignities of ghetto poverty. He developed into a powerful swimmer, practiced gymnastics and acrobatics, and went to the finals of a city boxing championship before illness forced him to bow out.

At the end of the day, however, as when it started, Ehrich Weiss was now just another Jewish garment worker. And so, it turned out, was Mayer Samuel, who worked for the same Broadway necktie cutter as his son. To the disgrace of the son his learned father had become a sweatshop sheeny. While manning sewing machines in an airless hovel, Mayer Samuel's health began to fail. The greenhorn, never able to learn English, was stricken with cancer of the tongue. Following an operation to remove the tumor, he died of shock, according to the doctors. Ehrich would recall that after the failed surgery at Presbyterian Hospital, as he tried to console his weeping mother, she replied, to his surprise, that if he'd had paradise for twenty-eight years he too would cry. Paradise he could not provide her, but he was determined to give her those material things his father had failed to. As soon as he became a vaudeville star.

It was after his father's death that Ehrich put away his running togs and applied himself as never before to magic. He developed with his brother Dash an escape called Metamorphosis, in which the magicians—one bound in a trunk, the other standing next to it—exchange places and outfits almost instantaneously. Those who saw the brothers perform the trick in the beer halls knew it was only an illusion—a curtain was quickly drawn and opened at the moment of the changeover—but *mein Gott,* those boys could move like lightning!

For Ehrich, the greater transformation was when he became Harry Houdini; the new moniker a tribute to his hero, the French illusionist Jean Eugéne Robert-Houdin—the forefather of modern magic. At that time Houdini began playing the dime-museum circuit. Within, patrons could find a chamber of horrors and waxworks of villains like John Booth cocking his derringer or Marat bleeding to death in his *baignoire.* Indecent contests were held—of the kind where fat ladies raced one another or Amazon Queens wrestled male volunteers. Some of these establishments also housed displays of grotesque medical specimens, and all had live performances in the curio hall. Houdini first presented his handcuff act there, but he was merely a sideshow performer.

It was the freaks these crowds had come for.

They came to see Unthan the Armless Wonder Man use his toes to play a violin or shoot an arrow at the ceiling. And they came for Mrs. Mattie Lee Price, the Electric Girl with spiritistic powers. Houdini had watched other occult acts like Mattie's, but she was the best of them. The waifish girl held a billiard cue extended while a trio of male volunteers failed to force it downward. She tapped a table with a walking stick and suddenly it rose on two legs and gyrated. With only the pressure of her hand, she caused a cane chair to move across the room while a heavy man was occupying it. Above all they came to see the beautiful Cuban Evatima Tardo entice a rattlesnake to flare up and sink its fangs into her milky arms and shoulders. Even Houdini was shaken when, after Evatima wrenched the serpent from her arm, a physician injected its poison into a rabbit, which instantly went into convulsions and died "in great agony"—grisly proof that the snake queen was no faker.

While Houdini never found a magician to mentor him, he acquired many tricks from these freaks to add to his arsenal. From Unthan he learned to use his toes like fingers; by observing the Electric Girl he grasped the rules of force and leverage; and the sword swallowers taught him to use his throat to conceal—and regurgitate as required—keys, lockpicks, and larger articles.

But it was Evatima whom he most admired, for she had this impenetrable aura. It was said that she could stop her heart from beating and control her circulation. She claimed to be immune to the germs of fatal diseases and oblivious to any kind of pain. To the astonishment of a committee of Chicago physicians, she casually stuck hatpins through her cheeks and knitting needles deep into her forearms. In Chicago, the City of the Fair, she met Houdini, and while nothing came of it romantically he was smitten by her mysterious power and gaiety. "I never had a pain in my life," she told reporters. "I don't know what an ache is. I am always happy, never sad."

Nothing seemed to faze her. Occultists believed that Evatima Tardo had developed the psychic gift of detaching from her physical to her astral body; thus, her mind was no longer connected to the torture. Houdini also wanted to learn to transcend the physical; but ultimately he came to realize she was vulnerable. As it turned out, she was immune to the venom of the cobra and the spider tarantula, but not the jealous lover. When that third and most dangerous species caught her cuddling in a Memphis restaurant with another man, he shot them both with a Remington revolver. Then he put a bullet through his own temple and joined them in that place where the big tent is struck and the barkers are silent.

The Magician in Love

*I*t was during his dime-museum days that Houdini first began to seek professional mediums. In séances attended with his grieving mother, he attempted to contact the spirit of Mayer Samuel, who had once believed communication with the dead was possible. Houdini pawned his dead father's watch to hire the mediums, but the messages they relayed from the life hereafter were catch-all sentiments. What he heard was spirit twaddle, clearly not the disembodied voice of Mayer Samuel. The disappointing results, not to mention Houdini's encounters with spooks on the flimflam circuit, were convincing him that there was no such thing as genuine mediumistic power. He had seen much in his short life, but no marvel that he found unexplainable.

This was twenty years before the ghostly War, when the virtuous Victorians, Lodge and Doyle, imbued the Spiritualist movement with science and fervor. In Houdini's youth, the séance was stigmatized as an illicit rendezvous in a back parlor. Psychic mediums often advertised their wares in the personals section of the *New York Herald,* such services being fronts, Houdini suspected, for prostitution, badger games, and other methods of extortion. Just when he began discrediting superstitious practices, though, he met a special girl who felt differently. There was no witch tale she did not believe in.

An eighteen-year-old Brooklyn girl of German origin, Bess Rahner was at a music hall when Dash Houdini introduced her to his brother, the senior performer in their magic duo. While just one year older than she, Harry felt the urge to shield her from his rough-and-tumble circles, including brawny Dash, as she was barely ninety pounds and looked like a child when wearing certain outfits. Bess had a lovely, slightly accented voice and large, naïve blue eyes that seemed unaccustomed to navigating the world of grown-ups. She was a seamstress for a tailor shop and a singer with the Floral Sisters. But given that her troupe played the beer halls on the Bowery, her innocent airs may have been more show than substance. Bess would one day joke that she sold her virginity for an orange to a destitute Houdini. Their courtship, such as it was, lasted only a couple of weeks before they exchanged vows and celebrated their matrimony at the carnival resort that was West Brighton.

There was good reason for their elopement. Bess's people were Roman Catholic, and her mother was horrified to learn that she had wed not just a Jew but a lowly showman. Cecilia Weiss, by contrast, hugged her son's wide-eyed shiksa bride and murmured that she was now her daughter. Still, it was a shock for Bess to be abruptly removed from her mother and ten siblings. She didn't really know her new husband; the Weisses' ways were foreign to her. And becoming Mrs. Houdini meant training to be a part of Harry's daunting magic act.

Houdini wanted to teach Bess to appear to be psychic, as well as assuage her fear of black magic. One night, he asked her to write the name— that she had never told him—of her dead father on a piece of paper and then burn it in a gas flame he lit. As he directed, she handed him the ashes. When he rubbed them on his thick forearm, her father's given name of Gebhardt instantly appeared etched on his skin in bloody letters. Bess screamed in horror and fled their tenement. "Silly kid, it was only a trick," he explained when he caught her outside and calmed her.

In time, he taught her the secrets of second sight and prestidigitation; he showed her how to slip into trances like a spirit medium and tell fortunes. He wanted her to replace Dash in the Houdini show, so that they could stage the kind of psychic act that was then the rage on vaudeville. "Professor Houdini" received the coin from the volunteer in the crowd. Bess on the stage revealed the date inscribed on it. He took the business card from the spectator. She announced the name and address on it. "The wonderful mystical demonstrations of Prof. and Mme. Houdini continue to be a source of wonder to all who witness their marvelous exhibition," a newsman applauded.

As Bess was more agile than Dash, the Houdinis would also develop an electrifying Metamorphosis. Yet they were still small-time. After three years of marriage, the couple had appeared in the Welsh Brothers Circus in

Pennsylvania, where Houdini performed as both a magician and the Wild Man of Borneo—a caged beast that crawled around in chains while spectators tossed him cigars and cigarettes to eat, and the ringmaster dangled a slab of raw meat just beyond his reach. For other ensembles or on their own, they had played the parishes of Nova Scotia, the curio stage in dime museums from New York to Chicago, and variety halls in the heart of Dixie. They added a comedy gig to their repertoire, and took a stab at burlesque and melodrama. Nothing seemed to capture the attention of the newspapers or vaudeville managers.

Bess grew despondent and was breaking down physically. When even the dime-museum stints began drying up, Houdini wrote the two great magicians of the Gilded Age, Alexander Herrmann and Harry Kellar, to request work as an assistant. They didn't need him. He approached four of the major New York newspapers and offered to sell to them, for the mere sum of $20, all of his prized secrets. There were no takers. He attempted to market by mail the special equipment he used for his conjuring routine. There were no orders. He opened a magic school. With the exception of an elderly Chicago businessman, he had no students.

His desperation finally led him to Dr. Hill's traveling medicine show, the lowest rung of entertainment. Barely able to afford the rail ticket, the Houdinis linked up with Dr. Hill in Kansas, where they performed on the wagon stage and occasionally in small-town opera houses. Between shows the magician sold toiletry articles and miracle elixirs. The Great Houdini had become a piker on the oily circuit. Yet his versatile gifts were not lost on Dr. Hill, who one day proposed something intriguing. With his flowing hair and inspired patter, Hill had the air of a wandering prophet. He wanted a different sort of act on Sundays, something to rouse the goddamn suds on Main Street. He asked if the magician could do a spiritist séance. Smiling confidently, Houdini said that he would raise the dead in every county.

The Spiritualist Ties

HOUDINI THE GREAT WILL GIVE SUNDAY NIGHT A SPIRITUAL SÉANCE IN THE OPEN LIGHT. So read the placards in 1897 when Houdini toured the prairie sticks. His spook show was imitative of the Brothers Davenport—two legendary magicians from his boyhood who seemed able to make instruments play while no living being had hands on them. In Houdini's replication of the effect, volunteers tied him within a cabinet, where a guitar, a horn, and tambourine were placed upon a table. He should not have been able to free himself to reach these instruments, yet when the light was dimmed a spook recital started. Later, the chamber door blew open, revealing him, still roped and chained, to be the psychic conductor, not the player!

In those days there was a merging of spiritism and stage magic. It was the custom for cabinet test mediums to be cuffed or collared before a dark sitting. Without such restraint a crooked spook might slip into a white robe and waxen mask to fake their apparition, use their foot to raise the séance table, or put the spirit trumpet to their lips and imitate discarnate voices. Mediums were the first escape artists. The *Scientific American* revealed that it was by no occult force that these miracle workers freed their shackles. In 1897 an exposé called "Spiritualist Ties" explained the means by which crafty psychics slipped their ropes, cuffs, chains, and spirit collars. The report spoke of false bolts, concealed keys, and the slack in any rope tie.

Although Houdini employed such methods, his mental phenomena became his real bread and butter. Occasionally he pretended to put Bess into trance so that the audience might ask questions of the spirits. But most often it was he, the celebrated Psychometric Clairvoyant, who contacted the Other Side. He thought of himself as a psychic detective. When performing in a town he toured its graveyards and took down names of the dead to throw out at his séances. Sometimes he was accompanied in his prowling by a local tipster who filled him in on tragedies and family histories. He combed through health-board records and frequented board-inghouse dining halls in order to cull gossip for his sittings. The dead were active when Houdini visited.

For all that, he began to see that whenever he gave a séance solely by his wits, with no cheating or informant to assist him, his work was still convincing. "No matter what I pulled, someone in the audience was pretty sure to claim it as a direct message. . . . When I noted the deep earnestness with which my utterances were received, and that I was being considered a medium of far more than ordinary psychic powers, I felt that the game had gone far enough." Mediums had been arrested for doing what he did: taking money under false pretenses. Houdini also realized that despite the easy money, spook shows were a waste of his abilities. He wanted to be a famous showman, not another duper of the gullible.

No spirit would be his savior. Practically as soon as he stopped the nec-romancy routine, he met the gruff maestro who changed his life. He was back playing the dime museums, this time in Minneapolis, when a Hun-garian stranger puffing a Cubana asked him and Bess to coffee after their act. He urged Houdini to abandon the little tricks; they were stock stuff. He pointed out that the magician had two stunts, Metamorphosis and his handcuff act, that no one else could touch. He offered to take him on if he would agree to change his program. And incidentally, he was Martin Beck, proprietor of the Orpheum Circuit, one of the largest chains of vaudeville theaters in the country.

Beck sat back and smiled presciently.

Soon after their meeting, Houdini gave away his prized pigeons and guinea pigs; there would be no more nights of pulling them from a top hat. His card tricks he would never abandon, but gone were many of the accou-trements of stage magic, as well as the mentalist act and the phantoms. The Houdinis had seen the last, they were sure, of Astral Station.

A new stunt found him at St. Louis Police Headquarters in the year 1899. The Great Houdini was stripped to his skin. His mouth was sealed with court plaster to prove no key or pick was hidden there. The chief of detectives and aides handcuffed Houdini's hands behind his neck and double-locked the neck cuff to his back. He laughed and bade them add more chains. They placed irons on his legs. Left alone for two minutes, he slipped them like a snake.

He told a dumbfounded audience of policemen and reporters that he had been studying locks all his life, and knew more about their workings than any man alive. He swore there was nothing supernatural to his craft. He explained that he was very strong.

"Feel of that arm!"

"It felt like a pillar of steel," reported the *St. Louis Post-Dispatch*. The paper compared him favorably to the Prussian strong man Eugen Sandow, hailed as the most impressive male specimen alive. They appreciated Mrs. Houdini too—for her pluck in Metamorphosis, her "soft little voice" and "big dreamy blue eyes." Bess had no costarring role, though, in most of the celebrated escapes that followed. Houdini vowed that he would leap cuffed and shackled from the Eads Bridge into the mighty Mississippi. As it happened, he would make as big a splash in the Mersey, Rhine, and Seine as any river in America.

Over the next twenty years the Handcuff King would escape virtually any kind of restraint. They locked him in a dreaded Siberian prison van, bottled him in a milk can, and entombed him in a block of ice in Holland. They shackled him to a spinning windmill, the chassis of an automobile, the muzzle of a loaded cannon. They put him in a padlocked US mailbag, roped him to the twentieth-story girder of an unfinished skyscraper, sealed him in a giant envelope, and boxed him in a crate nailed tight and dropped in New York Harbor. He emerged triumphant and smiling.

In March 1906, Houdini was stripped, double-cuffed, and ironed, and deposited in a cell in Boston's impregnable Somerset Street prison. In sixteen minutes he had broken out. He had opened not only his own but every cell on his block. He had made his way somehow through two iron-barred doors secured with complex locks. He had slipped into a cell on the first floor where his clothing was being kept, then walked unnoticed past guards at one of three possible jailhouse exits. In the prison yard, reporters and prison officials followed his footprints in the snow to the wall where they stopped.

Such feats caused many to wonder if Houdini could slip this dimension altogether. It was speculated that he could dissolve his physical molecules into the ether then reappear in an instant, free of his confinement. In reality there were brutal physical tests in his life of magic. But just as a medium often needed the privacy of her spirit cabinet to perform, so the Handcuff King had his vaudeville "ghost house"—the enclosure onstage where he might retire to free himself from a challenger's manacles. Conversely, he was known to appear at a magic show that imitated his own and challenge the escape artist to free himself from the same cuffs and restraints he used. He recalled how when one German pretender failed, he dragged him, still cuffed, to the footlights of a Berlin stage and ordered him to admit defeat or he would not release him. The nebbish had cried like a spanked babe. Houdini dealt that way with rivals.

The Great Leap

*D*uring the long period of Houdini's ascent there had been a metamorphosis in America. Even the small towns that he played were now electric. Automobiles had taken over the thoroughfares, and vaudeville halls were being transformed into movie palaces. The Great Houdini had become a hero of the cinema screen as well as an escape artist. In the two decades since his medicine show days, the magician had shunned spiritism; he was known instead for daring feats that were in keeping, so he told the press, with the laws of physical science.

But for all the applause he received, Houdini wished to move beyond his stratosphere of cinema and vaudeville entertainment. Unlike the champion boxer Jack Dempsey, whom some called a shirker, he had tried to enlist when war was declared and join the fight in Europe. No one begrudged that his age was against him, and with characteristic zeal he had contributed in other ways to the Effort. Houdini instructed sailors how to survive in the deep should their destroyer be sunk by the Kaiser's torpedoes. He showed up at Army canteens and performed for the doughboys. He staged elaborate vaudeville benefits and sold Liberty Bonds totaling $1 million. He donated from his own pocket to build a hospital ward for wounded servicemen, dedicating the wing to his dear deceased mother. The magician had done his part in the War for Democracy. Nevertheless, it bothered him that he had observed the show, so to speak, from the grandstand, while younger men did the fighting.

Unable to prove his mettle under fire, he was presented with an opportunity, late in 1919, to show what he could do in water. While filming a moving picture on Catalina Island in California, he took part in a real-life nautical drama. A small vessel had been disabled and was in immediate danger of capsizing or smashing into the rocks off Sugar Loaf Point. In response to the crew's distress calls, Houdini quickly secured himself to a line and dove into the turbulent waters. Shielding himself from the surf with a life preserver extended in front of him, he propelled himself with froglike strokes toward the stranded men—who, as if so directed, were waving and yelling for help. While onshore a crowd in front of the Hotel St. Catherine cheered the star's effort to save them.

The scene did not unfold as it would have in one of his melodramas. Exhausted, Houdini was cut on the rocks and battered almost unconscious. He had to be saved by deep-sea divers. It took a motor launch nearly forty-five minutes to cut through the waves and reach the party. Even so, he wondered to himself if he could have pulled off the feat when he was younger.

◆

Although he was forty-six in 1920, Houdini was admired for his strenuous magic at a time when the average male, according to H. L. Mencken, was "more like a rabbit and less like a lion." Teddy Roosevelt had died the previous year and with him went the rugged life the Colonel had once championed. "Americans were getting soft," F. Scott Fitzgerald wrote. Yet Houdini still expressed the tenacious spirit of the ghetto. The magician was a straight arrow, a teetotaler; he worried that to lose his edge might mean his days were over. He slept a mere four hours a night in his quiet townhouse on the Upper West Side of Manhattan. He ate blandly and in moderation. He had no children to distract him. His wife helped him train. His energies were devoted entirely to his escape art.

While Houdini had come a long way, there had been little compromise with middle age. His bushy hair was thinner and graying, his jawline slacker, yet his blue-gray eyes had lost none of their famous intensity. Even at this later stage in his career, his ambition was insatiable. It was his intention to inaugurate the 1920s by jumping handcuffed off Manhattan's Woolworth Building, the tallest building anywhere, and parachute down, while somehow escaping his shackles, to an area cleared out for him on Broadway.

His friend Orson Munn could imagine the spectacle. The publishing scion who guided *Scientific American* regularly escorted small parties up the electric lift to the fifty-eighth-floor observation turret of the Woolworth—

where his offices were—and with a view more breathtaking, he promised, than that of any Coney Island Ferris wheel. Despite the postwar slump, Munn expected a decade of progress. Thanks in large part to his father's client Thomas Edison, whose inventions Munn & Co. helped to patent, the movies were a thriving industry, the phonograph a household necessity, and any number of new marvels were anticipated by his magazine.

In the Rathskeller, an ornate eatery in the basement of the Woolworth, Houdini told Munn that unfortunately his great leap was deemed too dangerous. The city would not grant him a permit. He made it clear to the publisher, however, that 1920 would be a year of magic. He had a book coming out, *Miracle Mongers and Their Methods;* the release of his new movie to promote; and, more immediately, he was going to tour his favorite European country. For the first six months of the year, the Great Houdini was to fulfill bookings that had been canceled in Great Britain during the War. He also intended, while overseas, to look into the astonishing claims made by Sir Oliver Lodge and Sir Arthur Conan Doyle that they were communicating with their dead sons across the Barrier. And so, just as Sir Oliver arrived from England, Houdini made the reverse passage.

The American Mysteriarch

*W*hen Sir Arthur went to Portsmouth to see Houdini perform, he was revisiting a place where many things had begun for him. It was almost thirty years earlier that Dr. Conan Doyle set up the first home of his own in Southsea, a suburb of the great port, and opened his first medical office in a meager residence there. Even then he aspired to another occupation. The young physician had the ability to energetically pursue two goals simultaneously, and in Portsmouth he had produced his most unique creation—one that would allow him to end an unsatisfactory and unprofitable career as a doctor—his first Sherlock Holmes story: *A Study in Scarlet*. Doyle's critical faculties would often be compared to those of his fictional detective. When he was an unknown doctor, a supposed new cure for tuberculosis was introduced by Robert Koch, a respected German bacteriologist. Doyle was one of the few to call it a false hope. And he was proven right, unfortunately for his first wife.

Portsmouth was a place of many haunting associations for Sir Arthur. It was there he fell in love with and married a warmhearted and devout young patient of his named Louisa Hawkins. They would have two children, Mary and Kingsley; but Touie, as Arthur called his first wife, would suffer from consumption. She never lived to see the War with Germany, the death of her son, or her husband's transformation into the Saint Paul of Spiritualism. Doyle's psychic journey also began at Portsmouth. Having renounced Catholicism before he arrived, he took up, to Touie's chagrin, a study of the supernatural religions—Spiritualism and Theosophy. The latter sect was sullied for him when Madame Blavatsky, its leader, was unveiled as a brazen trickster by an investigation conducted by the Society for Psychical Research. Conversely, what drew Doyle to Spiritualism was the credibility, to his mind, of some of its adherents in Portsmouth, a martial city. When royal officers, sensible and sturdy, spoke of their convincing experiences with the séance, Sir Arthur took notice, though he found his own initial experiments with it unconvincing.

There were many memories for Sir Arthur, if not ghosts, in Portsmouth. Shortly after he, at the age of twenty-four, hung out his medical shingle at Bush Villas, his little brother, Innes, was sent by their mother to live with and assist him. As their father was not there for the boy, Doyle assumed the patriarchal duty, and he encouraged Innes's budding interest in the military. The brothers would stand in those days outside the post office, waiting for news of the campaign in Egypt; and at the harbor, they watched the troops embark for Africa to fight the Arabs or the Zulus, just as one day Innes hoped to.

By 1920, Innes was buried in Flanders, but to Doyle it made no difference where his brother's physical remains were kept—what comfort could anyone hope to find by communing with a gravestone and laying wreaths on granite? It pained the dead, he believed, to see their families mourn them. What they wanted, as much as the bereaved, was contact!

It had taken months before Sir Arthur was able to receive a message during a séance, but presently he claimed to be in touch with Kingsley and Innes as often as when they were alive in England. All that was needed to reach the dead, he said, was a gifted intermediary: the spirit medium.

◆

It was clear to any visiting American that the war his country was forgetting about still haunted England. Rationing was still in effect and limbless veterans rattled their tin cans on street corners. The very stature of Englishmen seemed diminished by the calamity. "Where are the monstrous men with chests like barrels and moustaches like the wings of eagles who strode across my childhood's gaze?" George Orwell would wonder. "Buried, I suppose, in the Flanders mud."

To these depleted Isles came the Great Houdini, the personification of American vitality. He arrived to find a country still in the throes of the Spiritualist revival. He had heard that Sir Oliver Lodge's testament on his communications with his dead son had been more popular in wartime Britain than the Bible. More than a year after the Armistice there was still an uproar over Doyle's *New Revelation*. Books on ghosts and supernaturalism were pouring from the presses. Sir Arthur was sparring with the Church over the legitimacy of the séance religion. Houdini had been corresponding with Doyle and had no doubt that the doctor turned author was genuine, but many occultists were up to their old tricks again, he suspected.

The papers had begun to complain of a plague of Theosophists, demonists, table rappers, and Tibetan sages. Having seen these actors thrive in his dime-museum days, Houdini recognized them returning like vultures after the carnage. Psychic arts once practiced by a young Houdini were again in fashion—the outcome of death the pressing question: "Did Private Tommy Atkins or Hans Boches or Johnny Crapaud, or now Sammy American, when he was killed in the trenches, pass forever away from the reach and communication of father, mother, wife, children or sweetheart?" the *Herald Tribune* had asked. Houdini pasted the article in his scrapbook sometime before leaving for England. There were really only two types of stories he collected: those on his escapes, and those on spiritism.

Houdini had empathy for those seeking consolation from the séance. Though he had lost no one close to him during the War, he still grieved for his mother, and his yearnings were in accord with the general mood of bereavement in England. But his grief was hidden. Like a shaman he turned his darkness into something magically cathartic.

Of all his stage escapes, Houdini believed the Chinese Water Torture Cell to be his greatest, and he declared it the culmination of his research and labors. It had taken him more than three years to develop and rehearse the aquatic escape, and when he had first introduced it to prewar audiences in Europe in 1912, the *Titanic* sinking had just incited a general dread of death by drowning. Often Houdini seemed able to channel a prevailing urge or fear into his performances; yet an English expert on physical mediumship, James Hewat McKenzie, insisted his liberation from the Water Torture Cell could only be effected by real sorcery.

As Houdini made his escape at the Grand Theatre in London, McKenzie had experienced "a great loss of physical energy . . . such as is usually felt by sitters in materializing séances." The magician's body was demate-rialized, McKenzie determined, enabling him to pass through the tank in which he had been incarcerated. What McKenzie had called "a startling manifestation of one of nature's profoundest miracles" still awed the crowds who thought they were merely watching a ripping stunt on vaudeville.

What was it like to drown this way? One had to wonder. Presently, at the Portsmouth Hippodrome, Houdini's attendants held their axes at the ready. If something went wrong, they were to smash the glass and rescue him. The orchestra took up "Asleep in the Deep" while all eyes regarded Houdini restrained upside down to a stock inside the tank. His face was bloated, his body clammy white under the wash of stage lights. He looked like a corpse resting in some bizarre Atlantean casket. For a few tense mo-ments the audience was allowed to watch through the glass panels as the top of the enclosure was soundly padlocked and bolted. Overflowing water drenched the rubber tarp on the stage and splashed the gumboots of the black-clad crewmen. A yellow canopy was drawn around the Torture Cell to preserve the mystery. Two minutes passed. A woman gasped, though the theater was otherwise unnaturally silent. Then came the moment of materialization. The curtain parted and there stood Houdini by the water chamber—liberated, smiling widely, his body glistening, his hair inexpli-cably dry. The audience rose ecstatically. None cheering louder than Sir Arthur Conan Doyle.

◆

Such displays of the impossible would soon convince Doyle, as they had McKenzie, that Houdini was himself a great medium—the very thing he claimed to be searching for. In their correspondence that winter and spring of 1920, Houdini said that he was willing to believe in spirit communica-tion, if only he could find a single genuine medium—one who would not resort to tricks when her psychic powers failed. Ever since his mother died, Houdini had been trying to find a clairvoyant who could reach her, and he regretted to say that his own séances thus far had been, without exception, a waste of effort. He had never found the same solace in the darkened room as Sir Arthur.

Over the years Houdini had made compacts with seven friends: telltale messages had been established, and it was agreed that whoever was the first to die would endeavor from the World Beyond to communicate through the séance. All of these other men were now deceased, yet no medium had produced the agreed-upon words. And so Houdini's doubts persisted.

After all of his own experiences on both sides of the spirit cabinet, as both spook-show medium and séance sitter, he was an expert, he told Doyle, on the tricks of phony psychics. He had personally sat with Bert Reiss, one of the most uncanny mentalists in America—the one clairvoyant even Thomas Edison believed authentic. Professor Reiss, as he called himself, was a grizzled German Jew who could answer written questions that were recorded out of his sight and then concealed in a drawer. No one had been able to ascertain whether he could read minds, had X-ray vision, or had the gift of psychometry, or divination via objects.

Houdini had unmasked him as a flimflam artist.

He caught Reiss red-handed in a lightning-quick deception, and according to his account, Reiss told him that he was the first to ever spot the method. The professor had used sleight of hand to work his marvels, and was as good in that regard as any magician Houdini ever saw on vaudeville.

Houdini suggested, in his letters to Sir Arthur, that the history of spiritism was one long tale of charlatanism.

"I see that you know a great deal about the negative side of Spiritualism," answered Sir Arthur, "I hope more on the positive side will come your way." But he warned Houdini that his attitude would have to soften if he expected séance results. "It wants to be approached not in the spirit of a detective approaching a suspect," he admonished.

While catching rogues and phonies was a sport Houdini relished, he did not want to appear eager to entrap or intimidate those sincere nonprofessional mediums whom Sir Arthur admired. He professed to be an open-minded investigator, and hoped, with Doyle's help, to gain access to any clairvoyant who might bring a single authentic word from his mother, silent these seven years beyond the veil.

Doyle said that he had spoken face-to-face with his dead son, twice with his brother, and once with his nephew—"all beyond doubt in their own voices and on private matters."

"It must be a wonderful feeling," Houdini responded, "to be able to converse with your son, or in fact, with anyone whom you loved in your heart of hearts. I don't mind telling you that your very seriousness makes me doubly interested to find the Truth, or solve the problem."

Seek and Ye Shall Find

*A*s the Great Houdini alighted from a motorcar in his gray duster on April 14, he appeared to Doyle more like one of those rugged German officers he had once raced in the Prince Henry Motor Exhibition, just before the War erupted, than a stage wizard in a top hat. The author of *The Sign of the Four* anticipated no such hostilities with his guest, who seemed through his actions and letters to be friendly and honorable. He had performed and bought shoes for hundreds of orphans in Doyle's hometown of Edinburgh; and the novelist's own children had never been more excited to welcome a visitor to their home at Crowborough.

Approaching the large estate with red tiles and five gables, Houdini was greeted by a page who escorted him to a sunny parlor where five Doyles— Arthur, Jean, and their three children—awaited his arrival. After accepting Houdini's apologies for his wife Bess's absence, the Doyles led him across a mahogany floor while the children gazed in awe at the man who walked through walls and caused an elephant to vanish. Sensing their excitement, Houdini plucked gold coins from the air and handed one to each of them—Denis, Adrian, and Jean Lena, whom they called Billy. It was a wartime trick called Money for Nothing, he told them, that he used to perform as his way of providing gifts to the doughboys.

The Doyles applauded the impromptu sleight of hand while Houdini, in turn, delighted in the place they called Windlesham. The immense hall where they stood was used by the family for billiards and music recitals, and also, said Jean, as a dance floor where 150 couples once waltzed at an Edwardian gala. The walls were decorated with portraits of English boxers, an original Van Dyck, and a stag's head covered with bandolier cartridges. What especially caught Houdini's eye, though, were the fantastic paintings of witches, ghouls, and faerie creatures—the work of an obscure Victorian artist, said Arthur; his late father, Charles.

Then, as always, they made a striking pair: the burly Scotch-Irish knight, Sir Arthur, speaking of his father the painter and Celtic faerie lore; and the short and stout Jew, Houdini, eagerly responding in an accent Sir Arthur thought was distinctive to the New York ghetto. What bound them was their mutual fascination with the outcome of death and, also, something nearly as sacred.

Charles Doyle had been unable to find a market for his occult portraits. The family had struggled and Sir Arthur grew up experiencing, as had Houdini, the humiliation of poverty. Both had wanted to redeem their fallen families and uplift their martyred mothers. As a boy, Sir Arthur had promised his mam that "when you are old, you shall have a velvet dress and gold glasses and sit in comfort by the fire." As a man, Houdini fulfilled a similar childhood vow when, after insisting that he be paid in gold coins for his performances at Hammerstein's Roof Garden, he happily deposited the treasure in the apron of his mother. Once he had even purchased and given her a silk dress made for Queen Victoria. When Houdini spoke of Cecilia Weiss, Jean had the impression that for all his bluster, he was like a lost boy looking for his mother. Despite some disappointing séances in the past, he now sought that reunion in England.

Other men whom Doyle knew and admired were not as open, he felt, to the practice of Spiritualism. While eating a half grapefruit, Sir Arthur brought up the recent death of Teddy Roosevelt—the most grievous loss to America, he said, since Lincoln was assassinated. Sir Arthur believed that Colonel Roosevelt had essentially died of a broken heart he need not have suffered after his son, Quentin, an aviator, was shot down by the Huns. Another friend of his, Rudyard Kipling, was traipsing through every cemetery in Loos, seeking the desolate comfort of knowing where his own son was buried. My God, lamented Sir Arthur, if they only knew—if they could only know!

After their lunch, Doyle brought his guest to the second-floor study. There Houdini saw a bust of Sherlock Holmes, and another of Charles Doyle's macabre paintings—a faerie shielding a butterfly from the talons of a monstrous raven. On the desk was a magnifying glass lying on a blotter, and to the left a mantelpiece holding pictures of soldiers arranged in order of when each had fallen. It looked to Houdini like a kind of shrine, draped with decorations the men had received for heroism.

Sir Arthur pointed out photographs of Kingsley and Innes Doyle, both of whom he said had been heard from recently. He then identified the first of the dead boys to come through at a séance—Jean's brother, Malcolm, who had been killed at Mons. His contact, through the mediumship of Lily Loder-Symonds, had been the first breakthrough for the Doyles.

Sir Arthur had once been dubious of Lily's powers, he confessed. She had said something at their first sitting, however, that had sent a chill down his spine. She claimed to see a soldier waving a gold coin and asking to speak to him. It was Malcolm. And that was the first time, Sir Arthur said, that he communicated with a dead man.

Lily could not have known, he explained, that he always carried on his keychain a prized gift from Malcolm—an antique guinea piece that he now took out to show Houdini. Dexterously, the magician rotated the gold coin between his fingers, and for a moment Sir Arthur wondered if he might cause it to disappear, like the sleight of hand he had displayed on his arrival. But he was only admiring the token of their reunion. A guinea, Houdini thought, was a small price to pay for a miracle.

◆

"Seek and ye shall find," Doyle exhorted. And seek Houdini did; his wary investigation of Spiritualism would intensify into an obsessive pursuit that would monopolize the remainder of his time in England. While Houdini had a promoter's knack for exaggeration, by his estimation he attended, on average, a séance a day during his six-month stay in Britain. Yet even the best of Doyle's mediums, Anna Brittain and Etta Wriedt, only came through with gushing whispers that relayed meaningless information from the Other Side. "This is ridiculous stuff," Houdini recorded in his diary.

Doyle attributed Houdini's inability to make contact with his loved ones to his own turbulent vibrations, which he was sure intimidated these sensitive ladies. Nonetheless, Doyle was confident that his friend was making progress in his search. As directed, Houdini sat with nonprofessional mediums, thereby avoiding the lechers who, according to Sir Arthur, were less prevalent in England than the United States, but just as devious. "Glad you are trying the Spiritualist churches," he encouraged Houdini, "because

sooner or later you will happen on some good clairvoyant." He only advised
that in his efforts to find her, the magician should "persevere and get it out
of your mind that you should follow it as a terrier follows a rat."

Houdini appeared to heed him. Though Mrs. Wriedt had warned that
the showman was "out to make trouble," most of the other psychics he
visited reported that he was well-behaved, a perfect sitter. Indeed, one medium in particular was pleased to perform for him. Before Houdini departed, he managed to participate in the British SPR investigation of the
French enchantress known as Eva C, the so-called Queen of Ectoplasm.
As her phenomena were purely physical, Eva was not the sort of medium
Sir Arthur supported. She brought no uplifting messages from the next
world—spirit communication was not in her repertoire. Rather, she was
known for manifesting clouds of ectoplasm that took the form of spectral
limbs and faces. For such ghoulish displays Eva C was the medium of the
hour.

Few psychics in Europe were as thoroughly and intimately tested as she.
The German researcher Albert von Schrenck-Notzing had probed her vagina before and after sittings to assure no fake ectoplasm was stashed there.
Houdini was often searched as invasively before his jail escapes, to ensure
that he concealed no pick or key inside the recesses of his body. No one,
though, had ever restrained him inside the device in which the research
officer of the SPR, Eric Dingwall, was the leading expert. Dingwall was
an author of a history of the chastity belt and the curator of ancient erotica
at the British Museum. Regardless, Houdini did not feel the expert had
adequately restrained Eva C.

The phenomena she produced came over a number of evenings while
Houdini and the others chanted *"Donnez! Donnez!"* There was a glowing
secretion from her nostrils, an ectoplasmic rod that projected from above
her eye, a filmy object that emanated from her mouth and then vanished
like magic, and once—the misty face of a phantom.

Houdini was both skeptical and captivated. He noted that Eva had been
searched by female members of the committee, albeit in another chamber,
and her orifices had not been checked in the way he deemed essential. He
told Dingwall that in his dime-museum days he had been taught by a Japanese acrobat to swallow and regurgitate a billiard ball. He had known a

freak who did the same with frogs, snakes, and other clammy animals. He suspected that Eva had concealed in her gullet, then expelled some time later, a slimy piece of ghost-white plaster. He was not yet convinced there was such a thing as ectoplasm. "Well, we had success at the séance last night, as far as productions were concerned," he reported to Doyle, "but I am not prepared to say that they were supernormal."

Sir Arthur had no similar reservations when it came to Houdini's own productions—his eerie escapes from supposedly foolproof restraints on stages throughout England. "My dear chap," wrote Doyle, "why go around the world seeking a demonstration of the occult when you are giving one all the time . . . My reason tells me that you have this wonderful power, for there is no alternative."

Aware of the artifice that he brought to his own performances, Houdini was not ready to pronounce any psychic genuine. Crossing back to the United States on the *Imperator,* he was still as skeptical of Doyle's messages as when he had arrived at Windlesham. Sir Arthur's wife, Jean, was convinced she had somehow been passed the gift of second sight from Lily Loder-Symonds, and Doyle made no major decision without consulting their dead loved ones. The Doyles, Houdini said, were utterly sincere in their beliefs. He doubted that Sir Arthur had gone soft in the mind, as the scoffers asserted. For he knew that even bright and worldly men were easily caught up in spiritistic mysteries. Once, during a séance aboard this very ship, Houdini had seen Teddy Roosevelt's shrewd eyes widen in bewilderment. But the sea does not give up its dead, he reflected; except by magic.

A Séance for Teddy

*I*t was on the *Imperator*, just before the Great War started, that Houdini met Teddy while sailing from England to America. Though men of different worlds, there was a tacit kinship between the Rough Rider and the escape artist: each had the curiosity and impulsive moods of a child; and each pursued his goals with relentless energy—what H. L. Mencken said of Roosevelt could just as easily describe Houdini, that he was "almost pathological in his appetite for activity."

Hoping to give the Colonel a thrill, Houdini wanted to leap handcuffed into the North Atlantic and free himself. The ship's captain forbade the antic, but while walking the deck with Houdini and discussing Spiritualism, Teddy suggested a different sort of exhibition: "Give us a little séance," he requested.

All his life Teddy held more with the Biblical miracles. He was an honorary member of the American SPR, though, and increasingly aware of his own precarious mortality. His recent ill-conceived expedition to the River of Doubt had been too much for him. Two of his party had died in the jungle, and he, delirious with a spreading infection and a 105-degree malarial fever, came within a whisker of being the third to be buried there. His health would never recover from the adventure.

Though Houdini rarely conducted spiritist sittings anymore, he was happy to oblige the ailing colonel. On the appointed evening, he requested that the lights be turned up for the séance to follow; he was not the kind of medium, he said, who prepared his manifestations behind a veil or in a spirit cabinet. Turning to Teddy, Houdini asked if he wished to put a question to the spirits. Eagerly complying, Roosevelt wrote it on a piece of paper shielded from the magician, and then folded and sealed it in an envelope. Houdini held up two "spirit slates," which looked like small chalkboards. Upon revealing them to be blank, he asked the guest of honor to insert his envelope between them. As instructed, Teddy told the audience his question: "Where was I last Christmas?"

Instantly Houdini untied the slates, revealing a multicolored map of the River of Doubt, the remote Brazilian estuary that Roosevelt had been navigating over the holiday. The Colonel roared in amazement. He had only just thought of his question; there would have been no time for such an elaborate ruse. "By George, that proves it!" he bellowed. Another wave of excitement hit when it was discovered that the message was signed by the late English journalist W. T. Stead, whose ghost was held responsible for the phenomena. A medium in his own right, Stead had sailed to America at the behest of the spirits, but unfortunately had booked passage on the *Titanic* and met a frigid end in the North Atlantic. Tonight he had evidently come through from Summerland; a friend of Stead's declared the signature authentic.

News of the séance was transmitted to New York and Washington. No one could understand how Houdini had done it. The morning after the séance, Teddy put his arm around Houdini and asked, man to man, if the phenomena the previous evening was "genuine Spiritualism." With a smile and wink, the magician replied: "It was hokus-pokus, Colonel." There ended Teddy's brief enchantment with the spirits. He died six months after his son Quentin was lost in an air battle; it was not for him to know the transcendent comforts of the new religion.

Part III

THE NEW WILDERNESS

⌗

The boundary between the two states—the known and the unknown—is still substantial, but it is wearing thin in places, and like excavators engaged in boring a tunnel from opposite ends, amid the roar of water and other noises, we are beginning to hear now and again the strokes of the pickaxes of our comrades on the other side.

—SIR OLIVER LODGE

Sir Arthur Conan Doyle

Sir Oliver Lodge

1922: Don't Let Them Tame You

In a short red dress that barely covered her thighs, the dancer pranced barefoot across the stage. Her dance, to the strains of a Russian ballet, was all the rage in Europe. This was not Paris. The Old Yankees found her performance more vulgar than a leg show at Scollay Square. When in defiance she bared her breasts to them, many of the offended walked out. The Harvard crowd and students from the art and music schools remained, cheering madly as she cried, "You were once wild here! Don't let them tame you!"

It was Boston's shame and sensation when Isadora Duncan gave her topless sermon at Symphony Hall. Days earlier she had presented the same program, without exposing her breasts, in liberal New York and was praised there as daring—one of the vanguard. This was not Manhattan. In Boston she was smeared in the newspapers, censured in the statehouse, and ridiculed in the drawing rooms of Back Bay. She was old and corpulent. Her breasts sagged. Her thighs were massive. Her speech—"This scarf is red and so am I!"— was Bolshevist incitement. When Mayor Curley banned her from the Boston stage, he was applauded by the Hearst newspapers. Even many of those, like Dr. Crandon, who rarely agreed with their Catholic mayor from the Mud Flats, believed he was right to banish Isadora Duncan. Let her preach mob rule to the Leninists she loved so much in her adopted homeland.

This was not Moscow.

◆

The Boston Brahmins loathed disorder and the prevailing isms—Socialism, Spiritualism, Modernism—of the times. They wanted the peace and normalcy that President Harding had promised to restore. Yet Dr. Crandon, no true Brahmin by bloodline, was a member of one of the old Plymouth families—a descendant of the spiritual dissidents who came over on the

Mayflower. His people were not first-tier gentry and his behavior was not always in accordance with the Brahmin creed: that one's name should appear in the newspapers just twice in a lifetime—a birth announcement and an obituary. The doctor's past divorce to his second wife, Lucy Armes, had been a news item. Moreover, in a city vehemently anti-abortion, he was not against feticide. His nascent interest in psychic research might also have been considered peculiar by some. It cannot be imagined that any Lowell, Adams, or Quincy ever dabbled with ghosts. Spiritualism was associated in past decades with free-lovers, suffragettes, and other radical cults. Despite that, Roy's beloved grandfather Benjamin had been a Spiritualist—a healing medium who sensed auras and prescribed botanical elixirs and invisible balms for the sick.

Dr. Crandon had not inherited these supposed psychic gifts, he told his wife, Mina. Never had he sensed bands of etheric light surrounding his patients, but then at Harvard Medical School he hadn't exactly been trained in prayer or second sight. He was dedicated to healing through more conventional means; and he focused so single-mindedly on medicine that after four years of marriage Mina felt that his profession came before her. When they took their evening walk through the Commons, the doctor often seemed absorbed in some medical crisis he did not wish to discuss. He was more apt to include her in the new obsession in his life. He had taken to the psychical research movement like a Jew to Marxism, remarked their friend Kitty Brown. He read journals on occult phenomena until late at night.

As for Mina, she was not the type to read quietly by her husband's side. Roy thought his third wife was like a chameleon in the way she had adjusted to his circle of Harvard and Gold Coast friends. Not that she blended in with them completely; some thought her pretty gay for a society wife. Accompanied by Kitty Brown she might cross Pinckney and explore the colony of artists and bohemians on the North Slope. There, in the speakeasies on Joy Street, *Don't let them tame you* became part of the vernacular. Even though it was Sir Arthur Conan Doyle, and not the red hussy, who caused the greater stir that year.

The Salt Highway

SPIRITUALISM TO WIN WORLD ASSERTS DOYLE
—*New York Herald*

*F*rom the hurricane deck of the RMS *Baltic,* Sir Arthur watched the skyline of his favorite American city emerge from the mist. Silhouetted against
a gray-violet sky, New York looked to him like some future metropolis, so
different was it from anything in Europe. He pointed out the three great
towers—the Singer, Woolworth, and Whitehall—to his three gaping children. As the ship rounded Battery Park, he felt both excited and uneasy,
knowing that a boarding party of reporters was awaiting his arrival at the
docks. Americans were led in their opinions by the newspapers, he realized.
Newspaper men here were keen for humor, and no subject was more easily
made fun of than spiritism. But it gave him some comfort to know that
on his previous visit to New York, two months before the War, he and the
press had gotten on famously. On an excursion to Dreamland on Coney
Island they wrote of his "Shooting the Chutes" and roaring with delight
on the splash-down. Of his gamely mixing it up with the flimflammers
and frankfurter men on the promenade. And of hundreds of men removing their hats, the band playing "God Save the King" while he and Jean
walked arm-in-arm through Steeplechase Pavilion. For her warm grace the
press dubbed Jean "Lady Sunshine." They had taken as well to Sir Arthur's
boyish enthusiasm, his unabashed awe of their city. But it was now April 9,
1922. This time Sir Arthur was coming on a religious mission. They were
already calling him the Saint Paul of Spiritualism. If that were so, he reflected, then the Hudson was his salt highway. He was sure that the Apostle
Paul, on the salt road he followed to Rome, hadn't encountered a more materialistic city. Would New Yorkers have a tin ear for the New Revelation?

He was buoyed by the prior success of Sir Oliver, whose own US tour
had launched a national fascination with spirit communication—a practice
that seemed to run contrary to the current trend toward trivial amusement.

A spirit message received at a séance weeks earlier back home in Crowborough further encouraged Sir Arthur: *"You have no idea what great and glorious work you are going to do. You will leave your mark forever upon America. We will all be with you, giving you inspiration and power and health."* The spirits had never led Sir Arthur astray. They were with him now, he believed, as the *Baltic* steamed slowly toward its moorings.

The first wave of newspapermen hit him before the liner had berthed. Boarding at the Narrows after the quarantine, an advance party sought out and cornered him. They were scruffy, importunate men in raincoats and fedoras. Flashes went off in his face. He could taste the powder. Pens came out—ready, he imagined, to be thrust at any chink in his aura. The keen senses of these men were alert, he felt, for any signs that their English visitor belonged in the nuthouse; that the War had cost him both his son and his sanity. Bellevue was just up the river. Would he drop anchor there? It wasn't just Sir Arthur's communications with ghosts that struck some of them as fanciful. He was now affirming the existence of faeries. He had put his reputation behind photographs a teenage girl had taken in Cottingley, West Yorkshire, of winged sprites dancing in front of her. Has Sherlock Holmes gone mad? many wondered. In fact, his direct, earnest responses had often disarmed the scoffers. Few doubted that he was still formidable. "Arthur is a massive man," said the *Herald,* "broad of shoulder and six feet in height. His hair is thin and brown, but shows no trace of grey. He is erect and the muscles that cover his enormous frame give one the impression that they are hard and powerful." He did not look like a man in his dotage, susceptible to charlatans.

Doyle found a windy doorway near the promenade deck where the flash smoke was not as intolerable. There he told the newsmen to fire away. What did he seek to accomplish on these shores? they asked. "To make a raid on American skepticism. To raid church and laity alike," he responded. As his children screamed at the sight of the Statue of Liberty, he said that Spiritualism was the "death blow to materialism." But were there really scotch and cigars in Summerland? Was there miniature golf there? What about relations between the sexes? they asked. Sir Arthur laughed heartily. It may have saved him. He did not know why, within Sir Oliver's four-hundred-page book on his communications with Raymond, some in America had seized on the brief message regarding otherworldly vices. Raymond was only saying that there was an etheric replica of everything in our world. Sir Arthur wanted them to know that while some mocked Spiritualism, it was the only faith to furnish proof of what lay beyond the veil. "It is not mere hearsay. I have talked with and seen twenty of my dead, including my son, when my wife and other witnesses were present," he told them. Had he brought any proofs? they pressed him. Come to my presentation, he answered. When they then asked what he would do first in New York he said, without hesitation, that he looked forward to seeing Broadway again. He understood that the lights there were brighter than ever.

The Men from Beyond

*I*n April a movie by and starring the Great Houdini premiered on Broadway. While *The Man from Beyond* played at the Times Square Theater, Houdini performed live immediately afterward. He was placing himself center stage amid the supernatural hullabaloo. If it is spirits you seek, he seemed to announce, then come see my picture! His press book promised that "audiences everywhere will welcome it as evidence that loved ones gone to the great beyond are not lost to us forever."

At the theater the Doyles saw first a close shot of the Bible with the verse John 5:28 highlighted: *Marvel not at this: for the hour is coming, in which all that are in their graves shall hear his voice.* A dead man then came to life: an arctic explorer, played by Houdini, who is resuscitated after one hundred years of frozen entombment on a lost ship. Brought back to New York, he encounters a young bride he believes to be the reincarnation of his former lover. Complications ensue when he attempts to part the veil and reclaim her. He must first escape the mental asylum in which her groom, a sinister doctor, has him locked up and tortured. After this and other predicaments are surmounted, Houdini saves his beloved from a canoe caught at the crest of the Niagara Rapids. This stunt he actually undertook—an unseen steel wire secured him from plunging over. The point of the movie is that an etheric cord still connects him to his heroine. There was also a surprising ode to Sir Arthur. The six reels conclude with Houdini reading verses from *The Vital Message*—Doyle's latest book on the "progression and immortality of the soul." *The Man from Beyond* was Houdini's attempt to merge his muscular form of melodrama with Sir Arthur's Spiritualism. *Variety* said, "The two things don't go together." Doyle found it the "best sensational picture" ever.

After the photoplay was over, the band struck up "Pomp and Circumstance" and Houdini bounded onto the stage all dash and fire. Cards vanished at his fingertips and reappeared in all parts of the theater. He swallowed a handful of sewing needles then brought them out threaded. He shouted, "Goodbye, autumn!" and made his heroine disappear in mid-air. From an empty bowl he pulled streams of bright-colored silk and giant flags of all nations. He shot off a pistol and yelled, "Hello summer!" The girl reappeared from the ether. He clawed his way out of a straitjacket as he had in his screen adventure. For the finale he brought out Fannie, a live elephant he had borrowed from the Ringling Circus, and made her vanish. Sir Arthur and others were allowed to come onstage. "Fannie!" the guest of honor called. But no one could find her.

◆

While Doyle had not come to entertain, his appearances in New York were a more popular draw than Houdini. He began with a series of three presentations to some of the largest crowds ever at Carnegie Hall. All the standing room the fire laws would permit, and many women in mourning garb or with gold stars pinned to their clothing. And there was Houdini perched by the stage. He had the nose, Sir Arthur felt, of a hawk, and the luminous blue eyes of a medium.

In a double-breasted blue serge and wearing gold spectacles, Sir Arthur looked both distinguished and sturdy. His feet seemed firmly planted on the ground, yet in his rolling Scottish brogue he spoke of ghosts and faeries. The miracles revealed in the New Testament had driven him out of the Church as a medical student, he said. Now mysterious wonders would draw all skeptics back to religion. He reminded them with a chuckle that he was supposed to know something about detective work. For him, this case was proven.

With awe he described the apparition of his mother at a séance in London. "Do you think a man doesn't know his own mother's face? I could swear by all I hold holy on earth that I looked right in her eyes." Jean Doyle, who had witnessed the moment, was seated onstage beside her husband. When he asked her to confirm the phenomena she did so assuredly. Proof? He told the audience about Kingsley. His death. Their reunion. He knew his own son's voice. He knew fact from illusion. Clear evidence, he insisted, was about to be presented. There were mediums in England with the gift for spirit photography. They were able to capture with cameras the world that psychics see. Here was proof the dead were with us, active and interested!

Suddenly the lights went out and the pictures started. The first showed a ghost gliding across a room at noon, holding in her hand a lighted candle. "The darkness of the theater, the spookiness, the uncanny effects produced by the pictures and the impressive sincerity of Sir Arthur as he told the history of the subject on the screen had a weird effect upon the crowd," the *Herald* reported. Houdini felt as if he were experiencing a séance for 3,500 spectators. It was unnaturally silent within the auditorium. He heard the popping of floorboards, the breath of his petite wife, Bess, sitting next to him. He felt her shudder as dead boys flashed on the screen one after another. There was a photograph of Kingsley's vaporous form smiling tenderly at his father. Loud gasps were heard in reaction to the image that followed. "On a divan sat Lady Lodge. Next to her sat Mrs. Leonard, a medium. Between the heads of the two women—thinly sketched but clear in every physiognomical detail—was the face of the dead Raymond." Next came another prim lady, who sat with the grim form of her son floating beside her. A bullet hole pierced his skull. Blood was pouring out of it. That was how he'd been killed at Ypres, Sir Arthur solemnly commented.

Some comfort for that poor lady, Houdini reflected. The picture that most interested him, though, was of the medium Eva C. Luminous rods shooting from her body held a table aloft during a remarkable sitting. This was her ectoplasm, Sir Arthur explained to the audience. It melted like "snow in sunshine," but when hardened it was powerful. Six men could not push that table down, he claimed. Houdini's eyes flashed but he kept quiet. No table was levitated during his séances with Eva C. He had never seen any of the effects shown in spirit photography.

Last in this spectral gallery "was the picture of a woman in a trance with six men looking above her head. They appeared to be startled. They had a right to be. Out of the sleeping body of the medium was coming a radiant creature who seemed to issue from the woman's shoulder like a wisp of smoke from a cigarette. The wisp curled upward and began taking form. Presently the legs and body of a beautiful woman were seen and then the head and shoulders heavy with unfastened hair. It wasn't a moving picture but if one followed the wisp of smoke one received the impression of a movie."

"You have seen the picture of an angel," Sir Arthur declared. "That's what that was, an angel."

◆

In presenting his images of the phantoms of dead boys swirling around the living, Sir Arthur spurred a new interest in spirit photography. The following day the *Herald* inquired what Dr. Walter Prince, America's most respected psychic investigator, thought of the phenomena. They found him at the Hotel Pennsylvania, participating in a psychic tea arranged by the Opera Club of America—a program consisting of music, psychoanalysis, the science of the human aura, Spiritualism, tea, and small rum cakes.

While sampling the refreshments Dr. Prince disclosed that the chief photographer of the prints Sir Arthur was exhibiting, William Hope, had refused to submit them for scientific analysis. For this reason, and because Hope was a professional medium, the expert was unconvinced. He conjectured that Hope's effects were due to either trickery, double exposure, or telepathy. Prince made it clear, though, that he had nothing but the utmost respect for Sir Arthur's "altruism and honest belief in Spiritualism."

Some felt differently about the British missionary. In a bellicose speech, New York's mayor, John Hylan, asserted that Doyle was out to fleece the country. "From all reports," he said, "the shekels are rolling in to him as fast as when he told how easy it was for the famous detective of fiction to get out of tight places." The English had tricked us into bailing them out of a horrendous war; and now Doyle arrived with his New Revelation—a call to arms, critics warned, for every shady medium in America.

As a former spook himself, Houdini knew how the flimflammers operated. He informed the *Times* how a false medium might lead a client into self-hypnosis, or by reading their facial cues could sense if they were onto something with their so-called spirit messages. He even said that some clairvoyants, if truly intuitive, might absorb "the telepathic wave from another's mind," and thus appear to channel the dead or read the future of the living. But he insisted that even a genuine psychic, if one existed, was tuning into the sitter, not the departed.

He said he had yet to meet a real necromancer.

When Thurston the Great made a lady float in midair without suspension, or Houdini escaped the death-row cells that should have held him, or depths that should have drowned him, it was not, they made it plain, *real* magic. The Society of American Magicians, of which Houdini was president, considered itself a voice of reason in this "renaissance of medieval superstition." The society threatened to ostracize any magician who claimed to possess real supernatural powers. Modern magic was "the natural enemy of spiritualism and of the occult." And Houdini's mandate was to expose any so-called Lady of the Darkness whose séances exploited the bereaved.

Yet there he was, reveling with the Doyles, linking hands with Sir Arthur's favorite mediums, and spouting occult themes in his new movie. Had he finally seen the Spiritualist light?

After one of Sir Arthur's lectures, Houdini escorted Lady Doyle along a side corridor in Carnegie Hall to rejoin her husband. They came to a padlocked door. Just as she turned to go back he reached out and "picked off the padlock as one picks a plum from a tree." It looked like he had magnetized it with a magic pass of his hand. She found the feat amazing. On another occasion, while riding in a taxi, Houdini showed the Doyles how he could detach his thumb from its joint, as if it were invisibly amputated. It was an illusion that almost caused Jean Doyle to faint. Hence, the magician wondered how this couple might fare in their search for mediums in America, if they were so impressed by sleight of hand. When they stopped by his home in West Harlem, he gave Sir Arthur a biography on Ira Davenport—he of the celebrated Davenport Brothers, the magicians whose nineteenth-century spook shows had merged the arts of spiritism and conjuring.

Houdini was doing exactly the opposite. His straitjacket demonstrations at the Times Square Theater required no dimmed light, screen, or curtain to hide his maneuvering. Instead he provided a more visceral spectacle: a torturous, contortion-like struggle. There was no pretense of harnessing occult powers. Unlike other magicians, Houdini revealed the trick and in so doing bared his spirit. Imitators had once tried to match him. So during the War, he had had another flight of masochistic fancy. He performed the straitjacket escape while suspended upside down some hundred stories in the air: "Top that!" he seemed to tell the competition.

"The life of an escape artist," he remarked, is "no bed of roses." One tussle with the jacket had done irreparable damage to his kidney. Another time the winds had sent him careening into a window ledge that deeply gashed his forehead. The most frightening mishap, though, occurred in Oakland, California, where the ropes on the crane that held him aloft became entangled and they couldn't lower him. He hung for almost twenty minutes that time, the pressure building in his skull, until a window washer tied a store of towels together and threw them to him—like a lifeline to a drowning seaman. This and other escapades were often caught on camera. For he had begun to offer in each city on his movie tour a prize to the best picture of the aerial straitjacket escape. The newspapers judging the contest received hundreds of photographs of Houdini contorting wildly in the air. And no filmy spirit beside him.

Séance by the Sea

*I*n June, Doyle faced his toughest critics when Houdini made him the guest of honor at the annual gala for the Society of American Magicians. Laughing heartily while puffing on his Limehouse perfecto, Sir Arthur appeared to enjoy their tribute to spirit vaudeville. When Houdini called for him to speak, the audience expected an impassioned call for communion with the dead, the spirit pictures. Instead, Doyle displayed moving images of monstrous creatures. They were dinosaurs; feeding, playing, loving, fighting with their fearsome teeth and horns—and tails that snapped a death blow to a rival. No one had ever seen anything like this on a movie screen. Many magicians believed that they were watching actual psychic pictures of beasts from another dimension. Doyle's "monsters of the ancient world or of the new world which he has discovered in the ether, were extraordinarily lifelike. If fakes, they were masterpieces," the *Times* marveled.

"How did you do it?" asked Houdini.

The next day Sir Arthur wrote him that the creatures were constructed by "pure cinema but of the highest kind" and were being used in *The Lost World,* a movie based on his book of the same title. His purpose in exhibiting the moving pictures without any explanation "was simply to provide a little mystification to those who have so often and so successfully mystified others."

◆

Sir Arthur's friendship with Houdini reached its heady apogee after the gala, when, just before sailing home, the Doyles invited him and Bess to join them for a weekend in Atlantic City. After arriving at the resort Houdini found his way to the hotel pool, where he taught Sir Arthur's sons to dive from the high board and float on their backs. He showed how he could submerge himself underwater for an astonishing length of time; his secret residing in the powerful inhalations and exhalations he practiced before the stunt. Like them, he had to breathe or die.

Later they joined the women by the ocean. While the children played with a beach ball and dashed in the surf, Houdini observed his Spiritualist friends. Sir Arthur was as upbeat as anyone he had known since Evatima Tardo. Lady Doyle told him that he had never uttered a cross word to her, nor to the children. The family was in almost daily communion with ghosts, yet Houdini felt a lightness in their presence; even the little ones told him they had no fear of dying. They spoke of their dead brother, Kingsley, in the Summerland—a place as real as any on Earth. Later Houdini was moved when one of the boys ran up to Jean, remarking that he was lonesome for her and wanted to give her a kiss. He did so caressingly on the mouth, then put his lips to each finger on her hand. It was as passionate a display of filial devotion as Houdini had ever seen outside his own home.

The magician's second day in Atlantic City was his mother's birthday. Appropriately his mind returned to the loss that had revived his interest in spiritism. Eleven years earlier, at a reception following a performance in Copenhagen, he had received the news from which he had still not recovered. His mother had suffered a massive stroke; there was no hope, wrote his brother Leopold, a doctor. The Great Houdini had instantly fainted in front of the press and two princes of Holland. He wept openly, and could barely walk without leaning on his wife.

In contradiction to Jewish law, Houdini had instructed his family not to bury Cecilia until he returned from Europe. After buying her the pair of woolen slippers that she had requested a few weeks prior to her death, he sailed back to say goodbye. Upon returning home he sat up all night beside her body in the parlor. That morning the Weisses buried her next to Mayer Samuel at Cypress Hills in Queens, with the slippers in her coffin. Once again his parents were together in their own world—and Houdini felt the urge to find them.

On the Atlantic City beach, he sat next to Bess—who looked girlish in a bathing dress of taffeta. She waved to the august Brit striding toward them with good news. He told them that Jean, who practiced that epistolary form of mediumship called automatic writing, had the feeling that Houdini's mother would come through that day. Gratefully, Houdini accepted the invitation to participate in a séance. The Doyles could not have known it was his mother's birthday. And for once he would sit with a medium whom he trusted. Sir Arthur apologized for not including Bess, but explained that the presence of "two people who were of the same mind, either positive or negative" might influence the results.

"Go right ahead," Bess said. "I will leave Houdini in your charge." Then the two men—Houdini in a frumpled white suit, Doyle in a trim dark one—walked back to the hotel while Bess awaited the outcome of the experiment. She closed her eyes to take a nap. Jean Doyle had once told her that in sleep the living may commingle with the spirits. Many a night Bess had heard her husband wake up, asking, "Mama, are you here?"

Perhaps this afternoon she might be.

Inside the suite, Jean was ready to begin. She asked Houdini to sit down while Sir Arthur drew curtains and placed writing pads and pencils on the table. Then began the intimate ritual. Sir Arthur bowed his head and said a prayer. Tenderly, he placed his hands on his wife's to give her added power. Houdini shut his eyes and listened to the lapping of the sea. Without having to be vigilant for trickery, he had never felt more open at a séance. Quieting his doubts, he tried to accept the Doyles' beliefs wholeheartedly. He had always been particularly fascinated with their notion of the etheric body. Often he was aware of a subtle force directing his physical movements, as though he were ahead of his body while walking the streets. At the moment he had a sense of that sort—as if he were floating. "If I ever had an astral body or soul, that soul was out of my body as far as it was possible and still live," he wrote of the sensation, "waiting for a sign or vibrations, feeling for the presence of my dearly beloved Mother."

Before long Jean sensed a presence. Her hand began to flutter; in an awe-filled voice she said that no force like this had ever seized her. She pounded three times on the table—the sign that Houdini's mother was the visiting spirit. She took up a pencil and with emphatic strokes put Cecilia's messages to paper. Sir Arthur tore off a page and handed it to Houdini. *"Oh my darling, thank God, thank God, at last I'm through,"* the communication began. Houdini looked pale and "deeply moved" as he read on.

The Doyles too were emotional; they knew what this reunion meant to the man in the white suit. *"I always read my beloved son's mind—his dear mind."*

Here was finally proof for him!

Five days later, in New York, Houdini told Sir Arthur that he had been "walking on air" since the séance. Sir Arthur understood the feeling. To experience authentic spirit contact was to be twice born. He wished to know, though, whether the Atlantic City sitting had changed Houdini's estimation of his own unusual powers—because something else happened there, and it had stunned the Doyles.

Jean had channeled fifteen pages of automatic writing, and Houdini seemed to accept every word to be as genuine as the cherished letters Cecilia once wrote him while he was on tour. Yet Houdini wanted the spirits to perform an encore. Just when Sir Arthur thought the séance in Atlantic City was over, Houdini had picked up a pencil and took a stab himself at automatic writing.

The word "Powell" immediately came through to him.

"Truly Saul is among the Prophets!" exclaimed Sir Arthur; for Dr. Ellis Powell, a Spiritualist friend of his, had died the previous week. Houdini had never heard of this gentleman, he later said, and was not aware that he had crossed over. He suggested that he was thinking of another Powell, an ill friend of his, a fellow illusionist.

He conceded that it was a strange coincidence.

In the parlor of Houdini's brownstone, Sir Arthur told him that the Powell explanation would not do. Did he still not recognize his gift?

Houdini smiled dubiously. The dead did not speak to him, but he had always wondered whether some invisible presence was protecting him.

He admitted that just before a dangerous stunt he listened for a voice to tell him when to dive or leap. "You stand there, swallowing the yellow stuff that every man has in him," he explained, "then at last you hear the voice, and you jump." He recalled that once he trusted himself rather than his guides and almost broke his neck.

Doyle had never heard Houdini come so close to admitting he was psychic. He sensed that his friend was on the right path now. *"I brought you, Sir Arthur and my darling son together,"* Cecilia had said in her message. *"I felt you were the one man who might help us to pierce the veil and I was right."*

That evening Mr. and Mrs. Houdini celebrated their twenty-eighth wedding anniversary with the Doyles. The four of them attended a glittering revue called *Pinwheel.* Wherever they went the stage lights followed. The show was interrupted when its impresario, Raymond Hitchcock, pleaded for Houdini to "do a little stunt." The magician demurred even as the crowd chanted his name. Settling the matter, Sir Arthur pushed Houdini onto the stage. Cries for his famous needle mystery arose. The performance of *Pinwheel* had stopped. Actors, crew, and chorus gathered around the stage to watch. Houdini swallowed five packages of needles then brought them up in a flourish all tied together. There was a thunderous applause. He bowed deferentially to his British friend. The spotlight then switched to Doyle.

The following day—their American adventure over, their last interviews given, their king snake, a gift from the Bronx Zoo, put back in its container—the Doyles gathered on the deck of the *Adriatic* to bid farewell to the throng of well-wishers and reporters assembled on the pier. And when the whistle sounded and the hawsers were cast off, Sir Arthur could feel satisfied about his mission. His optimism and fervor had resonated with Americans who were tired of a winter of Prohibition and humdrum politics. He had been received, wrote Horace Green of the *Times,* like "a breath of fresh air." He seemed to believe that a single proven medium was all that was needed; for "even if in the entire world of evidence, only one person were found capable of mediumistic materialization," Green observed, then the Rubicon was crossed.

For the time being, Sir Arthur took pride in the fact that it was not just Gold Star Mothers responding to his lectures; he had garnered respect from many of the reporters who he had feared would mock his work. There were indeed some who scoffed, and embarrassments and missteps had occurred, but overall he considered his tour a success. He had set lecture-hall records in New York, spread his message in presentations from the Eastern Seaboard to the Midwest, tested numerous American mediums, and hoped that he had won some new adherents to Spiritualism—most importantly, the magician he felt had been on the fence until Atlantic City. And really, it was generous for his friend to see him off. There was Houdini, waving briskly from the wharf.

The Prize

*I*n those days life was like the race in Alice in Wonderland," said F. Scott Fitzgerald, "there was a prize for everyone." Whether the award was for brains, grit, or grace, it didn't matter. There were prizes for transatlantic flight: Soon it seemed that every ex–Army pilot and Air Mail captain had eyes for European shores. Aviators and their flying machines were streaking across the front pages. Orson Desaix Munn's publication, the popular *Scientific American* magazine, had once sponsored contests for flight. It was the tabloids, however, that exploited the public's hunger for carnivalesque thrills. There were prizes for endurance: The dance marathon craze had begun. Americans were collapsing into one another's arms. The country was plunging toward hell in a handcart, the moralists warned. There were prizes for beauty: Sweethearts in wool swimming dresses graced the rotogravure pages of William Randolph Hearst's dailies.

From his offices in New York's Woolworth Building, Orson Munn ran a more respected press. He had nothing to do with the gaudier contests. Neither, though, was he among those offended by the first national beauty pageant—where teenage girls paraded past a maestro called King Neptune and his entourage of Nubian slaves. Before a crowd of 100,000 excited spectators assembled on the boardwalk of Atlantic City, the first Miss America was crowned—a beaming sixteen-year-old from Washington, DC. Seeing her face in the newspaper, Munn felt she bore a strong resemblance to the star Mary Pickford, whom he had met years earlier at a benefit during the War. Munn was himself married to a stage actress. A prominent New York socialite, he attended gala affairs. His work involved discussing and reading about subjects like Marconi's radio waves, the firepower of the latest battleship, and the twelve-cylinder car. Yet he had a flair for the rumba and spent his nights on the town. A tall, gangly, silver-haired man, he was ubiquitous in both scientific and entertainment circles. Two of his friends were Thomas Edison and Harry Houdini. He spoke fluently the language of both of their worlds.

◆

There were prizes for science. Even the lofty new discoveries in physics were brought down to earth when James Malcolm Bird, an ambitious *Scientific American* editor, presided over a competition in 1920 to find the individual who could best explain to the country just what Albert Einstein had discovered and what it all meant. It had not promised to be a major event. But with strong public interest in the latest scientific trends, Bird's contest caught on. A purse of $5,000 was put up—a sizable sum for the day; more prize money than had ever been offered toward science outside of the Nobel Prize.

Two years later, Bird was intrigued by that most controversial field of science—psychic research. A former mathematics professor at Columbia University, Bird had an intense, critical air. With his cloth cap, lean physique, and beaklike nose, he resembled Sherlock Holmes, and his observant eye noted the large splash made by the two crusading Englishmen, Lodge and Doyle. The paradox was tantalizing. During a period of a great surge in technology, spooks were in vogue. "The atmosphere of America contains more electricity than that of any other country and therefore more spirits," Sir Arthur had declared in Washington. He claimed that spirits were drawn to voltaic fields.

There was a prize for ghosts. Houdini's friend Joseph Rinn, a wealthy produce merchant and fierce debunker of mediums, had put up a large cash award if Sir Oliver Lodge could produce in his presence a convincing visit from Raymond or any other spirit. He later made the same challenge to Sir Arthur Conan Doyle. But the occult knights would not be drawn into a demeaning contest. The spirits, they made it clear, could not be summoned by coin. In an editorial, the *Boston Globe* concurred with Doyle and Lodge. "If there is a spirit realm accessible to the inhabitants of earth, the door to it will not be opened by a key of gold, for the simple reason that it could not possibly be that kind of door." Orson Munn felt otherwise. In the present environment he was certain that the golden key fit all doors.

Sir Arthur pursued a Grail, not a prize. Undistracted by frivolous challenges, he had just sold out seven New York halls—breaking Sir Oliver's record of six. His tour had then proceeded with an evangelical flair across the nation. "I take not one shilling of the proceeds of my lectures, so that I have no material interest," Doyle had told a crowd of 3,000 in Dayton, Ohio. "Approach this from a religious angle or leave it alone."

Although church attendance was down, a wave of fundamentalism ran at crosscurrents with Sir Arthur's spiritist revival: a choice between the Sweet Bye and Bye or Summerland. The leading Christian evangelist at the time was Aimee Semple McPherson, a brash, bob-haired sister who motored across the Bible Belt in her Packard touring car—her "gospel car"—inveighing against dance halls and occultism. From airplanes she dropped leaflets with the Words of Christ upon communities she visited.

There was a prize for religion. The moviemaker Cecil B. DeMille put a question to the masses flocking to the cinema houses. What picture did they most want to see? Through the *Los Angeles Times,* DeMille offered a large cash prize to the "Best Idea" for him to adapt to the screen. The country seemed mad for movies, prize contests, and motorcars. Yet by the end of DeMille's nationwide idea contest, he realized that many still wanted some Scripture. He immediately commenced work on the winning idea—a picture based on the Ten Commandments. It was to feature what he considered the most phenomenal event in history: Moses parting the Red Sea.

In New York, Orson Munn could still recall the days when church spires rather than office towers commanded the skyline. With its steeples and Gothic patterns, the Woolworth Building looked like a massive cathedral to him. It was a temple, though, of industry and commerce, and Munn's fifth-floor *Scientific American* offices were occupied by journalists with no previous interest in religious marvels. In mid-November of 1922 Munn met with his chief editors, including Malcolm Bird and Austin C. Lescarboura, in a charged editorial room. They assembled to discuss a recent challenge that Sir Arthur Conan Doyle had issued their magazine. He wanted the *Scientific American* to conduct an investigation of psychic phenomena. Being such a controversial subject, it required coverage by a reliable journal.

It was not that Munn and company refused to report on the supernormal.

As Doyle was aware, they did so frequently. By now the *Scientific American* was featuring reports on mediums in practically every monthly issue. But their approach was to present a contentious subject such as spirit photography and in that same issue have two experts offer divergent conclusions. The men of *Scientific American* presented no editorial opinion. They were, Sir Arthur implied, sitting on their hands—mutely observing. *Come, gentlemen,* he seemed to implore, *you won't determine a blessed thing in your offices in that skyscraper that Woolworth commissioned off the fortune he made on the five-and-dime store.* He encouraged them to become directly involved in séance research: to judge for themselves the demonstrations of those mystifying forces that Lodge, a frequent contributor to Munn's journal, had been unable to explain by natural laws. Doyle would not have to wait long to hear back from them. "The *Scientific American,*" Lescarboura wrote him, "accepts the challenge."

◆

Sir Arthur didn't know what a chord he had struck. To Munn and his colleagues it appeared he was questioning their reputation for zealous investigation. They were about to unmask Dr. Albert Abrams, who had swindled so many during the electronic-medicine craze. Bird and Lescarboura would determine that Abrams's famous apparatus, "the Dynamizer," was about as accurate in its medical diagnoses as a Ouija board. Resourceful journalists, they had a penchant for revealing to the public whether or not there was any substance behind a maverick scientist's claims. More than a magazine, the *Scientific American* was an agency committed to distinguishing genius from quackery, and to determining what lay even a half century ahead of the curve. Practically from its first issue in 1845, the magazine foresaw the motorcar. When it was only the stuff of fantasy novels they predicted the aeroplane. The work of Munn's predecessors was the stuff of legend. When Tammany Hall had ridiculed their calls for an underground rail system in New York, the *Scientific American* had dug a tunnel beneath Broadway and built one themselves. Through a pneumatic tube they sent a car surging back and forth via compressed air. It became a popular attraction. They had shown it was possible! They charged 25 cents a passenger for a ride on their thrilling transport.

Like his father, the previous publisher, Munn was a patent lawyer. For almost seventy-five years, three generations of the family ran a flourishing patent advisement firm that had helped license almost 200,000 new ideas and devices. Many of the great inventors had marched through the law offices that were next door to the magazine: Morse with his telegraph; Howe with his sewing machine; Gatling with his gun; and Edison, over the years, with a multitude of brilliant wares. Munn & Co. saw those things first. They considered it their mission to help Americans make sense of the latest technology. And now they had been urged to put aside the machinery and link hands in the séance room.

Malcolm Bird recalled that Austin Lescarboura was the first at the meeting to propose a contest. The idea was to crown a genuine medium, if one could be found, whose supernatural gifts would be confirmed by a committee of prominent judges—the top scientists, the savviest ghost hunters. An electrical engineer by training, Lescarboura had no taste for theater; he wanted the magazine to conduct a thorough scientific trial. Though his colleagues were in agreement, they sensed the investigation's commercial appeal. Thirty-five thousand contestants were answering DeMille's challenge. In the past, the *Scientific American*'s own contests had usually boosted circulation. And at that moment Munn was particularly interested in increasing sales. Even for the times he was remarkably profligate. He owned two opulent homes—an apartment in the Waldorf-Astoria and a Southampton estate. While attempting to travel by rail between Manhattan and Long Island, the Munns had once missed their train's departure. Orson Munn had thus proceeded to a nearby automobile dealership and purchased a luxury car—a silver Pierce-Arrow. The couple motored across the Queensboro Bridge in style that day. But he was about to leave his actress wife for a young dancer from Buffalo. He would soon be paying hefty alimony, so finances were a serious concern. Hope for increased revenue was not, however, the primary motivation for the psychic contest. The reputation of Munn & Co. had risen in the past, under the stewardship of Orson Munn's father and grandfather. Munn and his staff intended to make their own mark through the proposed investigation. "The idea of the *Scientific American*," one columnist wrote, was "to prove or disprove all the beliefs of spiritualists with one swishing swipe of its sword."

"On the basis of existing data," Lescarboura told the press, "we are unable to reach a definite conclusion as to the validity of psychic claims. In the effort to clear up this confusion and to present our readers with first hand and authenticated information regarding this most baffling of all studies we are making this offer." It was a purse of $5,000.* But those who sought to claim it, the *Scientific American* made it clear, should not be mental mediums. "We are not interested at present in the psychological manifestations," Lescarboura wrote Doyle, "because they do not lend themselves as readily to strict scientific methods of investigation. Furthermore there is greater interest, so far as the public is concerned, in physical phenomena." In other words, they were not looking for the sort of psychic who could come through with the name of a sitter's dead aunt's favorite cat. They wanted to test the physical medium—the kind of clairvoyant, once called a necromancer, who could make objects fly about the room and produce ectoplasmic forms. It was ghosts they were after. There were now "Rewards For Spooks," the *Los Angeles Times* reported. *A prize! A prize!*

---

* The magazine would offer two $2,500 prizes, one for physical phenomena and the other for spirit photography. Each would be worth approximately $35,000 in 2014 dollars.

The Ghost Hunters

*T*here was a ghost in Nova Scotia, a haunting in the county of Antigonish that sent shivers down from Canada. It began when the MacDonald farm was disturbed by a specter drawn to their adopted daughter. At first the visitations were not destructive. Raps and inexplicable bells were heard. Clothes and furnishings went missing. When the MacDonalds awoke to check their stock, they found distressed animals rearranged in stables. Their cows' tails were braided. What began as a nuisance soon became a recurrent nightmare. Fires with an eerie blue hue began erupting. Animals were murdered. Amateur spook hunters arrived but were no help; they too seemed scared and left bewildered. Then one evening thirty-eight conflagrations chased the family from their house. When a reporter and local detective arrived, they claimed to be slapped across their faces by the phantom. From the MacDonalds' farm, twenty-two miles by sleigh from anything resembling a town, the latest occult furor had erupted. Here might finally be the spook to defy science, many newspapers speculated.

Professionals were sent for. Dr. Walter Franklin Prince, of the American Society for Psychical Research, had never encountered a haunting he hadn't been able to explain by natural means. It was Prince's assignment to proceed with a team to Canada to see if he could solve the mystery. "A Party of inquisitive scientists now threatens to break in upon the quiet of the Antigonish ghost, whose fame grows with each new thrill he, or it, causes," the *Times* reported. Quoting Sherlock Holmes, cackling at his own jokes, and recounting tales of other rural hauntings, Prince—the fifty-nine-year-old psychic detective—was avuncular and patient. He rigged the MacDonald home with secret traps, in case humans and not poltergeists were the guilty parties. He sat in the parlor all night with a revolver, a camera, and a magnesium flash beside him. Neighbors expected at any moment to spy him fleeing from the place in horror. But nothing really happened. It was windy, a door blew open; that was all the phantom had to offer. On Prince's final day the MacDonalds' teenage daughter, Mary Ellen, sat blithely on the porch petting her kitten—the intruder was gone, she told her father. Prince had examined the burn marks on the walls, however, and determined how the outbursts started. According to him, Mary Ellen was the culprit, not the channel. In a possessed state, she had caused all of the phenomena. For the spectral slaps he had no explanation; the men may have worked themselves into such a frenzy that they either hallucinated or struck each other, he reported. Many were disappointed by the demystification of the Antigonish case. Mary Ellen, princess of flames, was committed to an asylum. And nothing more was heard of ghosts from that wild outpost above the border.

◆

Few had better credentials than Dr. Prince to judge a psychic contest. The Antigonish sleuth possessed two degrees from Yale and a keen knowledge of both magic and psychology. He was a former pastor who appeared to be less mystic than scientist. During a crankish, whimsical era, he remained a Maine farmer at heart—resolute and unimpressionable. After receiving Malcolm Bird's invitation to judge the *Scientific American* competition, he expressed both interest and reservations. Somehow, the idea of a prize challenge did not sit entirely well with him. Was this to be some highfalutin dance contest?

"I knew that investigations conducted by the *Scientific American* would attract much attention and excite criminations and recriminations," he wrote. "I deferred acceptance until I could consult my official superiors." As Prince soon discovered, though, the man whose consent he needed— William McDougall, president of the American Society for Psychical Research—had already been approached to join the *Scientific American* investigation. McDougall was boarding Munn's train. Prince was cleared to follow.

The ASPR was the sister chapter of England's pioneering Society for Psychical Research. In addition to presiding over both offices, Dr. William McDougall was one of the most esteemed psychologists working in America. His forerunner as both the president of the ASPR and chairman of the Harvard Psychology Department had been William James, who famously bemoaned that souls were out of fashion. As acclaimed for his intellect as his brother Henry was for his novels, James had been devoted to séance research, which he saw as the best hope for establishing an interrelationship of mind and spirit.

"Are the much-despised spiritualists and the Society for Psychical Research to be the chosen instrument of a new era of faith? It would surely be strange if they were; but if they are not, I see no other agency that can do the work," James wrote many years earlier. The father of American psychology, he was the inspiration, even after his death, for a new generation of ghost-chasing alienists that included McDougall.

Contrary to James's work, the general tilt in psychology was now toward the mechanistic approach. So McDougall had caused a stir when he wrote a treatise, *Body and Mind,* that stressed how humans are driven by a higher intention. A man of Scottish descent, McDougall never felt accepted in England—neither at Cambridge, where he learned, nor at Oxford, where he lectured. Sensing a "land of romantic opportunities," he came to the States in 1920, to take James's old position at Harvard. Due to James's influence, Harvard had always been the university in England and America most hospitable to psychic research. Nevertheless, Dr. McDougall tolerated no nonsense in the séance, and he did not hesitate to reach for an apparition, if by so doing he might expose a fraud in white muslin. Like Prince he rarely found mediums he could believe in. The Spiritualists were therefore hostile toward both of them.

There was some debate at this time whether psychic phenomena was the domain of psychology or physics. Because the *Scientific American* would be testing physical mediumship, they wanted a physical scientist. Austin Lescarboura had a good candidate. A former professor at MIT, Daniel Frost Comstock was a respected physicist and engineer. While less well known in the field of psychical research, he too was a member of the ASPR, and a zealous ghost chaser. Not yet forty, Comstock was suave and good-looking. Some found him as convivial as Munn, only smarter and younger. In his own way he too bridged science and entertainment; he was the inventor of Technicolor and founded that company. DeMille was to use Comstock's groundbreaking process for certain scenes in *The Ten Commandments*. Comstock, for his part, found Bird and Munn's contest to be an extraordinary production. He welcomed the challenge of substantiating a medium's power.

The author Hereward Carrington was also enlisted. Dr. Carrington had joined the ASPR in 1900 as a precocious nineteen-year-old embarking on what would be a lifelong psychic journey. He had cut his teeth investigating Lily Dale, an occult community and popular summer camp for those desiring a palm reading, a zodiac consultation, or a few sentimental words from the departed. At Lily Dale, disguising himself as a dupe with bad eyesight, Carrington sampled slate-writing mediums, materializing mediums, spirit photographers . . . a veritable smorgasbord of the supernatural arts. He tried them all, and all attempted to fleece him. So controversial was his exposé of the flimflammers' methods that the *Times* had featured his report. High-profile investigations were his bread and butter.

Carrington was an Anglo-American who lived in New York but spent considerable time in Europe, as well as the Orient. He was fastidiously well mannered, charming but elusive. He had a wife whom no one saw anymore and a PhD from a university in Oskaloosa, Iowa, that no one had heard of. At dinner parties—while the men discussed Ty Cobb's hitting streak or whether the Naval Treaty would hold—Carrington might sit with one of their wives, discussing that premonitory dream she'd had when she was twelve. Some thought him a crank. Carrington was one of the first to introduce Americans to a mystical form of contortion called yoga. He wrote scores of books, not just on clairvoyance but also on health and diet. He called for a return to the "natural food of man"—subsistence by means of raw fruits and vegetables. He had the wan, ethereal look of a psychic himself, but he was a former vaudeville magician who knew all the tricks and gaffes that spook mediums used in the séance.

By 1922 there was likely no researcher in the world who had investigated a wider range of supernatural claims than Carrington. He had tested the notorious Eusapia Palladino—a coarse, rotund, wily medium who levitated tables and shot cool breezes from an invisible third eye on her forehead. He had sat many years earlier with the uncanny mental medium Leonora Piper—the first to convince Sir Oliver Lodge and William James, among others, that it was possible to converse with the discarnate. And he had participated in the debauched magic rituals of the "world's most wicked man"—the poet and sorcerer Aleister Crowley.

Soon the *Scientific American* had assembled a jury of five: two distinguished men of science, two professional ghost chasers, and, most notably, Harry Houdini—who was finishing a book, *Magician Among the Spirits,* that chronicled medium fraud. Houdini was a special case. He claimed that Munn had agreed to clear all candidates for the judging committee with him first. "I am to know each and every man so selected," he informed Bird. Having never heard of Comstock or McDougall, he feared his reputation as a master of illusion would be ruined if the judges were to crown a sly impostor. He had far more at stake than the $5,000 prize the magazine was offering, he told his colleagues. Then he ruffled Bird's feathers by chastising the editor for not consulting him. He was further aggrieved by something Prince had observed: "The *Scientific American* was to have all the responsibility and take all the credit."

Houdini was telling reporters that the *Scientific American* challenge was *his* notion. In fact, it had been Austin Lescarboura's idea, it was Orson Munn's prize money, and it was Malcolm Bird's contest. Bird was the editor at the journal with the most knowledge of the psychic world. It was he whom the publisher had selected as director of this enterprise, and to him befell the task of choosing judges. Uncharacteristically, Houdini swallowed his indignation and fell in line. The press touted this to be "the greatest spook hunt of modern times." And he, claiming to be in pursuit of what William James had called a white crow—that rare, undeniably genuine, medium—was eager to be a part of it.

Part IV

THE SAXOPHONE AND SPIRIT TRUMPET

᛭

Awake and sing, ye that dwell in dust for . . .
the earth shall cast out the dead.
—ISAIAH 26:19

It was a time of miracles.
—F. SCOTT FITZGERALD

Malcolm Bird, producer of the
Psychic Contest

Announcing

$5000 FOR PSYCHIC PHENOMENA

A S A CONTRIBUTION toward psychic research, the SCIENTIFIC AMERICAN pledges the sum of $5000 to be awarded for conclusive psychic manifestations.

On the basis of existing data we are unable to reach a definite conclusion as to the validity of psychic claims. In the effort to clear up this confusion, and to present our readers with first-hand and authenticated information regarding this most baffling of all studies, we are making this offer.

The SCIENTIFIC AMERICAN will pay $2500 to the first person who produces a psychic photograph under its test conditions and to the full satisfaction of the eminent men who will act as judges.

The SCIENTIFIC AMERICAN will pay $2500 to the first person who produces a visible psychic manifestation of other character, under these conditions and to the full satisfaction of these judges. Purely mental phenomena like telepathy, or purely auditory ones like rappings, will not be eligible for this award. The contest does not revolve about the psychological or religious aspects of the phenomena, but has to do only with genuineness and objective reality.

This is merely a preliminary announcement. The names of the judges, the conditions applying to the seances, the period for which this offer will remain open, etc., will appear in our January issue.

1923: Speed

By now it was not enough to seize the day; many were seizing the moment. "Jazz it up" was the expression. It meant to pick it up. No music was faster. Even the foxtrot was considered too slow now. The Charleston would soon be arriving. Flappers were called "quick women." The battle cry seemed to be: Get what you can, for we all die tomorrow.

One giant figure embodied the notion that the country was on a spree. Babe Ruth gorged himself on eighteen hot dogs, blacked out, and woke up in St. Vincent's Hospital. THE BELLYACHE HEARD ROUND THE WORLD, *ran the headline. Everywhere people lived large. Sports were jazzed. The Yankees did not have to grind out wins. The Babe decided games with one mighty drive to the bleachers. Boxing had also changed. Fights used to go twenty rounds, even thirty. Now before the end of the first round Jack Dempsey had pounded his man to the canvas. Neither was football immune to brisk sensation. Red Grange revolutionized what had been a plodding game. There was no longer a need to advance downfield play by play. In a stadium built in Champaign, Illinois, to honor the War dead, Grange dashed to the end zone each time he touched the ball. "The galloping ghost," the press called him.*

A Jaunt with Kitty

*M*rs. Crandon excelled at no sport, though she loved a bracing horse ride along the Back Bay Fens. How wonderful it was to own and take out a horse again. On her mount she kept a pace that her husband found dangerous. For that matter, he always felt she drove her car too fast. During the War she had been a volunteer ambulance driver. In that capacity she was sent to the New London naval base that he commanded. After their marriage, Mina usually drove him around and too often he had to remind her there was no one dying in their automobile.

One day early in March, Mina went for a horse ride with her good friend Kitty Brown. They discussed Dr. Crandon's improbable interest in spirit mediumship, which was hard for either of them to take seriously yet. Her husband was a gynecologist, Mina joked; naturally he was interested in exploring the netherworld. But she told Kitty that a séance sounded like great fun. And she decided on a lark that she wanted one that day.

The minister of the First Spiritualist Church had been highly recommended by her friend Mrs. Richardson. "So entirely in search of amusement, I went with [Kitty] in order to gather some good laughing material with which to tweet the doctor." They showed up at their clairvoyant's door, still wearing their boots and riding breeches, and expecting that he would "try to put them off to a later date, or that they would meet some other easily recognized variety of mediumistic chicanery." Instead the minister seemed forthright and kept his ritual short and sweet.

Welcoming them into his study, he promptly went into a trance. Within minutes he was sensing spirits, among them a strapping, good-humored blond boy claiming to be Mina's brother. Her first thought was to wonder, What was this medium's method? How could he know of her dead brother in heaven? "If this is so," she said to the ghost, "give me some evidence that will identify you." She noticed that Kitty was staring over her shoulder, as if trying to picture the spirit that the medium saw behind her. Resisting the urge to look back, Mina glanced at her boots. Perhaps the medium caught that gesture. He said that her brother was reminding her of some trouble she had with her boots when they once went riding. Mina recalled her pony mired in a swamp as a child. When she dismounted she too became stuck, and her brother, always resourceful, had used a knife to cut open her boot and free her. She suspected that this is what happens with mediums. They make a hit and you fill in the rest of it. But what the minister told her next was even more surprising: Mina was being called to "The Work."

He said that she had rare powers and soon all would know it.

Thinking about the séance on her way home, it made perfect sense to Mina that her brother should be the one to come through to her, since they'd had a special bond—growing up together "in relative isolation from the other children." When he was a child, Walter was believed to have psychic gifts. He played at "table turning and spirit rapping"—the occult arts he had witnessed on his first trip to Boston. That is, until their father, pious Isaac Stinson, "set his foot down and firmly forbade it." The séance had been sacrilege in their home.

Since marrying Roy Crandon she had adopted the agnosticism of his enlightened circle. But while he considered mediumistic research a science, it was to her a curious trifle. "Many things were far from my mind, but few farther than spiritism," she later said. "I was interested in my home, my boy, in music and dancing, very much like any normal woman. And when the doctor my husband—began to read about psychical phenomena and tell me of it I rather disliked the subject."

Still bewildered, Mina told the doctor what had happened at the séance. His dismissive reaction surprised her. Dr. Crandon had been corresponding with respected professors and scientists. He declared himself "intellectually convinced" now of an afterlife. Yet he trusted no professional medium. No Spiritualist church. And no message dispensed by oracular ministers. "It's all a fake," he told her. She too decided that she had been hoodwinked. It was preposterous to think that the dead could come back, and that she might produce them. For a time she forgot what the medium told her.

A Square Deal for the Psychics

SIR ARTHUR CONAN DOYLE SEES EVIL IN REWARD OF $5,000 FOR SPIRIT
—*New York Times*

*M*alcolm Bird believed in no God, spirit, or discarnate voice. He saw his contest as purely a scientific enterprise, an investigation into a mysterious mental—yet natural—force. With all the talk of miracles, he believed that he and his colleagues at the *Scientific American* were the ones to use modern equipment and methods to answer the age-old question concerning the supposed powers that mediums possess. Let DeMille have the prophet Moses for his movie. What Bird invoked, when presenting Munn's contest to the *Scientific American* reader, was the most exalted psychic in the ancient world, the Priestess of Apollo.

For fourteen centuries a woman was chosen to be the Sun God's oracle, and pilgrims flocked to Delphi from as far as Asia to receive her counsel. The Oracle at Delphi inhaled magical vapors thought to emanate from the Earth's navel and then delivered her intoxicated forecasts from atop a cauldron in Apollo's Temple. Her words were incomprehensible and required a Delphic priest to interpret: men were rational; women psychic and ecstatic. There came a time, however, when one of her monastic men, the historian Plutarch, noticed the gases from the chasm were losing their aroma. Christianity had begun to flourish in Rome, and with the waft of the new religion the seeress's day was over.

◆

Even during the Oracle's reign there was debate, Bird claimed, as to whether she was "inspired or drunk or merely canny." So in 1923, with psychics once again conducting the rites of a religion, the argument resumed: one man's quack was another's Cassandra. "The controversy of today," he observed, "is essentially the controversy of 1000 B.C. translated into modern terms and given a modern setting." The difference, as the *Scientific American* saw it, was that the modern clairvoyant worked in a rational rather than superstitious world. If she wanted Munn's purse, she would have to face twentieth-century music, a score to be composed by some of the top psychic researchers and experts of the time—Prince, McDougall, Comstock, Carrington, and Houdini.

Bird admitted that it might be too ambitious to hope to solve the psychic riddle once and for all, but he explained that the contest's mandate was to answer the question for the present generation—many of whom were seeking mediumistic guidance as none had since the heyday of the oracle. Accordingly, the New York–based judges—Carrington, Houdini, and Prince—and the *Scientific American* representatives—Bird, Munn, and Lescarboura—gathered in the magazine's editorial room. While Houdini paced the floor or fingered a deck of cards, and Bird smoked Old Golds, the men exchanged views on psychics and framed the rules for the contest. Houdini wanted to employ thorough restraint to ensure no possibility of fraud. To his annoyance, Carrington insisted his control methods were too extreme, and the other judges agreed. Clairvoyants would be searched and rope could be used to bind them, it was decided, but not in the draconian fashion Houdini had in mind. "We do not wish to draw any picture of a medium trussed up like a roast fowl," said Bird.

But who and where were the great modern psychics? The first medium Bird wanted to bring to New York was Ada Bessinet, an Ohio seeress whom Doyle called the most outstanding physical medium in the States. In a sitting for him, she had produced the spectral face of his mother, wrinkles and all. Mrs. Bessinet summarily refused to sit with Houdini, however, and there was no immediate alternative. The contest needed Doyle's sanction, all felt, for the worthy psychics in Europe and America to step forward. "I place the announcement in your hands," Lescarboura wrote Doyle. "First, because your challenge has been instrumental in our making it; and second in the hope that you may influence some of the more prominent British mediums to come to this country for the good of the psychic cause."

It was "a square deal" they were offering the psychics. The mediums could work in complete darkness, Bird announced, and in a sympathetic circle. "We do not accuse the photographer of chicanery because he shuns the light, and insists that what light be present be red. We know also, if we will but admit it, that a hostile atmosphere does make more difficult the exercise of the mental faculties." As Bird had hoped, many psychics were assured by his statements. They were eager to win the endorsement of the prestigious *Scientific American;* the problem was that no credible mediums were in the ranks of those showing up at the Woolworth.

Among the first aspirants was a male medium who asked the magazine officials to lock the door to the room in which he was to be interviewed. Only then, in a low voice, did he confide to Bird that a spirit had channeled him the secrets to a marvelous machine for which he wanted Munn & Co. to pay him $25,000 to develop. He was dismissed without further questions.

The next candidate, an Italian barber from Williamsburg, Brooklyn, said that when it came to producing ghosts, turning tables, and talking with famous dead men—Shakespeare, Caesar, and Ben Franklin—he was better at the dark sport than any queen of ectoplasm. His offer was also rejected.

It was a parade, Bird felt, of crackpots, queens of mystery, and charlatans. An older female psychic who visited the *Scientific American* office told her interviewers that after many years studying the news sheets she had observed that citizens who got their faces in the papers resembled certain animals, a phenomenon that she believed Mr. Aristotle of ancient Greece had discovered about famous persons in general. To exhibit her case, the medium brought with her a bulging valise containing thousands of cut-out faces from the newspapers, each with an animal counterpart attached to it. Unfortunately, as she sat down her suitcase opened, strewing pictures over the floor and under desks. It took the office staff practically an hour, Bird reported, to retrieve them all for the distressed psychic. Her bid to compete for Munn's prize was, to her great disappointment, declined. One did not summon men like Comstock and McDougall from Boston or pull Houdini from whatever skyscraper he was hanging from or movie he was making to test some quack just off the train from Lily Dale or Cassadega.*

Doyle had warned them this would happen. Responding to the an-

---

* The two Spiritualist communities in the USA.

nouncement of the *Scientific American* contest, Sir Arthur—in a letter dispatched to Munn & Co. and published in the New York dailies—maligned the psychic tournament as "a very dangerous thing. A large money reward will stir up every rascal in the country." The more gifted psychic would be wary of a prize contest, he promised. "For the sake of the cause and their own reputations they would help you," he conceded, but only "if you got the personal support and endorsement of leaders of the movement."

As it happened, to involve *him* would not be an impossible task. Despite an aversion to the crasser elements of the contest, Sir Arthur was pleased "to see a journal of the standing of the *Scientific American* taking an interest in psychic matters." He had this in mind: that Orson Munn should fund an international search to be conducted by a savvy but fair individual. This man would scour both Europe and the United States for talented mediums. If the *Scientific American* were to send such a representative to him, Sir Arthur promised to give him entrée to the best clairvoyants in England, to essentially take him under his wing. Above all, though, Munn's agent had to be someone who was courteous and receptive—not the least antagonistic in the séance.

"Everything," he told them, "depends on your man."

◆

One month later, in early February, Malcolm Bird crossed the Brooklyn Bridge with two reporters who lived in the outer borough. Their conversation concerned in large part the preparations for the psychic contest taking up Bird's every working hour. Maybe it was the effect of the visit they had just made to a Broadway speakeasy, but there was something otherworldly to the twilight view from the bridge promenade. The clusters of yellow light beneath hazy domes and spires made the city seem a fairyland on opalescent water.

The evening's drinks notwithstanding, Bird's companions were sober materialists who gave little credence to the psychic revival. As for Bird, he liked to claim that he spoke "neither as believer nor as disbeliever" and would not make up his mind until better acquainted with the spirit medium. This was soon to happen; pursuant to Doyle's plan, Bird had recently booked passage across the Atlantic—where he intended to investigate the best clairvoyants in Europe.

Actually, Bird had reserved two possible crossings in order to ensure, depending on which mediums were available, the most opportune arrival. He also hoped to see something of London during his visit, but as it would turn out, he'd only get a glimpse of Westminster and Parliament, and not see the Tower at all, so busy was he with Doyle's psychics.

The first medium he met was John Sloan, a meek Scotchman whom Bird judged to have an intelligence "comfortably below the mean." This was the first séance the producer of the *Scientific American* contest had ever attended, and what struck him straightaway was his utter blindness when hands were clasped and the candles extinguished. A proper séance, as Bird was experiencing, is a sphere into which no light leaks, no human eyes adjust—as they might to a bedroom at night or to starlight. "One can stay there till kingdom come," he vouched, "and visibility will remain at the zero mark. One who has never attended a dark séance has in all probability never been in this sort of darkness."

Soon after the sitting commenced, voices came in a hushed whisper through the spirit trumpet sitting on the table and most assuredly not, Bird was certain, from the mouth of the medium seated next to him. When an invisible entity calling itself Captain Morgan took over the trumpet, things got "pretty thick." What happened next stunned the visiting American.

Although Bird had come to the séance incognito, the voice described him strolling across the Brooklyn Bridge with two companions three weeks prior! Captain Morgan claimed to have followed Bird's movements ever since the editor had made plans to visit Europe for work that the spirits deemed important.* Bird had reserved two tickets for his passage, the Captain revealed. The editor could not fathom how this wraith could utter things known only to a few colleagues with the magazine.

Racking his brain afterward, Bird could not determine any means of trickery; he later wired the friends with whom he had tramped to Brook-

---

* The spirit misidentified one of Bird's friends on the Brooklyn Bridge as a woman and was off by one day as far as the precise date of the shadowed excursion.

lyn, but neither could solve the mystery. How many blank séances had Houdini endured in his quest for spiritist proofs? Yet Bird, from the start, had something eerie to report under the credible masthead of the *Scientific American.*

Next, Sir Arthur directed Bird's European talent search to one of the most revered psychics in England. It was Gladys Osborne Leonard who first reunited Sir Oliver Lodge with his dead son Raymond; and Doyle said she was the best trance medium he knew of. The pleasant Mrs. Leonard would not be the star, however, of the *Scientific American* tests. Mr. Bird expected more for his thirty shillings. When the medium was possessed by the girlish spirit Feda, a number of discarnate voices were introduced to him—all murmuring that they had known him in life while cascading him with general information. Almost none of these personalities were the least recognizable to Bird—and a spirit channeled by Mrs. Leonard was way off in describing him. "I pause here," noted Bird, "to remark that this picture of me as a shrinking violet, highly sensitive to all sorts of delicate conditions is just about as whole-hearted a miss as any spirit ever made."

Whether wrong or right, these spectral voices were not what the *Scientific American* was seeking; theirs wasn't a contest of mental mediumship or second sight. Evan Powell, the Welsh channel through whom Sir Arthur first received communications from Kingsley, was more the model for their tests, as he produced not only messages from the dead but glowing forms and unambiguous physical effects. During an early-afternoon séance in London, Powell caused flowers to rise from a vase and caress each sitter's hand and face. While Bird suspected that Powell had slipped a hand free of his bonds, he was nonetheless impressed with the demonstration. "It is not inconsistent to speak of a given psychic performance as partly genuine and partly fraudulent," he explained. Regardless, Powell, whose gifts were being studied by the sympathetic British College of Psychic Science, would not commit to coming to America for more stringent tests.

On to the Continent, where Bird sat in Berlin with the mystifying Frau Vollhard. This dramatic medium, while kept under strict control, instantly materialized branches and large stones that struck the séance table. In their post-séance interview, Frau Vollhard's vivid blue eyes became even brighter when Bird converted the contest's prize stakes for her at 20,000 inflated marks per dollar. "But even for the purpose of winning such a colossal sum," he informed the *Scientific American* reader, "she would not sit in other than her own clothes and would not submit to more than a perfunctory search."

Just as he was ready to leave the Berlin apartment, and then Europe altogether, something else, rather terrifying, occurred when Frau Vollhard abruptly shrieked then revealed on the back of her hand spontaneous stigmata—deep bleeding punctures, as if she had just been bitten by a demonic creature. But the *Scientific American* committee would never examine such phenomena; the special conditions the medium insisted on—that her baggy clothing be allowed, her person remain uninspected—had marked her, like all other candidates presented to Bird, as unsuitable for further consideration.

The New Sherlock Holmes

During the 1920s, Sigmund Freud advanced the idea that the death drive, what he called *Todestrieb*, is intrinsic to our nature. As if to prove it, Houdini leaped, while others peered, into the abyss. While not one to dabble in the new psychology, Sir Arthur wondered whether the escape artist had an unconscious urge to join his mother in the next life. After their Atlantic City séance a trusted medium warned the Doyles that their friend's life was in danger. And how awful it is when a superhero lies broken on the pavement.

In New York a daredevil known as the Human Fly lost his grip while scaling the façade of a skyscraper. With the words SAFETY LAST—the title of the Harold Lloyd picture he was promoting—painted on the back of his iridescent white garment, the superhero seemed to hang lighter than air for a moment, then plummeted ten stories to the asphalt. The Human Fly died in front of 20,000 aghast spectators at Greeley Square—among them his twenty-year-old bob-haired wife, who would receive for her loss the $100 he was supposed to have been paid for the caper. "For goodness sake take care of those dangerous stunts of yours," Sir Arthur wrote Houdini. "You have done enough of them. I speak because I have just read of the death of the Human Fly. Is it worth it?"

Indeed, it was worth it! All of Houdini's wealth and notoriety came from performing dangerous feats; it would be far worse to walk the streets unrecognized than to fall ten stories. Yet he appreciated Sir Arthur's paternal concern for his welfare, especially since the relationship between the two was practically ruptured.

◆

He is "just as nice and sweet as any mortal I have ever been near," Houdini said of Sir Arthur shortly after their first encounter at Windlesham. Then came the marvelous times in New York and the culminating séance in Atlantic City. Soon, though, there were dark clouds in paradise: a rift had begun over exactly what had happened that afternoon in the Doyles' hotel room.

After returning to England, the novelist insisted that Houdini was transformed by the reunion with his mother, and that he had finally recognized his own power as a spirit medium: "Dear Houdini—Is there any truth in the story of Doyle that you got an evidential message from your mother through Lady Doyle?" wrote Eric Dingwall. "Also that you have become an automatic writer?"

The answer from Houdini was no, and he essentially said so publicly. On the day before the Halloween of 1922, he told the New York *Sun* that Spiritualism was nothing more than spook tricks, and mediums either crooked or hysterical. What prompted his statement was a challenge issued by psychics to their greatest foes: the magic order. It appeared that mediums foresaw the announcement of the *Scientific American* contest—for the General Assembly of Spiritualists made the reverse offer and put up $5,000 to any stage wizard who could produce eight psychic manifestations by deception.

Houdini accepted the challenge; it was becoming apparent that he considered the whole cult of spiritism to be his opponents and that he had never played it straight with the Doyles. His competitive juices flowing, he made headlines that infuriated Sir Arthur: DISAPPOINTED INVESTIGATOR SAYS SPIRITUALISM IS BASED ON TRICKERY AND THAT ALL MEDIUMS CHEAT AT TIMES—BELIEVERS SELF-DELUDED. Houdini was now slandering his religion, Sir Arthur felt, and by imputation his wife.

The press wanted a rejoinder from Doyle. "They sent me the New York *Sun*, with your article," he wrote Houdini, "and no doubt wanted me to answer it, but I have no fancy for sparring with a friend in public." Sir Arthur thought it undignified to reveal what had happened in Atlantic City, but he could not shake the vision of an awestruck Houdini receiving Jean's gift to him. He recalled his friend blissfully leaving the hotel room, clutching in his hand, after a decade of blank séances and disappointing results, the scrolls of automatic writing. "When you say that you have had no evidence of survival, you say what I cannot reconcile with my own eyes," Sir Arthur wrote him. "I know by many examples the purity of my wife's mediumship, and I saw what you got and what the effect was upon you at the time."

The spirits that had brought them together were precipitating their clash, and Houdini implied that his friend was not handling their disagreement sportingly. "You write that you are very sore," he answered Doyle. "I trust it is not with me, because you, having been truthful and manly all your life, naturally must admire the same traits in other human beings."

He then expressed the doubts—"The letter was written entirely in English, and my sainted mother could not read, write, or speak the English language"—that led him to reject Lady Doyle's communication. Houdini expected a genuine message from his mother to be in her native tongue—which Sir Arthur, who knew few Jews, assumed was Hebrew. Doyle explained to him that there was no language in the next life: psychics like his wife received transmissions in "a rush of thought." Trance mediums "might get the Hebrew through," he told him. "I don't think a normal automatic writer ever would."

Truly, their religious views were incompatible. "By the way," Doyle continued, "Mr. Bird told me that, in the very complete test given you by your mother, you found it incredible that she, a Jewish lady, should put a Cross at the top. The Cross is put by my wife above the first page of all she writes, as we guard against lower influences, and find it protective." Sadly, the escape artist was proving himself reluctant to make his greatest leap of all, thought Doyle.

After being asked to participate in Munn's spirit hunt, Houdini backed down from the challenge to produce by trickery the Eight Feats of Mediumistic Power. As one of the five chosen judges for the contest, he could not do open battle with the Spiritualists and claim to be impartial. Nevertheless, Sir Arthur complained that with Houdini's inclusion the *Scientific American* committee "becomes biased at once. What I wanted was five good, clear-headed men who would stick to it without any prejudice at all." But if Doyle had lost Houdini, he seemed to bond with Bird—the man upon whom everything depended.

They arrived from England together on April 4: the crusading Spiritualist and the *Scientific American* agent. The newsmen called Doyle's latest mission to America—his tour of '23—"The Second Coming of Sir Arthur."

However, judging from the reception that Malcolm Bird received, they were as interested in this "new psychic sleuth" and his international spirit hunt. "At a time when half of Europe seems to be dabbling in spiritualism and when there are thousands of converts to the idea in the United States," Bird's reports struck a chord.

He had seen a thing or two in the dark room. "Tables did jump off the floor, lights did appear, voices did issue from trumpets and mediums, vases did move through the air, all apparently because of some mysterious force the source of which has not been discovered. Mr. Bird said he saw everything which Sir Arthur said he would see, except ectoplasm, the strange substance which issues from the body of a medium."

Even so, Bird was surprised by the attention he received at New York Harbor. Just a few years earlier he had been a capable but obscure professor at Columbia University. Presently the reporters, of their own accord, had promoted him from secretary to "Chairman" of the *Scientific American* contest; they failed to realize that, rather than an expert and judge, he was only the coordinator of the psychic challenge. But having returned on the *Olympic* with Doyle, he was perceived as an important new player in the Quest Eternal. "I suggested to Mr. Bird that he come to me and place himself in my hands," Sir Arthur told the press. Having created one ingenious detective, he was seemingly molding another.

Bedfellows are rarely stranger than those made in the séance. Part of Bird's appeal to Sir Arthur had to do with something the European mediums had sensed: his presence was a boon to the harmonics of the gathering. One of Mrs. Leonard's spirits had prophesied that Bird was "eventually to do much work in the spiritist movement"; other spooks averred that he himself was a medium.

Malcolm Bird was making a name for himself and acquiring so much supernatural experience "that if he should criticize our movement, he is a critic whom we will be obliged to listen to with respect," said Sir Arthur. Conversely, Doyle warned that Houdini would "keep away every decent medium—for they are human beings, not machines, and resent insult . . . they do not go into an atmosphere which is antagonistic."

To reassure the psychics, Sir Arthur intended to sit in on the séances

Bird was organizing for May. He also told reporters that he would assist in the *Scientific American* search for that still-elusive prize-worthy medium.

Accordingly, Sir Arthur and Bird sat in a dark room in a rustic home near Lake Erie. The sleeping Ada Bessinet was slumped in the chair next to them, her breathing heavy and portentous. The room, however, was alive with her Odic energy. Spirit lights of yellow with a reddish tint darted over and around the heads of sitters. Then came a steam of grayish and transparent faces—thirty? forty?—that Sir Arthur strained to recognize before they faded. "I think that is Oscar [his dead nephew]," he exclaimed; another face with closed eyes he identified as his mother. Bird himself saw no familiar form—but then, he had lost no one close to him. This made him, he felt, a model observer: "I am unemotional in the presence of these phenomena," he wrote, "to what I conceive to be an extraordinarily cold-blooded degree."

But Secretary Bird did have an impulse for hyperbole. Convinced of the sincerity of a grandmotherly slate-writing medium Doyle had recommended in Indiana, Bird reported, "If she is a fraud, then there is absolutely no sense in believing anything creditable about any member of the human race . . . my whole sense of fitness rebels at the idea of this lady being a swindler." The committee judges were increasingly put off by such statements. Sometime earlier Walter Prince had sat with that same Indiana spook and found her work suspect. By commending psychics before any were tested, Bird sparked the fear in Prince that the *Scientific American* endeavor was becoming more journalism than science. The official experts in the contest—Prince, Carrington, Comstock, McDougall, and Houdini—worried that Bird's findings might be confused with their own. The editor was a greenhorn, muttered Houdini, an easy mark for spook fraud.

With each of Bird's reports, the *Scientific American* reminded its readers that his informal sittings were not to be confused with the committee's scientific examination of mediums. The New York press did not always grasp the distinction, though, between his preliminary survey and the rigorous tests to follow. Bird had sat in England for a spirit photograph with William Hope, who Prince and Houdini suspected was a faker. To their chagrin, Bird commented favorably on Hope's spectral pictures.

"It seems most extraordinary and it casts doubt upon all the forth-coming proceedings that Mr. Bird should announce himself as already convinced of the genuineness of spirit photography," editorialized the *Tribune*. They called for the truly scientific inquiry the contest had promised. Walter Prince, who did credit some of Bird's observations, issued his own shrewd reproof: "Mr. Bird, if he wishes to achieve the authority in psychical research which I invoke for him, must hereafter avoid falling in love with the medium."

The Crawford Experiment

*T*he Crandons gave a party with an unusual purpose that May. The dinner guests took their cue from Roy, who behaved more as a sober physician that night than convivial host. The butler, Noguchi, served but one glass of wine to each of the Crandons' friends, yet there was a feeling of anticipation, of electricity, in the air. For it was a pretty ghoulish activity that the doctor had planned. The weather, Mrs. Crandon commented, could not have been more cooperative. It was raining lightly outside.

Mina recognized that this evening would see the culmination of months of preparation by Roy. Before Sir Oliver Lodge had entered his life, her husband was as staunch an atheist, she felt, as her father had been a man of faith. He had once relieved her of her own religious baggage and pointed out to her the folly in worshipping a God conceived by primitive minds. Lately he'd begun saying there was more superstition in the Bible than in séance research. And he no longer dismissed what the medium had told her—that she possessed second sight. The doctor had visited that same Spiritualist minister, apparently giving no intimation of who he was, or that his wife had been by for a sitting. Again a spirit claiming to be Mrs. Crandon's dead brother had come through. Here, though, was the problem with mental phenomena—it was not suited to empirical proof. Chance, intuition, or deceit could explain the hits. Physical displays of mediumship were easier to test; they were either demonstrably real, Dr. Crandon reasoned, or brazenly false.

Of special interest to him were the séance experiments conducted in Ireland by Dr. William Jackson Crawford—a professor of mechanical engineering with a consuming interest in psychic effects. Dr. Crawford had sat with Kathleen Goligher, a nonprofessional clairvoyant, for a series of 170 séances in the attic of her family's Belfast house. Ectoplasmic rods that shot forth, he believed, from her genitals suspended a table high off the floor. He observed it rocking in the air as though borne on a choppy sea. He saw it suddenly turn sideways and revolve until upside down. All by the force of spirit operators who had chosen as their instrument this fey Irish girl. There was something called contact phenomena, which the Goligher circle had tried. They placed their hands on a table and collectively channeled a spirit that caused it to vibrate, move, and communicate by means of knocking or rapping. In effect, Dr. Crawford believed, they had brought the table to life.

With his technical tools—spring scales, pressure sensors, electroscopes— and discussion of reductions and force magnitudes, Crawford was the sort of skilled investigator who interested Roy. As was his penchant, he attempted to contact the scientist directly to elicit further information on his work. Alas, such an exchange was no longer possible. Dr. Crawford had drowned himself in a lake near Belfast. In a letter to his family, he did not blame the spirits for his suicide. "I have been struck down mentally . . . It is not the psychic work, I enjoyed it too well."

◆

Dr. Crandon's objective that May evening was to reproduce the Belfast experiment. "Contact phenomena are quite common," Crawford had said. "Nearly every family contains one member at least who is capable of producing them." Dr. Crawford had left behind a guidebook—to tilting and turning tables using psychic force—that Roy adhered to while planning his own venture into the unknown. He constructed a seventeen-pound table of rough wood according to the Crawford design. It was important that no nails were used, as the wrought iron was said to somehow interfere with the psychic magnetism. He had also purchased a red lantern to illuminate his library, as ectoplasm was most effectively formed in red light.

Dr. Crandon then invited a few close friends for dinner and a séance. By undertaking the experiment with his trusted circle, he felt that he eliminated the possibility of psychic fraud. Trooping up to the fourth-floor Book Room—one of two libraries in his spacious home—were guests with varying degrees of skepticism. Among them were Mina's friend Kitty and her husband, Dr. Edison Brown—two of the Crandon milieu of accomplished physicians and their wives. Curiously, the Browns were the two sitters that evening most disposed to accept the possibility of spirit communication. Less inclined to believe, but as game to try, was an old friend, Frederick Adler, who ran the building on Commonwealth Avenue where Dr. Crandon kept his medical office. Also present was Alexander W. Cross, whose diffidence seemed out of place among this usually lively crowd.

Cross was a troubled and easily rattled man. An Englishman from Canterbury, he carried with him a past that only the Crandons knew about. Aleck, as they called him, had worked for British customs in Shanghai for so long that he had virtually ceased to identify himself as a Westerner. It was during the Great War that his troubles began. While steaming back to England his liner had been intercepted by a German raider that held him captive for six months. When the vessel was sunk, Aleck escaped to the Danish coast. Somehow he made it to England and was given command of 10,000 Chinese coolies bound for labor at the French front. There he suffered trauma that made him unfit for civilian life. He was obese and in ill health when he made his way to Boston after the War. Dr. Crandon, his acquaintance from a previous visit there, did all he could to help. The doctor attempted to find Aleck work, and when this proved unfeasible he hired the poor fellow himself. Cross had a room in Cambridge but as often spent nights at Lime Street on the Book Room couch. Ostensibly he was Dr. Crandon's librarian, but Mina said that his true function was to keep their yellow cat out of mischief. Next to her, Aleck was the youngest of this séance circle. Tragically, he was also the closest to the grave.

◆

The six friends linked hands and rested them lightly on the Crawford table, just as the late scientist had advised. Crawford had also suggested that the ritual should begin with a prayer. Dr. Crandon left that part out. Mrs. Crandon voiced the flippant hope, however, that Crawford or some other spirit might find their way to the red lantern on Roy's desk. Clearly she regarded this activity as spooky fun. Her previous séance experience had not swayed her. Even Kitty, who had accompanied her to that post-ride fling with a ghost, doubted that anything extraordinary had happened that afternoon.

"By this time I was again pretty well unconvinced," Mrs. Crandon remembered. "But my friends, who had unconvinced me, now became very serious. Perhaps the red light sobered them. But to tell the truth they were all so solemn about it that I couldn't help laughing. They reproved me severely, and my husband informed me gravely that 'this is a serious matter.'"

An indefinite period of silence followed, heightened by the ticking of Roy's Quare clock. It was mysterious enough, linking hands in the dark with friends one rarely touched. The red glow gave Aleck's sanctuary the aura of an opium den, though nothing illicit was planned. Aleck shifted his bulk and drew a hard stare from Roy. These probes into the netherworld were not for the impatient. No ghosts were heard. None were really expected by the group hunched over the table. Something inexplicable was happening, though. Breathing and linking as one, the intention of the sitters had become an imperceptible force as much as a thought, and as the séance progressed—a quiver. The table gradually became animate. Dr. Crandon felt it was like putting his hand on the back of a dog. Suddenly the table slid slightly, then rose on two legs and crashed to the floor! In order to determine if one of their circle was a medium, each of the sitters took turns leaving the room. With Mrs. Crandon's departure the vibrations died. Her friends applauded when she reentered the study. The medium had been right about her. It was Mina, of all people, who had the supernormal gift; she who was the powerful instrument of some discarnate mind.

The Eve of the Hunt

*W*ith the *Scientific American* contest just a few weeks away, the New York press was blowing the spirit trumpet in anticipation. It was to be "the most thorough, scientific, and far-reaching spook hunt ever undertaken," announced the *Herald*. The *Times* called it "the Acid Test of Spiritualism." The *Tribune* christened the tests "The Great Spirit Hunt" and observed that "every open-minded person has been looking forward with interest to the investigations," for here at last was the "promise of truly expert and unbiased testing of the claims put forward in behalf of spirit photographs, ectoplasm and the rest of the current crop of spiritualistic doings."

There was still, however, no mention of a candidate. Even with Sir Arthur's support, "the well-known mediums—mediums who are reputed to possess the kind of powers which we desire to study—have not as yet come forward to aid us in our quest," the *Scientific American* reported in May. Despite receiving hundreds of applicants, Malcolm Bird worried that psychics were intimidated by the event at 233 Broadway, since shrouded back parlors were their accustomed stages.

While touring Europe Bird had encountered in Berlin a scientist with "the finest psychic laboratory in the world—and he can induce no medium to work in it with him." Envisioning the sensitive seated in her spirit cabinet while strapped to fifty-seven varieties of technical apparatus, Bird could well understand her absence. By now he wondered if the *Scientific American* had a similar predicament.

The committee's methods were as elaborate as any ever used to verify supernormal power. Aside from the vigilant jury, the candidate would encounter an array of modern monitors, gauntlets, and detectors. To ensure she was not concealing any earthly means for producing ectoplasm, the medium was to be thoroughly searched and then required to wear—rather than the white alb of her Delphic ancestor—a black bathing suit or potato sack (exactly which garment hadn't been decided yet) before entering her cabinet. Jury members would then tie her with rope to prevent her from using her limbs to aid the disembodied powers, and if the bonds were insufficient, there was a mosquito-net cloth to further restrain her. Light was anathema to the formation of ectoplasm—the *Scientific American* had conceded that—but the psychic's arms and legs would be marked with luminous radium spots so that the judges could track any suspicious maneuvers in the darkness.

These tests would not be compromised, as Bird felt some European studies were, by the faulty senses of bereaved sitters and aging researchers. If the *Scientific American* were to affirm the presence of disincarnate beings, it would be on a body of incontrovertible evidence. Walter Prince thought it unwise for Bird to reveal all their methods—what Austin Lescarboura and other technicians had devised would only cool the feet of the sought-after mediums. But if she were a true clairvoyant, why be afraid of benign scientific instruments? The induction coils, galvanometers, and electroscopes were for testing her electric field when the forces were active and also to determine if these so-called spirits were actually composed of physical matter. Munn & Co. revered new technology, and Bird seemed to take pride in describing the gadgetry their investigators employed.

All furnishings, he reported, had electric contacts to monitor any floating vase or levitating table. A phonograph with a directional microphone would be automatically activated should the phantoms cause a rap or whisper. And if any apparition formed, a camera with a powerful electric flash—in lieu of noxious powder—would not fail to capture it. Nothing was left out as the *Scientific American* converted its law library into a psychic laboratory. A chronograph was installed to register the readings of the instruments that were in turn monitoring the medium. Ready for use were kymographs, a sphygmomanometer, and other tools for measuring the respiration, temperature, heart rate, and blood pressure of the psychic—for the spirits were said to drain the vital forces from her abandoned body.

Such were the instruments when scientists had free rein in the séance. And with the apparent success of psychic experiments in Europe, it seemed just a matter of time before an American clairvoyant produced effects that registered on every dial while spectral orbs were photographed and a table floated over the upturned heads of five bewildered experts.

Part V

THE GREAT SPIRIT HUNT

⌗

. . . that it were possible
For one short hour to see
The souls we loved, that they might tell us
What and where they be.
—ALFRED, LORD TENNYSON

I came to myself within a dark wood where the straight way was lost.
—DANTE ALIGHIERI

The
JUDGES

Dr. Daniel Frost Comstock

Dr. Hereward Carrington

Harry Houdini

Dr. William McDougall

Dr. Walter Franklin Prince

The Wizards of Sound

To placate the psychics, Harry Houdini said that he would embrace Spiritualism if any medium should prove its claims. Having not yet given up on converting him, Sir Arthur suggested they visit the birthplace of his religion, the tiny town of Hydesville, New York—the sight of the phenomena that launched the first American séance craze: the famous spirit raps of 1848. The two men never made the pilgrimage, though Houdini was familiar with what had happened in Hydesville and said it was easily explained.

In the beginning was the rap. Rap—rap—rap! The late-night knockings woke the Foxes, ordinary farmers who had never before sensed ghosts in their house. The concerned mother, candle in hand, found her young daughters—Maggie and Kate Fox—in bed, conversing with the phantom that had caused the eerie sounds. Frightened and perplexed, she summoned other Hydesville residents, who were just as astounded by knocks that seemed prompted by the girls' questions to their invisible friend. An alphabet code was deciphered by a neighbor and from there on communications are said to have been established between the living and the dead.

With ghost seekers trespassing on the Fox farm, the mother sent her daughters to a Quaker home in Rochester. The spirit followed them there. Leah Fox, who lived nearby, became a leader of the budding spiritist cult by managing her little sisters' occult gifts. And when they visited New York City in 1850, the influential publisher Horace Greeley put the sisters up at his estate and gave them entrée to people of means; for them Maggie and Kate began to channel disembodied voices as well as knocks on furniture and walls.

As adults the sisters traveled many years later to England, where a venerable scientist, Sir William Crookes, was eager to study the case. According to Crookes, Katie produced raps on a plane of glass, a tambourine, and on his hands and shoulders. The noises were heard while she was suspended in a swing, enclosed in a wire cage, and after she fell fainting on his sofa. The raps were made on the roof of Crookes's carriage, inside a tree, and on the floor of the Lyceum Theater. "I have tested [the raps] every way that I could devise," Sir William stated, "until there has been no escape from the conviction that they were true objective occurrences not produced by trickery or mechanical means."

But even then the Fox sisters were seen as relics of a superstitious craze. It was no longer the Civil War era, when séances were held in the White House and the dead haunted the nation. Unfortunately for Maggie and Kate, who seemed lost in a void, this was also well before the twentieth-century Spiritualist revival. Star-crossed in love, exploited by their older sister, abandoned by patrons, they both took to the bottle. A shunned vagrant, Maggie was eventually paid to reveal the mystery behind the Hydesville sensation. The raps were heard at the New York Academy of Music, where her confession—that she caused the effects by the cracking of her toes—appeared to be the death blow to a movement already on the wane. And that was all Houdini needed to know about the Fox sisters, who launched a religion with their pranks and were buried in paupers' graves.

◆

Sir Arthur describes the Rochester Rappers as operating a "spiritual telegraph." Their powers were discovered just as commercial lines for Samuel Morse's receivers were being laid in all directions; and Rochester, home to Western Union, was then the hub of electric wire communications. In 1848 there was a mysterious link between the new technology and spiritistic phenomena—as if for every tap of the telegraph there was a corresponding rap from the shadowland.

Seventy-five years later there was renewed interest in establishing communications between two worlds. A telegraph operator in his youth, Thomas Edison was still touched daily by the pulse of Morse code. Since he was practically deaf, his young wife tapped it on his hand so that he could keep up with parlor conversation; if they attended a play she tapped the dialogue on his leg; and when they walked the Great White Way the din was barely audible to him. And yet, Edison was a wizard of sound. When Alexander Bell first presented the telephone, no one could hear through it—until Edison improvised the carbon transmitter that made voices louder. Now he hoped to construct an apparatus—a valve, he called it—that would amplify transmissions through the ether.

The inventor said that "the time will come when science will be able to prove all the essentials of what faith has asserted." Nevertheless, he abhorred occultism. Contrary to Lodge, he experienced no psychic breakthrough or transformation. "From my experiments with Sir Oliver Lodge and other scientists who believe that it is possible to demonstrate the existence of life beyond the grave, I cannot say that men live after death," he emphasized. "Our experiments brought no results that convinced me of the presence of the departed."

For this reason, Sir Oliver advocated contacting the dead through the spirit medium, the mental radio, rather than by any mechanical invention. Although no Morse code operator, Lodge heard his own odd tempo. As a youngster he had learned a five-finger piano exercise that became an obsessive tic in later years. While with company or alone he tapped lightly on the table—a habit he would take to his grave and hopefully beyond it. He sealed the melodic code in an envelope and deposited it with the SPR, with the idea that after his death a spirit medium would rap it on the séance table. In this way proving, after the envelope was opened and the notes revealed, that the human mind was the most powerful receiver.

By 1923, radio was the latest communications wonder. Marconi's wireless receivers would carry discarnate signals to the living, Doyle predicted. There was a curious parallel, he said, between spirit manifestations and the wireless: for were not both Hertzian waves and psychic transmissions carried through the all-pervading ether?

Unlike religions inspired by a prophet's holy vision, Spiritualism owes its genesis—and revival—to spectral sounds. A signal was received in the last year of the World War by George Valiantine—a down-and-out forty-three-year-old razor manufacturer who was startled by three peculiar raps at the door of his New York hotel room. No one was there when he answered the knock. Moments later, the disturbances were heard again, this time resounding through the empty corridor. A Spiritualist friend later told Valiantine that the knocks were the sign of a disembodied presence. She held a séance and the intrusions returned. The befuddled Valiantine, a man with no mystical tendencies, had "the gift" and was meant to develop it, according to a message from a dead relative. The small-time businessman suspected that the spirits had always been trying to reach him, for he had been hearing raps intermittently throughout his life, or so he later told the committee that invited him to seek the *Scientific American* prize.

The Jolly Medium

$\mathcal{M}$alcolm Bird often found that the mediums he investigated, no matter how gifted, were simpletons and rubes. In that class was George Valiantine of Wilkes-Barre, Pennsylvania, who was semi-illiterate, provincial, and inexpressive, yet channeled voluble spirit voices in eleven different languages. Like a human radio, Valiantine became known for his direct-voice mediumship—that is, he transmitted messages that seemed to manifest from space rather than by means of his own voice organ. To amplify the communications, two spirit trumpets were always placed on the table and in the course of the séance both megaphones might float above the heads of the sitters while emitting a spectral pulse.

Since the days of the Fox sisters, gifted mediums had attracted patrons to help them materially while they performed the Good Work. Valiantine's benefactor was Joseph DeWyckoff, a magnate more mysterious than the psychic himself—and a figure, despite his Spiritualist beliefs, as worldly and shrewd as Valiantine was folksy and jocund. Though he lived in New Jersey and was born a Russian Jew, DeWyckoff did not appear to belong to any particular place. He dropped hints of an adventurous past and was rumored to have done clandestine work in Cuba during the Spanish-American War. At present a lawyer, and a director of Vanadium Steel, he was one of the world's wealthiest believers in Summerland. He resided on an estate of over two hundred acres known as Arlena Towers—a pleasure ground with a nine-hole golf course and a private lake, where his discovery, Valiantine, liked to catch the pickerel and bass served up for breakfast. A lifetime associate member of both the SPR and ASPR, DeWyckoff, while neither bereaved nor a researcher, was on his own spirit hunt. The steel tycoon sat with many of the great mediums of the day both in Europe and the United States.

After hearing about the Wilkes-Barre seer, DeWyckoff invited him to

Arlena Towers for an exhibition of his work. Between séances Valiantine appeared to enjoy his taste of the high life and the felicity of his fascinating host. He stayed at the estate for seven weeks and like few clairvoyants who have sung for their supper, he produced a Babel of tunes. During his visit the medium amazed DeWyckoff, as well as his European servants and guests, with multilingual communications from their dead. "Xenoglossy" is a word Charles Richet invented to describe the phenomenon of spirits speaking in languages unknown to the medium who channels them, and not since the first Pentecost had a mystic manifested such a confusion of tongues.

George Valiantine was discovered by DeWyckoff around the time that the *Scientific American* was searching the world for psychic talent. Before long the medium was visited in Wilkes-Barre by two men seeking a demonstration of his effects: Dr. Gardner Murphy, head of the Psychology Department at Columbia University, and his companion, a reporter for the New York *World*. During their test séance, spirit trumpets rose and sailed about the room, disembodied voices were heard while blue and red lights bobbed about in space, and a ghostly hand touched the reporter's head then vanished as suddenly as it came. The two visitors were impressed, and both gave positive reports: the newsman to readers of the *World;* and Dr. Murphy, who was an alternate judge in the *Scientific American* contest, to Walter Prince.

Soon thereafter George Valiantine became the first official candidate to extend a spirit hand toward Munn's purse. The contestant was well liked; Valiantine, whom Houdini called "the jolly medium," appeared to be as sweet and guileless as a child. He often looked baffled by what he produced.

You Must Not Laugh

*T*he cleaning ladies who took over the fifth floor of the Gothic Woolworth Building each evening were too frightened to do their work. Strange rites were being conducted there. The women heard violent noises, a lady's scream, and the continuous murmur of men chanting hymns. The door and windows to the sealed *Scientific American* library, the source of the disturbances, were cloaked with black muslin to ensure the desired pitch-darkness for the activities inside. Malcolm Bird reported that the devilish sounds and black trappings "struck panic into the souls of those stationed on our floor; they were with the utmost difficulty prevented from fleeing the place." All this was embarrassing to serious researchers like Walter Prince. But the atmosphere was unsettling when George Valiantine was tested by the *Scientific American* committee of experts.

The psychic would have to channel his spirits through the steel marrow of the Cathedral of Commerce. To the sitters, though, it could have been a musty Victorian parlor where they waited for him to perform. In the dark all rooms are the same; and sitting in such a cryptlike state "for two or three hours had a curious effect," wrote a *Times* reporter. "There was a hypnotic suggestion in it, the eyes saw things that were not there, the nerves became tense and jumpy, and it was possible to understand why persons were convinced by the first touch of a 'spirit' hand or the sound of a 'spirit' voice out of the dark."

Aside from the reporter and medium, there was an imposing array of witnesses present for the tests. Chanting with the magicians and ghost hunters was Granville Lehmann of the American Telephone and Telegraph Company, who wondered, like many in the communications bellwether, whether the human brain could really receive messages from the astral plane. Also seated in the circle were Mr. Munn and his *Scientific American* staff, including Malcolm Bird and Austin Lescarboura—"the electrical detective" of the contest. At least two judges were there for each of the tests—either Hereward Carrington or his alternate, the local conjurer Frederic Keating; and Walter Prince, who attended two of the séances. But could Prince's failing ears make out what others heard? *Tap, tap, tap,* the staccato on the spirit trumpet, was often the first of Valiantine's other-worldly sounds. And when the phenomena started, the draining heat in the cloistered room only got worse. All the men wore short sleeves, including Houdini, who showed up baring his sculpted forearms for the final test séance, as if his muscles had any use in this contest with a spook.

"If all we hear about this man is true, he is one of the best mediums in the country," Bird told the press. Even so, the *Scientific American* wanted a convincing demonstration before summoning the entire commission—the Boston-based judges, Comstock and McDougall, were therefore not in the circle when the contest began on May 21. Also absent, due to his lecture tour, was Sir Arthur Conan Doyle. Which is not to say that Valiantine had no ally in the séance room; in attendance was Richard Worrell—the psychic's friend and protector from Wilkes-Barre. The Spiritualist was present to balance the energy of the doubters, and it was he who directed the proceedings, leading the Lord's Prayer and belting, above the others, the various songs the medium needed to bolster his force.

> *John Brown's body lies a-moldering in the grave*
> *John Brown's body lies a-moldering in the grave*
> *John Brown's body lies a-moldering in the grave*
> *His soul goes marching on*

Worrell was the first to sense the presence of a ghost. He said he felt the cold breeze associated with its arrival and smelled the fresh earth of the cemetery. After the singing faded, the *Times* reporter noted that the sudden cackling of the dead "made the hair rise on one's head." When they came, the spirit voices appeared to originate from above the sitters or beneath the séance table—it was no display of ventriloquism, Bird later said, since that ruse, based on misdirection of sight, not sound, is ineffective in the dark. Lehmann felt that if the medium's own vocal cords were the source of the sounds, then he made voices rebound from the floor and ceiling just as Marconi bounced sound waves off the sky.

On display was Valiantine's full aural repertoire: the high falsetto of the phantom Bert; the booming commands of the Indian chiefs Kokum and Hawk Chief; the trill of an opera singer named Christo di Angelo; and the whispers of Bobbie—Worrell's dead son. Returning from the higher plane where he was growing up, the invisible boy frightened a few at these tests. "Go about and touch them, Bobbie," directed his father. "Touch them all on the head with the trumpet, or touch them with your hands." The reporter observed that "it was startling after an hour of darkness to have something tap one's knee or hand." Not all the ghosts had so light a stroke as little Bobbie, though, and when Hawk Chief propelled the trumpet toward Bernard Walker, editor in chief of *Scientific American,* it nearly broke his glasses and his nose.

Two evenings later, Mr. Munn brought to the séance, rather than his wife, a dancer with whom he was smitten. When the girl felt a tap, she "gave forth a shriek," Bird recalled, "that might have been heard blocks away." Not only were the displays alarming the fainthearted, there were also a couple of tussles between sitters and the invisible beings. After sticking his foot out, Bird was reproached for "trying to trip a spirit"; and when Houdini was batted in the head the next night by one of the conical horns, he seized the assaulting object—later to be found broken in three pieces on the floor.

Valiantine was no trance medium; one could converse with him while he channeled the dead. A short and rotund man, he had a habit of saying "pretty good" whenever something pleased him—and that seemed to be most of the time. His effects included orange wisps of light that glowed like fire but oddly did not brighten the room by so much as the gleam of a cigarette. "Will they burn?!" cried Walker, jerking back his leg as one orb dove toward him but did not strike. There was also a guitar placed far out of the psychic's reach that twanged and traveled about the room. At that point, he felt satisfied with his performance. But then things went pretty bad for the jolly medium.

♦

Even before the psychic contest started, Walter Prince was dubious of Valiantine's direct line to Summerland. While Prince's own officer, Gardner Murphy, had recommended Valiantine, the ASPR had another report that cast doubt on the wonder-creator from Wilkes-Barre. "It all sounded suspiciously like trickery," noted Prince, "with which I had become familiarly acquainted." Malcolm Bird was at first more hopeful, but when Valiantine insisted on a dark séance he also smelled fakery. The candidate was a direct-voice medium—not a producer of apparitions—so why the need for a veiled demonstration? Valiantine also requested that the sitters not cross their legs during the séance, another condition that sent up red flags—for Bird knew that fraud mediums wanted to negotiate no roaming feet while they snuck under the table and tiptoed around in the dark.

Rather than express their reservations, the experts appeared to be in awe of the jolly medium. When the contestant spoke of the marvels he had produced for DeWyckoff and others, their reactions were: "Is that so?" "How remarkable!" "Can you just imagine a thing like that?" By golly, was George comfortable with these boys! Where was the scrutiny that the *Scientific American* had advertised? Their idea of control, the judges told him, was to saturate the carpet with talcum power so that any humans walking about during the séance would leave a pulverulent footmark. Though the medium assented, he warned that spirits leave trails too. He was concerned that "we would have an awful time getting the rug clean again," recounted Bird, "and perhaps we would better realize this and put the talcum in pans, here and there across the floor. We were deeply touched by this solicitude."

In truth, the *Scientific American* commission would have found it as absurd to layer the room with powder as they would to sprinkle it with faerie dust from the Cottingley Beck.* Their token attempts at controlling the medium were merely to distract him; in dispensing with traditional restraint and visible control they wound up giving him all the rope he needed to hang himself. Valiantine evidently believed that he was free to cheat,

---

* A rustic area in England where Sir Arthur believed that little girls had photographed real faeries.

as he hadn't read about—could he read at all?—the *Scientific American*'s methods for these tests.

Among the array of traps the investigators put out were ten hidden contacts that Lescarboura attached to Valiantine's chair. As long as the test-medium remained seated, a red bulb glowed in an adjacent room, where an office girl observed it. When on fifteen occasions it faded, she marked with her stopwatch the time and duration of the psychic's absence from his chair. Next to her was a Dictograph operator who kept a record, via Bird's loud commentary, of when manifestations occurred. The time intervals of the physical effects precisely matched the moments when the oracle left his throne. Thus the judges realized that Valiantine was faking the phenomena ascribed to Hawk Chief and little Bobbie. Rudimentary though also damning were the small luminous wall buttons that were visible only to Lescarboura and Bird. When an opaque body, presumably the stealthy medium, passed between them and the disks on the wall, the two editors observed an eclipse effect—and after each eclipse came one of Valiantine's miracles.

At the third séance, on May 24, Malcolm Bird engineered the coup de grâce. The invisibles were drawn to Bird—the fair-minded appraiser of mediums on both sides of the pond—tapping the secretary ten times with the spirit trumpet for each metallic touch received by others. "Hello, Malcolm," a spectral voice had whispered plainly. "Yes, this is Malcolm. Who are you?" he answered.

What followed were inarticulate sounds: if Valiantine's ghosts spoke many tongues, they could now be distilled into an unintelligible "wa-wa"—at least, that was how Bird described what he heard. When asked, however, if the spirit present was that of the deceased Harry Meyer, the voice clearly acknowledged that Bird was correct. Then Bird tried to elicit the details of how Harry had died. He envisioned his careless friend driving an automobile into a telephone pole. Or had he fallen off a ferryboat? "Come, Harry, can't you give me something about the manner in which you passed? Perhaps you can indicate whether you died a violent death? Was it an accident?"

It was most definitely an accident, affirmed the spirit that was again coherent when fed a few details of Harry's demise. Bird's inquiry was suddenly interrupted, though, by a snicker from Munn that provoked a louder outburst from Walker and Lescarboura. These men realized that Bird had never known any individual named Harry Meyer, and they could no longer suppress amusement at their colleague's attempts to draw audible words from a mumbling wraith, which then fell into the trap of proving its own nonexistence—except in Bird's imagination.

The candidate may have sensed then, with his circle in stitches, that the experts had been playing him like the phantom tune on a fiddle. As the exhibition turned to comedy, Worrell reprimanded the sitters. "Friends," he said, "I must really ask that you treat this seriously. After all, this is a religion to many persons, whether you believe in it or not, and it deserves respect. This is the most sacred of all things . . . Please do not laugh."

"Yes, that is so," piped Valiantine in his low brogue. "You must not laugh." But while the committee members—Carrington, Houdini, and Prince—had comported themselves respectfully and not been the ones to react like underclassmen at a Ouija party, the proper atmosphere for spirit converse was lost. Worrell complained that he had not sneered like these men when Valiantine brought his dead mother through. He admonished them for mocking the spirits. Bird, meanwhile, wondered if Worrell would ever finish his sermon—while in the control chamber the girl stared expectantly at the red bulb.

A Waste of Science

*V*aliantine's day was over. It was not long before the *Scientific American*'s first contestant, whose name reporters usually misspelled to match the holiday, realized that none of the experts present at the Woolworth, least of all Houdini, were enamored of his gifts. For Houdini the evening contained more brazen jugglery than test-worthy mediumship. Whatever unusual feats this psychic might produce in a less stringent environment, his séances for the *Scientific American* committee confirmed that he was not their shining candidate.

Although more exhibitions were scheduled, Valiantine abruptly departed on the evening of May 24—never to return. Having solved the case, the *Scientific American* wanted the story of their first inquiry to be an exclusive. Until the magazine published its finding, the sitters pledged not to say what had transpired: when the séance is over, by Orson Munn's edict, the trumpets are silent; even the *Times* agreed not to print anything before the *Scientific American* announced its verdict. Understandably, then, Bird was disturbed when a member of the committee preempted his own report on the unveiling of Valiantine, and shamelessly stole the magazine's thunder.

By the end of Valiantine's performance, the Great Houdini looked, uncharacteristically, to be nothing more than a supporting player. Except for that wicked clout from the trumpet, the ghosts, for the most part, stayed clear of the judge most hostile to spiritism. But few things rankled Houdini more than to be ignored, and he denied any vow to keep quiet. Two days after Valiantine's final séance, the magician called the newspapers and revealed the Woolworth mystery—even explaining the covert electrical devices that Lescarboura had used to trap the psychic, which of course reduced their future effectiveness.

Houdini's reason for the exposé, he said unconvincingly, was that his friends in the magic order had taunted him for falling under the spell of

Valiantine. Hence, he spoke first and pulled no punches with the jolly medium. "I never saw such awkward work in my life," he asserted. "There wasn't a chance at any time that this magician fooled us." By his account, Houdini was instrumental in unmasking a crook. "I think those people ought to be put in jail for preying on the most sacred of human emotions."

While Houdini sought to stamp his name on the proceedings, Malcolm Bird was adamant that they were no place for glory-seekers. When called for his response to the story, Bird said that Houdini had violated the trust of the committee with his loose-lipped condemnations. "And please say," he declared, "that Mr. Houdini is through right now as a member of that Committee." The star expert had not been fired from anything since the days of his beer-hall act—yet this 125-pound former mathematics professor had apparently booted him from the jury. HOUDINI IS OUSTED AS A SPOOK HUNTER, trumpeted the newspapers.

The magician's allegations especially outraged Richard Worrell, who claimed that Valiantine had set off the sensitive contacts on his chair by shifting his weight during the charged demonstrations. Did Houdini expect the subject to stay unnaturally still for three hours in a corpselike state of rigor mortis? When a medium is possessed by spirits, movement is said to be involuntary; and Valiantine's backers still considered his effects prizeworthy. Worrell wanted the medium X-rayed during the next séance (for what purpose, he did not specify); they would then bathe him in red light inside his cabinet, he proposed, so that the committee could photograph spirit forms in all their radiance.

Contrary to the press report, the medium had not been chased out of town. With Valiantine at his side, DeWyckoff showed up at the offices of the *Times*—and there explained that all mediums lose material form while producing ectoplasm. It was this loss of weight, he insisted, rather than the subject sneaking away from his seat, that had been registered by the fancy apparatus. But despite such objections, the *Scientific American* was through with DeWyckoff's psychic. Bird concluded, in his own report on the candidate, that Valiantine "failed to give any evidence whatever that his mediumship is genuine." Speaking for the judges, he announced "that his mediumship stands rejected, and that his claim to the prize and to the Committee's further attention stands vacated." Sometime later, though,

Bird would offer a more nuanced take on Valiantine: "My own personal opinion is that he quite probably has genuine subjective powers, and attempts the fraudulent production of physical manifestations to go with his 'spirit messages.'"

As expected, the newspapers had the final word on the controversy. The *Times* called the committee's exposure of Valiantine "the neatest bit of ultra-scientific, detective work ever brought to bear upon phenomena supposed to have their origin in the intangible, spiritual world." The *Tribune* concurred that "it was not a very auspicious beginning for the spirits." But the paper also stated that it was "A Waste of Science" to test a medium whose "perambulating trumpets and whacks from Indian spirits . . . were old stuff in the General Grant Era."

The editorial particularly chided Bird, the "impresario of the occasion," for dismissing the most competent judge on the committee. And for the first time a respected daily questioned the motives and expertise of an inquiry that, for all its scientific pretense, seemed "largely concerned in securing effective publicity." The *Tribune* observed that—"amid this vast amount of fraud and trickery of the mediumistic world there may well be a remnant of genuine phenomena. Upon that possibility hang theories of great potential significance to mankind. It is a tragedy that every effort to test the existence of spirits should meet such difficulties in living up to a true scientific standard."

The psychic tests, however strict in procedure, could never rise above the quality of the candidates, Bird decided. And so the search went on to find a better class of medium. Toward that end, William McDougall had not been idle in Boston. A short time after George Valiantine was discredited, the Harvard psychologist began to test a young Beacon Hill lady who had only recently discovered she was psychic.

The ABC Club

*I*n late May, just as the *Scientific American* judges were dispensing with their first candidate, Mina Crandon began to exhibit her own, previously latent, psychic power. At the first séance hosted at 10 Lime Street, she had appeared to be more surprised than anyone by the revelation that she alone caused the table effects. Her husband, who had been as incredulous, wanted to see it happen again. So one week later, on June 3, the circle formed for further experiments in his den. By now the party had taken to calling itself the ABC Club, as all at the prior sitting—Drs. Crandon, Caldwell, Brown, and their wives; the devoted Frederick Adler; and Aleck Cross, the troubled Englishman—had surnames that fit. Dr. Mark and Josephine Richardson were the only new additions to the circle. While their name did not conform to the group appellation, the Richardsons had already played an important role in convincing Roy of the scientific merit to this work; and they took on the important responsibility of recording the events.

The Richardsons were two of Dr. Crandon's closest friends. Mark and Roy had met fifteen years earlier, when both were examiners for the same medical insurance company. Around that time a heartbreaking tragedy occurred, when the Richardsons' two young boys died of polio three weeks after contracting the disease. Devastated, the couple saw Boston mediums who attempted to contact their sons. A skeptic at the time, Dr. Crandon had always felt the Richardsons were blinded by grief; one could only walk along the river with those dead boys for so long before it was time to let them cross. But the Richardsons did not let go. For years they were the only Spiritualists among Roy's friends, and he saw in Mark the same paradox he would one day encounter in Sir Oliver Lodge. A notable scientist as well as a physician, Richardson was a pioneer in the development of a vaccine for typhoid fever; he described séance phenomena in the same clinical tone with which Roy once heard him lecture on the cultivation of the typhoid bacillus from rose spots. At present, of course, Roy thought he had been too closed-minded when Mark spoke of the continued existence of his sons.

Dr. Crandon asked his guests to quiet their minds. Mina, wearing a pleated light-blue frock, tried to do the same as the white lights were turned off. During a prolonged silence, the red-lit room began to feel colder and the atmosphere thicker. A series of sudden tilts and jerks of the table began. At first the spirits spoke only through table movements—one turn meaning yes and two no—when questions were put to them by the circle. But when Dr. Crandon proposed that raps to which he assigned a code might be a more effective means of communication, the invisibles agreed. The noises were neither the kind of cracking retorts that the Fox sisters had once manifested nor the tinnier Bessinet variety; these were a series of more muted taps that amplified into a percussion when the physicians applied a stethoscope to the table. And there sat Mina—shivering as the disturbances intensified.

Evidently the spirit of a Mrs. Caldwell, mother to two in the group—Kitty Brown and her brother Frederick Caldwell—had taken possession of the table. What happened next, however unbelievable, was attested to by everyone in the circle. As if dragged by spectral force, the table suddenly lurched toward Caldwell. Whether invisibly propelled or not, the effect was terrifying. According to the séance record, the table pushed Caldwell out of the den, through the dark corridor, and into the Crandons' bedroom, where it forced him onto the bed—after having smashed walls and rumpled all the rugs in transit. While Aleck went into hysterics, and Josephine screamed, the other sitters followed the table that was chasing Caldwell. "On request for more the table started downstairs after him," wrote Dr. Richardson, "when we stopped it to save the wall plaster." Dr. Crandon didn't want to see his home wrecked by the poltergeist—which was what seemed to have been unleashed.

To what else could stunned witnesses attribute such phenomena? Roguish spooks were known to sneak a foot under the séance table to make it rise. But even had Mrs. Crandon—presumably no Mrs. Houdini in disguise—been playing a trick, there was no way she could have engineered the movement of that heavy piece of furniture with her satin pump. Or were four respected physicians and their wives collectively hallucinating?

All members of the ABC Club dismissed the idea they were seeing things that night.

Six days later, something less sensational yet more important in the development of the Crandon mediumship occurred. Roy had proposed a new way of communicating between the spheres. Raps would no longer suffice; instead, he wanted Mrs. Crandon to go into trance and vocally produce the messages, many of which seemed to come from her dead brother, Walter. She resisted this new experiment, which her husband said was inspired by the contact between Sir Oliver Lodge and Raymond. As awed by the effects as the rest of the sitters were, she did not want to miss anything by being induced into sleep. What's more, she was afraid of being possessed by the dead visitors.

"I will do nothing of the sort," she told Dr. Crandon.

For the first time Mina's wishes clashed with her husband's zeal for psychical research. To settle the matter, Roy put the question to the spirit that seemed to be the dominant presence at the séances. "Little sister will do exactly as big brother says," the doctor entreated. Minutes later, Walter indicated through table raps that he wanted to try the experiment.

For a while all hands remained on the table, the only noise a faint series of knocks. Then, as one, all heads turned to Mina, who was making odd noises in the scarlet light. She sat, as if in an opium haze, touching the sides of her face. She sighed and began to sway. Suddenly and loudly a guttural voice unrecognizable as her own cried out: *"I said I could put this through!"* It was her big brother, Walter, and though other invisible souls came through that night—the dervish spirit of Mrs. Caldwell, the lulling voice of Roy's grandmother—Walter controlled this sitting as he would most others at Lime Street. According to the record, when Mina came out of her trance, her face was moist; but not, it was thought, with tears or perspiration. She had been secreting ectoplasm—the substance of discarnate life.

While nothing miraculous occurred during that séance of June 9, an important contact had been made. Skeptics of Spiritualism have always maintained that something is suspiciously absent when loved ones return. Disembodied personalities may lack identifiable qualities—the mannerisms, intelligence, pep, and humor of corporeal life. Often the dead are obsessed with mundane objects they may have owned while alive—a brooch, an article of clothing, a childhood penknife—and their communications, such as they are, sound so mawkish and interchangeable that, if the words of those passed on are any indication, we are all torpid zombies after death.

In the case of the return of Walter Isaac Stinson, lost to Mrs. Crandon since a railroad accident in 1911, none of these criticisms held. Those who had known Mina's older brother swore that the ghost retained all the vitality and charm that he had in physical life; and in the course of providing proofs of his existence, he seemed to be having a pretty good time. Scientists would find it refreshing that in the solemn séance room, fun was had whenever dead Walter arrived. Usually the spirit was affable, as had been the man, except when encountering a sitter he did not like; then he became truculent, a force to be feared. There was no angelic presence; it was not his style to communicate platitudes, or the terse precepts from dead Indian chiefs that so many spirit guides produced. Walter spoke as he did while on this Earth; he could be coarse and profane. Yet he had more liveliness and personality than many of his sitters, the Crandons felt, and when he was present one might forget they were communicating with a disembodied mind.

For Mina, Walter had once been a guiding figure, who taught her to ride horses on the Stinson farm in Picton, Ontario, and to later negotiate Boston—the "hub of the universe" to them—after the family emigrated there when she was a teenager. Though he was five years older, Mina considered him her best friend until his horrible death at the age of twenty-eight. A railroad fireman on the New Haven Line, Walter had been riding a locomotive that jumped a switch—toppling off the tracks and into the sand. Pinned between the cab and tender, he was slowly crushed to death in the Harwich yard.

Twelve years later Walter was a powerful presence at 10 Lime Street, which is not to say that his phenomena lacked grace: the stronger the channel, the more elevating the séance program became. On the Sunday of June 17, one week after Mina's first attempt at trance-mediumship, the ABC Club again joined hands. Walter had promised at the previous sitting that tonight he and Roy's uncle Elliot (an admiral whose Arlington funeral the Crandons had attended on New Year's Day) would demonstrate something that would exhaust the medium and amaze the guests. At this séance, after

Mina had reluctantly slipped into her trance, Walter asked Roy what had most affected him when he watched his favorite uncle put into the earth. The doctor answered that it was the playing of "Taps." *"Your Uncle Elliot stood beside you there as you listened,"* whispered Walter. Then the voice directed the circle to *"have patience"* as a long wait was in store. The red light remained on and all could see Mina, her blond head bowed forward as though praying. It was with an air of triumph that she finally lifted her face and smiled ecstatically into the gloom. She squeezed the hands of the sitters next to her; then came an ethereal rendition of "Taps" "as on a bell so pure as to bear no vibration—almost as though breathed out without the use of an instrument." It was a moving yet chilling manifestation of the hymn to dead fighting men. Two weeks later Walter repeated the tune for an honored guest: William McDougall was present, the world's greatest English-speaking psychologist, said Roy, and a judge for the *Scientific American* prize.

◆

If ever a medium were baptized by fire, thrown into the spiritist controversy so soon after the discovery of her clairvoyant gifts, it was Mina Crandon. Roy's otherwise well-adjusted wife seemed to be possessed by a supernatural force—her effects more dazzling than the traditional whisper through the spirit trumpet or the floating orb of translucent light. Still, it is remarkable how quickly she became the star of psychical research. Less than a month after the ABC Club's first séance, the experts at Harvard appeared to sense the ozone-like waft of ectoplasm from across the Charles River. Dr. A. A. Roback, who knew Roy professionally, was the first outside investigator to participate in the experiments when invited for the séance of June 24. The fastidious Roback, a Harvard psychologist with a thick German accent, was told how the table had manifested incredible power, how it forced itself into the laps of sitters and chased one out the door of the study and down the hall. This all sounded to Roback like so much spirit humbug. Sometime later, when Mina brought the table to life, he slunk to the floor—from where he shone a flashlight at the medium and her sitters, in this way verifying that no human hand or foot was causing the piece of furniture to gyrate and circle madly; as if confused, a sitter later observed, by the strange Jewish professor crouched beneath it.

While there was no place in Dr. Roback's worldview for the occult, he found no evidence of flimflam or pathology. Accordingly, he asked the chief of Harvard Psychology, Dr. McDougall, to help solve the Lime Street mystery.

During the first few months of Mina's mediumship, the psychologists participated in a number of her séances. Walter gladly welcomed Dr. Mc-Dougall as someone respected on the higher plane for his work with mediums. Even so, in their attempts to establish a natural explanation for Mina's manifestations, the investigators found themselves in a kind of contest with her spirit operator, since they wanted to prove that with vigilant control they could stop the phenomena.

For all their efforts, the ghosts still haunted the place.

Mrs. Crandon could not whistle to save her life, so it was perplexing that Walter usually announced his arrival with a nebulous whistle. The sitters also heard at various séances a noise that sounded like chains being dragged across the room; raps resounding on furniture, the walls, the door; and piano notes struck by Walter that seemed both too immediate and too ethereal to be accounted for by the Steinway on the first floor. As Roy's experiments continued, Mina mastered the direct voice—which meant that by midsummer Walter conversed without the use of the medium's vocal cords. Dr. Ralph Harlow, a Harvard-educated ghost hunter unassociated with McDougall's team, said that he "was present many times when Walter's voice was as clear as that of any person in the circle. And it was absolutely fascinating and startling to hear him wander about the room. At times his voice would be close to my ear, whispering some very personal comment about me or my family; at other times it would come from a far corner of the room, or from outside the room, beyond the door piled waist-high with books, or from the center of the table."

Unsettling as the vocal phenomena were, the table was where the action occurred. Could Walter perform true levitation? he was asked during the séance of June 23. The spirit responded that he didn't know but he would try! A tense wait ensued as Walter gathered energy from the circle. Brown, Adler, and the medium would be put on the scales after the séance and found to have lost weight, but the spirit had apparently made good use of their physical essence. Just moments after Dr. Brown "sensed that the table was about to rise," so it did—by supernormal means it was thought, as none could discern in the red room any limb or article holding it aloft. At first the table had risen only by a few inches and very briefly—a display that paled to what Eusapia Palladino, the former queen of table manifestations, was said to have achieved when she was in good form. But it was Walter's modus operandi on the higher plane, as on Earth, to build in methodical stages, as he might a railroad line. Two months later, after steady progress with this demonstration, he was raising the Crawford table for as long as a minute, and shoulder-high.

Thus far Mina seemed able to cause both furniture and inert sitters to take on animate life and there was often a raucous energy when she was in trance. On two occasions a neighbor climbed onto the table in an attempt to stop its quaking, but it bucked him as a bronco would a cowboy. The ghost of Walter Stinson liked to dance with the table—meaning that he made it tip and move to the foxtrot music he requested on the Victrola. If not in trance, Mina was apt to break into laughter, a habit that vexed Dr. Crandon. But Walter did not want his sitters to behave like mourners. *"Don't sit like ramrods,"* he instructed them. *"Let the kid giggle if she likes,"* he chided Roy.

They did whatever Big Brother said.

During the sitting of June 30, Walter directed his circle to carry the table downstairs and into the parlor, where it was reported to have tilted on two legs and played on the piano a simple tune that a deceased friend of Dr. Crandon's had composed while alive. Walter also had stunning tricks he did with his four-legged wooden toy—especially when in the company of Mark and John, the Richardsons' dead little boys. Once, the two phantasm children and their older guide caused the table to pulsate so violently it shattered—*"Richardson and Stinson, wreckers!"* cried Walter. The roughest phenomena, though, were reserved for those who got on the spook's bad side.

Soon the ABC Club was utilizing most of the traditional articles employed for séances, and Mina often sat in a curtained, wood-framed spirit cabinet, which is said to provide the needed darkness and privacy for ectoplasm to materialize. Kitty's husband, Dr. Brown, was cautious in attributing what they had witnessed to spiritistic force, and it was he who often sat next to Mina and kept control of her hands and legs. On one occasion, with Dr. Brown occupying the cabinet with the psychic, it began to shake and move about the floor. Deafening knocks were heard and the curtain pole slashed downward, inches from Brown's head. Then the whole structure spontaneously burst apart.

It was rebuilt into a version sturdier than before. During a red-lit sitting one week later, with Dr. McDougall now controlling Mrs. Crandon inside the cabinet (and he a far tougher audience than Brown), again the pole shot out with hostile force. When the sitters tried to replace it, they claimed to be resisted by an invisible presence that shattered the cabinet a second time. The nine screws that held the structure together were soon discovered neatly stacked in the corner—an orderly touch to the poltergeist effect, and the work of little Mark, Walter said. Mrs. Richardson was then heard to comment that while on the earthly plane her son was always good at picking up his toys.

◆

No member of the ABC Club was as disturbed by Mrs. Crandon's work as Alexander Cross, and he reserved the right to leave the circle when the more violent effects began. Broken years earlier by the War, recently abandoned by his wife, Aleck was the middle-aged neurasthenic case whom the Crandons charitably employed. After witnessing all that the medium wrought, he had become a Spiritualist practically overnight. He seemed to hold Mina—a nurturing presence to him—in affectionate awe, despite her being nineteen years his junior and, he believed, a witch. Aleck did not see her as a spell-maker in the Salem sense, yet he and Roy had noticed at one sitting aurora-like flares shooting from her fingertips; he had heard her issue prophecies in trance that came true in short order; and he was beguiled by her automatic-writing scripts. Mina was now manifesting scrawls from the spirits in English, French, Swedish, Dutch, Greek, and poor German—as well as a note in Latin that was translated by a blushing classics professor who said it was too obscene to record. She had also produced for Aleck, who had spent almost thirty years adventuring in the East, a message in ideographic Chinese; it was from a General Kuen, who addressed him in a childhood nickname that schoolmates who thought he had the eyes of a Chinaman had given him while growing up in England. How could she know what they had called him as a boy?

Mrs. Crandon, who said she disliked creeds and isms, had no urge yet to convert anyone to Spiritualism, let alone this middle-aged orphan. Her husband viewed the séance from a scientific rather than religious angle, but Aleck often had an emotional reaction to the ghosts. As time went on, Mina's sittings weren't enough to sate his growing fascination with the occult; he sought out other mediums as well—one of whom he brought home.

For the first time a psychic other than Mina was asked to help conduct a sitting at Lime Street. Mina could barely suppress a laugh as the obese clairvoyant from South Boston lumbered up the stairs to Roy's den. After hands were linked the charmer began shaking the beads she removed from her neck while transmitting plaintive ghostly whispers and scribbling illegible messages on her pad. The circle considered her performance more entertainment than anything else, but taking Mina's cue, all were polite to Aleck's guest.

Later Mrs. Crandon went into trance and produced something Walter had been promising for weeks—that little John Richardson would make music for the group. What followed sounded like a one-finger piano lick by the spirit of the little boy, so faint it was heard by only half the room, yet they felt no piano could produce such an unearthly sound.

At the next sitting, one week later, there was speculation that the guest medium had somehow altered the usual atmosphere in the séance room, for another invisible seemed to usurp Walter's place as the spirit that manifested for the ABC Club. Mina abruptly complained that a cold hand had gripped the back of her neck. Ducking forward, she felt it grasp her chin— and it was apparently a female presence as she sensed scented hair brushing against her face. She began to shiver as cold air, at least to her mind, began buffeting the spirit cabinet. Nothing like this had ever happened before. The medium was not in trance and in the red light all could see she was shaken. Aleck was even more alarmed. The sitters on either side of him noticed that his hands had become cold and clammy, and then he began to cry.

It was not just the sittings that spooked Aleck; he was carrying his new belief in Spiritualism to "ridiculous extremes." Every mundane piece of good fortune that befell any of the group was the gift of Mina's spirit guide; every subtle noise in the house was to him the work of Walter or the Richardson boys. One time Mina's young son John Crandon had struck the piano in the parlor, and it gave Aleck a start—as if he could no longer distinguish between the notes of living and dead boys.

The Dark Side of Summerland

*T*here was magic in West Harlem, where in his fine brownstone the Great Houdini showed off a talking teakettle that answered in a ghostly whisper any question put to it. There were treasures in the wizard's lair, where on display in his long front parlor were the once-potent wands of famous dead conjurers; the bronze that would one day ordain his grave; and a statuette of Sarah Bernhardt, who he said had once asked him to restore her amputated leg, so sure was she that he was supernormal. Visitors to 278 West 113th Street felt transported from the commonplace. The Houdinis cultivate a house of mystery!

Of all rooms in his townhouse, Houdini himself found most enchantment in the space where he claimed to spend five months a year researching his publications and inventions—the cramped top-floor sanctuary that he called his favorite place on Earth: his library. A source of pride for Houdini, the apartment was no decorous nouveau-riche book room like the kind Gatsby's guests ogle. Aside from the voluminous Spiritualist works, he had amassed one of the finest, though disordered, private theater collections in the world, including prized items of John Wilkes Booth, the mad assassin, and Edwin Booth, who was haunted by the dead that came to him in dreams and during séances. One day Houdini hoped to match the trove of the Brahmin Robert Gould Shaw, the renowned Harvard collector. He took pleasure in receiving men like Mr. Shaw in his library. His collection meant that he was not some crass virtuoso from the ghetto: he was as erudite as any high-and-mighty Brahmin.

But Houdini never showed Shaw or any other visitor the only article that he stipulated should not, upon his death, be sold at any price: a lost artistic diary that contained the comparatively worthless macabre sketches of that failed Victorian artist Charles Doyle. According to Sir Arthur, his father channeled the supernatural beings he drew and painted. If so,

Houdini felt that Charles's tragic fate, kept secret by the Doyles, was in keeping with those who communed too often with the happy phantoms.

The Handcuff King had his own inner demons; it took as dark an imagination as Edgar Allan Poe's to conceive of the predicaments from which he fought to extricate himself. There were gruesome items in Houdini's library. In an envelope in a desk once owned by Poe, he kept graphic photographs of Chinese captives, men and women, butchered at the stake. Houdini could only wonder if their astral doubles had mercifully slipped away from their torture. He had always been privately fascinated with the malignant forces in society—pogroms, crime, and insanity . . . His great ambition was to defeat, as he did in his photoplays, a great menace to humanity. Toward that end, he had of late been poring over material for *Magician Among the Spirits*, his exploration of the darker side of Summerland.

Seated among his valued books, stacked in towering piles above him in his study, Houdini looked more like a well-built scholar than the heroic escape artist on the billboards of cinema houses. He eyed with disdain an article on how the great Howard Thurston, whom some considered a more outstanding magician than he himself, had just converted to the Spiritualist cult. "During a recent series of tests," Thurston reported, "I was astounded on several occasions by the unmistakable presence of a very definite supernatural influence which seemed to be attempting to transmit some sort of a message to me, or through me."

Unlike his rival, Houdini flouted the spirits, whether good or evil, but he was inclined to demonize crooked mediums. Accordingly, he collected—as ammunition to be used in a campaign against the occultists—newspaper accounts of spirit crime and tragedy. Arrayed on Poe's desk were some of the most disturbing articles in his arsenal.

In a case of "radio telephone spiritualism," a Mr. Robert Hose of Chicago slit his wrists while under the influence of a discarnate voice coming through the ether. While in San Francisco, a Mr. John Cronyn used his revolver to dispatch his two sons to the astral after the spirit of his dead wife told him to send them to her. In Brooklyn, one Thure Vigelius, a studious young chemist, was working on a book called *The Hereafter,* and by inhaling doses of chloroform he believed he traveled there. Tragically, on one of his research trips Vigelius had crossed too far: "Visits Hereafter for Book Material and Never Returns," the *World* disclosed.

There were items in the wizard's lair that would appall Sir Arthur Conan Doyle—reports that suggested his latest American tour was not all plaudits from newsmen and teary applause from Gold Star Mothers. Had Sir Arthur painted the life beyond too vividly? Some were in a great hurry to enter Summerland, and Houdini thought Doyle was encouraging them to get there. The press had begun to connect Spiritualism to lurid crimes—suicides and child murder.

In Newark lived a woman named Maud Fancher, who believed that from the spirit world she could help her husband find a brighter future. Mrs. Fancher did not want to deprive her two-year-old son of his mother—and so, three days after Doyle spoke at Carnegie Hall, she poisoned him with Lysol. The spiritist convert then took a dose herself and died two days later in a hospital. SHE COULD QUOTE SIR ARTHUR, read the headline. "Damn Spiritualism!" her husband cried to reporters.

Doyle explained that Mrs. Fancher had misunderstood the Spiritualist message. He began to speak against suicide at every lecture. There was no shortcut, he insisted, to the hereafter. Houdini, meanwhile, began to compile other reports as tragic.

A Mrs. Edith Miller Busby gassed herself at her home in Atlantic City; shockingly she took her three young daughters—dressed for their passage in party frocks—with her when she slipped across the Borderland. She left a note saying that she was "not a material person" and a quote as well: "What if the soul could cast the earth aside, And naked on the air of Heaven Ride?"

There was also included in the magician's collection the case of a Mr. Herman Light of Omaha, Nebraska, "who filled his library with the writings of Sir Conan Doyle and other spiritualistic authorities." According to the article that Houdini filed, Light, who missed his recently deceased wife, craved the spiritist paradise so desperately that one night he forced his son to drink a poisonous elixir, then took a fatal draught himself. As the double cortege passed by the next day, Light's neighbor, another recent novitiate to the séance religion, put a shotgun to his mouth so that he too could enter the plane where lost lovers reunite and all orphans find their mothers.

Faces in the Sky

The undiscovered country, from whose bourn
no traveler returns, puzzles the will.
—*Hamlet*

*T*he missionary who had returned on the *Olympic* could not, as they say, cross the same river twice. He felt that Manhattan had somehow changed since his last visit: its avenues were blighted with potholes; Central Park was dirtier; New Yorkers more wound up by the saxophone and stock tip. He too looked different. The press noted "a subtle change in Sir Arthur's appearance since his last lecture tour here, a year ago. A dreamy expression blurs the keen eyes that are searching every day into mysterious realms. As he paced up and down in his suite at the Biltmore last night—a huge, shaggy figure, with ruddy cheeks and hair barely frosted with gray—he seemed remote and visionary, in spite of his great stature and his hearty manner."

During his previous tour Sir Arthur had given a cogent, Holmes-like presentation on the case for spirit contact. This time his urgings at Carnegie Hall were more evangelical. "I have a vision," he said while closing his eyes and holding his brow intensely. What he saw was Spiritualism emerging from the mist of doubt and criticism. This would coincide with the decline of a church not designed for modern people. "How else could ten million young men have marched out to slaughter? Did any moral force stop that war? No, Christianity is dead," he declared. The movement to unite faith and science would take hold most strongly in the country that—thanks to the Fox sisters—had started it. He called this new sect the Church of America.

To publicize his mission, he presented what he called "the greatest spirit photograph ever taken." At Carnegie Hall he projected a lantern slide of a crowd of men with bare heads bowed, gathered around London's Cenotaph—all paying homage to the war dead. He indicated with his pointer a small party separated from the rest of the mourners in the picture by a shaft of light he claimed was ectoplasm. The select group were mediums planted among the Armistice Day throng. The spirit photographer, Ada Deane, had captured a manifestation that required the combined forces of those psychics.

With the next photograph the mood in the auditorium instantly changed. Sir Arthur tapped his pointer against the sky above the Cenotaph monument. Visible now were scores of disembodied faces: some vaporous, others so clear as to be recognizable by loved ones, and all wearing "the fixed, stern look of men who might have been killed in battle," reported the *Tribune*. "There was something about this photograph, and the conditions under which it was shown that was so eerie, so weird, so supernatural that it impressed even the scoffers."

The image of resurrected soldiers caught on Mrs. Ada Deane's plate was too much for some in the audience. Even Sir Arthur seemed taken aback by the volume of gasps and frightened cries. A hysterical woman in the back wailed, "Don't you see them? Don't you see the spirits?" Sir Arthur halted his presentation while Lady Doyle went to calm her. Her reaction was not to the spirit picture, she told Jean, but rather to the presence of something unearthly in the immediate atmosphere. There were ghosts, she said, hovering over Sir Arthur. The glorious dead all around him.

After viewing Doyle's proofs, Hereward Carrington was approached by the *Herald* for his opinion on the Cenotaph faces. The *Scientific American* had a prize for spirit photography—that Ada Deane had been invited to seek—as well as psychic phenomena; and as it happened, few investigators were as familiar with the English mediums whose cameras registered what the eye could not. The previous summer Carrington had sat with Mrs. Deane for a spirit picture in her London studio. The unmasker of the rogues at Lily Dale had taken "every precaution and examined everything" while testing the spectral portrait maker. "I took my own marked plates, removed them from the camera and developed them myself." No ghost showed up in his exposures. Yet while posing for Mrs. Deane, Carrington, whom some considered psychic himself, had envisioned a nimbus of light projecting from his right shoulder. To his astonishment a semblance of what he imagined, like an etheric flare, showed up in the developed picture.

On the same trip he sat for the other popular spirit photographer, William Hope, and in the developed photographs a woman's glowing face was visible next to him—his unknown astral companion.

Despite these effects, Carrington was dubious of Sir Arthur's Armistice Day phenomena. While granting that a few authentic psychic photographs existed, he believed that most were fraudulent. And like his fellow committeemen, Carrington was wary of newsmen associating his views with Doyle's. Above all things, he wished to be regarded as a serious researcher. A few days after Sir Arthur's appearance at Carnegie Hall, he gave his own lecture, far more thinly attended, at a small theater near there. "The next world is a mental world where we create our own environment," Carrington avowed. His subject was "Dreams." The fantastic images that every mind created nightly.

In New York, Jean gave a radio sermon on Spiritualism that was heard by 500,000 Americans. The Doyles then took to the road, with the intention of visiting the places—Cleveland, St, Louis, Chicago, and the western cities—they hadn't made it to in 1922. Bird joined them in Ohio for the examination of Ada Bessinet, yet she still refused to come to Manhattan for the contest. Regardless, every time the *Scientific American* agent wrote favorably on a psychic it was "one more point gained in this uphill game," tallied Sir Arthur. "They cannot continue to think that I am a credulous fool so long as my observations are corroborated by such a man as Bird." To that end, a spirit picture was worth a thousand words. In addition to the Armistice Day phenomena, he displayed at every talk on his tour a photograph of Bird staring dispassionately into the camera, unaware of the wispy forms beside him.

◆

In a Cleveland hotel banquet hall a gimcrack band played ragtime. Couples shuffled zombielike in the center of an enveloping crowd. The girls' dresses were rumpled and soiled. Their ankles were swollen. They stopped only briefly to syringe their bloodshot eyes. Sir Arthur was told that the dancers had been at it for over twenty-four hours. While impressive as a display of spunk he sensed an aimless desperation to it all. Returning to his room, he told his wife what he had seen. It was somewhat seedy, they both agreed, but morbid curiosity drew him back to the hall the next evening. The same couples were still on the floor, performing their mechanical one-step before what appeared to be the same leering crowd. The women rested their heads on their partners' chests. They seemed to be sleeping while their feet moved resolutely on. Sir Arthur left before the dance derby was over. Later he heard that it went on for more than seventy hours; that one contestant had fainted; that two others in a similar competition in a nearby town had gone mad and died. All for some paltry award.

♦

The Colorado Rockies were a rugged place to plant the Spiritualist standard, but Sir Arthur had always thrived in high altitudes. "There are unsolved mysteries at every turn," he said, and, as fate would have it, a great mystifier was passing through the territory. While stopping for their respective engagements in the Mile-High City, Doyle and Houdini crossed paths. And for every magic performance at the Orpheum that the Great Houdini gave, Sir Arthur made his case at the Ogden theater for life beyond the grave.

But there would be no psychic showdown in the old mining town. The two men were as amiable with each other in person as contrary in print. Pleased to reunite, Houdini and the Doyles (again Bess was indisposed) motored together along a mountain road then picnicked under the shade of green ash trees. That evening a rejuvenated Bess went to hear Sir Arthur present his "Proofs of Immortality." She listened raptly while he lectured. She marveled at his spirit pictures; she gasped at every ghost. Mrs. Houdini later told Sir Arthur that he spoke so fervently, she feared he would burn himself out before he reached the West Coast.

As for Houdini, who performed himself that night, he was gratified to hear that Sir Arthur's talk, while well attended, was no sellout. Doyle was a miracle monger, he said, who packaged his wonders with conviction and erudite words. Nevertheless, the magician believed that his own feats paled next to the novelist's enduring fame. "Doyle is a historical character and his word goes far," he admitted to Bess, "in fact much further than mine."

Sir Arthur would give one hundred talks in forty days during his tour of '23. In Salt Lake City, while trying to convert the Mormons in the Tabernacle, he staggered and, as Bess had predicted, nearly collapsed. The famous organ played hymns while he paused. The Mormons—whom he had portrayed so lewdly in *A Study in Scarlet*—cheered happily when he got to his feet and projected the spiritist proofs that, unlike Joseph Smith's Golden Plates, were available for all to view.

His next stop was Los Angeles, a city where European writers came to sell their souls. But Sir Arthur had no Sherlock Holmes scenario to shop. He told newsmen that Spiritualism was more important than Bolshevism or the movies. He called it "the greatest thing that ever came out of America." Then he toured the studios. As the Doyles strode across the replica of a Great War battlefield, complete with scarred trees and fetid craters, he admired how closely the set mimicked what he had seen in France. The filmmakers' lavish constructions were like parallel worlds that came to life under mercury-vapor lighting.

Not long after leaving California, while touring lower Canada, Sir Arthur heard from Dr. Le Roi Crandon. Following the initial séance experiments on Lime Street, Roy wrote for advice in developing his wife's mediumship. In response, Sir Arthur warned him about attracting dark spirits—"undesirable elements"—that could harm the medium if his circle was not composed of "religious Spiritualists." What was needed was a "guardian control" to shield Mrs. Crandon from hostile influences.

"My little circle," the doctor answered in July, "have now become all religious spiritualists and I feel that we have a guardian control in the brother of the Psychic." Dr. Crandon assured Doyle that in death, as he had in life, Walter was looking after his kid sister. *"Do you think I would let anything happen to her?"* Big Brother had promised. The new convert to the faith was eager to have Sir Arthur meet Walter. Would the British expert come to Boston?

Regrettably, Doyle could not make it to New England, but an important connection had been made. Dr. Crandon was the kind of Old Bostonian Sir Arthur had always respected, and Mrs. Crandon would soon replace Houdini as his great psychic hope. The Doyles had nothing to say to the magician now: not after he told an Oakland reporter that Sir Arthur was under the spell of a notorious rogue.

To Sir Arthur, this was a particular sore point, as it revived an incident that had almost ruined his previous tour. In the spring of '22, the Doyles had sat in New York with the sought-after Mrs. Thompson of the First Spiritualist Church and her reverend husband. Three days after performing for the Doyles, the couple was arrested for defrauding their sitters. In reaction, Sir Arthur said that he had quickly recognized the couple he sat with as spook crooks. The ghost identifying herself in an Irish brogue to be his mother was actually Mrs. Thompson disguised in filmy white robes. It had been humiliating, though, when the *Graphic* published an illustration of him on his knees, kissing his fake mother's glowing white hand.

I Am a Winner

*H*ad Houdini's rash exposé of George Valiantine killed the *Scientific American* contest? It seemed unlikely that other mediums would "risk their reputations—and their livelihoods—by submitting themselves to the investigation of observers who command the resources of modern science and are willing as well as able to use them," said the *New York Times*. "This is a regrettable consequence of Mr. Houdini's hurry to convince his jeering friends that he was not such a 'simpleton' as to be taken in by tricks that any professional 'magician' could duplicate and improve upon. Except for that, probably half a dozen Valentines could have been exposed, and the impressiveness of the disclosures would have been far greater."

Stung by the censure of both the *Scientific American* and the newspaper of record, the magician quickly made amends with Malcolm Bird: HOUDINI PRESTOS HIMSELF BACK IN SPIRIT HUNT, flashed the headline. "I'm positive that mediums won't hesitate to come forward," he assured the press. "They're sure to get a square deal. Valentine got the squarest deal he ever got in his life."

For a while it appeared that Houdini was wrong. Months went by without any further séances in the *Scientific American* library. Until finally Bird invited the reverend of a Spiritualist church in Ohio to pursue the psychic award. He called her the flower medium, but she was something of a mystery: no one he knew had ever witnessed her exotic work.

The Rev. Josie K. Stewart had collected eight hundred testaments to her psychic powers over the years. She presented her bona fides to the touring Doyle, who had recommended her, without a sitting, to Malcolm Bird. Mrs. Stewart would later tell reporters that the spirits warned her to expect a hornet's nest if she accepted Bird's offer to be tested in October in New York. She saw it as her mission, though, to face the scientists and experts there. And so, with a valise containing the glowing appraisals of her work, the flower medium came to perform in the library where George Valiantine had been summarily exposed.

Mrs. Stewart, in a brown satin frock with squirrel trim, caused heads to turn when she entered the offices of Munn & Co. A plump, high-strung woman, she had thick red-brownish hair and piercing dark eyes. On her fingers were gold bands from the various men to whom she had given her hand over the years. The medium was married, having been divorced twice, but her husband had not accompanied her to New York. She was adorned with other rings and shiny bangles on her arms. It was no small task for her to remove them all. At which point Mrs. Bird, Mrs. Lescarboura, and three female stenographers conducted, as best they could, the inspection not only of her anatomy but all of her ornaments and clothes.

Nervously, the Rev. Josie Stewart then faced the circle that included the ubiquitous *Times* newsman; a female friend of the psychic; Messrs. Prince, Carrington, Bird, and Lescarboura; and other representatives of Munn's journal. Like Valiantine, Mrs. Stewart was voluble while linking hands. She had a specialty that she described: in clear light she would channel written spirit messages that manifested on plain cards. Her modus operandi was to place on each card the petals of a flower, their coloring matter to be used by the psychic operators as ink. Immediately she sought the gentleman in the circle with the proper magnetism for the effect to work. She placed cards on the heads of her various sitters. Unfortunately, no one had the right vibration. The séance was a blank. The medium spoke instead of the marvelous things she had done at other times and places and what she would do at her next demonstration.

Jam tomorrow and jam yesterday, Bird reflected, *but never jam today.*

The flower medium had more confidence at the second test séance two days later. Rubbing her hands together like a pianist before a recital, she said there was strong electricity in the room. As was her ritual, Mrs. Stewart chose a flower, this time a moss rose, from a bouquet on the séance table. She plucked its petals and inserted them in between each card that the spirits were to use in their communications. Rolling up her sleeves, she told the circle, "Folks, I am going to get it. I feel what seems like a wave." The medium then proceeded to Hereward Carrington and placed the cards with the rose petals on his auburn head. Dr. Carrington was used to receiving cards and flowers from women, Bird supposed, and she had clearly singled him out as the "battery" for her psychic force.

The reverend of the First Spiritualist Church breathed deeply while histrionically bringing her hand to her brow. She asked for water and then guzzled two glasses full while keeping the cards and petals on Carrington's head. All waited for her to lay down her deck and show the authentic spirit messages that would be her winning hand—the royal flush of messages from Spirit Land. Finally she handed the cards to Bird. "There may be some writing on them," she said.

To her consternation, the cards were blank. Just then Mrs. Stewart's friend, who had come all the way from California for the event, felt compelled to defend her. Facing the committee when the lights were raised, she said that while the medium's power was weak today, she had seen something phenomenal in their hotel the night before. They had heard voices and saw a blazing green cross on the ceiling. "Didn't we, Josie?" she beseeched the medium.

Jam tomorrow and jam yesterday, Bird mused, *but never jam today.*

Carrington suggested they wait a few days so that the psychic could find peace of mind before trying again. But when they gathered on October 15, the committeemen again saw the medium wilt like flowers in fall. Her performance was becoming increasingly melodramatic and peculiar. While she used a "battery more often than not," Bird reported, "she often omits this feature; and she does many unorthodox things with the cards. She puts them to her own head." There was no charge. "She parades about the room with cards in her right hand and her left extended ostentatiously." There was no charge. "She sits at her table and fingers the cards and turns them over and fairly plays solitaire with them." When turned over, they were blank. Finally Mrs. Stewart concluded that the Woolworth Building was not fertile ground for her botanical effects. She instead suggested an afternoon demonstration outdoors. "She yearns for nature," observed the *Times.*

A séance in some flowery meadow in the light of day? Why not, said Bird, who wished to do anything within reason to accommodate the sensitive's needs. Hence, the commission gathered next in a residential garden overlooking Long Island Sound. It was a crisp day. After being searched, the flower medium requested an overcoat, which the *Times* reporter graciously produced for her. The investigators scrutinized her every move as she bent to the earth and picked phlox, asters, and ferns to lay on each card handed to her by Bird. "This is my last chance," she declared. "I must make a success."

The reverend placed one of her gold bangles on a card. Moments later she snapped her fingers like a vaudeville conjurer. Nothing happened. The committee sat attentively in the sun for ten minutes. Nothing happened. She tried scattering a few of the cards in the nasturtium bed. There they lay, still blank. She placed a card on Lescarboura's head and then removed it with a "he won't do" expression. She felt the aura of the newsman but said that he was "not electrical." Once again her hopes lay with Carrington. A card was placed on his head. Still no writing materialized.

Then came Mrs. Stewart's last attempt to win the psychic prize. "Folks, I must ask you to gather round me," she announced. "Come draw your chairs right up to the table where I am sitting. Others of you stand behind me." She asked Carrington to place his hand on the back of her neck while she clasped the hand of the elderly lady whose daughter was hosting the séance. Breathing deeply, the reverend pleaded for the spirits to arrive. "They must come now; they must. You women will pray that they will come, won't you?" Moments later she cried ecstatically: "See! Do see! There they are now, Mr. Bird, look at the cards and see what you can read. The waves passed through and through me."

There was writing at last. *Truth crushed to earth shall rise again,* read the first card in a script of heliotrope and pink—the colors of the flowers the medium had placed in the deck. Other messages were signed by dead mystics like William James, and W. T. Stead. The communications essentially said that finally verifiable spiritistic proofs had been brought through. Astounded by what they saw, the sitters surged around the medium. She had attempted a feat usually done on spirit slates, but the mechanism of slates allowed for hidden pencils and other opportunities to cheat. This was an entirely different effect. In plain light and in front of the sharp eyes of Prince and Carrington, Reverend Stewart had just produced spirit messages on a number of the *Scientific American*'s own cards! There was no writing instrument or any other means to explain the simultaneous appearance of the messages. They were ascribed by trusted newspapers, if sometimes glibly, to the finger of ghosts.

SPIRIT MESSAGES IMPRESS SCIENTISTS, the *Times* headline read. WOMAN'S TEST DECLARED PRIMA FACIE EVIDENCE OF COMMUNICATION WITH THE DEAD. Malcolm Bird announced that "we are sufficiently well impressed to proceed further." First, though, the supernatural proofs were eagerly examined. As soon as Munn's staff returned to the Woolworth, they put the spirit writing through a series of laboratory tests: chemically, to determine the material in the flower ink; microscopically, to ascertain if a writing instrument had been used; and spectroscopically, to find out if there was ectoplasm. "It is possible that our tests may show ectoplasm in the writing," Bird told the press. The commission also studied motion pictures that had been filmed of the medium's every move—the hand may be faster than the eye, Lescarboura believed, but the camera was faster than both.

For months, said the trusted *Hartford Courant,* Munn's prize money "seemed sure of remaining safe with the *Scientific American;* but now there may be at least a hairline crack between the $2500 and the assets of the journal." Bird, the Holmes of spiritism, had spent much of the evening with his eye glued to a microscope, trying to ascertain the mystery of how the spectral writing came to be. After the laboratory analysis, the commission was ready the next day for another display of psychic writing. Once again the séance took place in the *Scientific American* library. Fresh off her triumph on Long Island and confident that she had already won the prize (she didn't know what "prima facie" meant, Bird commented), the flower medium had never been more merry. "Oh," she chirped, "I feel good this morning. I ought to get lots of writings. Anybody want to search me to see if I have anything concealed on me?" Bird said that they could dispense with the examination today. "Ah," exclaimed Mrs. Stewart, "no one looks suspicious this morning. Everybody is smiles."

They smiled as they had at George Valiantine before he went down in flames.

The candidate rolled up her sleeves, exposing her milky arms. She took several deep breaths, then drank copiously from her water bottle. Abruptly she blurted emotionally: "I'm a winner. I know that I am a winner. My angel friends said to me the night before last, *Have no fear—we'll see you through.* Someone said that every century has its psychic. Someone said that Jesus was one and Joan of Arc another and some have been kind enough to call me the psychic of this century."

With that, the spiritist martyr arranged flowers on the cards with her usual ceremony while continuing to bare her soul to the gentlemen seated around the mahogany table. "If you knew how serious this is to me—I tried to serve the spirit world and now I am trying to serve the scientific world." Someone mentioned, rather provocatively, that Harry Houdini, presently touring in Kansas, was eager to see her spirit writing. Mrs. Stewart retorted that she hoped no one expected her to go before a mountebank. "This is my religion and my science. I am not catering to that class of people."

The reverend recalled a harrowing experience before a committee of magicians, which she had already described in some detail before. Even the mention of Houdini seemed to affect her magnetism. Where now was the magic of yesterday afternoon? The contestant placed cards successively on the heads of Lescarboura, Bird, and the rest of the *Scientific American* staff while begging the researchers to solve the mystery. "I wish some cool scientific person would tell me how I get this writing," she murmured. "I don't know. Will you, Mr. Bird, see if there is any writing there? No? Too bad! Too bad! Then I guess that I shan't take that $2,500 prize home. But I must get my mind off that prize—no money in the world could pay for a living truth, one that will tell whither and why. No sir!"

She must have known then that the cards would always be blank in the *Scientific American* séance room. The reverend was becoming frustrated with the sitters, who seemed less accommodating than they had been on Long Island. "It is terrible to conform to all the rules," she complained, "all the rules and regulations and then to be turned down by the unseen. It is more than trying; it is vexing."

On the verge of tears, she gathered her friend who had witnessed the flaring green cross in their hotel room. They left to pack for her trip back to Cleveland. But though she had failed again at the Woolworth, Mrs. Stewart was sure she had done enough to win the contest. Bird had the sense that the medium was already "mentally spending our $2,500." Munn, however, wasn't writing the check.

It had not taken long for Bird to see that their candidate was a cheat.

Cards were up her sleeve. When days earlier she returned the deck to him following her first blank séance, he noticed that five in the stack were missing. He anticipated that at a future sitting they would reappear with prewritten messages in flowery ink. Later, during the sitting on Long Island, Reverend Stewart did something that he felt gave her a chance to retrieve what she had pinched. After the psychic writer had been searched, she went to use the bathroom while the commission assembled on the lawn. Upon returning she complained of the cold. The reporter had provided his bulky German overcoat with outside pockets, Bird noted, "big enough to swallow the Woolworth Building." It was then Prince whispered, "Now, we are going to get some writing." The medium must have found a blind spot in the vigilant eyes—and camera—of the committeemen. No one saw her make the switch. "You know magicians claim, and rightly, too," Bird told reporters, "that the hand is quicker than the eye." Five messages were produced minutes later—on five counterfeit cards. "The texture, weight, color and thickness all were different under the microscope than ours."

Sir Arthur wished to know, after studying Bird's scenario, why the medium used five substitute cards if she had pilfered the originals. The editor could only surmise, but he believed Mrs. Stewart had made copies of the cards she swiped, brushed messages onto them at her hotel, then produced them in the garden with a look of devout wonder on her face. The cards were substitutes. The *New York World* reported that no spirit operators wrote on them with ferns and violets. "The bubble of mysticism created by Mrs. Josie K. Stewart, the Cleveland medium, in a sunlit garden in Bay Side L. I., was shivered yesterday when it was brushed by the harsh finger of science."

"Another mediumistic failure," Bird determined. "Her claims to further attention and to the *Scientific American* award stand vacated."

Mrs. Stewart was enraged. The reverend complained to her Spiritualist congregation that she had been forced to conduct séances in New York for fifteen cigar-smoking men in a noxious atmosphere of smoke and intimidation. She said that her inquisitors had made her strip nude in front of strange women who examined her. She threatened through the press to bring a suit against Munn & Co. for saying that her messages from the departed were fake. Malcolm Bird responded that the journal would be "tickled to death" if she wished to take her case before a higher court.

The Spookess from Chicago

MAN BITES A GHOST AND UPSETS SÉANCE
—*New York Times*

*W*ithin two weeks the Cleveland seeress was forgotten. Now Mrs. Elizabeth Tomson of Chicago, the third aspirant for Munn's prize, was the psychic in the spotlight, and she an old-time mystifier of the Anna Fay vaudeville variety.* The latest candidate produced from her cabinet myriad snowy white forms, all of which Houdini insisted were phony. Yet even he would admit that in her cunning way she was formidable. In London a decade earlier, the medium had been challenged by a skeptical inventor to manifest from a spirit cabinet in which he would restrain her. Sir Hiram Maxim was famous for inventing the prototype of the machine gun that would send thousands of bullet-riddled young men west. Was that not enough to break hearts, that he also had to deny the spiritist consolation of life after death? His draconian bonds had seemed more appropriate for one of Houdini's escapes. He put the medium in a black body stocking to inhibit any access to fake ectoplasm. Then his people tied her, sewed her, taped her, chained her, and sat her within the inspected psychic cabinet. It took one hour before Mrs. Tomson cried that she was beaten. She had produced no apparitions and lost the competition. But when Sir Hiram parted the curtains to her booth, he received the fright of his life. Coiled above the medium was a large snake, poised as if to strike him.

Mrs. Tomson produced just the sort of dime-show spookery that attracted medium baiters. When she came to Manhattan in 1920 for a public test séance at the Morasco Theater, it was "all I could do to keep J. F. Rinn

---

* A theatrical, charismatic medium of the Gilded Age, Anna Eva Fay purchased a shipping company, a gold mine, and a marble quarry in California on what she earned contacting the departed.

from breaking up the performance," Houdini remembered. Before the days of the *Scientific American* contest, Joseph Rinn had been more of a nemesis to crooked mediums than the Great Houdini. And that evening the bellicose Rinn had an ugly exchange with the Broadway impresario Raymond Hitchcock, who defended the psychic after she claimed from the stage that Sir Oliver Lodge had endorsed her.

When later queried by Houdini, Sir Oliver said that Mrs. Tomson's spook act had been rejected by his English SPR investigation. Undaunted, the Chicago psychic still sought the applause of scientists, and the highest stage for a publicity-seeking spook was now the *Scientific American* library. Mrs. Tomson had been the first medium to petition to be tested by Munn's commission. She was reluctant, though, to return to the city where debunkers like Joseph Rinn had hounded her from the stage lights and attacked her in the newspapers. Aware of her dilemma, Bird tried to persuade her. Despite her detractors, Mrs. Tomson was the only notable psychic in the world willing to be tested by the jury, and as a materializing medium she would give them an opportunity to judge the most sensational of spiritistic effects—the fully formed apparition. This psychic produced visible forms—not raps, whistles, and vague messages from the departed.

What frustated Bird was that the medium wanted publicity but feared judgment. She and her elusive husband, Dr. Tomson, kept themselves in the news by exploiting the public interest in the *Scientific American* challenge. There were features in Midwest papers that said she was off to conquer the committee in New York; one story even announced that she had already won the psychic honors. Bird suspected that the Tomsons were the source for these rumors. The medium told him that she couldn't afford the trip to New York even though the *Chicago Tribune,* which supported the *Scientific American* investigation, offered to finance it. Months went by and still Mrs. Tomson wavered. Finally, around the time of Halloween, she came to New York and pronounced herself ready to be tested.

The Tomsons promptly invited the committee to a Sunday-evening séance at Raymond Hitchcock's estate in Great Neck. Given such short notice, only Bird and Dr. Prince could make it. They arrived to find the sitting attended by about thirty individuals, mostly theatrical people. Despite that,

Dr. Tomson wanted the demonstration to be an official *Scientific American* test; he was upset that the full commission was absent. Bird explained that he and Prince were there as guests, not judges. This wasn't a sitting that would satisfy the rigors of their program, he protested. A respected surgeon searched Mrs. Tomson prior to the exhibition, but Bird remarked that he only inspected her vagina and not her rectum or esophagus—orifices that could conceal the gossamer material from which fake ghosts are fashioned.

Not long after the usual hymns and hand clasping, Mrs. Tomson manifested spirits in glowing robes that were recognized by some in the circle who were led to the cabinet. Hitchcock identified a white-bearded face as either his uncle or grandfather, Bird noted incredulously. Then "a woman was reduced to a condition of emotional crisis by her very positive recognition of her mother's face and voice." The sitter was kissed and embraced by the astral form of her dead mother. Yet when Bird and Prince had their respective turns to approach the cabinet—their hands clasped by Dr. Tomson to prevent them from touching the ectoplasm—and the curtains were dramatically parted, they thought their ghost looked suspiciously like the medium who was supposed to be sleeping inside it. One face that Bird saw hovering in front of the cabinet was so unformed that it might have been anyone a sitter imagined. Could it be that the medium provided the etheric clay, Bird wondered, with which the observer mentally molded a loved one?

Three days later Dr. Tomson showed up at the *Scientific American* offices to inspect the premises in which his wife was to perform that evening. He found the arrangements unsatisfactory, complaining that there was no place for the medium to disrobe and be examined. Bird took him to a room sequestered for that purpose, which had running water. Upon further discussion, it was clear that the library itself was the source of Dr. Tomson's unease. A law library apparently lacked the psychic atmosphere. When Bird responded that it would be impossible to find another location at the last minute, "the doctor very kindly offered to take the load off my shoulders; Mme So-and So, a friend of his, he was sure would offer a room in her apartment."

Resisting the urge to laugh in the occultist's face, Bird insisted that the séance take place on *Scientific American* ground and according to its regulations. In reply, Dr. Tomson grumbled that both the journal's conditions and its choice of judges were not to the liking of Mrs. Tomson's spirit operators. "I finally reminded him," Bird wrote, "that we weren't submitting ourselves to his test, he was submitting to ours; that if he didn't like our rules, he needn't play the game at all." Dr. Tomson took umbrage at Bird's hard line. He issued an ultimatum: the sitting was to be where he determined, or not at all. Consequently, a few hours before her test séance, Bird called up the committeemen to inform them that Mrs. Tomson's test sittings were canceled.

The next day the doctor reappeared at the Woolworth to see if Bird had changed his mind. As a compromise, the editor said that he would allow Mrs. Tomson to be tested at Orson Munn's apartment in the Waldorf. The offer did not satisfy Dr. Tomson, however. Not only did he still want to choose the location, there would only be one demonstration, he stated, after which a verdict would be expected from the commission. Exasperated, Bird accused the Tomsons of wanting to avoid the apparatus concealed behind books and in the walls and floors of the library.

Dr. Tomson did not deny it. His wife, he said, was pretty tired of dubious scientific trials and uncouth physical examinations. Then why, Bird asked, had she entered the *Scientific American* contest? The doctor said they hadn't. Then what was he doing in Bird's office? He didn't seem to know exactly. Moments later the angry spiritist walked out, accusing Munn & Co. of running a scheme, financed by the Catholic Church, to defame genuine mediums. The editor rose and followed him out into the hall. The Tomsons had never intended to face the committee! Bird shouted. He later reported that "aside from these minor items, we agreed perfectly upon all points."

Soon Bird was thankful that the Tomsons had backed out and not tainted the psychic tests with their vaudeville apparitions. Two days after the confrontation he had with her husband, Mrs. Tomson was invited to give a séance at the Church of Spiritual Illumination. There she walked into a more severe trap than anything the *Scientific American* would have laid for her. The congregation were Brooklyn Spiritualists who suspected humbug. When one in their flock was led up to Mrs. Tomson's cabinet, his arms securely clasped by the doctor, he proceeded to take a bite out of a ghost and came away with a mouth of white gauze rather than ectoplasm. A scuffle broke out between parishioners and the medium's party. Mrs. Tomson fled in her bathrobe; she and the doctor departed the church without making a collection. The next day they beat it back to Chicago.

Spiritualists themselves could be more hostile than magicians to fraud mediums. Sir Arthur would write Bird that he was grateful to the committee for exposing "a wrong one" when they rejected the Rev. Josie Stewart. The National Spiritualist Agency had years earlier banned both Mrs. Stewart and Mrs. Tomson. The irony was not lost on Secretary Bird that the *Scientific American* was investigating mediums even the Spiritualists did not believe in. It hadn't yet been necessary to even summon the full commission for a test. He was heartened, though, by a brilliant new light on the horizon.

Ain't We Got Fun

But in her web she still delights,
To weave the mirror's magic sights,
For often through the silent nights,
A funeral with plumes and lights
—ALFRED, LORD TENNYSON

*J*ust before Malcolm Bird visited Beacon Hill, most of the Western world observed the holiday that marked five years since the Great War ended. Armistice Day fell that year on a Sunday, a day the Crandons usually held séances. And in honor of the veterans, Walter whistled "Taps" for the ABC Club, and the "Last Post" for Aleck Cross, the Englishman.

In New York, Orson Munn took part in less macabre activities. Having recently divorced his wife, the publisher was free to cavort openly with his girl, Caroline. The couple watched the Civil War veterans amble up Fifth Avenue, and the flying parade of airplanes over Broadway. Later they attended the Victory Ball at the Waldorf, which was draped with a thousand US flags and the colors of the ten Allied nations. The Follies performed a historic tableaux there, after which guests danced in the grand ballroom. The silver-haired Munn and his agile companion pulled off an inspired foxtrot to "Ain't We Got Fun."

In London, Sir Arthur witnessed thousands of the bereaved gather at the Cenotaph—the scene of the mass spirit return that he had made famous. This time no ghosts were photographed as all bowed their heads for the traditional two minutes of silence. But at home, the Doyles had just received unnerving messages from a spirit that communicated through Jean's automatic writing. This personality, called Pheneas—a leader of men who had died thousands of years ago near Arabia—spoke of another catastrophe. The War, as Sir Arthur observed, "has not had any very marked effect." Because little had changed and materialism was rampant, Pheneas warned of something *"Worse than Atlantis."*

The prophecy wasn't surprising to Doyle, who saw a dark undercurrent to jazz culture. Americans were caricatured as reveling since the Peace, while the English fretted over their crushing war debt to the House of Morgan. During his American tour, though, he had noticed that the US papers were "full of alleged change of climate, encroachments of ice, and general signs of a glacial epoch." Disciples of Doom were on every soapbox. Popular books like *Whither Mankind* called the calamity unavoidable. Yet Sir Arthur believed that the worst scenarios could be averted if Spiritualism took hold in the way the movement's pioneers and first prophets had envisioned.* They had said long ago that humanity would be converted by a widely convincing display of spirit communication.

---

* Andrew Jackson Davis, the Poughkeepsie Seer, had visions that appeared to foretell the coming of the Fox Sisters' phenomena when in 1847 he predicted a powerful demonstration of mediumship that would usher in a new era of "spiritual communion."

The Helson Report

Sit in a theatre, to see
A play of hopes and fears,
While the orchestra breathes fitfully
The music of the spheres

—EDGAR ALLAN POE

*E*xamining séance reports while seated by a window in the dining Pullman, Malcolm Bird noted flashes in the night that resembled spirit lights, making his trip to Boston feel momentarily like astral travel. But even in as amorphous a place as the séance, Bird appreciated the precision in these records. He had heard a good deal about the Beacon Hill medium via Doyle, who was in close correspondence with Dr. Crandon. En route he read two first-person reports on her activities: one from Harry Helson, a Harvard psychologist who was helping William McDougall investigate her; the other the séance minutes from Dr. Crandon. The observations of the two men were relatively similar; it was their conclusions that were worlds apart.

As if to prove that time does not exist in his dimension, Walter had been routinely stopping the clocks at 10 Lime Street. It flustered Aleck Cross when Mina's dead brother made mechanical devices—clocks, Victrolas, electric lamps—go haywire. And it perplexed the Harvard psychologists when such feats were exhibited on command. Often Walter would ask a sitter when they wanted time to freeze. Later on, the grandfather clock in the parlor, and other timepieces, were discovered to have stopped at the appointed minute. Dr. McDougall could not divine the method for the clock effect, or for anything else that Mina manifested. With proper control, though, he was still invested in the belief that he could stop her phenomena, which would go far to explaining them.

On the night of November 3, the Harvard investigators arrived at Lime Street for dinner and a séance. There was an especially tense air at the gathering and a lack of the usual pre-séance conviviality. After the main course was served, knocks were heard, according to Helson, from the up-stairs rooms that no one occupied. Helson and Mina went to investigate and found nothing amiss, but the sounds had so disturbed Aleck Cross that he left the house without finishing his dinner.

A short time later the investigators proceeded with their plan to seal the residence. They asked the servants to leave and then bolted all three entrances. The doors leading to the cellar were sealed with wax impressed with Dr. McDougall's thumbprint. All closets, trunks, and bureaus were inspected. The professors looked under every bed and beneath the sofa pil-lows; what they hoped to find there was not clear to a bemused Mrs. Cran-don. After checking the clocks for trick devices, McDougall locked and pocketed the key to the grandfather clock that Walter particularly liked to enchant. There had never been control like this at Lime Street. Mina later remarked that it was as if they suspected her of something far worse than leading séances.

Finally all were ready for what promised to be a showdown between Walter and Dr. McDougall. The sitters gathered in the dim red light around the table, the investigators controlling Mina, and immediately the disturbances began. Five loud raps were heard, as if taunting the men who thought they could put an end to the mediumship. The table jumped toward a few in the circle, stopping inches from McDougall's chest. Shift-ing to the psychic, it became animated like a pet dog. Tilting on two legs, it froze in that position for half a minute. By the system of raps on the floor, it issued greetings and answered questions from the sitters.

At 9:30 all heard the signature notes of Walter's arrival, a remote whistle that carried the first two bars of "Souvenir." Raps and scratches were heard and strange laughter. After the noises faded, the medium retired to her cabinet, one of her hands controlled by McDougall, the other by A. A. Ro-back. Helson reported that throughout the evening Mrs. Crandon was re-strained in this manner. Fronting her booth was a thin black drape through which the investigators could see her silhouetted in the scarlet light. They observed no suspicious movements or other signs of deception. For their benefit, a further method of control was suggested by Dr. Crandon. The sitters and psychic filled their mouths with water: demonstrating in this way that none of them produced the voice of Walter. Roback attempted to say something but could only gurgle. After their inability to speak while the ghost did was established, one by one the circle expelled their water. All except the medium; Walter bragged that he would talk until his sister was blue in the face. Then she laughed, to Roy's irritation, and spewed out her water.

Soon the mood changed dramatically. The church clock in the neighborhood struck ten while Water echoed it with ten strokes of his *"celestial clock."* Next he produced "Taps" on an invisible chimelike instrument. A dinner gong was placed on the floor of Mrs. Crandon's cabinet. With her securely held, it rang. Minutes later Walter addressed Dr. McDougall. What time did he want the parlor clocks stopped? the ghost asked. McDougall said that around ten thirty would be to his liking. Walter then asked him if he trusted Roback. Of course, McDougall answered. Accordingly, the voice directed Mina and Roback to go downstairs and check to see that the clocks were still running. When they returned, the medium was put back in her cabinet—which suddenly became charged with energy. The booth shook and tottered toward McDougall. But Walter pushed it only so far. Just as quickly all was quiet. Four raps on the floor followed, his signal for good night. The lights were turned up and Mrs. Crandon emerged from her cabinet, fully alert and smiling.

Downstairs, the researchers discovered that all the doors were still locked, the wax intact, and the two clocks in the parlor frozen at 10:30. Helson was dumbfounded. Yet it was he, at the next séance one week later, who grasped at a thread in an attempt to discredit Mrs. Crandon.

Bearding the Lion

There she weaves by night and day,
A magic web with colours gay,
She has heard a whisper say,
A curse is on her if she stay
—ALFRED, LORD TENNYSON

*T*he sky was low and ashen and Harvard Yard deceptively serene as Mina walked toward the building with the brick columns for her November 15 appointment with Dr. McDougall. His was the office in Emerson Hall that William James once occupied, and she supposed that McDougall wanted her to feel chastened by summoning her there. The news was not good. Her husband had been given the choice of relaying the finding of the Harvard investigation to her directly or sending her over to Emerson Hall, so that McDougall might carry out the "delicate office." When he chose the latter option, Mina had not seemed especially concerned. Whatever the psychologist's finding, she felt they had nothing shameful to answer for, whether in this world or the next life.

Her present impression was that at least her interview would be cordial. While never one for small talk, Dr. McDougall greeted her amiably enough. However, with a commiserating look in his eyes, he said that he was suspicious of her psychic work. He clearly wanted an admission from her of some sort. When she challenged his allegations, he got rather patronizing. The chairman of the Harvard Psychology Department had been a major in the British Army during the War; his duty as a psychologist had been to distinguish the neurasthenic cases from the shirkers. He was concerned now for her well-being; the pressure they had all put on her to manifest spirits was driving her to cheat, he implied.

She hadn't faked anything, she protested. How could she, when during the sittings she was unconscious—dead to the world, if he would pardon the expression. Grimmer now, disappointed at her lack of remorse, Mc-Dougall insisted she was not dishonest; it was only that an innocent joke had gotten out of hand. Resolutely, the psychic denied this. He'd been beside her during the séances; he'd held her hands and her feet, she reminded him. How in heaven's name was it even possible to cheat?

After more exchanges along these lines, McDougall switched from a paternal approach to that of a prosecutor. He said that he would have to expose her to Roy if she didn't come clean. Mina answered that whatever Dr. McDougall did, she and her husband would continue to hold séances and converse with Walter. Smiling in bewilderment, she said that her brother's spirit was as real as any psychologist that haunted Lime Street. At that moment McDougall reached into his desk and brought out the evidence that he claimed proved otherwise.

He held in his hand a sinewy piece of thread. To his chagrin, Mrs. Crandon burst into laughter. She now realized it was all a game. Dr. McDougall, recent president of both the American and English SPR, had no natural explanation for her phenomena. Walking out of his office, she was struck by the absurdity of it all. McDougall wanted to hang her with a thread? She doubted that his mentor, William James, would have stooped to such burlesque.

◆

That afternoon, the Crandons met Malcolm Bird at the Back Bay Station. The medium looked strikingly different in her gray brocade jacket from what he was expecting. The female candidates the editor had thus far considered for the *Scientific American* program—Mesdames Bessinet, Stewart, and Tomson—were middle-aged, stout, and unrefined. In contrast, Mina was a youthful blonde, he observed, with fashionably bobbed hair. Comfortable behind the wheel, she drove them directly to Lime Street.

They had barely sat down for dinner—the Crandons, Bird, and Aleck Cross—before Mina brought up her interview with Dr. McDougall. It sounded to Bird like the bearding of the lion of Harvard Psychology in his den. She said that he had subjected her to a medley of threats, cajolery, kindness, and persuasion in trying to get her to concede false spookery. She did a fine imitation of McDougall haranguing her like an underclassman caught cheating on an exam. She appeared to be hurt and confused, though. What did he think she had to gain from faking psychic manifestations?

"It was impossible for her to talk about anything other than the allegation of fraud, or to listen to anything else for more than a minute at a time," Bird remembered. She was reacting with the genuine indignation, he thought, of one falsely accused. But if Lime Street was—like the committee's other cases—another dead end, he didn't blame Dr. McDougall for wanting to get there sooner rather than later. Bird was as determined to find out whether Mina was genuine or a cultured impostor. He told her he knew that Harry Helson had discovered a thread attached to a stool that Walter was supposed to have propelled across the room. In response she produced a piece of string for Bird, though not the actual piece of evidence. If he were to find it on the floor after a séance, what would he think? she asked him. He said it looked to him like the raveling from a rug. But what about this matter of it being tied to a chair?

Helson, she flared, had not found anything tied to a chair! He didn't? puzzled Bird. From the other side of the table, Roy insisted that he was ready to accept a plausible explanation for his wife's effects, but none of the psychologists had come up with one. Then Aleck described how Walter tore the spirit cabinet to pieces around McDougall, and suggested there were bad feelings between the ghost and the alienist.

While touring the house after dinner, Bird recognized one strong impediment to any investigation. Ten Lime Street had an elaborate layout, and he knew that it would not be easy to secure the place for a controlled experiment. "It possesses an architectural complexity (largely the result of extensive remodeling) which surpasses belief," he noted. "There are two flights of back stairs, affording four independent points of access to the front of the house; there is a butler's pantry with a dumb-waiter. The whole house fairly teems with curious closets, crannies, cubbyholes large and small, blind shaftways, etc., the utility or necessity of which is not always apparent. The more mysterious ones doubtless occupy space that hung heavy on the remodeler's hands, but even when one has formulated this idea some of them are very puzzling."

The couple, he felt, were less eccentric than their residence. Even as the evening progressed and the conversation flowed naturally toward its macabre channels, Bird found the Crandons engaging and refreshingly rational. When he spoke of his aversion to the occult, he knew that Roy understood his language. The doctor had a strong grasp of physics and chemistry. And Bird was as impressed with the Crandons' obvious social credentials. A stranger to their sphere, he was of much humbler origins. Bird's roots were in Brooklyn, where his father had been a carpenter. It was his gift for science and mathematics that had advanced him: to Cornell and Columbia, and now to his position at the journal. For all his studiousness, though, Bird was no "scientific iceberg," and he would soon have a good rapport with the medium. Whoever said the Boston gentry were stuffy, he reflected, had not spent an evening with the Crandons.

If Mina were the mistress of a den of tricksters, as McDougall had hinted, then she was ready to show her guest how the plot was master-minded. "She has a sense of humor quite as wicked as my own," Bird real-ized. "My visit at this time was made into one continuous circus by the fashion in which that confederacy theory was batted about the house." It began when he explained how magicians use horsehair to invisibly levitate objects; hence McDougall's theory as to how she caused the table to rise. Amused, Mrs. Crandon led Bird on a search for damning evidence. He was in stitches as she pointed out various features of the Lime Street architecture or its furnishings, and gravely explained its role in the ruse. They looked for threads and horsehairs under ashtrays and teacups. They sought out ac-complices in the closets and lifted up rugs that might cover trapdoors. At one point Mina dramatically thrust open drapes behind which one of her coven might hide, though she claimed to have no idea whom that might be.

The Crandons' maid, Lydia, was too scatterbrained for flimflam, she decided. Lydia would walk into a séance and blurt to the Harvard investi-gators that she forgot to crank the Victrola that played the spectral sounds. Aleck Cross was too clumsy to tiptoe about in the dark. Bird and Mina agreed that it was the Japanese butler who was her partner in crime. "If we cracked one joke about strings we cracked a hundred," Bird wrote. He believed their horseplay was her way of dealing with the strain that came of her visit to McDougall. She captivated Bird as no medium had before. But the *Scientific American* was not offering a prize for ethereal beauty and charm. He sought to discover her methods, he later said, by getting her to let down her hair.

As the magazine's psychic detective, Bird was thought to be "bad medicine for fake ghosts." In fact, Dr. Crandon suggested that the Harvard researchers may have been in a hurry to expose Mina before Bird got the credit for unveiling yet another hoax. As it turned out, the Boston medium would not be thwarted by a thread; she was vindicated practically as soon as Bird took on the case. Harry Helson, the investigator who plucked the string from the floor, stopped by Lime Street the day after Bird arrived. He said that he wanted to make amends. Just as Roy had conjectured, Helson admitted that he had been too eager to solve the mystery that was puzzling his department. The string had not been attached to any object; he claimed to have been misquoted on that score. He produced the incriminating thread and conceded that it was identical to the rug fringe Bird showed him. With no other evidence, Helson apologized for offending the Crandons. The witch was absolved. Later McDougall called to say that he was withdrawing his accusatory letter. He too apologized. By Bird's account, it hadn't been a good showing by the Harvard boys.

The following day, Bird visited the lion in his den. "I can't seem to impress upon these impulsive young men that they mustn't get ahead of their research," McDougall said. He also confirmed with a grudging smile that Mrs. Crandon's version of her unpleasant interview with him was "substantially correct." But contrary to what McDougall might expect, the Crandons were willing to continue with the Harvard tests. Neither he nor Helson was to be banished from Lime Street. Most psychics Bird knew, including Ada Bessinet, refused to sit with researchers who expressed doubts about their work. It was to her credit, both men agreed, that Mina was willing to perform again for the wary Harvard group. What had made him suspicious from the beginning, McDougall confessed, was how unusually clever the lady seemed. Bird responded that psychics need not be morons to be genuine, though he wanted to avoid any assumptions about Mrs. Crandon until he had a chance to sample the goods.

That night he heard the hair-raising whistle and greetings from Mina's dead brother for the first time. Walter's mannish voice was so different from the medium's that Bird could not imagine the same vocal cords producing both sounds. He could see, though, that both siblings liked to banter. To Walter, the important New York visitor was "Birdie"—a writer to be made fun of for his quaint attire, as Bird dressed like an Oxford don. Yet aside from the vocal effects, the ghost was not active. Roy explained that the medium's force was unaccountably weak.

At the sitting the next evening, they weren't favored with a visitation for some time. What was the matter? Kitty asked. When finally the Crawford table began to move, something was different. Walter typically turned the table in a circular motion. It moved this time in more of a straight and jerky fashion—a sign that an unfamiliar spirit was in control. The intruder would only communicate by the old method, abrupt tilts that spelled out yes or no. Churlishly, it answered no to every question put to it. All were relieved when the energy seemed to change and Walter returned. The table started dancing to the circular movements that were his trademark. But Big Brother did not stay; soon the other personality was directing the psychic. A frightening male whisper—*"Break the circle, quick!"*—was heard. It was like all hands abandoning ship when the sitters pushed away from the table. Only Mrs. Crandon remained—oblivious in her trance to any danger. Without waking, she urged her nervous friends back into the circle. Thinking that unwise, Dr. Crandon turned on the lights to wake her. She abruptly went into a seizure. Her body jerked wildly, her limbs thrashing against the spirit cabinet. Her face took on a feral expression. She spewed curses "in tones of the mud gutter," Bird observed, "rather than the Back Bay." Suddenly, the intruder barked, *"Get the hell out of here!"* as Walter tried to come through. To all appearances there was a struggle for control of the medium. "It was obvious that, genuinely or fictitiously we had to do with an evil possession," Bird realized. He didn't know whether a priest or psychologist was more needed on Lime Street.

The following night the Harvard group was invited to sit with Mrs.

Crandon once again, both at the dinner table and for a séance. Dr. Mc-Dougall thought it improper to return so soon after offending the psychic, but Roback was there, along with Helson and Gardner Murphy—the alternate judge in the *Scientific American* contest. As the séance proceeded, the researchers realized that the medium was in no better form. She demonstrated only the least impressive table effects; the mysterious intruder was still preventing her brother from manifesting. Bird found it more disturbing that the table continually shot toward *him,* confirming the suspicions of the medium's friends: that the *Scientific American* editor, being the only stranger to the circle, was responsible for attracting the dark spirit. He was taken aback by their attitude. The psychics had often considered him an energizing presence—he was not used to being thought of as a demon carrier.

It was decided that he and the Harvard group should leave the house, to see if the medium was less inhibited without them. Stepping outside the Crandons' front door, Bird lit a cigarette and stared up at the red-hued room where Walter was presumably battling the other wraith. A full moon shone overhead; and as the scientists took their late-night stroll, Bird wondered if it was more to blame for the medium's hysterics.

In the meantime, Mina's friends were able to contact Walter. He told them that the interfering force was on a lower plane, closer to them than he was—therefore it was easier for the intruder to control the medium. Big Brother said the situation was only dangerous if Mina slipped into trance. It was OK to hold séances, he allowed, as long as she was conscious. But if he said to break the circle, then they had better break it, he warned.

At the séance the next evening, Bird sat with a circle on pins and needles. Seeing how vigilant the ABC Club was, lest she slip into trance, Mrs. Crandon teased, *"The goblins'll get you if you don't watch out for me!"* She had as much fun with the scientists. When the table moved slightly, Helson complained that he was tired of that kind of phenomena. He wanted Walter's more exciting stuff. "Let's get on to levitation and the music," he urged. It was a remark that Bird felt disqualified the Harvard rug hopper from psychical research—if his previous misconduct had not already done so. Mina explained that she was helpless without her magic thread that lifted tables and pulled piano strings. At this crack, they all laughed—

even Helson. Moments later, Aleck Cross began acting strangely. No longer alarmed, the sitters found it amusing when he left the circle. A short time later, Gardner Murphy announced that he had to make a train back to New York and departed. The commotion led Mina to wonder if Walter had ordered them to break the circle. Yet her brother had not returned.

All agreed that they would try a final time to contact Walter. The sitters were still chattering when Roy turned the lights down. Bird soon noticed that Mina had become silent. Someone announced that she was in trance. Before any of them could wake her, the intruder was back. The medium made anguished noises. She kicked over her chair and toppled onto the floor, overturning the spirit cabinet. Dr. Crandon warned that in this state she couldn't be allowed to break the circle. At his command, four of the men struggled to hold Mina. Her resistance was fierce, though the seizure was shorter than it had been the previous evening. She came out of it moaning, as if waking from a disturbing dream. If she is faking this, thought Bird, she ought to be in movies.

On his way back to New York, Bird mulled over what he had seen. Dr. McDougall had indicated that this case might have more to do with abnormal psychology than supernatural possession. He had sensed something illicit in the relationship between the spirit and the medium. At one sitting, Walter told his sister to remove her corset, as the stays were impeding his force. She complied, according to McDougall. Riding on his train, Bird pictured her undressing in the scarlet light while the Harvard professors watched her every move.

Much about the case would have interested Dr. Freud, the psychologists decided. As for Bird, he was impressed with the sincerity of the medium, and he found her unusually gifted, even if he had witnessed none of the physical effects that baffled the other researchers. It worried him, moreover, that Walter had open contempt for the Harvard team. *"It takes a crook to catch one,"* the ghost had said of the investigators trying to discredit his sister. Yet for a change it was science on the defensive. Two nights earlier, while walking down Beacon Hill with the alienists, Bird heard Gardner Murphy interpret the case according to the Freudian model. Walter was the Id—a primal force unleashed in the darkness; Mina the Ego—the ghost's conduit; and the investigators, particularly McDougall, the Superego that would not abide Walter, for his effects were a violent assault on a scientist's beliefs and authority. The idea that a ghost might really exist was hard to swallow even for many psychical researchers. They believed in supernormal phenomena while doubting that discarnate beings were the cause.

Whatever was at the root of the clash, Bird saw that it made great drama. Back in New York, he informed Orson Munn that there had been a war between the Crandons and the Harvard scientists. Who won? Mr. Munn wanted to know. The medium won, Bird told him.

The White Dove

And moving through a mirror clear
That hangs before her all the year,
Shadows of the world appear.
There she sees the highway near
—ALFRED, LORD TENNYSON

*T*he appearance of the malefic spirit that Bird had carried like a bug to Beacon Hill was thought to be only a temporary setback to the Crandon mediumship. But even if Mrs. Crandon shook it off, Roy was wary of the invasive attention that came with the *Scientific American* tests. The Crandons had just gone through a war with McDougall, and were not sold on Bird's psychic tournament. Despite that, they were ready to work with other scientists. In December, the only month that Roy could get away from his medical practice, he and Mina planned to visit France and England, where they would hold séances for the venerable European researchers. "There was accordingly little time for peaceful resumption of the Lime Street routine after the war," wrote Bird. Under a dark pall, Harry Helson tried to test the medium. He arranged a séance at the Harvard Psychological Laboratory, and left the ABC Club alone there with Mina—so that she might orient herself to a new environment.

The sitting started with promising table action, yet Walter indicated that he was not in control of the psychic. Then one in the group foolishly brought up Bird, the mention of whose name seemed to cause a disturbance. Walter gave the signal to break the circle. The séance was over. The bells of Harvard's Memorial Church would not toll that night to ghostly accompaniment. Days later the sittings were resumed in Roy's den. Though the intruder was gone, Mrs. Crandon produced little more than verbal communications from her brother. Then, on November 25, Walter promised to do something showstopping.

He would cause a live dove, he said, to pass through the walls of 10 Lime

Street. If the thing were done, it would be another bolt hurled at the skeptics. While such "apports," as researchers called them, were often faked, some believed that certain mediums had the power to manifest objects and even living creatures directly from the ether. Those who credited the effect speculated that dematerialized animals and articles could be conveyed through the molecular interspace in walls and closed doors, then restored to solidity as they appeared on the séance table. It was the psychic equivalent of Houdini walking through walls, and Mrs. Crandon had never done anything like it. When Walter announced that he would try an apport, the ABC Club was thrilled; though there was chuckling when one sitter suggested that the ghost apport a kitten instead, and Kitty Brown requested a human baby from the fourth dimension.

They were not laughing the next evening, when—as if from thin air—a live dove arrived in the séance room. The creature—*"a companion for Birdie,"* Walter murmured—perched on the edge of the table, unnaturally motionless and calm. The next day inquiries were made at various pet stores to see if a particular blonde had been recently shopping for birds. Evidently she hadn't been seeking one.

Kitty adopted the animal. When eventually shown the dove, Malcolm Bird found it the most serene creature he had ever encountered. For about six months it lived with the Browns until, to Kitty's distress, it mysteriously died one morning. Mina consoled her that it must have been a carrier pigeon and ready to return to its dispatcher. After burying it in the Browns' backyard, they wished it a happy journey back to Walter.

Sensationnel

A most remarkable instrument: London envies Boston her possession.
—SIR ARTHUR CONAN DOYLE

Sir Arthur recalled the scene vividly. As if apported from some more joyful place, the woman in the black velvet wrap emerged through the turning doors and twirling her pennant flags waltzed about the hotel lobby. Kingsley was dead. She waltzed slowly. When the maroons roared she left. The War was over. Five years after her victory dance, Sir Arthur stood in the same hall. He had not yet met the Crandons but immediately recognized them when they entered the Grosvenor Hotel. They spotted him too and Mina waved gaily. No introductions were necessary when Sir Arthur greeted the medium he had been waiting for.

◆

The Crandons' first stop, after debarking the *Olympic* one week earlier, was Paris, a city of psychic light, where mediums were tested by pioneering researchers like the Nobel-winning Charles Richet, the astronomer Camille Flammarion, and Dr. Gustav Geley—who displayed at the Institute Metaphysique his prized molds, casts, and photographs of ectoplasm. Many who had visited Geley's society, including Bird, were awed by his proofs of the fleeting substance that all psychical researchers were trying to capture and examine. Roy considered it more of a priority to see Geley's collection than anything in France. It was a delight to drink wine again in public, lunch in the Bois, and walk the grand boulevard. For the most part, though, the Crandons spent their trip in dim rooms.

Mrs. Crandon had never endured such strict control as Messieurs Richet and Geley imposed at her demonstration of December 8, 1923. Throughout the séance her hands and feet were held by the two French scientists, who both sat with her inside the spirit cabinet, resting their heads on each of her shoulders to make sure Walter's voice was not her own. Independently, it seemed, the ghost whispered one of his humorous poems. Minutes later he made the table dance and then levitate while a music box played. The parlor was lit with the brightest red to which Mina had ever been exposed, yet the researchers saw nothing to suggest deception. Dr. Geley's associates applauded the phenomena. They yelled *bien* and *encore,* as if Mrs. Crandon were the Josephine Baker of the spiritist circuit. When the table manifestations were over, loud raps were heard on the cabinet. The entire structure then imploded on the scientists and the psychic inside it. Mina would always remember Geley—who died in a plane crash a few months later—crying *Sensationnel!* while examining the debris of her cabinet.

◆

When Mina was still a child, Dr. Le Roi Crandon came to England to take on his first surgical post, at Guy's and St. Thomas' Hospital of London. Twenty-five years later, on this strange new venture, the doctor had returned with his third wife to meet scientists he hoped might explain what the Harvard group had not. All the world's psychical institutes were in elegant white townhouses, it seemed to the Crandons, with pictures of the first ghost hunters on the parlor walls. Their initial stop in London was the British College of Psychic Science, the brainchild of Hewat McKenzie, who believed that Houdini really passed through water cells and brick walls. McKenzie and his wife were Spiritualists, and not known to be as rigid in their controls as the English SPR. If Mrs. Crandon were a clever fake, then she might have latitude to pull some sleight of hand at the college. Yet aside from a few faint raps and whistles, her first sitting for the McKenzies was a complete blank.

The Crandons' next appearance was at the SPR, the institution that had once discredited Eusapia Palladino, among other touted spooks, after she had dazzled the scientists in Italy and France. More recently, Eric Dingwall and a new generation of SPR officers had disenchanted Eva C, the Queen of Ectoplasm—when, with Houdini present, she did little more than disgorge gauzy bile from her mouth. It was Dingwall, amateur magician and curator of medieval erotica, who now controlled Mrs. Crandon during her first séance for the SPR. Among those attending was also the Hon. Everard Feilding, another seasoned researcher and dabbler in magic. The investigators used a trick séance table, Malcolm Bird was later told, with a shelf that would immediately collapse if physical pressure were applied to it. Even so, Mrs. Crandon made the table rise and float six separate times. At Dingwall's request, she even levitated it twice in clear white light. None in the circle had ever before seen that particular effect—contrary to the ritual, when the lights were turned up, she continued to perform. That evening Mina went back to the McKenzies' for another séance at the college, where this time Walter made a twelve-pound table dance and rise in full light while a Victrola piped jazz. The McKenzies called her levitations unprecedented. They and Dingwall welcomed the arrival of the Boston psychic.

News of her triumphs also impressed the scientist who had originally inspired Dr. Crandon's experiments. Sir Oliver Lodge would soon tell colleagues visiting the States that the two things they must see were Niagara Falls and Mrs. Crandon. She was said to have rare magnetism. When on December 12, at the Stead Psychic Center, the medium sat for Ada Deane, photographer of the Armistice Day miracle, every plate showed ectoplasmic forms around her—one of which Mina said was her brother, Walter, recognizable by his blond wavy hair, slightly twisted mouth, and scar above the left eyebrow where a horse had kicked him. It was indeed Walter, his mother in Boston later affirmed. All of this was gratifying news to the detective writer who had arranged most of Mrs. Crandon's European demonstrations, the supportive guide who had followed her progress from afar.

All roads to the spirit world—Houdini's, Bird's, and now the Crandons'—led to Sir Arthur's door. At his suite in the Grosvenor, Mina gave her last séance of the trip. She sat in a rug-covered cabinet, veiled behind a three-way screen that made her feel as if she ought to receive confessions from the three other people in the room. With her limbs extended from the enclosure, her clasped hands resting on the square séance table, and her feet restrained in Sir Arthur's lap, she went immediately into trance. There was no music, though the persistent rumble from nearby Victoria Station was as evocative of Walter, the former railroad worker. Tonight he arrived quickly and with force. He levitated the table to a record height thus far, and when Dr. Crandon turned the lights up, none could discern what kept it in the air. With blinding darkness restored, the darting presence whistled in Sir Arthur's ear, behind Lady Doyle's back, and then more distantly, as if he were leaving the room. But he was not. With no warning Mina's cabinet began to pulsate, the rug falling on her head. Dried roses that had been on a shelf were transported through the air. Though Walter had spared the Victorian couple none of his coarsest jokes, he left a flower at Jean Doyle's feet as a token of his affection for the old girl.

In the séance room, as well as over dinner, Mrs. Crandon made a fine first impression during her visit at the Grosvenor. Both in terms of talent and refinement (few had any inkling she was country-bred), Doyle considered her to be of a different class from most psychics. Her husband was an esteemed surgeon and she a dashing girl; although, as Brahmins went, both seemed rather modest. Mrs. Crandon said that she could not credit many of the effects ascribed to her, particularly that during her séance a bird had been apported from another sphere. Her spirit control, on the contrary, was brash and lacking any sublime quality. "Walter has a wealth of strong language and makes no pretence at all to be a very elevated being," Doyle wrote. Even a racy spirit had use over there, however, and he perceived what that calling might be: Mrs. Crandon and Walter would be excellent subjects for the *Scientific American* challenge. As Sir Arthur had feared, the confrontational style of some of the judges was anathema to the fragile psychic constitution. Yet he had heard, via Bird, how Mrs. Crandon stood her ground in the confrontation with McDougall—how she had deflected his accusations with grace and humor. She was a rare breed, in Doyle's estimation, a sensitive with mettle. And in her dead brother she had a powerful guardian. She would not be intimidated, Sir Arthur felt, by enemies of spiritism—the traducers of mediums.

The Boy Medium

BOY MEDIUM PUZZLES EXPERTS
Committee Says Phenomena Produced by Italian May Be Genuine.
—*New York Times*

*E*usapia Palladino, the great medium of the prewar period, had something none of the recent pretenders could claim—the backing of respected researchers such as Carrington, Lodge, and Charles Richet. The scientists reported that the coarse and corpulent Palladino, a Neapolitan peasant with fiery, protuberant eyes, could move furniture about the room by some unknown power. With a commanding stare she drew the séance table toward her or raised it in the air. Seated in her chair, she purportedly levitated herself while sitters clung to her; she raised a fist and violent raps were heard as if, said Lodge, someone were striking wood with a heavy mallet. And when the psychic emitted a breeze of cold air from a cleft in her forehead, it was joked that the slight Carrington was carried away by it.

Certain that Signora Palladino was ready for a bigger stage, Carrington had brought her to America in late 1909 for a series of ballyhooed exhibitions that some said fattened his wallet. He had negotiated a magazine deal with *McClure's* and was charging for an evening with Eusapia a hefty $250 a séance. Unfortunately, her psychic channel had somehow been lost or corrupted in the passage from the Old to the New World. By the end of a disastrous New York tour, the newspapers were calling her an unmitigated fraud. Her disappointed supporters still maintained that Palladino, though apt to cheat when frustrated, had produced unparalleled effects in Europe. But Eusapia was no longer the hope of the psychical research movement. She died just after the War, though her spirit was said to possess a medium who had inherited her power.

◆

The papers called him the Boy Medium. To the *Scientific American* judges, he was Nino Pecoraro—a pale, muscular twenty-four-year-old Neapolitan immigrant who, when his physician discovered that the boy possessed the Gift, had been employed as a drugstore clerk. After having spent two years helping Pecoraro develop his clairvoyant powers, Dr. Anselmo Peccio presented him to Munn's commission.

Dr. Peccio, it occurred to Bird, was as drawn to spirit mediums as magnates were to chorus girls. When Carrington brought Eusapia Palladino to America, Peccio had hosted her séances at the Hotel Theresa in Harlem. At present it was the Boy Medium enchanting guests in the Italian doctor's suite; yet he needed looking after in a way the late Signora Palladino had not. The boy had terrifying nightmares, and ghosts were said to appear by his bedside. He was known, Dr. Peccio attested, to jump out of his window whenever the dead gave him a fright.

Pecoraro first came to the attention of psychic researchers in 1922, when he gave a séance for Sir Arthur in Washington, DC. Among the sitters were Carrington and an Italian debutante named Aida, who looked ready to bolt for the door should a ghost appear. To Aida's distress, soon after the lights were turned out a chilling breeze wafted from the spirit cabinet that held Pecoraro tied to a chair. Minutes later an impassioned spirit was heard; "Aida! Aida!" it roared—so suddenly, Doyle recalled, "that it made us all jump from our chairs." Articles of Pecoraro's clothing flew from the cabinet and landed on the séance table—the medium's collar, his belt, his crumpled shirt. The spirit then called for Aida to enter the cabinet. "Oh, no, no, no!" cried the petrified girl. Though nothing else remarkable happened that night, the medium had shown enough promise for Doyle to recommend him to Malcolm Bird. By the time of the psychic contest, Pecoraro had also sat with an unimpressed Walter Prince at the offices of the ASPR. Two of the three New York judges were therefore familiar with the third official candidate for the prize.

Dr. Peccio had developed the Boy Medium specifically so that he could channel Eusapia Palladino and continue her work. Nino would attempt to produce for an American research committee what his spirit control failed to in life: unassailable evidence of the power of the psychic mind. Typically his demonstrations resembled an old-time spook show complete with spectral music and floating instruments. Because he was known for such physical effects, the judges did not treat him with the kid gloves used for the other candidates. None of the covert devices that had monitored and trapped George Valiantine were attached to the Boy Medium's chair. Dispensing with the technology Houdini had compromised, the judges instead trussed Pecoraro like a dangerous criminal or crafty escape artist. After his hands were encased in heavy mittens sewn to his coat sleeves, he was instructed to clasp his elbows with the opposite mitt—straitjacket-style—while Carrington bound his arms with picture wire, and his torso and legs with long lengths of rope knotted to his chair. Despite this predicament, Pecoraro looked so unfazed that Bird began calling him "poker face."

The stoic Pecoraro, having never learned English, was more apt to communicate with the dead than with any of the jury members. When he went into trance, the voice of Palladino did the talking—her Italian translated by Dr. Peccio, the intermediary between the medium and the committee. This personality, the doctor warned, was as mischievous a spirit as she had been a medium, having stolen $35 from his billfold when the lights went out. Since then the ghost had been repaying him, he explained, by apporting dollar bills onto the séance table. Are our wallets safe? asked one journalist. Yes, replied Dr. Peccio, who had pasted in a scrapbook the singles Palladino had produced at various séances, along with a ledger of what the wraith still owed him. Yes, echoed Bird, who was sure it was a larger purse—Mr. Munn's money—that the candidate hoped to spirit away.

Unlike the previous contestants, the Boy Medium made a strong first impression. The lights were barely extinguished when Pecoraro startled a circle that included the New York judges, the journal staff, the inevitable *Times* reporter, Dr. Peccio, and three respected Manhattan physicians who were studying the case. Within the cabinet were placed a collection of instruments that the bound medium should not have been able to reach. Yet bells rang at once, a tambourine clanged, a whistle shrilled, and the spirit megaphone blasted through the curtain of the cabinet, tilting the séance table. A crescendo followed, where all instruments seemed to play simultaneously, while a trumpet voice wailed. Fifteen minutes later, Eusapia implored the sitters to talk and sing, as intermittent raps and assorted notes from the instruments were heard. The séance ended with an earthly crash and then a shriek. Inside his cabinet the investigators found the hysterical Pecoraro, still bound but capsized in his chair. His nose was bleeding profusely. Quickly they cut him free, so that Dr. Peccio could attend to his injured psychic.

At the next pitch-black séance, the instruments were placed this time on a table outside the cabinet. Again they were played and manipulated. The bell was thrown at Bird's feet. The table rocked violently just as some in the circle saw a glowing hand form outside the medium's cabinet. The hoarse voice of Eusapia vowed that a full materialization was in store, but the spirit often promised more than the medium produced. The séance ended with the common excuse for a failed effect: there was a hostile presence, complained Eusapia, that stanched her energy. While she did not name him, all knew that she blamed Walter Prince—whose open doubts had offended her. Prince appeared to be validated, though, by what happened next. The last thing Eusapia said was that the medium had been agitated and his bonds disturbed—which they were, as the experts soon found out. While still restrained, it was evident that Pecoraro had frantically tried to escape. His gloves were in disrepair and had bite marks, as if a dog had been chewing on them. In Prince's view, the medium might have been able to slip them; but if that were so, it puzzled Bird why there were no fingerprints on the musical instruments. Another intriguing discovery was that the psychic's trance appeared to be genuine. While Pecoraro was unconscious, the physicians had stuck pins in his calves without provoking any reaction. When they opened his eyelids and shone a flashlight into his eyeball, he did not recoil.

"We regard this case as unusually interesting," Bird told the press, "and believe that the medium does not practice conscious fraud." Nino was like a character in a Poe tale, tormented by some subliminal terror. In staff meetings at the *Scientific American*, it was suggested that he had either hypnotized himself during the sittings or fallen under the spell of the faintly disreputable Dr. Peccio.

By this time the experts were certain that Pecoraro, whether deliberately or not, was presenting a spook show. When Bird's assistant had sewn Nino's gloves to his sleeve, he was almost asphyxiated, the editor reported, by the stench of garlic on the medium's breath. When a powerful blast was later heard from the trumpet, some in the circle detected the same offensive aroma. It should have been the spirits, not Pecoraro, who were communicating through the megaphone; Bird doubted the sitters had smelled "celestial garlic." More incriminating was that the psychic's bonds were always found to be slightly loose after his demonstrations. Bird had never encountered a medium who took so long, after the séance was over, to come out of his trance and allow his cabinet to be searched. This was because Pecoraro needed time to restore the bonds he had escaped, Prince contended. The medium had nevertheless performed his magic while tightly controlled. The experts hadn't been able to stop him. The *Times* called him "the most promising contestant to date." In consequence, Orson Munn decided to summon his expert on escapology.

Houdini was performing in Little Rock, Arkansas, when he received the wire urging him back to New York. His first reaction was irritation with Bird, who had not bothered to inform him that another psychic was performing for the jury. This was what came of excluding him from the proceedings: the commission was stumped. Not a deliberate fraud? he scoffed. Pecoraro's dark sport was not practiced while unconscious! Even though he was booked, Houdini decided to cancel his engagements and return to the metropolis. Finally he would have the opportunity, or so he imagined, to put his stamp on the contest: to save the journal from disastrous embarrassment.

Like no psychic the committee had yet investigated, Houdini saw Pecoraro as a throwback to his sawdust days. He believed the medium was doing the Davenport act, the performance he had once mastered. Sitting in the train car that carried the Houdinis, as Dr. Hill's wagon once had, across the prairie, the magician could hear the barker. He envisioned Pecoraro on the dingy stage. *Hurry, hurry, hurry! Step right up to see the Boy Medium. Just one thin dime, ten coppers, two nickels, the tenth part of a dollar! Come see the Italian Occult Expositor. This tent for Pecoraro!* Bird's latest candidate was an escape artist. And nothing rankled Houdini like a performer muscling in on his territory, let alone one who claimed his feats were supernormal.

◆

The arrival of Houdini at the *Scientific American* offices was a great surprise to almost everyone. Yet the psychic's poker face betrayed no fear of the expert now supervising the test séances. Houdini was impressed by Nino's well-developed chest and shoulders; he said the medium had a better physique for escape art than he did. And he had an unspoken message for the strapping Italian psychic: *You will not take the prize.*

On the evening of December 18, there began what Walter Prince saw as a match between escape artists. As Houdini went into action, Dr. Prince quickly recognized—as did most of the eighteen other observers in the library—that he truly was the master of his profession: the Einstein of the science of deception! As Houdini directed, Nino's hands were placed into gloves that were stitched snugly at the wrists; the gloves were then sewn to his undershirt; the psychic's arms thrust into a jacket that was reversed; the mitts sewn to the sleeves of the coat; the coat to his trousers; and for the last sartorial bind, the contestant's collar was strung snugly around his wiry neck. Throughout the process, Houdini tried to limit the medium's discomfort. If Nino did feel that his bindings were severely applied, he never complained. He stared blankly into space: hypnotized already, or so it appeared, by the master of escape.

The Great Houdini was just warming up. He told his audience that they should not restrain the medium in the way the commission had previously—for "even a tyro could get his hands loose from sixty yards of rope." Explaining how the long lengths gave an escape artist slack, Houdini lashed Nino with dozens of short pieces of rope. He made a labyrinth of loops around the contestant's body then tied them with square knots that left lengths long enough to bind him to the chair. Next the chair was secured to the baseboard of the cabinet with a metal strap, a wire cord, and sealed with wax. It took more than ninety minutes for Pecoraro to be controlled to Houdini's satisfaction. Studying his handiwork, Bird was in awe. While he had always tried to ensure the comfort and indulge the whims—a garden for the flower medium!—of the psychic candidates, he did not think that Houdini was manhandling the Boy Medium. It was fair, Bird felt, for the committee to make cheating an excruciating proposition for Nino. Anyway, what was a gauntlet of rope to those who left their bodies? When his work was done, Houdini said that he could not guarantee the medium wouldn't get loose, only that he would never get back.

Not long after the circle formed, the raspy voice of Nino's spirit control was heard from the psychic cabinet. While the ghost at first expressed no hostility toward Houdini, there was a galvanic tension in the library. Previously the spirit of Palladino had been remarkably good-humored during the sittings. She hadn't sulked, cursed in Italian, or exhibited any of the other disagreeable habits she had while alive. She had seemed particularly pleased to reunite with her old manager, Carrington, telling him that what she once did as a medium she now directed from the Other Side. As Houdini expected, the ghost that had been so active during the prior tests did nothing this time but talk. Eusapia complimented him on the thick web he had spun around the psychic. She said that she would manifest despite his best efforts to stop her. But the séance was a blank. When she asked for the circle to sing, no instruments came to life. An hour into the sitting, a few weak and suspicious raps were all she wrought.

The frustrated Eusapia complained that Houdini had bound Nino like Christ to the cross. Angered by the slur, the magician had to be restrained by Bird from going after her. Later, Dr. Peccio also objected to Houdini's control methods. He said the medium was in pain, that his circulation was cut off. Only if he tried to escape, Houdini shot back. Once more Bird backed his expert. The wails from the cabinet he ascribed to the anguish of defeat.

By the end of Nino's third séance, the *Scientific American* staff agreed with Prince—who had called the effects "particularly stupid" from the beginning—and Houdini; the Italian candidate, whether consciously or not, was another false medium. Only Dr. Peccio, stating that he should be made a member of the jury, had not given up on his discovery.

Another sitting for Nino was arranged a few days before Christmas; this time without Houdini present. Unsurprisingly, Eusapia was in better form. The instruments blared. The curtain to the spirit cabinet billowed like a sail. "Marvelous, is it not?" Dr. Peccio boasted. When midnight came the medium went into hysterics: he frothed at the mouth then burst from his chair, ripping his bonds apart. Peccio later declared that his psychic ward had now done enough to win the prize. "I am entitled to the $2,500," the doctor said—as if he had orchestrated everything. "I want it. He has given convincing proof. Absolutely. The money is as good as mine." To his disappointment, the committee wasn't satisfied. Bird announced that they needed to see more from Pecoraro. Further tests were arranged for January. But when the doctor found out that Houdini was going to be present for them, he and his psychic failed to show up to take their medicine.

Part VI

THE WITCH OF LIME STREET

⚜

The world is eagerly awaiting a universal religion.
—CECIL B. DEMILLE

The orthodox seem less inclined to scoff.
—*Time*

When the lights were out and we sat around that table in pitch
blackness or in the faint glow of a dim red light we witnessed some of
the most strange phenomena ever seen by humans.
—S. RALPH HARLOW, RECALLING THE SÉANCES AT
10 LIME STREET

Mina Stinson Crandon, born August 28,
1889, in Picton, Ontario

Walter Stinson, died August 7, 1911, in Boston

1924: An Evening on Lime Street

Imagine yourself invited to one of Dr. Crandon's evenings, including an invitation to dinner. Down in an old historic section of Boston you would find his house, suggesting memories of many historic things that occurred in Boston. After the quaint little Japanese butler admitted you to a charming parlor you would find yourself face to face with a handsome, middle-aged surgeon who knew the secret of hospitality and put you quickly at ease. Something about the pleasant expression in his blue-gray eyes that looked so clearly and honestly in yours would suggest to you other men of his profession of character and ability. If you had come prepared to be critical and hostile you would find it hard to keep that attitude towards so charming a gentleman.

When Mrs. Crandon was presented she would completely upset all preconceptions of the famous medium. A very attractive blonde with a charming expression and excellent figure the "Witch of Lime Street" proved to be a thoroughly feminine lady with the best traits of a mother and housekeeper. Her vivacity, with the doctor's poise and dignity, made them a delightful pair for an enjoyable dinner. Both had a diverting sense of humor and the conversation would never lag.

After the meal, which frequently involved a little wine that warmed your heart, you would be invited into the library. There the atmosphere was that of literary Boston—comfortable chairs, books everywhere. . . . Probably while the doctor was talking with you some of his friends would drop in for the séance of the evening. You might meet Dr. Mark A. Richardson, who had some reputation for work he had done on typhoid vaccination. You could not fail to like him. A representative of New England's best ideals would be the impression he would give you. Certainly you would not be led by what you knew of his career or by his manner and conversation to think of him as a magician's assistant. Nor would his wife give rise to any such idea. . . .

After this social hour you would find yourself going with this interesting group up to the séance room. However you might feel about ghosts and goblins you certainly would feel that you were in for a diverting evening. In the dark room you would meet the most intriguing personality of all. True, he would be only a husky whisper. But what could he whisper!

—Dr. Henry C. McComas, a Princeton psychologist who investigated the Lime Street phenomena

◆

Boston had no brash celebrities or stars; it was known instead for its bright minds at MIT and Harvard. The Red Sox had traded Babe Ruth and the Blue Stockings drove Isadora Duncan from their city. For the time being the Crandons managed to avoid publicity, though what was happening in their séance room could not be kept entirely quiet. Whether the guest was a Harvard psychologist or Beacon Hill neighbor, the Crandons' gatherings became a sought-after invitation when Mina returned from Europe. Roy lamented in a letter to Roback that so many were now attending the Sunday sittings, they "were in danger of becoming vaudeville!" While that was the last thing he wanted to happen, the demonstrations could be riotous.

For all the screams and laughter, one of Roy's experimental goals was to effectively muzzle the ABC Club. He and Dr. Richardson hoped to demonstrate that Walter's distinctive voice and chortle could not be produced by any in the séance circle. Richardson would thus introduce his famous voice cut-out machine: a mechanism to prove no one opened their mouth while the spirit was supposed to be talking. By this process, which Mina likened to a group pacifier, a rubber nipple connected to a U-shaped tube was held in the mouth of each person in the séance room—all of whom were instructed to blow through its opening until columns of water ascended in one arm of the tube and descended in the other. When balance was reached, the sitters and psychic were told to use their tongues to close the hole in their nipples. All in the circle were thought to be silenced by the device: if anyone should open their mouths, the air pressure fell, causing water to displace in the free arm of the luminous U-tube. Mina thought it fortunate that séances were conducted in the dark, since it would have driven her to mute hysterics to watch her friends clench on their nipples while Walter repeatedly whispered, *"David dug a deep and dirty ditch,"* or *"George is an extraordinary jazzy jay-bird, by jingo."* Dr. Crandon, who failed to see the humor, would claim that the unusual device achieved its aim. When in use it apparently gagged the sitters but not the ghost.

◆

To ring in the beginning of 1924, a gong placed out of the psychic's reach began to chime. After delivering a blow to Aleck Cross's chest with the hammer, Walter struck the instrument to the accompaniment of jazz on the Victrola. It would be a year of ghostly taps, ectoplasmic hands, and floating roses for the sitters—and of mysterious elliptical lights that flashed like darting eyes when Walter introduced his psychic animals. Although she had not yet committed to be tested by the *Scientific American* committee, Mrs. Crandon, as if preparing for a debut, began to expand her mediumship. In England and Germany, there was a scientific fascination with a phenomenon called telekinesis. Mediums in Europe, such as Evan Powell and the Schneider brothers, made vases and lampshades levitate and move about the séance room. Early in the year, Mina added these effects to her own program.

By then Mina and Walter's mother, Jemima Stinson, had begun attending the Sunday séances. And a psychic named Sarah Litzelmann was sometimes invited, as her presence seemed to boost Mina's power. With her arrival there began a strange flirtation between the ghost and the girl. "Walter, I have brought you three red, red, red roses," Sarah announced at a dark séance a couple of evenings after Valentine's Day. Walter answered with a rustle from the spirit cabinet, and a burst of chilling ardor. *"I have brought you a yaller, yaller, yaller rose,"* he murmured. After he repeated this refrain to two other women in the circle, Kitty Brown and his mother, single yellow roses materialized in the ladies' laps. On another occasion, with Mina controlled, two carnations were placed on the séance table. When they began to move, and Mrs. Richardson expressed the urge to smell one, it was carried "with almost lightning speed around the circle," grazing faces and tapping heads and noses, before floating underneath her chin and remaining there.

"Are you having a good time? Isn't this a great party we're having?" Walter played with more than flowers. In March, reports described an ashtray slithering across the séance table, rising to the ceiling, then gliding to the spirit cabinet and rattling against the walls while Mina, slumped in her trance, was restrained by Drs. Crandon and Richardson. Walter said he took his force from the minds of the sitters, though he complained that their mental strength was inadequate.

While the Harvard group continued to investigate Mina, they were unable to explain her new manifestations. Flowers caressed the ladies or slapped the faces of the researchers. Sitters were tickled, pinched, and had their hair pulled. Scientists had their trousers tugged by something that felt fuzzy, diaphanous, icy, or in other ways inhuman. Sarah Litzelmann was "pecked at, as if by kissing lips"; Mrs. Richardson felt something like a cobweb envelop her face; a digit like "an animal's paw" stroked her calf and ankle. Another in the ABC Club, Frederick Adler, was startled by a buzzing sensation against his leg. *"Yes, like a flea,"* Walter whispered. "Scratch it, then," challenged Adler, whereupon he instantly felt something clawing him. When Dr. Crandon wondered if this were a spoof, Walter struck his brother-in-law in the ribs ten times. With each invisible blow the ghost whispered, *"I'm spoofing you, am I?"*

"Laugh," Walter implored. *"If you can't laugh at anything else look at yourself in the mirror."* One night, on request, Walter produced an ectoplasmic finger with glowing bones, as in an X-ray photo. It raised and lowered like a gavel, making a tap on the table as it came down, then a luminous mass went over the side of the cabinet and six blows reverberated. "The best sitting yet," Dr. Richardson recorded.

"There's a wild night ahead." Walter liked to tease Roy, and other sitters, by warning that spiders and furry worms had been unleashed in the pitch-darkness. *"It's like that in hell,"* the ghost cackled. Sensing something crawling over his lips, Dr. Edison Brown slapped at the invisible insect. When Aleck Cross began to whimper, he received a strike across his palms. Mina felt a form like a cat rubbing against her legs.

At another gathering that winter, the medium manifested two triangles of light, like curved wings, that Walter said was a bat named Suzy. *"She lugs me around,"* joked the ghost; *"I went to Europe on Suzy."* Suzy flapped in the face of Roback, but seemed more gently inclined to Dr. Crandon's sister, Laura, whose shoulder it perched on while the others calmed down. There were other animals, "psychic livestock," that Walter introduced to the circle, but the occult menagerie was not complete until Mr. Bird returned to Lime Street.

Margery

Be sure a future moves slowly toward its final augury,
Proclaiming sure and certain hope,
Outshining faith of Priest and Pope—
Revealed by grace of Margery
—CAPT. QUENTIN C. A. CRAUFURD, AN AWED
VISITOR TO LIME STREET

A single validated case of spirit communication and Sir Arthur Conan Doyle would be vindicated, but how many exposures would it take before the anti-Spiritualists—magicians, fundamentalists, Menckenites, and hardboiled scientists—no longer had to see mediums featured in the newspapers? Bird observed that readers who wrote to the *Scientific American* were equally divided between skeptics and those sympathetic to the psychics. The magazine had been inundated with letters commenting on the committee's handling of Pecoraro—some complaining that the psychic's bonds had been too tight, others that he should have been tied more severely. But those who pointed out that clamor and competition inhibited spirit phenomena were starting to irritate a staff that was "excessively weary," Bird wrote in his column, "of having these truisms dinged into our ears by every occultist Tom, Dick and Harry." Bird did not want it alleged that the commission was bullying sensitives, nor that the *Scientific American* was involved in a religious inquiry. Psychic phenomena, in his opinion, were not miracles. "If they happen," he asserted, "they certainly happen through the operation of laws and causes as definite as those which produce a series of explosions in the cylinders of an automobile engine." The problem, as Bird saw it, was that the *Scientific American* was stuck with lemons.

That winter—following the magazine's exposure of Dr. Albert Abrams, the infamous electric healer—Bird was ready to return to a spook hunt that had bagged only the worst sort of quarry. "If one examines our experiences of the past fifteen months in search of a generalization," he reported, "one must be struck by the lack of quality in the mediums who have come forward." The *Scientific American* contest was designed to test the world's great psychics. So where were they?

In an attempt to galvanize new candidates, Bird published a statement by one of the occultist Tom, Dick, and Harrys—a Spiritualist who warned of the opportunity his movement was squandering.

"What are you going to do about the *Scientific American* investigation?" the man had beseeched the National Association of Spiritualists at a meeting of that council. "Here is the best chance you have ever had to prove to the world that these things happen. If you do not take advantage of it, the world must and will conclude that you stayed under cover because you knew that you had nothing to show."

Hear! hear! Bird wanted to respond. Christianity was launched by apostles who went bravely to the lions. Did not one reputable medium have the courage to face a skeptical magician and a few sympathetic scientists? At Munn's behest, the magazine published in bold print the names of the famous psychics Bird was most interested in bringing to New York—including Evan Powell, Ada Deane, William Hope, and Miss Ada Bessinet of Ohio. He said that Munn & Co. would pay their way and put them up. It was now or never for them to step forward.

The only worthy respondent was Dr. Le Roi Crandon, whose wife, still unknown to the public, had not been mentioned in the challenge. But though she was ready to be tested, Dr. Crandon feared that the Woolworth setting would be a circus; nothing of merit could be determined there. Instead he offered to bring the commission to Boston, so that the séances could take place in a calmer environment. He even invited the New York judges to stay at Lime Street while they sat with Mina.

The news that Mrs. Crandon was ready to throw her cloche into the ring pleased Bird. The Boston lady was likely their last hope, he told Munn, for investigating a worthwhile psychic. Unlike the other candidates, Mina never took a dime for her work, and the Crandons had generously offered to fund the tests in Boston. In return, Bird was willing to make special arrangements for them. Bringing mediums to the *Scientific American* offices, where they were expected to stand and deliver, was not working, the editor admitted. It was in keeping with the scientific method to work in stages with a psychic, Bird also conceded, before she was asked to give a definitive demonstration. Moreover, the Crandons did not want their name in the papers. To address that concern, Bird offered to give the candidate an alias. Her middle name was Marguerite—why not call her Margery?

Margery they called her; and Margery she became. Soon after the agreement was made, Walter composed an ode to Bird through his sister's automatic writing.

> *There was a young man from New York.*
> *As a scientist he was a whale.*
> *The mediums came from near and far,*
> *For him to put salt on their tail.*
>
> *And he did it without any doubt.*
> *And he did it with very great glee.*
> *And would you believe it: the son of a gun*
> *Is chasing with salt after me.*

Dangerous Games

Sweet lad, O come and join me, do!
Such pretty games I will play with you:
On the shore gay flowers their color unfold,
My mother has many garments of gold.
—JOHANN WOLFGANG VON GOETHE

The Crandon test séances were not hindered by the presence of children in the house. The couple's foster son, for reasons unknown, was no longer living with them. Other prospective adoptees would be brought to Beacon Hill, but as none remained there for long, it was speculated—out of the Crandons' earshot—that the spooks drove them out. Only John Crandon, eleven years old when his mother became a test medium, grew up at 10 Lime Street. Though John's biological father lived just a few miles away, the boy was raised by Roy and had been given his name. During séances he was tucked away for the night, protected from what he later called "dangerous games."

Ghosts are said to be drawn to sensitive beings: they possess fragile young women and make mischief with children—like the Fox sisters from Hydesville. Yet there is no record of Walter preying on John or any of the orphans who stayed with the Crandons. The children were believed to be safe. In profiles of Margery so little is mentioned of her son, it is easy to forget that he was in the residence at all. Until his adolescence, however, John was usually there—and while his mother led séances, he was sleeping, or trying to, next door.

The doctor wanted to quell any suspicions that, as in the case of Maggie and Kate Fox, the Lime Street phenomena were caused by puerile pranks. As a precaution, the servants were sent to the movies or confined to their quarters on séance nights. John was locked in his room, though no one thought to shield him from the ghoulish sounds. If Walter was active, the raps and whispers and the crash of furniture, followed by Aleck's screams, frightened the child on the other side of the wall. Once John heard wood being torn violently apart. The next morning, he discovered the debris of the spirit cabinet, which he vaguely understood to be his mother's work.

John's anxiety worsened as the mediumship progressed. Eventually, the Crandons' friends suggested to them that Lime Street, the new mecca of psychical research, was not the best environment for a child. The doctor, who anyway admired the old boarding schools, decided that Andover was the place for John, and there he would be sent. But John and Mina remained close, and the boy worried about her well-being. Dr. Crandon, an obstetrician, had not been Mina's physician when her son was born; he had never cut the umbilical between her and John.

Older and less frightened by the spirits than John, the Richardson children occasionally attended the Crandons' gatherings, and they were enchanted for a lifetime by what they saw. It began with Noguchi flashing a broad smile when greeting the Richardsons at the front door, then escorting the family through the dark passage and up the creaky stairs. As they passed the first landing, the children noticed the Victrola that Walter was known to bewitch. They were next led into the book room, to greet the guests with whom they were about to link hands. The pre-séance receptions were held in a warm and rustic space—decorated with nautical art and attended by individuals with titles like judge, doctor, and captain. Dr. Crandon might be poised in a corner, speaking to one of the distinguished Europeans who came to visit. And by the fireside, entertaining guests, was the pretty psychic herself; in her one hand a cigarette, in the other a pen with which she dashed automatic writing.

When the doctor gave the word, the sitters were directed upstairs. There, in the fourth-floor séance room, researchers checked their equipment and cameras in the red light while the others took seats around the famous table. The scratchy Victrola played "Souvenir" or, later in the decade, "Happy Days Are Here Again." Before long the medium was snoring loudly in her trance. The light was turned off and they waited for Walter to arrive.

"I can still almost hear his voice in my mind's ear," Marian Richardson would later say, "a hoarse masculine whisper." To the young girl and her parents, "Walter came through as a real person." The Richardsons dismissed any notion that the ghost might be an invention of the psychic; on the contrary, he was a tangible being, their intimate friend and advisor. "Hello, Walter," the circle chimed; and with contact established, the ghostly hijinks began.

"He flitted from sitter to sitter, touching each one lightly," Marian recalled. "He would extract objects from their pockets, or put things in, so delicately that the victim never noticed it. He seemed especially to tease Dr. Crandon and would sometimes tweak his hair quite sharply. The long-suffering brother-in-law would violently start, swear—and then say meekly, 'Thank you, Walter.'" It was strange, not only to the children, to see the doctor made that docile.

◆

When Malcolm Bird returned to Lime Street, in April of '24, the Victrola played "Yes! We Have No Bananas," a silly and infectious tune that was heard everywhere at the time. For a people discovering Freud, the Bananas song carried subliminal meaning, for it was often joked that virile men had become a vanishing breed. In lieu of popular warriors or explorers, New York had given a scientist, Albert Einstein, a ticker-tape parade. Bird had watched from his office window as the little Jewish professor waved reticently to the masses on Broadway.

"I've never seen such a bunch of stiffs in my life," Walter ragged his circle. *"Talk about dead people, my God."* He liked to tell "us humiliating things about ourselves," Bird said of the dialogue between researchers and the ghost. At times Walter made cracks about the scientists' poor grooming habits, hearing deficiencies, sluggishness—the generally feeble qualities of his elders. In contrast, Big Brother "almost bristled with forceful personality," and joked about being more romantically active than any of them. On one occasion when Margery gave a blank séance, Walter had a reason for his absence: *"I had to take my girl to a strawberry festival."* Both his youth and libido had evidently survived. "Walter, when you are relaxed do you surround yourself with youth and beauty?" a Christian pastor had asked.

The other guests could almost picture the wink Walter gave them when he replied: *"No, I am not relaxed when youth and beauty are around. I am under fifty."*

Cruder things were communicated and, in the name of good taste, stricken from the record: "Walter is familiar with all the ordinary cuss words," Bird reported, "and some extraordinary ones." While in trance, the medium could be as vulgar. Possessed by Walter she did and said things that would otherwise have been off-limits in this man's city, where a woman could neither enter most speakeasies nor sit on juries. A society wife was not supposed to swear or smoke—yet Margery, while believed to be unconscious, channeled a coarse and irrepressible spirit control.

One of the more amusing features of the sittings was the exchanges between Walter and Dr. Crandon, who tried to control the proceedings as he might a surgical operation at Boston City Hospital. But Margery could turn the tables on him through her brother's presence. It was part of the repertoire for the ghost to release the curtain rod from the spirit cabinet, then poke Roy with the pole. During one sitting the doctor was stroked, pushed, caressed—even, at his own suggestion, given a "kick in the face." Thank you, Walter. Another time the Richardsons recorded that "a large and muscular hand" appeared to descend upon the doctor's head, ruffling his hair. Whereupon, according to the report, he "came as near to hysterics as a professional man should."

Walter Stinson was called a "he-man," the "big boss"; and when raps were heard in the séance room, these were caused not by the agency of little girls, as with the Fox sisters, but by "the teleplasmic materialization of his brawny arm and fist." He not only dominated the séances; in time he made his presence felt in the Crandons' bedroom.

One night, while Dr. Crandon and his wife lay in bed, the couple "were bombarded with innumerable raps" that came through louder than those produced in the séance room. The sounds manifested from the floor, walls, ceiling, and telephone, Roy later wrote his father. Curtains on the canopy bed were torn apart, a chair five feet away was pushed toward the couple. The room began to creak and shake. The plush mahogany chair tipped over, "scattering Margery's clothes everywhere." When the light was turned on, only a few raps were heard. After the doctor turned it off again, the effects returned. There were raps on the mattress springs, and the sensation that a formless body had gotten under the bed; "then the whole foot of the bed was lifted from the floor."

"It was not," the doctor noted, "a pleasant experience." In general, though, the mediumship provided less harrowing thrills. The spirits had brought untold mirth and wonder to Lime Street.

Thank you, Walter.

Kisses from the Void

Four members were present last night; the control was perfect;
the phenomena went on serenely.
—DR. LE ROI CRANDON WRITING DOYLE ON THE SCIAM TRIAL

*A*s Malcolm Bird stood on the outside of the circle, watching the medium seated within her black, open-faced cabinet, he sensed wariness from a group that still blamed him for the setback the previous November—when a hostile force was drawn to the séance room. Was that to be the case once again? Bird wondered. Clearly Margery could dazzle her friends, even those who were scientists, and confound a few university psychologists; she could impress a few, mostly geriatric, European experts; but when it came to sittings with a representative of the *Scientific American,* would she once again conduct blank séances and blame it on some superstitious devilry?

Soon after the room went pitch-dark on April 11, he had his answer. The demonstration began with the ghost's clarion-like whistle, the likes of which Bird had never heard before. Later he learned that Walter conveyed myriad moods—pleasure, remorse, amusement, boredom, and anger—with different tones of his signature whistle. He had a variable pitch with which he might greet each particular sitter, and a fading note to signal he was leaving. In lieu of the whistle Walter had recently announced his appearance with a far-off yodel, but tonight the ghost arrived boisterously—whistling as the saxophone played madly on the Victrola.

Already Bird sensed a different energy since his visit to Boston in the fall, so he hoped to finally witness the effects that he had heard about in reports from Harvard, France, and England. Capturing proof of a full apparition was a kind of grail that the British SPR researchers were seeking; and since returning from Europe, Dr. Crandon was determined to see Margery generate an ectoplasmic form—a spirit as vivid to the eye as Walter sounded to the ear. Bird had been told that Walter was developing his sister's powers expressly for that phenomenon. The first step, the ghost said, were the spirit lights he'd started producing. Walter had warned sitters not to start or panic when the bright flashes began to dance around them; instead he encouraged them to laugh. *"We can walk on the vibrations made by your laughing."*

Though the demonstrations were "both comedy and serious physics," there was a general sense of awe when the lights appeared—some in a cloudlike mist, others in the shape of globes, diamonds, tubes, or clovers. Several sitters described a bright wave as like the voracious flames in a Cubist painting; and with their appearance was "undoubted progress toward materialization." While these phenomena are easily faked—and as readily exposed by psychic investigators—no sleuth ever caught Margery, or any in her circle, flashing an electric torch; no magician at her table would ever rip a glowing form from the air and then reveal a buoyant object daubed in Ghost-Glo paint.

In fact, what Bird saw that night and for years to come truly amazed him. For an hour the lights came—"variable in brightness, in size, in shape"—accompanied by cool breezes with sufficient force to billow the curtains; at other times the flashes were accompanied by raps or whistles. Oddly, the lights were not seen by every person in the room—at least, not at the same time—so Bird was left to wonder if some individuals had sight more finely tuned to Margery's apparitions.

Following the light show were table manifestations of the kind the psychic had exhibited in Europe. Three times, with Margery controlled, the table flipped over and rotated back to its upright position. Then it tilted on two legs, like a dog expecting a biscuit after a trick. Having had enough of that, Walter began to build force within the spirit cabinet. Spectral touches were felt; a tapping on McDougall's head, a contact on his knee. Minutes later, Margery's booth began to quake. With the wing to the cabinet now flapping and the structure shifting and tilting, Bird got on the floor to help McDougall and Roy maintain control of the medium. With dignity barely intact, he was able to keep her hands firmly gripped—yet to his shock his hair was grasped and pulled. Dr. Roback, whose commission was to catch anyone sneaking about the room, confirmed that no person was behind Bird. Either the medium used her teeth, or Walter was responsible for the assault.

Bird had little time to fully consider the matter, as something more remarkable then happened. Walter had evidently gotten hold of the luminous curtain pole—which came unloosed from the sockets at the top of the spirit cabinet—and slammed it with a hair-raising thud on the table. While it alarmed Bird to see it pointing inches from the psychic's chest, what followed was spectral entertainment. Suzy the bat appeared—a sphere of wing-shaped light that began to flutter, click, and dance on the séance table. When Walter maneuvered the curtain rod to rest at a steep angle— one end on the cabinet, the other braced on the table—the winged light tobogganed up and down the pole. When the bat disappeared, Margery's invisible brother spun the pole in slow, mesmerizing rotations, like a drum major.

The next sitting was as perplexing. The pole was transported through a maze of arms and legs in such a complex way that Bird felt it was either carried by a number of accomplices or had to truly penetrate matter. One thing he knew for sure: Margery, with all four of her extremities controlled, was not the pole carrier. Bird could not identify a culprit. During both the Harvard and *Scientific American* investigations, a sentry, usually McDougall's assistant, was stationed by the door to prevent any intruder from sneaking into the séance room. And to ensure that none of the sitters were up to mischief, Roback continued to quietly patrol. "The presence of such an observer, likely to bob up any moment at just the wrong place," said Bird, "would wreck the morale of any fraudulent operator."

As in Europe, the *Scientific American* official was not only considered a positive influence on the séance battery, he was one of the few investigators for whom a spirit showed any affection. When a couple of sitters began to whisper during Margery's performance, Bird hushed them with a "tsk-tsk" that Walter apparently mistook for a kiss. For the rest of the evening, and well into the year, Walter made a smacking noise or tsk-tsk at the mention of Bird's name. When he was present, the ghost blew him kisses from the void.

◆

The committee intended to treat Margery like a promising candidate whose supernormal gifts, if she really had any, were to be developed and tested in stages. Because William McDougall was a member of both the SciAm commission and the leader of his own active investigation, his Harvard group fell under the auspices of the magazine—with Dr. Roback made a non-voting member of the jury. It was agreed that Margery would sit for various combinations of the committee before Bird assembled the full imposing quorum, if need be, to judge her phenomena. Members of the ABC group were allowed to be present, though they would not be for much longer. Margery would soon have to draw her force from a circle composed of professional investigators.

Secretary Bird took full advantage of the Crandons' offer to accommodate any representatives of the *Scientific American,* or judges of the contest, who wished to stay with them. He saw Margery's hospitality and the doctor's generosity as a testament to the Crandons' dedication to the inquiry. After the séances, large parties often went out to dinner, and Bird noticed that Dr. Crandon always picked up the bill. By the same token, Mark Richardson, one of Roy's closest friends, said that for all the meals he had at the Crandons' house, he could almost never get the medium to dine with his family in Newton. Ever the hostess, Mina was rarely anyone's dinner guest—she was the madam of this occult salon, the elusive siren of her society.

From April until late August, Bird would make eight separate visits to Boston. He came with his wife—"Lady Bird," as Walter called her—who helped Margery prepare her gatherings; or with Austin Lescarboura, Bird's fellow editor and quack exposer; at other times Hereward Carrington accompanied him. "There is a deep groove on the map between Westfield N.J. and Boston," Bird jested, "worn there by my numerous passages of 1924 over this route." During the spring and summer, Bird—to the neglect, he admitted, of his other journalistic responsibilities—spent a total of fifty-seven days and nights at 10 Lime Street.

◆

At this time Dr. Crandon was in close contact with Sir Arthur Conan Doyle, who had "plowed these deep furrows in our country and sown the seed that was expected to reap a harvest of mediumistic activity." Margery, whom Doyle called "the centre of American hopes," was thought to be the prize of the harvest. But that depended, Dr. Crandon believed, on the sanction of the *Scientific American,* a "materialistic and coldly scientific paper." For as soon as the Committee admitted the validity of psychic phenomena, "the whole matter at once assumes a kind of respectability," Roy said, "for many of the morons who inhabit the Main Street of America."

The two men had differing views on the producer of the psychic contest. Malcolm Bird had disappointed his former guide to the spirit world by harshly exposing every psychic who had performed at the Woolworth. Regardless, "My present impression of Bird is a little more favorable than yours," Dr. Crandon told Sir Arthur. Though Bird enjoyed causing a stir, Roy found him to be "at least half scientist and half newsman."

When Sir Arthur was Bird's age, he created a consummately dispassionate figure in Sherlock Holmes. Yet the moody Baker Street detective, to whom Bird was likened, could not abide banal life and sought escape through the opium needle. There was something of that same duality to Bird, whose occult adventures had been fostered by Doyle. If Bird considered himself unmoved by psychic manifestations, he was still drawn like an addict to the Crandons' red-lit séances. While not a supporter of the spirit hypothesis, it took the editor only five sittings with Margery before he concluded that she had genuine telepathic powers.

During one SciAm gathering, while he and Carrington held their hands over the closed mouths of the Crandons, Bird admitted to feeling the first gooseflesh of his life when Walter verbally beckoned and whistled to him from across a room that held no possible confederates—only a couple of respectable Beacon Hill matrons. Bird found it wicked when Suzy fluttered in Roback's face—rattling the usually stoic German psychologist by crawling in his hair or poking him with the flowers she carried in her talons. He was moved by some of Walter's more subtle effects, as when the spirit caused a single rose petal to slowly fall from the ceiling, brushing his cheek before landing by his hand on the séance table. He had to suppress a laugh, though, when Walter cussed a blue streak before a circle of visiting clergymen. "Is that the language of the fourth dimension, Walter?" a preacher asked. *"Some of the things you believe to be solemn are really to be laughed at,"* Walter answered. At a later sitting, the voice indicated that scientists were just as misguided. *"You might be better up an apple tree counting the leaves,"* he advised them.

At a demonstration that spring, Dr. Crandon produced a megaphone from his yachting days for use as a spirit trumpet, and Bird was among those humiliated when the spirit caused it to rise from the table and perch, in turn, on the head of each scientist in the circle—a dunce cap for the *"damn fools"* sent to study him. The luminous megaphone then floated "with marvelous speed" toward the ceiling and into the spirit cabinet, where it flew back and forth, knocking against the walls—like a bird trying to escape its cage.

Margery might have felt just as confined there. Having her home besieged by psychic investigators, for whom she had to perform, was starting to tell on the medium. In late April she suffered bilious headaches, nausea, and vomiting before a scheduled séance. "We all tried to dissuade her from keeping her engagement for this evening with the *Scientific American* sitters," Bird wrote, "but she regarded the occasion as a highly scientific and highly important one, and she insisted that if she permitted illness to interfere with it, she would be seriously discredited in the eyes of the committeemen." Her determination that night was not reinforced by her disembodied brother. When Walter came, he remarked that *"the kid"* had no force and the circle was futile. The séance proceeded weakly, alternating between red and dark light, until Margery abruptly excused herself to vomit. Shortly after she returned, Dr. Crandon was called away—as was not unusual—to remove an appendix. Bird suggested they break up the gathering, but Walter said to remain a little longer. Dr. McDougall kept Margery's legs in his "usual vise-like control," her hands held by the scientists on either side of her, while she moaned frailly. Before long Bird sensed, and then tried to resist, a growing pressure on the table that seemed to emanate from its very structure. When he weakened, the table suddenly toppled over, spilling onto the floor the megaphone and all the detritus of the scientists—their instruments, scales and Dictaphone, and the ukulele Walter liked to play. It was a convincing exhibition, thought Bird, by a medium in poor condition.

Catch Her If You Can

$\mathcal{A}$ decade before Houdini was making it a part of his repertoire, Hereward Carrington gave a Broadway exposé on the methods of mediums before an audience at the Lyceum Theater that included twenty-three newsmen. "Mr. Carrington, with the sweetest smile shown by any male performer this season," gushed the *Tribune,* "and with hair of the lightness of spun moonbeams; dainty of figure, finished and burbling of voice, stood in the midst of skulls and crossbones." Before the ghoulish scrim, the fair sleuth rhapsodized on death while delivering an effect-a-minute spook show featuring floating tambourines, spirit hands, slate messages, and phosphorescent forms. After the one-night engagement his wife, Helen, who had played Grieg on the piano as the curtain raiser, revealed to a reporter that "Mr. Carrington is a very strange mixture. He is the most healthy minded thing, but loves skulls. I sometimes think he must be very deceitful—he does these things so sweetly and easily."

Her husband's surface charm, as Helen had hinted, could be as misleading as a spirit faker draped in muslin. Aligned with no one, Carrington was an opinionated judge of psychic talent whom Houdini saw as his rival on the *Scientific American* jury. One of the younger experts, Carrington was a lithe forty-two due to his practice of yoga, but since he began his career in psychical research as a nineteen-year-old, he may have had more years actual experience as a ghost hunter than any of the other committeemen. The newspapermen assumed that he was one of the ASPR representatives, since at one time he had been an important officer there. His mentor with the ASPR had been the trailblazing James Hervey Hyslop—president of the society for two decades until, after suffering a crippling stroke, Dr. McDougall succeeded him. But the autocratic Hyslop had fired Carrington, then his research officer, for using company time to write his sundry books on Eastern mysteries, vegetarianism, and juice fasting. Carrington's relationship with the ASPR was further soured when he brought Eusapia Palladino to New York.

Dr. Hyslop disapproved of both the publicity surrounding those demonstrations and the test medium, whom he thought a fraud and hysteric. After Palladino was indeed caught faking her séance effects by a team of Columbia professors instructed on how to entrap her by Houdini's medium-busting friends Joseph Rinn and W. J. Davis, the vindicated Hyslop wrote his former protégé a letter of admonishment that essentially said: *I told you so, Hereward.* Carrington felt the incident at Columbia University was overblown by the press. But whether Eusapia was a bona fide channeler or shameless cheat—or both, as Carrington believed—she was the last medium he publicly endorsed.

◆

Another frequent houseguest at 10 Lime Street, Carrington stayed with the Crandons on six occasions, for a total of forty-four days and nights, during the spring and summer of '24. On one visit he accompanied Fred Keating, the magician who was an alternate judge in the contest.

Before his first visit to Lime Street, Carrington had read what sounded like far-fetched reports on the mediumship: Had the spirit cabinet, with Margery seated in it, really been dragged all over the séance room by an invisible carrier? Carrington suspected that Drs. Crandon and Richardson, despite their professed adherence to the scientific method, were exaggerating. Yet during his first sittings, which were composed only of committeemen, he witnessed the same type of phenomena. While Carrington held one of Margery's hands and controlled both of her feet, the medium's booth was "shaken as a rat by a cat," as Bird put it. At another séance, with Carrington and Bird firmly in control of the psychic, "the cabinet was battered about all over the apartment, pushed, hauled, shoved and ultimately by great good fortune, it got pushed over so that it completely blocked the door of the séance room." Hurled to the floor, Bird somehow managed to maintain his grip on both the medium and her husband. Sitting vigil by the door, McDougall's secretary warned that the cabinet was being forced into the hallway. Its left wing was then wrenched off "with the utmost violence." When the raucous effect was over, the lights turned up and Bird extricated, there sat Margery, fresh as a daisy.

"I have never heard her draw a hurried breath in the séance room," Bird reported. Examination of the battered cabinet showed that the screws had been torn out rather than unscrewed. In disbelief, Dr. McDougall speculated that a man with an ax snuck into the room and had a whack at it. Offended by the accusation, Roy countered that the culprit was likely "a negro dwarf concealed in the fireplace." McDougall's assertion became comic grist for Margery, who often reminded the assistant guarding the doorway to remain alert for her ax-wielding, black-robed confederate. The man with the ax became the euphemism, even to members of the committee, for the accomplice who had to be involved if Margery were a charlatan.

Mrs. Crandon's forte was the motion of objects without apparent cause. Anything not tied down was liable to move or take flight during the séances, while, adding to the Wonderland effect, the band played on. Whether Walter was in a violent mood or delivering one of his soothing poems, the Victrola piped his favorite songs. The ambience was something else the Crandons had brought home from Europe, though Walter's preference for popular songs was a departure from the traditional séance hymns. And the continuous play, or rather intermittent activity, of the Victrola produced another of the mysteries that baffled the committeemen.

When Walter cried something like *"John, get off of that!"* it was a sign that his phantom tagalongs, the dead Richardson boys, were playing with the Victrola; the mischievous brothers seemed to delight in making the machine slow and flat, then pick up speed again or stop. Carrington could not explain how it happened. There were times when he or Fred Keating, flashlights in hand, stood by the Victrola and made sure no one approached. Still the music fluctuated weirdly—apparently at Walter's command. Austin Lescarboura, the magazine's electrical expert, took the machine apart and claimed that he had fixed the problem. At a séance sometime later, the jazz played normally until Walter remarked that half his energy came from music. The song sped up as he spoke. Then the song stopped. Agents for the manufacturer came by and declared the motor and phonograph in proper working order; but what warranty protects a sound box from the interference of an ectoplasmic hand? Mina wondered. That very night, the saxophone slowed until it sounded like the wailing of a succubus. It was magic to the ears of Dr. Crandon.

The committeeman Daniel Comstock—the former MIT physicist who had only recently become involved in the case—had the Victrola looked at by electricians in his shop. After some tinkering, they gave it "a blanket guarantee." Despite their assurances, at a séance that night the machine stalled, slowed, and began to overheat. Afterward Comstock and his assistant, Will Conant, secretly replaced the motor. But when the séances reconvened it flatted during "Souvenir"—Walter's favorite song. Comstock and Lescarboura checked the source of the electricity, because the music often began to die just as a spirit light faded, or speeded up as it flared. As Carrington reported: "Investigation of the wiring in the house failed to disclose anything which could account for these results."

Neither could a trickster solve the mystery. Fred Keating, a popular stage conjurer, admitted he had no explanation for a spirit cabinet thundering across a room, then bursting apart. Where were the wires to convey it? The confederates to drag it? He found most impressive the spirit lights that swooped across the séance room like a comet while Walter called for control. The magician "came to scoff," said Dr. Crandon, "and remained to pray."

When Margery was at her best, or worst for that matter, there was no telling what weirdness might unfold. At the sitting of June 11, the light effects became as much burlesque as spook show. After she had smashed yet another cabinet, "Psyche," as Dr. Crandon called his wife, "retired to rearrange her clothing and her hair." In the dressing room, Dr. McDougall's secretary witnessed her alarm at discovering a glow that extended from her bra strap toward her left breast. At Margery's request the secretary fetched Carrington, who spotted something else—a luminous spot on her right shoulder that faded as he observed it. They returned at once to the séance room and presented this latest oddity to the experts. Walking to the moonlight by the bay window, Margery unloosed her robe, while the investigators—Bird, Carrington, Keating, Comstock, and McDougall—took turns examining the light patches by rubbing their fingers against the sparkle on her skin and undergarment. No residue came off on their hands; it was not, they decided, zinc-sulfide paint. And if she were cheating, they did not think she would have alerted Carrington to the incriminating spots. Looking dazed, Dr. Crandon sat down by the séance table as the room lights were turned up and dimmed again. Then something happened that unnerved the men even more than the violence to the cabinet. There was a whisper, *"Good night,"* and a ghostly cackle—"practically in our faces," Bird recalled. "My God! That's Walter," McDougall exclaimed. At that moment—practically two a.m.—the phosphorescence on Margery vanished, except for a minute sparkle that dwindled from a stain to a freckle.

♦

Experiments at Lime Street were almost never daytime affairs. "We went to bed in the small hours and got up not too long before noon," Bird reported to his publisher. Since Dr. Crandon was at his medical office during the weekday, Margery was often alone with investigators whose company she began to enjoy. After her experience with the stuffy Harvard professors, the arrival of the New York committeemen—Bird, Keating, and Carrington—was like a fresh breeze on Lime Street. Keating had magic; Bird a fiendish wit; and Carrington—or *"Carrie,"* as Walter called him— unusual charm.

Carrington's gaunt, ethereal appearance and faint English accent made him seem, to Kitty Brown, like the tragic hero in a Victorian novel. It was Carrington whom the ABC Club wives wanted to sit next to at dinner. And with each conversation, Margery and her circle discovered another odd wrinkle to him. He did not drink liquor. He subsisted for the most part on raw fruits and nuts—and for weeks at a time on nothing but juice cocktails. It was important, he said, for mediums to maintain a steady nervous system and he encouraged Margery to drink less alcohol, a suggestion she humored then soon forgot about.

Like Bird, Carrington became fast friends with the Crandons. They both thought this a great advantage in determining whether the mediumship was authentic. The committeemen who stayed at Lime Street had carte blanche to search any room and an intimate knowledge of their subject's routine. Bird had never heard of a psychic making her home—indeed her entire life—as open to an investigation. Apparently, she had nothing to hide.

"Catch her if you can," said Dr. Crandon.

Despite months of trying, William McDougall never caught the medium in fraud. Yet the psychologist had theorized, to her face, that objects in her sittings were transported by strings, and that the destruction of her spirit cabinet was caused by a stealthy intruder with an ax swung expertly in the dark. One of the cardinal rules of the *Scientific American* tests was not to condemn the psychic without ironclad evidence. Despite that, Dr. McDougall was not shy about voicing whatever suspicions came into his head. It was difficult, though, to provoke real ire in Margery. She had forgiven her foe for the accusations in his office, and during séances a kind of banter had developed between them where she responded to his incredulity with wit.

One evening the researchers were surprised by what sounded like chains being dragged across a floor—as Dr. Crandon imagined Scrooge must have heard when the ghost Marley came to him in shackles. When Margery started, McDougall interpreted her flinching as an attempt to loosen his grip. The psychic responded that she was supposed to be controlled, not dead, and she would not be held accountable for having human nerves. But aside from the odd exchange or two, the Crandons noticed that McDougall was protesting less. After one extraordinary effect, the researcher said to Margery that "if it happens again I shall leave this house an altered man." It happened again. And so Dr. Crandon wondered if McDougall would cease being to the investigation what Scrooge was to Christmas just before he was transformed by a ghost.

The Tipping of the Scales

*I*t had been agreed that the two Boston experts, McDougall and Comstock, would lead the committee's initial testing of Margery. Yet since she was a physical medium, the physicist Comstock had the equipment and expertise to take the investigation more in the direction the *Scientific American* wanted: toward the examination of her effects rather than their psychological cause. Given the magazine's preference for hard science, McDougall was not going to win the topical debate over whether the study of psychic phenomena fell under the auspices of psychology (Harvard) or physics (MIT). Comstock therefore got his way, his overbearing streak mitigated by enthusiasm: it was easy to argue with him but hard to stay sore for long. Even Walter liked him, though he said the physicist's fussiness depleted the séance charge.

Voluble and spruce, Daniel Frost Comstock had the air of a genius, the imprimatur of MIT—until recently his employer—and the aura of Hollywood, an industry experimenting with his Technicolor invention. Having just applied his colorization process to several scenes in Cecil B. DeMille's *Ten Commandments,* he now turned his attention to capturing proof, supported by photography, of mediumistic marvels. As the Margery trials progressed, Comstock began to overshadow McDougall, as well as every other committeeman presently involved in the case. From April through August he attended fifty-six séances with Margery—more than anyone else. "He made more real contributions to the scientific consideration of the mediumship than all other observers combined," wrote Bird.

Comstock presented greater challenges to Margery, if she were a fraud, than the Harvard alienists who poked around in the dark, controlled her arms and legs, and sought—unsuccessfully, she said—to get inside her mind. Whereas they carried little more than flashlights into the séance room, Comstock brought cameras to capture what was invisible to the human eye. At MIT he had conducted ocular tests that indicated another Boston psychic perceived an unnaturally wide spectrum of color. His idea was to develop an ultraviolet camera lens to reveal the world that clairvoyants see. Unfortunately, Comstock's first subject died before he could experiment with her, but the special quartz lenses and mercury-vapor lights—like the kind used in moving pictures—were among the equipment he used at Lime Street. If anything shady was happening there, he was sure his cameras would detect it.

Along with the new apparatus, Comstock brought changes to Margery's program. Séances were sometimes held in his apartment in case Dr. Crandon had concealed any insidious devices within the walls of 10 Lime Street; and a new spirit cabinet being developed by the committee was supposed to be "inaccessible to fraud." But the real shift came with the new tests Comstock had designed. His idea was to invent tasks for the medium that could not be caused, or matched, by flimflam, and to focus control on the object of Walter's power rather than its mediumistic source. If phenomena were produced in a "closed and sealed space," it was far less important, Comstock believed, to restrain the psychic and monitor her friends.

Walter said that he would try to generate the proofs Comstock wanted, though when it came to what he could manifest on any given night, he warned that he was as ignorant as the scientist. "That's some ignorant, Walter," Comstock chuckled, just as he unveiled something more rudimentary than anyone had expected.

A simple chemical balance was what he placed on the séance table. He promised it could be used, in a fraud-proof way, to validate the same invisible force with which Walter shattered cabinets. *"Those damned scales,"* as Walter would call them, were sealed in a glass or celluloid cover to prevent any human hands from reaching them. Future models would have moving parts made of brass or wood—negating the possibility that their motion might be caused by a trickster's magnetic tool.

This was the trial Comstock introduced. Instead of raising the table, he asked Walter to levitate a pan or manipulate the scales in some other way. At first the ghost wanted the cover removed for a practice test, a condition that raised a flag of suspicion. Yet even without the cage, no one could explain how Walter, in visible light, made an empty pan lower while the weighted pan rose. At that point Aleck Cross, of all people, interrupted the discussion by clearing his throat.

"May I have the floor?" Cross asked.

"You may have the entire house," the ghost said with a laugh.

All heads turned to Cross, who suggested that one of the researchers try to push down the weighted pan. Carrington and Bird both tried successfully, though the researchers had the sensation of pushing against an opposing force. They asked Cross if he wanted to try, but he only smiled queerly, as if awed by the state of unbalance his friend Walter had caused.

At another séance, with the scales illumined by red light, Walter asked Comstock if there were any way the scientist could make one pan rise and the other stay grounded while both were empty. "No," Comstock replied without hesitation. After doing just that, Walter boasted: *"Comstock, I've got you; I can get out just as easily as I can get in."* With the glass cover in place, and weights having been placed on the west pan, Walter balanced the scale by applying his force to the east pan. At other test séances he produced the same effect with weights of a three-to-one ratio, four-to-one, then topped off at five! *"Have we got them running!"* Walter crowed while making the pans oscillate to jazz rhythm. His powers had never been so directed toward one particular effect. When Carrington observed that the ghost had a scales complex, Walter responded that the MIT professor had one first.

"You asked for balances, and you're not going to get another damned thing until the balances are finished," Walter said. After those and other proofs were furnished, they would not hear from him again, the voice warned. A man could die twice, he quipped, and when he left their plane, this time for good, he hoped they would put a new inscription on his grave: *"Here lies a scientist, faithful unto cabinet and scales."*

Their laughter was interrupted by Walter's next communication: *"Gee, little Mark is in the scales."* The pans began bouncing as the Richardsons' dead son had his fun with them, and photographs were automatically snapped. Comstock's cameras captured a halo over one pan, just as little Mark caused it to oscillate. At other times they caught mysterious flashes and patches of light around the scales or hovering near Margery. One picture that Bird hoped to be "recognized as a landmark of psychic science" showed a numinous cylinder on one of the pans that evidently caused it to rise—the prism, said Dr. Crandon, through which Walter directed his force. Margery thought it looked more like a gin glass.

At a séance shortly thereafter, on June 21, the medium produced her best work with a chemical balance that was sealed in its cage and loaded to a six-to-one arrangement. While the Victrola played the lively "Linger Awhile," the scales bounced up and down with "the utmost vigor," or froze in perfect balance despite their weight disparity. After the demonstration, there was an argument between Dr. Crandon and Comstock over whether the scale mechanism had been thoroughly examined prior to the test. *"Oh, what's the use,"* Walter was heard to whisper. And never again did he play with the scales that had been tilting in his sister's favor.

♦

Dr. Crandon said that Margery could produce exactly what the committee called for—a simple yet fraud-proof exhibition of her psychic power. "When Walter swings those balances under the cover . . . this will end the investigation," he had promised Sir Arthur. The balance tests were now being contested, to Roy's dismay, by the inventor who had once boasted of their infallibility. The caution of scientists did not, however, douse Roy's optimism. For all their strict conditions, he believed his wife's demonstrations were generally impressing the commission. Margery had produced both "simple as well as complex physical phenomena which cannot be gainsaid," he informed Doyle, who eagerly awaited news of the journal's latest, and most important, psychic trial.

"I've made another plaything for Walter," Daniel Comstock announced. The latest invention the physicist placed on the séance table was simple like the others: a bell and battery wired to a telegraph key (later a lever board) that when depressed caused the apparatus to ring; it was the device that would develop, upon further modification, into his famous bell box. The challenge presented to Margery was to make the bell ring without touching it physically. In defense against the possibility of preparation for the trial, she was apparently not made aware that Comstock was going to present her with a new test object.

The very night he produced it, she mastered it convincingly. While Bird controlled the psychic, the bell rang suddenly—as if to signal a new round in the contest between her and the scientists. Bird believed the effect was Margery's pièce de résistance: "the climax of the mediumship, so far as sheer inescapable validity." With her hands and feet controlled, she caused the bell to ring in long and short peals, singly and repeatedly. Walter, her invisible operator, seemed to have complete control over its functions. "You ask it to ring," Bird reported, "and it rings. You ask it to stop and it stops."

There were times when one of Margery's sitters, usually the farthest one from her, grabbed the bell box and left the circle. It rang as he walked away from her. Carrington clasped her hands and covered her feet with his own—"to prove that they were in her shoes where they belonged." The bell rang while she laughed. He put her feet in his lap. The bell rang. A luminous plaque was placed over the contraption for the purpose of revealing any shadowy hand or device that might cause the phenomena. None were evident when Walter rang it with his invisible terminal. The bell was secured inside a box. It still rang. The medium and her bell box were moved to Comstock's apartment. It rang there too. In darkness, as well as in visible light, the bell box blared. Margery made it ring in Morse code but did not transmit anything like the famous message that had once heralded telegraph technology: "What hath God wrought?" Instead, the message delivered was more distinctive to Walter: *"Are all the scientists here damned old fools?"* Once, though not in the presence of the commission, a sitter asked Walter if he could reveal his etheric hand depressing the button. Mark Richardson reported that a shaft of light, in the shape of a finger, suddenly extruded from Margery's lap; and when it reached the bell, it sounded.

◆

Even before the scales and bell experiments, Dr. Crandon knew that Bird believed in Margery's work. In truth, the editor was no closer to accepting the spirit hypothesis. He could more readily attribute Margery's revelations to an unknown subconscious force than to her dead brother. Regardless, the mandate of his investigation was not to determine the cause of psychic phenomena; it was to prove or dismiss their objective occurrence. It made no difference to Bird whether the spirits returned. What mattered was that Margery's work appeared to transcend known physical laws. And when the commission could not explain a medium's effects, she was supposed to be awarded the prize.

Margery was brave, trustworthy, and overwhelmingly convincing, in Bird's estimation. On a drive back to New York, Carrington said he felt similarly, and if the vote were that day his would be cast affirmatively. Keating, while not a voting member of the commission, was also a believer; the magician saw no hocus-pocus in the Crandon mediumship. Comstock was on the verge, Bird felt, of endorsing her. McDougall was softening. Prince was a mystery. But while the secretary needed four votes to declare Margery a winner, the idea was not for each of the five committeemen to decide individually; they were supposed to render their decision as one unified body.

So that left Houdini.

It had been a bad idea, Bird had once warned Munn, to put a man on the committee whom the spirits considered a mortal enemy. A match between Houdini and Walter would dignify science about as much as Jack Dempsey and Luis Firpo slugging it out at the Polo Grounds.

As the weather warmed, Bird was hopeful that by the summer he would be announcing a breakthrough in psychic research. Yet he and others still felt an unaccountable chill at the Crandons' gatherings. Many times he heard sitters say they experienced a loss in body heat during the production of phenomena—as if the medium were somehow siphoning the energy of her circle. *"When I use your brains,"* Walter explained, *"there are cold breezes and a drop in temperature."* Those "arctic breezes from nowhere," as Bird described them, were an important feature in the Margery séances. The cold gusts reminded Carrington of the kind Palladino used to produce, even though she supposedly emitted the current from a cleft in her forehead, while no one could determine the precise origin of Margery's more blustery effect. Generally, the winds came from the direction of the cabinet, blasting the curtains apart and bracing the circle. When Bird first experienced the breezes, they came with psychic lights that wafted across the séance room. "These were of considerable force," he reported; "distinctly cool," and as real as anything nature produced.

To measure the phenomena, Dr. Crandon installed a mercury thermometer that confirmed it was advisable to dress warmly for the séances. When Walter was active, the temperature in the room might drop as much as twenty degrees. The scientists objected that the thermometer placed in the spirit cabinet was far from fraud-proof: Margery could have secreted a magnet on her person, they theorized, and used it to send "the float kiting up the minimum side."

For all their monitors, the temperature of the medium herself was not determined, but Walter was believed to take most of his energy and heat from Margery. If she practiced deceit, Comstock remarked, it was with a cool constitution. When Austin Lescarboura controlled her hand during the séances, his own hand, normally hot and damp, "was chilled to an icy temperature positively uncomfortable for us to touch." Bird often controlled her other hand as the cold winds streamed from the cabinet; and to prove that the current was not issuing from her body, she blew warm puffs of air down his neck.

House of Crimson

*I*n Walter Prince's dream, the doomed young woman begged him to hold her hand while she was beheaded—as if by a guillotine. One of his hands was in her hair and he could feel the bloody dampness. His other hand was caught in teeth that clenched his fingers—fastening then refastening; her disembodied head would not release him. The next day, he discovered while reading the *Evening Telegram* that a woman named Sarah Hand, a mental patient on leave from an asylum, had—at the same time as his dream and not far from his home in Flushing, Queens—laid her head on the rails in front of a train, which decapitated her. She had wanted to prove, she said in a letter the authorities discovered, that her severed head might exist consciously, apart from her body. Following his own investigation of the case, Prince determined that his premonition was hard to attribute to chance. Her photograph resembled the woman in his nightmare.

This was not the only time that Prince had a personal psychic experience. Proofs of mind acting on mind came to him in the manifestation of his own harrowing dreams, though he had not had any like them recently. He had no intimation that anything was amiss during the period of the *Scientific American* contest. He was a troubled man, but they were natural worries that plagued him in May, when he first visited 10 Lime Street.

If Margery had any tricks up her kimono sleeves, then Dr. Prince, known for solving the Antigonish hoax, was considered the most qualified of the ASPR investigators to expose them. According to Doyle, Prince was an arch-skeptic. At least one medium had won Prince's deepest affection, yet he had the reputation for being detached and uncompromising. He disapproved of the casual contact between the researchers and Margery— the lively sublunary activities that were taking place on Lime Street: Carrington dancing with the medium; Bird playing charades with her friends. Neither did he trust experiments devised by a Tech physicist who knew nothing of magic, hobnobbed with Hollywood moguls, and tried to habituate a spirit to his fancy cameras.

The one psychic whom Dr. Prince believed in was named Theodosia. Years earlier he had discovered that the disturbed young girl, a victim of brutal abuse, had extraordinary mediumistic powers. He wrote a 1,300-page report on her various personalities. Then he adopted her, and tried for the rest of his life to heal her. Recently, in a public debate with Houdini, Prince challenged the magician to match the raps that Theodosia had produced at his Flushing home. Uncharacteristically, Houdini demurred. He was sure that the phenomena in the Prince house were easily explained but did not wish to call the researcher's daughter a fake.

Prince appeared to be drawn to distraught females, or they to him, but he was wary of the dangerous side to a medium's hysteria. He had seen such mayhem in Antigonish, when an unstable young woman almost brought her family's home down like the House of Usher.

◆

There was a reason why Prince, the most respected of American psychic researchers, had never, like the Englishman McDougall, been made president of the ASPR; for he was, as Bird described him, "one of those in whom rugged intellectual honesty sticks out like a cactus." Prince was scrupulous, critical, and deliberate in thought and action. A former minister, a psychologist, a stickler for accuracy in a nebulous field, he was remarkably disciplined. The Antigonish sleuth said that he hadn't played a game in twenty years; he hadn't fished in thirty. What he didn't mention was that the previous year had been the most difficult of his life. His wife had suffered through nine operations for cancer.

For all his present misfortune, Mrs. Crandon did not find Prince to be dour or morbid. He liked to crack jokes that were old hat, and reminded her of the pious, earthy men she knew as a child. Probably since the moment he was born into a fast-changing world there was an anachronistic quality to Dr. Prince. He arrived on Beacon Hill like a Maine farmer to a dance at the Chilton Club. More accurately, he was a Bulldog in a house of Crimson. With two degrees from Yale, he was every bit as sophisticated as the Crandons' Harvard friends. And he was more scholarly than any of the new generation of psychic researchers. Yet he was the investigator Walter often referred to as *"a damn old fool."*

Margery's demonstrations, at their most raucous, were a "regular six-ring psychic circus," waxed Malcolm Bird. At one séance the editor heard a bell ringing; a tambourine illuminated by spirit light shaking; Walter whispering and whistling through the spirit trumpet; a psychic dog barking; and Margery laughing; "all at the same time!" There was some concern, though, as to whether Prince would hear any of this.

After endeavoring to make dinner conversation with the new investigator, Roy discovered that he, like Thomas Edison, had a hearing impairment that effectively detached him from the rest of the world. Prince was never satisfied with the way his hearing aid functioned and said that he had written to the various manufacturers complaining of it. Ultimately, though, he did hear Walter's clamorous effects. He also witnessed many of the most dramatic phenomena: the spinning curtain rod; the movement of heavy furniture; the destruction of the spirit cabinet; and the playing and flotation of a ukulele that landed in his lap, causing him to exclaim: "I have a psychic baby."

But as the tests progressed, Dr. Crandon sensed that Prince was not as awed by his wife's phenomena as Bird, Carrington, Comstock, and Keating. At times the ASPR officer exasperated Roy even more than the suspicious Harvard psychologists. When Prince witnessed an astonishing effect, he blamed it on the faulty control of Carrington or Bird, yet when he took Margery's hands, the curtain pole continued to gyrate, the table to dance, the scales to swing,

Prince was not especially liked by his colleagues, and Bird complained that he offered no suggestions for advances in the psychic program, as had Carrington and Comstock. Moreover, Prince did not seem to consider the Margery case as important as the rest of the commission. He refused to stay with the Beacon Hill couple, maintaining that the ASPR could afford him sufficient, if not fancy, room and board. He seemed as disinclined to fully acquaint himself with the case, Bird observed, as to get to know the Crandons. His first visit to Lime Street ended, Bird felt peremptorily, after only a few test séances. Through Margery's automatic writing, Walter expressed his own frustrations with the ASPR expert: *"What use can lights and ghosties be, when Princes come and will not see."*

For all these reasons, there was a noticeable lack of rapport between Prince and the Crandons. The psychic bell ringing did not appear to move him. He never saw or heard enough to satisfy him. Walter said that, like some old horse, the ASPR should retire him. Margery faced a formidable challenge in winning over the crusty New England minister, as her spirit control did not cotton to *"this man Prince and his vibrations."* Adding to the tension, the Crandons were hurt when someone mentioned that Prince did not entirely trust them. Before one séance that took place late in the SciAm investigation, Prince told one of his colleagues of a vision he'd had the previous evening: Dr. Crandon, he joked, would sit on the medium's right (his customary position) and phenomena would ensue. The crack somehow got back to the doctor, who did not appreciate Prince's insinuation that he was an accomplice in fraud. "A mean and uncalled for implication," he wrote Sir Arthur, "showing a mind too sclerotic for research work."

Prince's vote was crucial—Bird did not think Margery could win the prize without it; but no medium, except for the one the impaired ghost hunter adopted, had ever really convinced him. Prince also seemed to have little confidence in his fellow researchers. He trusted no phenomena that occurred without his direct control of the medium and her environment. The old Puritan would not be satisfied, Dr. Crandon told his friends, until he was a committee of one, and the tests were under the auspices of the ASPR rather than the *Scientific American.*

During the séance that occurred after Prince's sarcastic premonition, Walter was in unusually bad form: he made the Victrola behave weirdly but could not activate the bell box as he had previously. "Walter, last week you rang the bell most every night in red light," Dr. Crandon said with a tinge of disappointment. *"Yes, with an entirely different circle,"* the spirit answered. *"All friendly."* So that he might adjust to Prince's energy, Walter asked the ASPR officer to prolong his trip to Boston. When Prince refused, the mood was grim in the Crandon circle. Prince had just witnessed a series of essentially blank séances that made prospects for a favorable vote from him unlikely. Hence, Walter made what seemed like a rash offer. The medium was never known to perform in the day, yet her brother invited

Prince to a séance at Lime Street the next afternoon, to be held in the day-light considered anathema to the production of ectoplasm. Furthermore, per Walter's instructions, the bell box was to be under Prince's control and this time he would be alone with Margery.

Walter had proposed a séance for one, even though Prince was said to block his phenomena. "We all do not see how this can be done," the doctor wrote in his séance report, "but it will be tried nevertheless." While it worried the Crandon circle, Walter was keen for the challenge: *"I'll give the old buck the surprise of his life,"* the voice assured them.

At 2:30 the next day the trial started. Dr. Prince drew the curtains, although sunlight still shone into the room. He arranged the degree of light himself, then examined the bell box and explored the medium's lap. Satisfied that all was as it should be, he sat directly across from Margery, with no table between them; their feet in contact; their hands clasped in each other's; the bell box held vigilantly in the investigator's lap—as if he were the guardian of the Hope Diamond and she the world's most cunning jewel thief. But if Margery were indeed an impostor, it would be difficult for her to reach for the prize without Prince observing her. Though subdued, the room was bright enough, he later said, to see "anything the size of a pea" in the space between him and the medium.

After sitting for a while in silence, whispers were heard as the psychic began to receive messages—one of which was from Prince's now deceased wife, whose ailments in her last days included, as Margery accurately related, a persistent chill which now afflicted the medium. Prince watched her shivering, and expressed, with emotion that surprised her, the fear that she "might die." Promptly he covered her hands to warm them and pulled her robes around her. Then came a shattering crack near the west wall as Walter's voice warned, *"The kid is too cold."* A fifteen-minute break was taken, and a coat and tea fetched for Margery. After another search, they took their previous positions for the séance. And there they waited. For an hour nothing happened. Prince wondered if this was Margery's gambit, to simply outlast him. The minute he nodded and relaxed his grip, the bell box was hers for the taking. If so, she underestimated the Maine farmer. He was ready to sit with her all night, or until she cried uncle. That scenario was obviated by the sudden noise of the bell ringing, ringing, ringing—a noise that carried downstairs to the parlor, where Dr. Crandon sat with company that saw him smiling intensely.

According to Margery, Dr. Prince then declared, "My God it was the bell box." After the investigator checked the device, and found nothing wrong with it, they resumed their vigil. "The control is perfect. Walter, ring it now," Prince challenged. Five minutes later the investigator looked into Margery's eyes, as if to make a remark, but was interrupted when once again the bell box rang. With the second demonstration, Prince had heard enough. "I examined the space between the medium and myself," he later stated, "without discovery." He then escorted Margery across the hall to her bedroom, where he experimented with the bell box, and asked the medium to disrobe. He explored her dress and petticoats but found nothing incriminating. By Margery's account, he said that he could think of no other way that the bell box could have rung other than by supernormal agency. In Prince's own report, he maintained that it would still take a few more experiments, with similar results, "to satisfy me of that."

As he left her house, Prince was unusually affectionate with the medium. After he hugged her, she watched from her front door as he got into the taxi that drove him toward South Station. Just because there had been a matinee performance, though, did not mean the evening event was canceled. At a séance after dinner, the appearance of Walter was greeted by "cheers and rejoicing." When asked what had caused the loud crash during the afternoon sitting, the spirit replied that he *was breaking the ice for Prince.* He said that the stunts in daylight were difficult for him to produce but he had not wanted Prince to return to New York without something to shake his skepticism. After the successful demonstration for the ASPR investigator, Margery's brief slump was over. That evening the psychic and her brother were marvelous. The ukulele and megaphone floated near her head, then rattled against the cabinet. The instrument was later transported over the circle, at which point one of Comstock's lights flashed; a sign that a photograph had been taken of the ukulele that was floating in a firmament of eerie crimson.

All the Muse That's Fit to Print

WOMAN ASTOUNDS PSYCHIC EXPERTS
—*New York Times*

SCIENTIFIC INVESTIGATORS WON BY DEMONSTRATIONS
OF RICH WOMAN MEDIUM
—*Brooklyn Eagle*

FOUR OF FIVE MEN CHOSEN TO BESTOW AWARD
SURE SHE IS 100 P.C. GENUINE
—*Boston Herald*

*U*ntil recently the casual reader of the *Scientific American* did not expect, for his thirty-five cents, to find stories on parlor séances and hauntings. It was a journal of science and technology, not occultism. But there was a world of difference, Bird often pointed out, between the supernatural and supernormal. Margery could very well be a genuine medium without actually being in touch with discarnate spirits.

In the present environment, that was like endorsing Biblical miracles while denying a belief in the Divine. Whenever mysterious forces were discovered, it activated the urge for supernatural communion in some vestigial region of the human mind—or so it seemed to Bird, who sat at his typewriter while looking at photographs of spectral lights and heavy objects that hung in the air, defying gravity. It occurred to him that *Scientific American* journalists had always sought to debunk just this type of curiosity. Under the leadership of the two prior generations of Munns, they had likened spiritism to carnival flimflam and medieval sorcery. Yet there had also been occasions, Bird knew, when the magazine substantiated discoveries that seemed too fantastic to be true. A part of its mission, and now his, was to demystify the new frontiers of science.

When Wilhelm Röntgen discovered the X-ray, and presented proof in the form of spooky photographs of his wife's skeleton, it had the appearance of a dime-museum stunt that elicited much ridicule on both sides of the Atlantic. Shortly after his announcement, though, the *Scientific American* claimed that Röntgen's work would not only revolutionize the diagnosing of disease, it might eventually be applied to "cosmic questions of the utmost magnitude." While this was well before Malcolm Bird's tenure at the magazine, he believed experts were now close to validating a psychic force that, at the very least, would legitimize a new branch of psychology or physics. Bird therefore wanted to relay more than a good ghost story when, in the summer of 1924, he told the world about Margery.

"The Lady about whom this story revolves is the wife of a professional man of prominence in the city of their residence," he began his *Scientific American* article. "Her brother was regarded as psychic while in this life. After his death, curious things began to happen." Supernormal effects were channeled through the sister and controlled by the brother, he explained; and with the "systemization" of her clairvoyant gifts, Margery had produced "objective phenomena of great distinction."

Bird forcefully addressed the possibility of chicanery—and why the unsavory assumptions about spirit mediums did not apply to Margery. "The favorable moral factors of the case it is impossible to exaggerate. I consider them stronger than in any contemporary instance of physical mediumship." At last the commission was working with a respectable lady—rather than the trumpet babbler from Wilkes-Barre, the cagey seeress from Ohio, or the ward of the doctor from Harlem. Unlike the other candidates, Margery had no cloudy past or material motives. "The psychic is so much a lady of refinement and culture that to speak of this feature gives one who knows her a lively sense of bad taste," he averred. "It follows that the mediumship is wholly private, nonprofessional and free from the odor of money."

Not only did Margery "pay the freight" for the committee's relocation from New York to Boston, she was going to donate the prize money, should she win it, to further psychic research. She had already paid a higher price in other ways. Though averse to publicity she had sacrificed her former serenity and privacy. "Dislocation of the family life by all this is acute," Bird reported, "and the psychic's role as mother of her twelve-year-old son is seriously hampered, to her keen realization and concern."

What sustained her was the encouragement of her inner circle. While Bird created pseudonyms for all the characters, he made it clear that Margery's supporters were "substantial people of affairs, both materially and intellectually." Four were physicians, and one (Mark Richardson) an innovative scientist whose research on influenza had earned him a place in *Who's Who in America*. They were convinced Spiritualists, Bird said, but wary of the religious side of the movement.

As for the ghost, while Walter could be truculent, he "displays keen interest in the scientific side of the case, and in the mechanism of his own manifestations." Without discussing the quality of entertainment that the séances provided, Bird observed that the spirit had "the same keen humor that is noted in Margery as a person."

In the two articles he wrote about the Lime Street investigation, Bird cast himself as an active researcher as much as a journalist. He covered Margery's work with the restraint expected of a scientific publication, but it was clear what he wanted to convey: the commission's impression of Margery was "distinctly favorable." Finally the *Scientific American* had found a medium whose phenomena were prize-worthy.

◆

Even though Bird knew the report on Margery would be controversial, he and his colleagues had still "underestimated the general interest in our work." Once the dailies picked up the story, readers wanted to know more about the Boston lady who might be the world's first scientifically verified medium. If she truly had passed the jury's tests, it would be an important development in the quest that Lodge, Edison, and others had taken up: to establish communications with dead souls. There was a journalistic hunger for more information on Margery, her brother's ghost, and the phenomena—an occult mania not seen since the Fox girls, seventy-six years earlier, made the séance a popular domestic pastime.

Orson Munn was not crowning his winner just yet, though. A few newspaper stories emphasized something else that Bird had said: definite proofs had not yet been given. The commission was preparing an ultimatum for Walter. The plan, according to an incredulous *New York World* editorial, was "to tell him to quit playing with the furniture and the musical instruments and to give a real demonstration, such as closing an electric-circuit gap in a sealed jar or tipping a scale protected from tricky touch."

Anyone following the story would have concluded that the ghost had already done that. In July, the *Times* heightened expectations when it reported that the committee was "unable to find the slightest evidence of fraud" in the psychic's manifestations. MARGERY PASSES ALL PSYCHIC TESTS, read the headline of record.

As Bird had expected, his star judge reacted strongly to "the barrage of publicity." It appeared, to Houdini's dismay, as if the *Scientific American* editor spoke for the committee. Bird did not speak for them. Certainly he did not speak for Houdini. He spoke for the magazine. Bird, however, was the only one associated with the contest making public statements; like some sideshow piker, the Great Houdini had been left off the main stage. An important inquiry was taking place, and he the only committeeman excluded. Yet the newspapers were reporting that Margery had convinced the experts, which suggested that she had also impressed him. When he read about the case, Houdini "immediately exploded." The *Scientific American*, the jury, and the magician himself were "being made ridiculous," he cried. He wanted to go to Boston and expose the high-class sorceress immediately.

Bird responded with a letter reminding Houdini that the original idea was not to bother him with the new case "unless, and until, it got to a stage where there seemed serious prospects that it was either genuine, or a type of fraud which our other committeemen could not deal with." As they had now reached that stage, Bird and Munn did, in fact, want to talk to Houdini. Could he "run in," at his convenience, to lunch with the publisher? It was hinted that he should not rush over to the Woolworth too quickly, though. Munn was out of the office until the following week. Bird was busy for the next few days. It might be better to call first.

When Houdini did finally confront Munn, the publisher told him that he had been trying to reach him for a week, "but Bird had been side-stepping the matter." This came as no surprise to the magician who complained that he had been excluded from the Margery trials so that Bird could push the other judges toward a favorable verdict. Denying this, Munn called his editor into the office to refute the charge directly.

By Houdini's account, he asked Bird if Margery was going to be awarded the prize.

"Most decidedly," Bird answered.

"Mr. Bird," Houdini flared, "you have nothing to lose but your position and very likely you can readily get another if you are wrong, but if I am wrong it will mean the loss of reputation."

Houdini turned to Munn, who he felt respected him as an expert on spirit humbug. He had to be permitted to sit with Margery, he told the publisher. If she were a genuine medium then, given the reports he had read—about a live pigeon transported through matter, and so forth—she had to be the "most wonderful in the world." But if she were given the prize money and later found to be an impostor, then her endorser "would be the laughing stock of the world."

That was why they had asked to see him, Munn acknowledged. They wanted Houdini to go forthwith to Boston.

Bird tried to hide his displeasure at the magician's war readiness. The other experts had worked with Margery for three months without detecting trickery. "He would now step in," Bird wrote, "locate in two sittings the deception which had eluded them for fifty, and with one magnificent gesture would save the committee."

After Houdini left the journal's offices, the editor had a private conference with Munn. The showman had just called his colleagues incompetent at best, and dishonest at worst; he had already formed the opinion that the medium was a huckster. Bird warned that Houdini was going to wreak havoc on the Margery tests. Recognizing that danger, Munn decided to accompany the magician to Lime Street, and ensure that he was "on his good behavior." So on July 22, the day after the most positive *Times* story yet on Margery, Munn and Houdini traveled by train to Boston. Bird, who drove, had arrived there one day earlier.

Upon hearing that Houdini's visit was arranged, Margery became noticeably nervous and excited. Dr. Crandon wrote Doyle of the turbulent atmosphere on Lime Street.

Tonight Houdini and Mr. Munn, owner of the Scientific American, *sit with us for the first time and will stay for several days. I*

think Psyche is somewhat stirred by it internally because of Houdini's
general nastiness. She is vomiting merrily this morning. However,
some of her worst days have given the best sittings.

Dr. Crandon had received alarming reports on the magician whom
Doyle called a clever liar and medium baiter. Sir Arthur wondered if Walter could "rise above" the trickster's negative energy; whether Roy could
work with him was just as uncertain. Even before Houdini came to Beacon
Hill, something was shifting in the way Dr. Crandon dealt with investigators. Feeling that some of them were out to persecute his wife, he was not
as cordial as the trials continued. On the verge, Roy sensed, of Margery's
winning the contest, he required that the committeemen sign copies of
their notes after every sitting and leave them with him, so that if they later
made statements inconsistent with their observations, he had the material
"to crucify them."

The doctor was through "wasting any time in compliments or polite-
ness," he wrote Sir Arthur. "It is war to the finish and they know I shall
not hesitate to treat them surgically if necessary." If this was the way he
felt about the investigators who shared some of his own metaphysical beliefs, then prospects for a civil relationship with an arch-skeptic did not
seem likely. Houdini was an anti-Spiritualist who disdained the faith of the
Crandons and Doyles. Roy, in turn, was no friend to Houdini's religion.

Like many in his circle, Dr. Crandon was wary of aliens—the immigrant wave that might turn the United States into an eastern European nation. At the Yacht Club he was known to make some pretty severe remarks
about Jews, and he expressed, before he had met him, much the same hostility toward Houdini. "My deep regret," he wrote Sir Arthur, "is that this
low-minded Jew has any claim on the word American."

On the eve of the escape artist's visit, Walter composed a poem that
augured conflict. *"Harry Houdini, he sure is a Sheeny, A man with a crook*
in his shoe. Says he 'As to Walter, I'll lead him to slaughter' 'But,' says Walter,
'Perhaps I'll get you!'"

A Dead Man Rising

"LUCK, NOT MAGIC," SAVED HOUDINI FROM DEATH
—*Boston Herald*

*I*t was once the wizard's role, as the wise man in his feudal shire, to ferret out witches and counter their spells. Yet in 1924, if the newspapers were to be believed, the Witch of Lime Street had the upper hand. HOUDINI THE MAGICIAN STUMPED flashed one headline. A showdown appeared imminent between Houdini and the medium who was receiving the kind of publicity for which he had always seemed willing to risk his life. When a younger Houdini had escaped a packing crate dropped from a barge into New York Harbor, *Scientific American* had called it "one of the most remarkable tricks ever performed." Lately Orson Munn's journal was praising another wonder creator—a magician in disguise, if Houdini was right.

Margery's challenge was to prove that her brother lived after death, while the Great Houdini's feats were designed to persuade the masses that he faced annihilation if he failed *his* test. In every escape he was feared lost then rose again. Once, in California, they had trussed and buried him under six feet of sandy soil. Emerging bleeding, pale, and dazed, he was the "perfect imitation of a dead man rising." Another time, in Australia, upon leaping manacled and chained from a bridge, he dislodged a corpse on the river floor that burst the surface next to him. Believing it part of the act, the spectators had applauded the Lazarus effect.

Now Houdini and Orson Munn were en route to Boston, a city that had always presented the escape artist with even stranger and more macabre challenges. They caged him in an iron witch's chair. They put him in a straitjacket outside Keith's and watched as he dangled from the tower, one hundred feet in the air. Before the mayor and scores of other onlookers, he was rolled in two sheets by attendants from a Worcester asylum, strapped to a cot, and had a dozen buckets of ice-cold water poured on his body. He slithered out nonchalantly. Restrained in cuffs and irons, he was stuffed inside a dead, reeking 1,600-pound sea creature and dropped into Boston Harbor. He escaped like Jonah from a whale.

When traveling in those days by train, Houdini used to do push-ups in the aisles or pull-ups between the cars. After returning to his seat, he would soon feel the urge once again to exercise or perform. This time he would not need his strength, so he decided to forgo such lighthearted gymnastics. His mission was to deliver a report to the committee, but he was not cut out to be a passive observer in the dark. His impulse was to do something more, to expose the medium that very night, even if Malcolm Bird was not inclined to write about it. When he and Munn disembarked at South Station, Bird was waiting to drive them to Lime Street. As they walked through the terminal, Munn saw passersby greet Houdini with amazed smiles, and he brightened as they called to him.

Everything Lovely

*T*he arrival of Munn and Houdini was like another flare in the meteoric rise of Margery; for all of Roy's reservations she was now receiving a new tier of guests—two luminaries in their respective worlds of publishing and entertainment. While Houdini's presence made her understandably anxious, she was proud to receive him in her parlor. She had become aware of researchers like McDougall, Prince, and Comstock only within the last year, but the Great Houdini had been a star since she was a child. Moreover, he seemed, like her, a little out of his realm among intellectuals and scientists. The name McDougall had meant nothing to him, he admitted to her, until the Harvard professor had been chosen as a judge in the psychic contest. And it seemed that McDougall, like the other judges, was not eager to attend a sitting the magician was managing. The psychologist had not responded to Bird's calls about this gathering. As for Carrington, he'd left Boston before Munn and Houdini arrived. Prince had pressing business in New York. Even the affable Comstock sent a proxy—his assistant, Will Conant—for Houdini's first séance with Margery.

Given Houdini's boisterous reputation, Margery was pleased to find that he could be almost as polite as Carrington, as curious as Bird, and more enchanting than Keating. Before her husband arrived from the office, she gave her New York guests a tour of the neighborhood; and despite being on opposite sides of the Borderland, she and Houdini appeared to get on famously. Everyone believed they were of different social spheres, but Margery was more of an outsider to Beacon Hill than most visitors imagined.

During their walk, Houdini discussed the loss that had driven him to explore the spirit world. While Bird had always found it maudlin when the magician spoke of his dead mother with adjectives such as "beloved" or "sainted," Margery was sympathetic to Houdini's frustrations with the mediums who had failed to contact his loved one.

Everything was agreeable to Houdini. At dinner he did not appear to be the loutish medium baiter whom Roy had described. Instead, Margery found him rather dignified; a feeling that, on the surface at least, seemed mutual. In his diary that night, Houdini praised the Crandons' good taste and noted Margery's beauty—which explained, he said, Bird's glowing reports on her mediumship. Though determined to be the one investigator immune to the Boston Circe's spell, Houdini seemed to be having a swell time at Lime Street. He was amused when Margery, who had heard it from Sir Arthur, asked him if he too were a medium. While denying that claim, he told her of the voice that guided him when he stood precariously on a bridge—how he awaited the guardian-like prompting before leaping into the abyss. He also seemed impressed with Dr. Crandon, who had proudly showed him the finest private collection of Lincoln memorabilia in Boston. Houdini, in turn, could boast of his holdings on Booth, the scoundrel who had assassinated him.

After an inspection of the house, Houdini said that he found nothing suspicious. Accordingly, on that evening of July 23, Margery gave her first demonstration for him and the small circle that included Munn, Bird, Conant, and the husband who seldom left her side in the séance room. Roy was considered to be practically a second medium, Houdini was told, as Margery needed his presence on her right. Yet if ever a psychic were caught between opposing forces, one energizing and the other potentially depleting, it was Margery—since Houdini was on her left that night, controlling her extremities on that side. The dark gathering began with the usual disembodied whispers and whistles, then Walter confronted the publisher and magician. *"Very interesting conversation you men had on the train. I was there. I can always be where my interests lie,"* the voice taunted.

Before the visitors could respond, Walter went straight for Houdini, warning him that he was directing contact onto his right leg. For the record, Houdini confirmed the touches there. Some time later, after an intermission and a reassembling of his circle, Walter called for *"control!"* At that moment, Margery shifted away from Roy and toward Houdini, so that he could control both of her hands and feet. With the medium thus immobilized, Walter announced that the spirit megaphone was floating in the air. *"Have Houdini tell me where to throw it,"* the voice said. "Toward me," Houdini commanded. Instantly the trumpet landed at his feet. Walter then ordered Bird to guard the door against any intruders. Before he could obey, the cabinet was hurled "backwards violently," Houdini reported. If Margery and the magician had met on agreeable terms, the ghost was having none of it. *"You—Munn and Houdini—think you're pretty smart, don't you?"* Walter sniped while proceeding to assail the New York guests with his effects. The Victrola slowed and stopped. A luminous plaque that had been placed on the bell box rose, lowered, then oscillated back and forth. For the climax, the bell box rang—seemingly of its own accord—while Margery was clasped by the magician who felt, she imagined, every fluctuation of her pulse and twinge of the nerves in her extremities.

Houdini had not sat idly while Walter was active. During the demonstration he had placed both of Margery's hands between his knees and explored the bell box for signs of manipulation. When he later refastened his hands on hers, he ran them up to her shoulders to ensure he was indeed holding the medium. She sensed he was uncomfortable with more intimate contact. In one report, from a previous séance, it had been noted that "Carrington explored the medium's lap," but Houdini eschewed that kind of groping. Neither would he have been among those committeemen who had once lined up by the bay window to examine the glowing spots on Margery's chest—as if upon her bosom lay the answer to the Lime Street mystery. But while Houdini was less invasive with the psychic, he had no compunctions about imposing his will on the proceedings. Earlier that night, when the red light was turned up, he exploded at Bird for releasing one of his hands from the circle. When a sitter breaks the chain, it is considered debilitating to the séance battery. Houdini had other reasons, though, for ordering the editor to keep his hands on the table and away from the medium.

Aside from that flare-up, Margery had not found the magician to be a hindrance. Afterward, the Crandons were pleased with Bird's impromptu report that mentioned good control and a steady production of phenomena. The document was signed by Orson Munn, his editor, and, without disputing it, Harry Houdini.

The star expert made no statement when the sitting was over; he appeared pensive, as if mentally reliving what he had witnessed. The Crandons were therefore hopeful that he, like the magician Keating, had come to scoff and left believing. And leave Houdini did, at least for the rest of the evening. Unlike Bird and Carrington he considered it impossible to stay at the medium's house, break bread with her frequently, and then "render an impartial verdict." Nevertheless, Margery felt her demonstration had gone well, and anticipated a favorable response from him. What the Doyles had once tried to do in Atlantic City had passed to her; and that night she had delivered more than the stream of Victorian platitudes that Jean Doyle had once given him. Margery had displayed hard evidence—physical phenomena that would make her the equal, Keating once said, of great illusionists like Thurston (who came to believe in her) and Kellar, if she produced her effects deceptively.

After the séance, Bird drove Munn and Houdini back to the Copley Plaza Hotel. No one got out of the car when they parked on Beacon Street, as this was where the sitters had agreed to hold their "postmortem." Turning to face Houdini in the backseat, Munn demanded his opinion of Margery.

Without hesitation, Houdini delivered his verdict: "All fraud—every bit of it." He promised that at the next sitting he would expose everything, although there was still something he hadn't worked out. "One thing puzzles me," he admitted. "I don't see how she did that megaphone trick."

Bird refrained from defending the medium. Rather, he offered one of Prince's speculations: if she were cheating, Margery might have balanced the megaphone on her shoulder while it was supposed to be floating. "It couldn't be in her lap," Bird maintained. "This was open to exploration."

"It couldn't be on her shoulder either," Houdini responded, as he had checked there during the manifestation. Abruptly, as Bird recalled, "an expression of relieved triumph" spread over the magician's face. Now he called it the "slickest ruse" he had ever uncovered. Margery did not have supernatural powers; she could not really have suspended the megaphone in the air—for Houdini that was a given. Neither could she have kept it on her shoulder. There was only one other possibility: the medium had balanced the instrument on her head, then launched it toward him.

Bird found his scenario absurd. How could this society wife pull off a feat that would have challenged even a vaudeville conjurer? He wanted to know how she made the bell box ring, if everything was fraudulent. With her foot, Houdini insisted. He explained that he had worn a rubber bandage around his calf during the rail journey to Boston. By the time they arrived at Lime Street his calf and ankle, as he intended, were swollen and sensitive to Margery's foot, which rested next to his during the séance. During the sitting he had noticed her pull her skirt up well over her knees. Every time she slid her ankle or flexed her muscle, he felt the subtle movement through her silk stockings; he felt this happen precisely when the bell box sounded. Margery, he said, was a cunning impostor. What about the stopping of the Victrola? Munn offered. That was easy, Houdini said: someone got up and stopped it.

So it was not enough that Margery was balancing trumpets on her head, thought Bird, and ringing bell boxes with her feet while the star expert was supposed to be controlling them. Houdini now asserted that she had accomplices who broke the circle and darted over to manipulate the music player. It could not have been Dr. Crandon, Bird affirmed, for he himself was controlling Roy during the phenomena. At this remark, Houdini bristled. Why had Bird broken the circle? he inquired. "For exploring purposes," claimed the editor who often seemed to have his hands on the medium, Houdini hinted, when it was unwarranted. As the meeting ended, he left a strong suggestion that Bird was Margery's confederate. Hours earlier the two men had exchanged a cordial handshake at South Station; by the end of the evening they were open enemies. While Munn and Houdini checked into their hotel, Bird drove back to the Crandons'.

◆

The next day Margery confronted Houdini about a conversation that— unless Walter was right when he said he was everywhere—she should not have been able to divine. Hurt and disappointed, she accused Houdini of making vile statements against her; it would only tarnish his own name, she warned, if he followed through on his promise to try to expose her at the séance that evening. Begging her not to attribute what she knew to her psychic sense, Houdini asked her which particular bird was whispering in her ear. After admitting that Malcolm Bird was her source, she made Houdini promise to keep quiet about it.

Proceeding directly to Munn and Bird, Houdini accused the editor of compromising the investigation by informing Margery of the committee's discussions. Bird denied that he was revealing anything to the Crandons. Who was calling him a snitch? he demanded. Reluctant to completely break his promise to Margery, Houdini said that he had put two and two together when he saw her and Bird talking privately. The former mathematics professor snorted at that deduction, telling the magician he had gotten his numbers wrong.

◆

Photographs were taken that day, which Margery would urge Houdini to keep private. Outside her home she stands beside the white-haired, well-coiffed publisher; behind them, leaning directly over Margery (he had to stand atop something unseen to enter the picture), is Bird—lean, bespectacled, and somber. Next to Margery, and the focus of her enigmatic gaze, is Houdini—stout and graying, a little ruffled in his dark suit. After that, Houdini took a snapshot of Margery smiling primly in a doorway, her hands behind her back, her hair and white frock radiating sunlight. Then someone took an intimate picture of Houdini and Margery posing alone near her front door. Though known to be formal and demure with women, Houdini leans close to the medium. Standing almost in profile to the camera, he holds her hand and smiles at her affectionately—while she has turned to him as if expecting a kiss.

◆

If Houdini planned to expose Margery on July 24, then Lime Street, where she worked her best magic, would not be the setting for her fall. The next séance took place at the Charlesgate Hotel at 535 Beacon Street, in Daniel Comstock's apartment. That evening Margery stood in the physicist's bedroom while removing—as part of a regimen of more stringent control—her green dress and undergarments. Gladys Wood, Comstock's secretary, thoroughly examined her person and clothes, then searched the medium's genital region and between her toes; she shone a pocket torch inside her mouth and when Margery let down her blond hair, Gladys searched there. Turning off the light, she inspected the medium's body, particularly her chest, for the luminous spots that had once puzzled the committeemen. She found nothing within Margery's vagina, concealed in her mouth, or sparkling on her skin that would explain how spirit cabinets were torn apart, megaphones floated, and tables levitated. Assured that the medium was clean, Houdini and Roy, waiting in the makeshift séance room, proceeded to clasp her hands when she was seated in her cabinet.

Also present in the locked room within the suite were Munn, Bird, Comstock, and Conant; and Walter, if one believed in his existence. *"Ha, ha, Houdini!"* the spirit cackled, just as Houdini reported that something was touching his right knee. After the spectral contacts came a series of Margery's finest effects: the cabinet quaked and moved across the floor, the table rose, the megaphone moved, the Victrola behaved weirdly, and raps were heard. At a moment in the proceedings when Houdini, Conant, and Bird declared the control to be perfect, the table became animated and turned over, knocking the bell box to the floor. Minutes later, Walter instructed Orson Munn to sit up. Admitting that he had been slouching, Munn was impressed by Walter's perception of his posture in the pitch dark. With control of the medium once again established, the publisher was startled when the bell box rang and stopped. Walter asked him how many more times he wanted it to ring. "Five times," requested Munn. Five rings were immediately heard. After which the ghost, signaling that the demonstration was over, whispered *"Good night"* to the Charlesgate circle.

◆

A dramatic effort to prevent or expose the phenomena had been expected from Houdini; yet he hadn't interfered with the test. Deferring to Comstock, he hadn't snapped this time at Bird. After the Crandons left the hotel, the magician explained that during the séance he informed Mr. Munn that he "had" the medium, but was advised not to expose her, as the time was not right. Regardless, Houdini claimed that the psychic had performed every trick in her repertoire. Margery had leaned forward to raise the table with her head; she had once again worn the megaphone like a hat before hurling it into the air; she rang the bell box with her feet.

Later he reported that the medium "is unusually strong and has an athletic body." She had the powerful constitution of an escape artist, he implied, not the ethereal aura of a psychic. Earlier, he had been surprised when it took so long for the bell box to ring. According to Houdini, Margery had revealed her predicament to him when she said, "You have garters on, haven't you?"

"Yes," Houdini had replied.

"Well, the buckle hurts me."

It was then Houdini realized that the buckle had caught the medium's stocking, so that her ankle was pinned to his. When he unloosed the buckle, he claimed her foot shifted and the bell soon rang. By this point he wanted to go directly to New York and tell the newspapers about Margery's slippery feet, as well as how he had caught her with her head under the table (she said she was looking for a hairpin, he claimed)—and the myriad other ways he saw her cheating. Munn, Bird, and Comstock insisted, however, that no statement would be allowed. Displeased, Houdini wanted to know why it was OK to immediately expose the other candidates but not the Beacon Hill psychic.

"It's different this time," Bird replied.

Later, Houdini handed Munn a letter he drew up, stating that Margery was "one hundred per cent trickster or fraud." Outraged by the statement, Bird said that Houdini had not fulfilled his guarantee to catch the medium, because he could not. The Crandons also felt vindicated by the two demonstrations Margery had given for the entourage from New York. In their view, Houdini had come to Boston determined to discredit her. He had "said many nasty things behind the psychic's back," Dr. Crandon wrote to Doyle. Yet he had left without curtailing her work. To counter Houdini's accusations, Roy had his signatures on séance reports that said the magician controlled Margery while the manifestations occurred. "The clouds break a little since yesterday," Dr. Crandon told Sir Arthur. "Houdini and Munn . . . have signed the complete notes of both their sittings without reservation. These sittings are so full of clean-cut psychic phenomena that any subsequent denial would indict these men before all the world."

Following the contentious tests, it was evident that Margery had survived Houdini's first challenge: she had stood up to the notorious bugbear to spiritism. "Houdini is apparently all that you and other gentlemen have ever said of him," Roy told his English ally, "to which I should be pleased to add a choice collection of adjectives which you may assemble from the White Chapel and the East End. Nevertheless, I think we have him."

If Houdini could not stop the phenomena—and he had abstained from trying this time—Margery would receive the prize. As final proof, Dr. Crandon suggested to Bird and Doyle the possibility of "the one-man circle." He wanted Margery alone in the dark with the trickster, and let him stop her if he could. "Who knows, perhaps we shall add Houdini to this list of magicians who have become spiritualists," he said. In the end, however, Roy decided that Houdini, who he thought was crooked as a dog's hind leg, would probably insert his own toe in the bell box to prevent it from ringing. It was better, the doctor felt, to have other judges present so that both the medium *and* Houdini could be supervised. Another round of sittings, this time for the entire jury, was thus arranged for later in the summer. Bird expressed confidence to Roy that Margery would do just fine: "The Committee will sit in Boston in September. Everything lovely."

A Shake-Up in the Contest

If these people were on the level they wouldn't have to perform in the dark . . . More power to Houdini to run the fakirs out of business.
—*Providence News*

*W*hen the midnight train carried Harry Houdini and Orson Munn from their first sittings with Margery to the teeming Grand Central Station, the publisher felt his mood shift accordingly: it could not have been a grayer, steamier, more prosaic July morning. Houdini, though sleep-deprived, had been reliving his encounter with Margery. She was a savvy operator, he said, and it had taken all of his considerable experience in flim-flam to unveil her methods. As the two men parted outside the terminal, Munn recognized that they were at a crossroads in the investigation: the credibility that was the lifeblood of his family's publication was at stake. He would be forty-one years old the next day, far younger than the magazine that had recently been entrusted to him. He was sweating and uncomfortable. Reading the *Times* on the drive to the Waldorf, he saw that the sweltering heat was causing abnormal behavior. By police estimates, hundreds of thousands fled the hot spell on a working day, descending on Coney Island—and 50,000 remained there to sleep, like an exhausted army, on the beach. Munn could not help but wonder if the much-anticipated approach of Mars—riding closer to Earth than it had in a century—had something to do with the infernal weather and general upheaval.

Publisher Munn was in a quandary: though he respected his editor, Houdini's suspicion that Bird was the Crandons' carrier pigeon disturbed him. The September issue of the *Scientific American* was supposed to contain another report on Margery—Bird's most positive yet on her medium-ship. It would be a great embarrassment if Bird commended Margery just as Munn's chief expert exposed her as a charlatan. At no small cost, Munn therefore decided to pull the story from the presses. Houdini had successfully clipped Bird's wings; Munn would now have to decide between Margery's advocate and her debunker.

Matters came to a head at the *Scientific American* office days later—when Houdini showed up with a report on Margery that he withheld from Bird. "I told Mr. Munn that Mr. Bird tells the medium everything," Houdini recollected. During this exchange he got Bird to admit to Munn "that she wormed things out of him by cross-examining." Afterward, on the phone to Walter Prince, Houdini boasted that Munn refused to show his own editor the document. In his efforts to usurp Bird, Houdini found an unlikely ally in Prince, who had hitherto seemed less opposed to Bird than to Houdini's grandstanding attacks on spiritism. That August Prince and the magician would square off at the Saint Mark's Church in a raucous public debate over the validity of psychic phenomena. But Prince found Houdini no more excitable and boastful that night than during committee proceedings; he later said that "in the genial sunshine of his presence, one hardly minded these peculiarities."

"It is, to say the least, an extraordinary partnership," remarked Bird, who had no idea how revolted Prince was by his public adulation of Margery, as well as the commercial aspirations of the magazine that sponsored the contest. "I have become disgusted beyond the point of endurance," Prince wrote Eric Dingwall—the SPR investigator who had tested Margery in London.

Seizing the moment, Houdini urged Prince to come over to the *Scientific American*. Two doors from Bird's office, they asked that Munn prohibit his editor from giving statements on the committee's findings without the assent of themselves and the other committeemen, and they insisted that Bird no longer be referred to as "Secretary of Judges." It was misleading to the public, they explained, to associate him by title with the jury. Faced with the threat that his two expert judges were ready to quit, Munn agreed to their conditions. The producer of the *Scientific American* contest was now reduced, in the eyes of Houdini, to a clerical position. "Mr. J. Malcolm Bird will never again write for the committee," he informed Dingwall. "You ought to see the piffle," he said of the article he had convinced Munn to squelch. "It is terrible."

While Houdini had no issue with Bird's presence at the séances, Munn, fearing a dustup, decided to ban him from the next round of tests. Bird might have heard one too many of the siren's songs, thought Munn, and drunk too much of her potion. Whatever the cause, Bird's reputation as a neutral observer and thus the magazine's had been compromised. If the journal were to err, Munn wanted it to be on the side of the doubting Thomases.

It was now Houdini's contest.

"Houdini and Prince simply constituted themselves the mouthpieces of the committee," recalled Bird. They were "dictators," who "got together, agreed on a program, and jammed it through as far as they were able." Bird lamented that the mediumship he had been instrumental in developing and unveiling in stages—the trust and rapport that he had carefully cultivated between the magazine, the Boston subcommittee, and the Crandons—would be destroyed by the rampaging wizard. Houdini wanted to take the priestess off her throne. He said that manual control of the medium wasn't working; yet Margery, a Beacon Hill matron, was not some Italian drugstore clerk—you couldn't handle her like Pecoraro. With that in mind, Houdini and his assistant, Jim Collins, designed a humane mechanism for restraint; it was a great surprise they had in store for Margery. "We are going to have a final séance with her," Houdini wrote Dingwall. "And in this séance she is to be stopped."

Who Is Margery?

MEDIUM MEETS TESTS
"Margery," Wife of Prof. Crandon, of Harvard, First to Demonstrate
Spirit Forces Under Scientific Control
—*New York Mirror*

No evidence of fraud was found, and the moral factors were all in
favor of the medium, who has put every convenience at the
disposal of the investigators.
—*Time*

*T*he summer of '24 was the hottest Margery could recall. Relief was not in sight, she supposed, until the *Scientific American* contest was over, and she missed getting away from Beacon Hill, even though she purportedly left her body nightly. She wanted to escape the stifling séance room by motoring along the South Shore or sailing on their schooner, *Black Hawk*. But she rarely complained about the endless gatherings; with the deciding tests scheduled for late summer, this was not the time for leisure and distractions.

The showdown between Houdini and Margery had become an international story. According to many of the reports, the *Scientific American* judges had decided to award the Boston psychic the prize unless Houdini could change their minds, and their next encounter would apparently not be as cordial as the one in July. MARGERY TO RASSLE WITH THE HANDCUFF KING, declared one headline. SPIRITISMUS IN PRÜFUNG (Spiritualism on Trial), a German newspaper announced. Tabloid reporters had become like a Greek chorus, goading the players toward a fated conflict in the dark.

Despite the provocation, Margery and Houdini were still on good terms. "I have been hearing some very nice things about you lately," she wrote him, "so I am glad to be able to say I know 'The Great Houdini.'"

While many of those contacting the Boston medium had their letters intercepted and answered by Dr. Crandon, Houdini and Margery began a warm correspondence when he sent her the Lime Street snapshots and told her how much he enjoyed his visit there. The photographs that showed them delighting in each other's company were like doves of peace, considering the brewing animosity between Houdini and Margery's supporters, but she asked, "in view of the fact that I hate publicity, never to use any of those pictures or show them publicly. Dr. Crandon and I know that you are a gentleman and will respect our wishes in this matter."

Although her wishes were honored, the yellow press did not abide by the code to which she held Houdini. "One day I was in town shopping when my eye fell on an afternoon paper," she recalled. "I nearly fainted. There was my name on the first page in those bold, black letters the Boston papers love so much." Later she discovered that a reporter for the *Boston Advertiser* had followed one of the researchers to her home and figured out who lived there. From then on all knew the true identity of the mysterious candidate for the *Scientific American* prize. The *Advertiser* revealed her address as 10 Lime Street; for Margery there was the embarrassment of everyone knowing that "Margery" and "Mina" were one in the same:

> Who is Margery?
> For over a year the world has buzzed with speculation concerning the identity of the Boston woman who has startled scientists with the most astounding feats of mediumship ever witnessed.
> She stands today revealed as Mrs. Le Roi. G. Crandon, wife of professor of surgery at Harvard for more than fifteen years and the author of a number of scientific volumes.

The Hearst papers posted a photograph of Margery, never more genteel, next to one of Houdini fettered by balls and chains. She had become just the kind of rotogravure item that had no place, Dr. Crandon had warned, in a scientific trial. Refusing demands for interviews, the Crandons instead allowed Hereward Carrington to speak for them. From their parlor, he told the *Boston American* that voices, cold winds, and astral bells were not the jury's province. It was the gravity-defying scale test, and others like it, that were the mark of this investigation. Still, the newspapers glorified Margery in ways that embarrassed Bird and Carrington.

> A year and three months ago the *Scientific American,* conducting an investigation into the claims of mediums, offered a series of prizes of $2500 each to any medium who, in the face of the most heart-breaking tests, could establish irrefutable proof of spiritistic communications.
>
> Scores, attracted by the tempting offer, presented themselves, advanced their claims and were laughed to scorn by the scientists.
>
> Then came "Margery."
>
> She complied cheerfully with every exaction and test . . . with the one request that at each séance her husband be permitted to hold her hand.

Whether or not the commission was convinced, the Boston and New York newspapers had found their medium. "The woman may be genuine, as they say," Houdini told *The World.* "I will not commit myself until the tests are over. But there will be further tests. A case of this kind excites too many people, disturbing them, and giving them hope for communication with the dead. If Margery can give that communication, all right; but if she can't, I want to do something more for humanity than entertain it."

Houdini's involvement with the case helped put Lime Street on the map, but a higher class of artist, in Dr. Crandon's estimation, would ultimately find the place. "To experience the events at 10 Lime Street was not only to get glimpses of wonderous, unexplainable things; it was to meet some of the most outstandingly curious minds in the nation," said S. Ralph Harlow. When in town, William Butler Yeats liked to stop by—and one day he and Roy, who became his doctor, joked about the yellow fever that gripped reporters who wrote about Margery. "I have had my first cold," Yeats noted. "Dr. Crandon cured me with tabloids and whiskey. . . . Séance very remarkable."

The Pulitzer Prize–winning novelist and ASPR researcher Hamlin Garland would also come eagerly to Lime Street. "If one quarter of the marvels reported from here are true," he wrote, "this is the most important psychical laboratory in America." What he encountered in no way disappointed him. Garland found Dr. Crandon "scholarly in appearance, slender, low-voiced, and graceful, entirely in keeping with his book-walled study." His interest in the doctor was outshone a few minutes later, though, when "the widely celebrated Margery came in—a lovely young woman charmingly gowned. She was much younger than I had expected her to be. She was indeed hardly more than a girl.

"She showed no signs of the many grueling tests to which she had been subjected," Garland observed. "She was not only smilingly at ease but humorous in her replies, and yet, beneath her gay mood, I caught now and then a hint of serious purpose." During their séance, the investigator was as charmed by the ghost who called him *"Garland, my boy,"* and regarded him as a *"reg'lar fellow."** Awed by the ensuing effects, Garland would become another champion of Margery's work, though he found it savored of "commercial magic."

---

* Garland's sitting would not take place until May 1927.

A Man As Light As a Feather

All witchcraft comes from carnal lust, which is in women insatiable.
—*Malleus Maleficarum*

*W*itches, supernatural beings, have always been imbued with super-normal desires. In their flight, their nightly passage, they ride on brooms or pitchforks, cooking sticks and other phallic objects. In myth, they attempt to defeat men through seduction. And there was something almost superstitious in the voluptuous power Houdini ascribed to Margery. The nebbish scientists could not resist her.

◆

"Why, he's a pink one," the Crandons' maid said of Hereward Carrington, branding him effeminate. "He has rouge, cold cream, lipstick in his room and uses it all the time!" So maybe that was why he came to the summer sittings "looking like a million dollars," Margery surmised, while the other researchers entered perspiring and left humiliated by Walter for their lapses in hygiene. Carrie had his own room at Lime Street and often went there to refresh himself during intermissions. But there was something odd and unseasonable in the way he dressed. In the summer, while the other men wore short sleeves to the séances, he piqued Margery's curiosity by wearing layers of heavier clothing.

He was prepared for the cold breezes, he told her.

Carrington was as exotic as the places he had visited. One morning he discussed a trip to Egypt and the mystical traditions there. He explained to Margery that according to *The Egyptian Book of the Dead,* the heart was the only organ to survive physical death; it was weighed against a feather in the afterlife and must be light—unburdened by the weight of guilt or sin—for the soul to survive. That day, while Roy was at the office, he taught her basic card tricks and how to make coins disappear. She was impressed with his deft sleight of hand, and, as Carrington saw, a quick study.

They talked about the medium Palladino, and Carrington's examination of her in Naples. He described his work without the scientific pretense she was used to from the others. But he had his own affectations—like the way he pronounced *séance* and *clairvoyance* like a Frenchman, and *Palladino* like an Italian. He had lived in places she had always wanted to visit, if only Roy could get away from his medical practice for more than two weeks a year. Carrington was single, unencumbered, his marriage over. She felt no guilt at what developed. On the contrary, she thought Roy would approve of their budding friendship. "Wouldn't you like to kiss me?" she asked Carrie as they embraced in front of her husband and other members of the ABC Club.

"What was I to do?" he wrote. "She was there in my arms."

The next day their affair began, but it was hard to find privacy. They often went for long walks on the promenade, where one afternoon Carrington asked her to elope to Italy with him. She let him down gently, as he seemed rather fragile to her. He had tuberculosis, which she felt explained the woolen underwear and two vests beneath a shirt and sweater in summer. Roy believed that Carrington's emaciation was the result of his crankish diet rather than any disease. Whatever the cause, the investigator was wasting away and ashamed of it. He was as light, Margery discovered, as a feather in her palm.

Onward, Psychic Soldiers

The committee would tie Margery up like Times Square traffic in
the rush hour, but that made no difference. They would set traps for
Walter but he was never caught once.
—*New York Daily Mirror*

No Houdini, your methods will not prevail. Spiritualism is
advancing by leaps and bounds, and not the world the flesh and the
devil, not even magicians can prevent it.
—*Light: A Journal of Spiritual Progress & Psychical Research*

*W*hile Houdini prepared to end Margery's run, "the big show," as Bird
called it, attracted a new set of séance-goers: a business titan and a respected local journalist. In August, Joseph DeWyckoff arrived in Beacon
Hill to witness Margery's phenomena. The steel mogul who had sponsored
George Valiantine, the committee's first candidate, marveled at Walter's
"triple stunts"—in which the ghost whistled or sang through the megaphone that appeared to swim through the air like a fish while playing the
tambourine that floated near the ceiling, or rang the bell—all with the
medium under DeWyckoff's firm control. *"Continuous performance, good
as Keith's,"* whispered Walter.

The loftier phenomena were still in development. Progress was made
toward the full materialization of a discarnate soul when a small orb shaped
like a face, perceived to be the spirit of Mrs. DeWyckoff's dead friend
Sadie, hovered near the magnate's wife. It was then DeWyckoff realized
that his international quest to find a powerful medium was over. Deeply
affected by Margery's work, the DeWyckoffs became intimate members of
the Crandon circle, although their relationship with Roy would have been
implausible were it not for their mutual interest in psychic phenomena.

Unlike the cerebral physicians in Roy's circle, DeWyckoff, a Russian
Jew, was tough and unyielding as Vanadium Steel—his industrial prod-

uct. Years earlier, he had been known to settle quarrels with his fists or his walking stick. At present he communed with spirits and gave benevolently to mediums. But the Crandons did not need DeWyckoff's money. *"Don't tempt mediums by giving them presents,"* Walter admonished him.

◆

In August, the conservative *Boston Herald* began to cover the Margery case more extensively than any other newspaper. And Walter Stewart Griscom, a thirty-six-year-old scribe from an old Philadelphia family, was the *Herald*'s chief reporter on the beat in Summerland. With no prior knowledge of spiritism, Griscom could not fathom why mediums kept megaphones on the séance table, nor the reason they gave their demonstrations from within a curtained cabinet that looked like a fitting stall at Filene's. Yet the reporter had certainly heard of Daniel Comstock—with whom he arranged an interview at the physicist's Cambridge laboratory.

"Dr. Comstock regards psychic research as the baby science of 1924," wrote Griscom. "And the attitude of the public regarding it," he quoted the physicist, "is identical with the attitude of the public toward electricity, toward radio, toward every new science that has ever been perfected." Why then did some scientists, and one notable showman, believe mediumistic phenomena to be impossible? asked the reporter.

"I didn't say it was possible," Comstock responded. "I only said it was true."

Griscom next took a ride to "quaint old Lime Street," knowing that this was not a section of town where one expected to find a practicing psychic. Margery was indeed in rarefied territory. "Should Mrs. Crandon win the $2500 prize, as it is generally conceded that she may," he wrote, "she will be the only real 100 per cent medium in this country."

Having arranged the meeting through Harvard contacts, Griscom hoped to land the first newspaper interview with Margery. Instead, he was greeted at her door by Hereward Carrington, who was there "for purposes of scientific investigation." The reporter was led through the parlor by Carrington, then into the cool dining room where Margery waited.

Unlike other newsmen pursuing her, Griscom did not smell of tobacco or look as if he had slept in his suit. But for all his geniality, he got nothing from Margery. When he asked her directly if she had already won the prize, she smiled elusively and replied, "No, not yet," then referred further questions to Carrington, who said that as a matter of fact there was "only one more test to apply to Margery to establish her as 100 per cent genuine." While Carrie praised her mediumship, Griscom jotted notes with the dexterity, thought Margery, of an automatic writer.

It rankled Houdini that Comstock and Carrington were speaking publicly about the case while he, for the most part, was abiding by Munn's order to keep quiet. Even more disturbing to him was a Margery feature in his favorite paper, the *New York World,* by Fred Keating—a fellow illusionist and alternate member of the jury. Keating said that he was baffled by the misty green lights emanating from nowhere; and the violent demolition of Margery's chamber, after which Bird had to be pulled from its wreckage like Buster Keaton when houses topple on him. Other laudatory reports, by newsmen who had never been to Lime Street—declaring the PSYCHIC POWER OF MARGERY ESTABLISHED BEYOND QUESTION—did little to deflate the messianic hopes of her more devout followers.

"The earth is in a very strained, tormented condition at present," the spirit Pheneas warned the Doyles in August. "It is like a pot boiling over with the lid on it. It may thrust the lid up." Lady Doyle, who channeled Pheneas, wrote that when the catastrophe struck, the multitudes would flock to Margery for "knowledge & hope & comfort."

Houdini, on the other hand, was seen by many occultists as the Antichrist to Spiritualism. Some in the movement saw the spirit medium as a Virgin Mary surrogate, forming spirits out of an ethereal substance thought to emanate from her vagina. They considered it sacrilege when Houdini began unmasking and defiling psychics.

Houdini "is racially a Jew," the *National Spiritualist* pointed out. To emphasize that message he was referred to as Weiss—a name he had not gone by since he was a teenager. "Mr. Weiss may pass as an expert conjurer of ephemeral importance to humanity," the occult journal opined, "but he can not qualify as an expert on matters belonging to the realm of Spiritual powers. His Special Sphere is trickery for his own financial gain."

From his higher pulpit, Walter said that defeating Houdini mattered more than the outcome of the psychic contest: *"More important than to get a favorable award is forever to wipe Houdini off the map as a ghost hunter."* The voice warned that the magician was plotting a dastardly trick: he was going to conceal an obstructive object in the bell box, so that even Walter's pseudopod would not be able to ring it. He told DeWyckoff to be on guard; and to mobilize his circle Walter led them in his variation of the Christian hymn.

> *Onward, psychic soldiers,*
> *Marching as to war,*
> *With the cross of Science*
> *Going on before!*

Enemies on two planes were allegedly after Houdini. Upon his arrival in the Hub, "he was shadowed by hostile interests," a Boston tabloid reported. "He refused to be seen at his hotel. Meeting a friend at the Back Bay railroad station, he held his conversation in a telephone booth, declaring that he was being watched and that they might be overheard." And that night, in the séance room, Walter whispered, *"I will take care of Houdini."*

Houdini's Box

Four out of the five men selected as a jury are thoroughly convinced
that the Boston woman is 100 percent genuine, and it is believed that
announcement of the award will come within a very few days.
—*Boston Herald*

Houdini announces that he will not commit himself until the tests
are over. For the general run no verdict is awaited with greater interest
than his.
—*Buffalo Enquirer*

I held both her hands and feet and still she manifested," Houdini wrote
Prince of the July séances with Margery. One month later it was time for
her to either conclusively demonstrate her psychic powers or for Houdini
to prove she faked them: "We can't both be right," he stated. If he had his
way in the August sittings, there would be no spirit raps, table levitations,
or spectral lights. But he did not appear eager to lay a trap for the medium, as the committee once did with Valiantine, by allowing her enough
freedom to attempt flimflam, and then expose her in flagrante. His intention was to prevent the phenomena from happening altogether. Houdini
wanted a blank séance, Bird warned the Crandons. He was hatching "a
very deadly plot" against Margery, Sir Arthur later affirmed. There was no
other way, the Crandon circle felt, for him to stop her from winning the
psychic contest.

Walter, who knew all, advised a way to deal with their nemesis. In the
dark, "Houdini could only win by a blank and hence he would by trickery
insure a blank," Roy explained to Sir Arthur. "Walter solved it by announcing he would give them nothing hereafter except red light phenomena."
As both the secretion of ectoplasm and production of spook tricks are
believed to require darkness, Walter's strategy defied the spiritist ritual,
whether practiced by earnest mediums or swindlers. According to Bird,

it was Houdini who inexplicably insisted that the lights be kept off at the August séances. "He gave no reason," recalled the editor, "for this extraordinary stand."

Whatever his motives, Houdini promised that he would not hinder the psychic program. "I want to give Mrs. Crandon every possible chance to make good, and if she possesses any psychic power, I will be the first to assist her in proving her genuineness," he wrote Comstock. He and his assistant, Collins, had developed an apparatus for control that would be "comfortable for Mrs. Crandon." He hadn't "the slightest wish to interfere with anything," he informed Dr. Crandon.

As for the two committeemen with whom Houdini was likely to clash, they still thought he had no business in a scientific trial. Having already made up his mind about Margery, Carrington saw no point in upsetting the séance atmosphere by knocking heads with his antagonist. Shortly before Houdini arrived in Boston, he left Lime Street. Once again McDougall was also out of town. Despite Munn's hopes for unity, Margery would not perform before the full jury.

While lecturing in Canada, McDougall made his own case for what Dr. Crandon wanted—a true metaphysical science. In his view, physical science could not address the greater mysteries—"For the atoms are gone," he said; "matter has resolved itself into energy; and what energy is no man can tell." Inspired by McDougall's argument, the *New York Herald* said that "religion is once more becoming respectable for an intellectual." Then why, Bird wondered, was the psychologist absent when a spirit medium was so close to receiving scientific sanction?

Munn and Comstock had asked Houdini to develop a method of restraint for Margery that was both foolproof and humane: an apparatus that would not inhibit the delicate formation of ectoplasm. To that end Houdini—master of escape from milk cans and torture cells—may have drawn too much from his own line of work when designing Margery's cage. Charged with the commission of controlling without disturbing the medium, he had constructed what was henceforth known as Houdini's box.

One reporter later called it "not unlike the stocks used for punishment purposes by the ancient puritans"; another saw it as "a cross between a pillory and folding bed on Tuesday night"; a third likened it to an "electric bath cabinet." But there was a logic behind the odd invention. Houdini and Collins had constructed a new kind of cabinet—one that allowed the darkness and privacy deemed necessary for the psychic while curtailing any impulse to cheat. They presented an oak box that sloped upward at the top, like the roof of a house, and contained apertures though which the medium's head and arms stuck out.

Bird, among others, feared the design was too restrictive: "the use of this cage involves the assumption that the psychic force either issues from the medium's head, or else is capable of penetrating an inch of wood," he pointed out. Prince too thought it might be impossible for the medium to perform in Houdini's box. But game as always, Margery was willing to try—even if Dr. Crandon considered Houdini's new restraint a brutish and unprecedented attempt to prevent manifestations of the spirit life. The irony of it was not lost on Walter, who composed a piece to make light of the predicament escape artists, corpses, and now his sister shared.

> *I'll sing ye a little song tonight,*
> *A song from a box that's closed:*
> *For the scientists have locked it tight,*
> *They are out to do and know.*
> *But ye can't shut a Ghost in a box for long:*
> *I'm sure to be raisin' me voice in song.*

When Munn suggested that Bird transport the box to Boston by automobile, Houdini objected that he would undoubtedly allow the Crandons to examine and find a way to undermine it. He didn't want to give them access to the box until the medium was locked inside it. So he brought his box by train to Boston himself, assembling it on August 25 in Comstock's apartment—where Walter would attempt to do what he had to every other cabinet in which his sister sat: demolish it.

Upon seeing the cabinet for the first time that evening, Margery's first request was that the six-inch-wide screen be replaced by a solid block of wood. Houdini reacted with dismay. The screen, to be placed over the region of her lap, was designed to allow her ectoplasm a point of release into the room, he explained. Margery countered that Comstock had said that if she were a fraud, she could extend wires through the screen to ring the bell box. Each time Houdini made the case for the screen, the medium repeated: "Comstock said, perhaps I could stick out wires." When the phenomena came she wanted no talk of threads, concealed wires, or anything else her critics had grasped at to discredit her.

Houdini suspected that she knew the real reason for the screen: to grant him a window into the bodily region where the tools of a false medium's trade might be hidden. Part of the answer to the Margery mystery, he believed, lay in the inventive use she made of her anatomy. He doubted if the secretaries and wives—least of all Bird's wife—who searched her prior to séances looked very carefully between her legs. The medium's argument was a sound one, though, and Houdini relented. There would be no screen in the cage.

The second of Margery's conditions was that before the demonstration for the committee, her special sitters—the DeWyckoffs, Aleck Cross, and Roy's sister Laura—had to form a "friendly circle" without the jury present. Her group needed to establish the proper atmosphere in the room, she said, and then attempt to contact Walter. Without her brother's consent on the cage, there would be no tests, she warned. Houdini agreed to this as long as he and the other judges could stay until she was securely locked in the box. While he did not say so, he thought Margery was angling for time and privacy, in order to plot a way to defeat his fraud-proof cabinet.

With the program agreed on, the medium stepped into the black box and Houdini lowered the wooden flaps, each with a half-circle that formed the opening through which her head extended. Gently, he helped her thrust her arms through the slots created for them, then locked the padlock cover. As she had requested, Munn, Comstock, Houdini, and Prince quietly left the room just as the lights were lowered. Assembling in the hallway, they heard Walter's whistle and Margery's laughter. The ghost urged his friends to *"be of good cheer."* He whispered that he *"would take care of everything."*

At 9:45, Margery's partisans, led by DeWyckoff, exited the séance room. Walter had given his OK to Houdini's black box—the sitting could commence immediately. In the agreed-upon fashion, the jury formed around the table. Houdini controlled Margery's left hand, Roy her right. Seated outside the circle, Prince grasped the handhold between the Crandons, while Comstock and Munn completed the chain. The table arranged, the red lights were turned off. Just eight minutes later, a violent, splintering noise was heard. It was the sound, Comstock realized, of Walter tearing his sister's cage apart.

The front of Margery's box had been forced open in the dark. Quick to deny the spirit a victory, Houdini explained that the fixture was secured with brass tacks: anyone leveraging their shoulders could sit in the cabinet and muscle it off. Exasperated, Dr. Crandon stood up. Neither Houdini nor Prince, he stated for the record, had given any indication that they felt the medium tense or strain—as she would need to have done in order to physically cause the phenomena. On top of that, Houdini had already admitted that any effects occurring while Margery was in the fraud-proof box had to be genuine. If the box was that secure, then how could he accuse Margery of such crude shenanigans? Houdini's offer to demonstrate how easy it would be to force the front of the cage over the staples did little to mollify the doctor. Comstock was himself miffed that the supposedly stalwart oak box could be that easily manipulated. So heated were the exchanges that Walter ordered the committee to leave and the friendly circle reinstated. After his gang returned, the spirit whistled "with his best cockiness."

At 10:35, the committeemen were invited back, with the Crandons' friends this time retiring to the back of the room—from where DeWyckoff glowered in the darkness. Though tempers had quieted, Dr. Crandon asked if Houdini had a flashlight on him. In the tone of head of surgery, the doctor warned that any white light might endanger the medium. Houdini assured him that he had no flashlight and offered to be searched if anyone doubted it. Roy dropped the matter, but there was more awkwardness when the Crandons finally realized that Bird, who they assumed was uncharacteristically late, would not be attending the test séance at all. They were given no reason for his eviction from the circle.

Exactly eight minutes later, there was another disturbance when Walter hissed, *"Houdini, you think you're smart, don't you? How much are they paying you to stop these phenomena?"*

Having canceled bookings to sit with Margery, the showman was offended. "I don't know what you're talking about," he said. "It's costing me $2,500 a week to be here."

"Where were those contracts?" Walter persisted.

"Buffalo," Houdini was about to answer when Comstock interrupted.

"What do you mean by this, Walter?" asked the scientist. "This talk isn't psychic research."

"Comstock," the voice responded, *"you take the box out into white light, examine it, and report back. You'll see fast enough what I mean."*

After doing this, Comstock announced that a rubber eraser had been stuck between the clapboards on the bell box; it now took four times more force to cause it to ring. The Crandons would later blame Houdini for trying to squelch the effect, as he was the last to test the apparatus; and they noted that the bell box had been fixed in almost precisely the way Walter had predicted days earlier. For now, though, no accusations were exchanged. Houdini swore that he hadn't tampered with the bell box. He asked Walter if the spirit thought he had. A stony silence ensued until, at 11:01, the séance ended.

If Houdini was right about Margery being a lady magician in disguise, then his fraud-proof box had not lived up to its name. He was adamant that she would not succeed again in breaking his cage. The next day he and Collins reconstructed the box in Comstock's apartment, adding thick metal staples, hasps, and padlocks to secure the top. Now let the ghosts walk! Houdini told his assistant that he had seen the Crandons huddled next to the cabinet after the séance ended. They appeared, he believed, to be measuring the opening between the top flaps for her head. It was too narrow, they had previously objected, even though Houdini felt there was ample space for the medium to stick her svelte neck out.

As Houdini and Collins worked on the black box, a third man entered the premises and approached the séance room. At that moment the phone rang, like a bell box that Walter had activated. Entering the hallway to answer it, Houdini encountered Comstock's assistant, Will Conant, who was used to entering the apartment as he pleased. Accusing him of spying for the Crandons, Houdini chased him out. He trusted no one friendly with Margery—least of all silent intruders who hovered by the séance room while he worked on the psychic's box.

Despite the rift, Houdini discovered that Margery rarely made critics feel unwelcome at Lime Street. After his run-in with Conant, Houdini arrived to inform the Crandons and their guests that all was ready for the séance that evening. The exchanges between Houdini and the psychic were refreshingly pleasant away from the Charlesgate. Margery even asked the magician, who admitted he was exhausted, if he wanted to take a nap upstairs rather than retire to the Copley. After accepting her offer, he followed her upstairs to her absent son's bedroom.

She told him that John would be thrilled to know the Handcuff King had slept in his bed. Houdini replied that he would like to meet John sometime and entertain him. Privately, though, the magician could not understand why the Crandons sent their son away from home while any scientist who could quote William James was welcome to stay there.

Three flights down, while Roy conversed amiably, Orson Munn was under no illusions that anything had changed. The Crandons and Houdini had not relaxed their mutual suspicions, though he was glad to see their clashes confined to the séance room. Sometime later, Munn heard Margery descending the staircase. Joking that she had just tucked Houdini in, she rejoined them in the parlor. Prince seemed to lighten in her presence. Roy resumed discussing a nautical adventure. The waters were deceptively calm now, thought Munn. Sail on, Dr. Crandon.

Showdown at the Charlesgate

For life is full of boxes, closed,
And death follows right along.
The only difference that I can see
Is, you sing in your box when you're gone.

—WALTER

Dr. and Mrs. Crandon knew every move that we were making.

—HARRY HOUDINI

*T*he committee could not have chosen an eerier locale than the hotel at 535 Beacon Street that rose like a castle over Charlesgate Park and its scraggy Muddy River. With its green oriel windows, stone spires and turrets, and interior courtyard, the Charlesgate Hotel was an emblem of Victorian medievalism. But the magician who walked into the green-and-gold lobby did not think a medium would have any more luck with her dark art there. When he left the elevator carriage and entered Comstock's apartment, he was surprised to see the individual he considered largely responsible for propagating her psychic humbug. Waiting for him was Malcolm Bird, who wanted to know why he had been banned from the Charlesgate séances.

At a meeting in Comstock's office, Houdini told Bird that he was not welcome because he had "betrayed the Committee and hindered their work." The Crandons, waiting down the hall, could hear every word of the ensuing argument: Houdini accusing Bird of undermining the psychic investigation, the editor denying the charge and retorting that Houdini was a blundering tyrant. Munn, who disliked acrimony, would have to either appease his editor or openly side against him. It was better for Bird not to participate in the séances, the publisher reluctantly decided. Whereupon, according to Houdini, Bird immediately resigned from the committee, realizing that no one trusted him.

Bird told it differently. He said he gave up his title because his situation was untenable: he could not continue to function as secretary and still oppose Houdini. Regardless, Prince was summarily elected as the new secretary of the contest. Bird then found himself in the humiliating position of having to retreat from the apartment and abandon the enterprise that he, more than any single individual, had created and advanced. "When do you leave for New York?" Houdini asked. "You go to hell!" snapped Bird, and then left after saying goodbye to the Crandons.

The commotion that Sir Arthur warned would ruin the *Scientific American* tests appeared to have shaken Margery. Yet she was ready to attempt another demonstration for the jury. Retiring to Comstock's bedroom, she removed her dress, slip, and stockings. Standing as naked as Houdini when searched before a jailbreak, she was examined by a female stenographer, who vouched that there was nothing on her person that God had not given her. Then, having slipped back into her garments, she entered the séance room and stepped into Houdini's box. The same group as the night before—Dr. Crandon, Comstock, Prince, Munn, and Houdini—surrounded her, while the stenographer sat in an adjacent room with sliding doors kept partially open, so that she could hear Mr. Munn dictate what followed. The locks to the cabinet were examined by the jury, and the bell box by Houdini, who stated that the medium could not reach it. Punctiliously, she requested that it be moved even farther from her black cabinet, but Dr. Crandon said that it was fine where Houdini had stationed it. Then came a reshuffling of the circle: a game of musical chairs that would have been amusing were the atmosphere less volatile. Houdini wasn't going to allow the doctor to control his wife any longer. Prince therefore assumed Roy's customary position on Margery's right. In reaction, Dr. Crandon insisted on a strict control for the escape artist. While Houdini seated himself on Margery's left and grasped her hand, Comstock, the sitter most sympathetic to the Crandons, was entrusted with the control of Houdini's left hand, left foot, and head. To accomplish this, he placed his foot atop Houdini's, then held the magician's hand high in the air, resting his elbow on Houdini's shoulder and leaning their linked hands against his head. At this point they were more intertwined, observed Munn, than Spanish dancers at the Lido-Venice nightclub.

Houdini suspected that the Crandons wanted to ensure he didn't have the range of movement to detect psychic trickery. But their object, they had said privately, was to prevent him from planting anything in the bell box or the cage that might incriminate Margery. To Munn, it appeared as if both Margery and Houdini were on trial. After he locked the door to the hallway and the light was extinguished, the most contested of Margery's test séances began. Houdini had a hunch she would attempt to smuggle into her cage an instrument to ring the bell box, which she would access while the box was being locked and before her hands were restrained. As the sitters linked hands, he watched her face carefully. By her expression and the way she tensed her neck, he determined that she was reaching for something she had dropped on the floor of the locked cabinet. Thus the magician repeatedly irritated Prince, and offended the medium, by reminding him not to let go of her other hand.

"What's the matter with you, Houdini, that you keep on saying that?" Margery demanded.

"Do you really want to know?" he asked.

"Yes," she replied.

"Well, I will tell you. In case you have anything smuggled in the cabinet-box, you could now conceal it."

"Well, do you want to search me?" she proposed.

"No, never mind, I am not a physician."

With Margery's permission, Houdini stuck his hand into her box, discovering nothing suspicious, though he could not reach to the floor— where he believed she had something stashed. But if Margery were indeed cheating, she now demonstrated why she was the match of any Ten-in-One-Show trickster who lived by their wits.

Almost immediately the medium went into trance. Walter's shrill whistle signaled his arrival in the séance room, and at once he began his attack.

"Houdini, you are very clever indeed but it won't work . . . I suppose it was an accident those things were left in the cabinet?"

"What was left in the cabinet?" the magician asked.

"Pure accident, was it? You were not here Houdini but Collins was."

Before Houdini could answer, the ghost flew into a rage. *"Houdini, you goddamn son of a bitch. Get the hell out of here and never come back; if you don't I will. What did you do that for, Houdini? You're a bastard for putting up a plant like that on a girl. There is a ruler in that cabinet."*

A collapsible ruler would be just the tool for Margery to activate the bell box beyond her reach, and Houdini believed that Walter's outburst was a sign that the medium was frustrated and trapped. It was chilling, however, what Margery's dead brother said next. *"You won't live forever, Houdini, you've got to die. I put a curse on you now that will follow you every day until you die. And then you'll know better."*

Houdini did not react to the curse. More disturbing to him was that the ghost had called him a bastard. "If a man would have said that to me, I would clean the floor up with him," he later threatened.

According to Dr. Crandon's report—which Bird, Richardson, and Doyle would publicize—Houdini reacted more like a whimpering cad: "I don't know anything about any ruler; why would I do a thing like that? Oh, this is terrible. My dear sainted mother was married to my father."

Houdini, of course, denied Dr. Crandon's account of how Walter caught him laying a plant on Margery, and how he cowered when found out. Roy claimed that Houdini bent forward with his head in his hands and cried, "I am not well. I am not myself." In a letter to Sir Arthur, he even conjectured that the trickster might have swiped the ruler from his son's room when he took his nap that afternoon.

Contrarily, in Houdini's report, this was a triumphant moment in his campaign against psychic fraud. Margery was still in her box, most likely with a pilfered device on the floor. She was trapped red-handed, he thought. No one appeared to doubt that a ruler was in the box. It was one of Walter's few claims the Great Houdini did not deny.

Houdini and the Crandons are generally in agreement on what happened next. In effect, Comstock broke up the tussle between the magician and ghost. He told Walter that his accusations and threats were detrimental to psychic research. He reminded him that rulers are used in box construction and it was reasonable to believe that one was dropped there by mistake. Since Walter had accused Houdini's assistant of the act, Orson Munn summoned the old stagehand to answer the charge. Standing under the carmine light that made all the sitters look indecent and ghoulish, Collins produced his own folding ruler from his hip pocket. To bolster his assistant's statement, Houdini made him swear on the life of his mother that he had nothing to do with the one in the box.[*]

Whatever lay in the cabinet, Houdini no longer seemed worried about it. The instrument would have no bearing on any effects that might occur the rest of the night, he promised, as the control would be too tight. Once again hands were linked and, at 9:45, the lights turned off and the séance reconvened. The atmosphere was "volcanic," Comstock later said, with the entire circle "on edge." When Walter returned, he apologized for his nasty words and asked for them to be removed from the record, but, *"being the brother of the kid,"* he said he had to defend her. In the meantime, Margery was sweltering in a box that contained no ventilation; it may have inhibited the secretion of ectoplasm, but not her perspiration.

Leaning toward the medium, so that she could feel his breath in her face, Houdini said that he could be stripped nude, searched, and locked in the box, his hands held by Dr. Crandon and herself, yet he would still ring the bell box, tie knots in a handkerchief, and rattle a tambourine.

"That would not prove anything," Comstock retorted.

"It would prove that these things could be done by trickery," Houdini declared.

Margery insisted that Houdini would have to smuggle a tool into the box to perform. The conjurer smiled in the dark: *Like you did,* he thought. He maintained that he could perform these marvels without concealing any device. "Your husband, Dr. Crandon, can search me as only a surgeon can, and I will guarantee to do these things. Do you want me to do it?"

---

* The Houdini biographer William Gresham quotes Collins, years after Houdini's death, providing a different account of how the ruler came to lie in Margery's box: "I chucked it in the box meself," said Collins, "the Boss told me to do it, 'e wanted to fix her good." Smiling slyly, the old magic assistant said, "There's one thing you got to remember about Mister 'Oudini in his last years. For 'im the truth was bloody well what 'e wanted it to be." However, Collins's supposed admission should be taken with at least one grain of witch's salt. Gresham's source for the story was Fred Keating, who endorsed Margery and had a grudge against Houdini.

She did not. She only said that if Houdini could do such wonderful things, he must possess psychic powers himself.

"I wish I did," he answered, as if disappointed that she did not want to see his tricks.

Later, when it was clear the séance was a blank, Margery grew irritated. She accused Houdini of trying to ruin her for his own financial gain. She knew that he was going to give a performance at Keith's just after the test séances were over, and it was theatrical motives, she complained, that drew him to her work.

Houdini responded that he had booked the show in June, long before the sittings had been arranged. Furthermore, he "was in demand all over the world" and could dictate his own dates. He said that he could change them, if she wanted him to, even now.

Not long after this exchange, at a few minutes to eleven, Houdini finally suggested they turn the lights on and open Margery's box. After she stepped out of it, he found, sure enough, a ruler on the bottom that folded up into a six-inch length. Munn noticed that Margery looked depleted, while Houdini was energized: as if he, rather than the psychic, had absorbed the séance charge. And yet, Dr. Crandon recalled that after discovering the ruler, the magician cried, "I am willing to forget this, if you are!"

The doctor's account of Houdini expressing tacit admissions of guilt had a false ring to those who knew him. In fact, neither the Handcuff King nor the Spiritualists were going to let the incident lie. "I do not think," Sir Arthur later said, "that it should be forgotten or that it will be forgotten." But the Margery mystery was not Sherlock Holmes's case. The next morning, Houdini wrote Walter Lippmann at the *New York World* to say that he had unmasked the medium whom Bird had "failed to detect" in forty sittings. He had "stopped her manifestations. One more séance this eve. & will be back if nothing happens."

◆

The next day Margery granted the *Herald Tribune* her first press interview, though she avoided discussing her contest with Houdini. She was even less forthcoming about her past. "Mrs. Crandon refused emphatically to tell anything of her childhood, although it was suggested that this might throw some light on her claimed powers." Yet the medium seemed "eager for conversation not related to things psychic." The box that curbed her phenomena had not dampened her zeal. "An attractive figure sitting at the wheel of her large automobile or receiving in the handsome home that is tucked away in the eminently respectable Back Bay," she was the girl next door, provided the girl was "vivacious and comely" and her home a vortex for the ghosts of the departed. What had happened, though, at the Charlesgate séances? Where she had recently produced psychic terminals that battered cabinets and elevated tables, now her force seemed weaker than a dead galvanic battery. Her powers being a mystery even to her, she could not say why they were failing, but the test séances, she reminded her interviewer, were not over yet.

◆

The group that sat together in the Margery séances, no matter how in-harmoniously, also ate together. Despite the strife at the Charlesgate, the medium dined with Houdini after her newspaper interview, along with Munn and Prince, at a suburban restaurant that was safe from prying eyes and newspapermen. This time, however, the tension between Margery and Houdini had not diminished overnight. Dr. Crandon sat next to his wife at séances because she said he calmed her, and that afternoon, while he at-tended to his medical practice, Margery seemed agitated at a dinner that included none of her admirers. By Houdini's account, she was sure that he was going to denounce her to his Boston audiences. She warned him that her supporters—led by Joseph DeWyckoff—would turn violent if he at-tacked her from his vaudeville pulpit.*

---

* In the confidential report that Houdini submitted to the commission he makes no mention of Margery's threats. His account of this conversation appears in a pam-phlet he published two months later, that revealed how he exposed the tricks of the Boston medium.

"If you misrepresent me from the stage at Keith's some of my friends will come up and give you a good beating."

"I am not going to misrepresent you," he replied; "they are not coming on the stage and I am not going to get a beating."

The medium was not consoled, as Houdini recalled. She repeatedly told him about her twelve-year-old and how she did not want him to grow up and read that his mother was a fraud.

"Then don't be a fraud," he advised.

When the Crandons appeared that evening for the final sitting at the Charlesgate, Margery, looking refreshed and never more feminine in her green kimono, expressed the hope that they might have "a good-natured séance." Houdini, meanwhile, who had brought an athletic suit, seemed ready for a physical contest: the dark sport of trapping crooked psychics. He wanted to prove he carried nothing—flashlights, rulers, and so on—to concern the Crandons, hence a getup that was like a bathing costume. Alas, Margery told him that his street clothes were sufficient for the gathering—a plea that denied the circle the fitting image of Houdini clad for manly competition seated next to the medium in her boudoir attire.

But when the lights went out, his might was diminished. All his career Houdini had been developing his prowess, as if for some consummate test of his strength and wiles. Yet while idolized for his strenuous feats, he had an infertile union with his wife. His most ardent relationship had been with Cecilia Weiss. Bess, for whom he prided himself on being "a good boy," became more mother than mate. Though Houdini had a secret affair with Jack London's widow, he exhibited a curious prudishness with women: it was rumored that he was uncomfortable kissing his movie heroines, and was incensed when years earlier two of his brothers formed a love triangle with the same lady.* At present Houdini felt threatened by a medium who was openly seductive, as if he and Margery were replicating a mythic contest—male strength and rectitude versus female sorcery.

---

* Houdini's brother Nathan lost his wife, Sadie, when she fell in love with their older brother, Leopold.

Margery had tried to vamp him in her own son's bedroom, he told Prince, and when seduction failed, her husband purportedly tried to bribe him at the final Charlesgate séance. "While we were waiting there for something to happen and her reputation depending on my report," Houdini recalled, "Mrs. Crandon said she hoped that I would be seized in a trance, which would be a wonderful thing." The doctor then added that if Houdini were entranced that evening, if the magician could only see the spiritist light, he would give $10,000 to charity.

"It may happen, but I doubt it," Houdini said.

When friends of the Crandons heard of the accusation, they found it absurd: the righteous Dr. Crandon would not have attempted to bribe Houdini, let alone at a test séance in front of the jury. The charge was another of the magician's attempts, they believed, to defame the couple. No one contested the lack of mediumistic phenomena, though, on the evening of August 27. The group sat for some time while Margery moaned and perspired in her box, but there were no manifestations. Not a single desultory rap. No whistles. No ringing of the bell. No shaking of the cabinet.

Houdini had apparently prevailed. He had proved that when he applied his control the revelations stopped. It was disappointing for Roy to see his wife so inhibited by Houdini's box that nothing happened. Where was Walter? The jury waited for an hour, but there was not a word from Margery's spirit guide. Her final séance at the Charlesgate was all darkness and silence, and the discomforting suggestion that death is an eternal blank.

The Postmortem

*I*t must have been a spirit's invisible hand, as much as Malcolm Bird, that guided Mina Crandon from privileged obscurity to the front pages. While she had never aspired to be the avatar of the Spiritualist revival, she took on the role when the committee of judges had seemed ready to endorse her powers. The contest in which she participated was the platform, distinctive to a wishful age, for an inquiry into spiritistic phenomena. However much Bird denied that the ultimate goal was to determine whether the dead survived—declaring instead that the magazine only wanted to find a genuine clairvoyant—to the press the venture was the Quest Eternal. All of the candidates claimed to draw their occult forces from the spirits, and all had swiftly been declared delusional or fraudulent. Then came Margery, the medium who had led ninety-three séances, many of them said to be convincing, that were observed by various members of a jury of experts. Had communications with departed souls finally been proven? "While thousands of persons interested in spiritualism throughout the country are besieging the office of the *Scientific American* for an answer to their question, excited by the publicity given the investigation of Mrs. Crandon," a Hearst reporter wrote, the "answer remains the same."

"No," said her champion at the magazine. Although Malcolm Bird had attested to her psychic powers, he could not attribute them to any discarnate agency. "I do not mean that the theory of spirit forces as a possible explanation would not be considered, but this theory would be only one of countless possibilities."

But had Margery at least demonstrated bona fide supernormal powers before the committee?

"No," said Harry Houdini.

While the Handcuff King respected Orson Munn's order to keep quiet until the proceedings were over, in his confidential report to the commission, his triumphal postmortem of Margery, he determined that all of her effects had natural causes.

"I charge Mrs. Crandon with practicing daily her feats like a professional conjurer," he said, adding that her training as a secretary and cello player made her "resourceful to the extreme . . . She is not simple and guileless, but a shrewd, cunning woman." Without making clear how her music practice and secretarial experience abetted her mediumship, Houdini claimed to know a fellow trickster when he saw one. Margery had mastered "some of the slickest methods, I have ever known," he wrote Harry Price, an interested investigator with the English SPR, "and honestly it has taken my thirty years of experience to detect her in her various moves."

The experts and other informants who had been at the Charlesgate tests disclosed enough for newsmen to presume that Houdini had dealt a mortal blow to the hopes of the *Scientific American*'s only legitimate candidate. "The sad report comes from Back Bay that a formal test of Margery's power before the scientific jury turned out to be a blank séance," said the *New York Tribune*. By all indications she had lost the big prize that had seemed to be hers for the taking. "We are still far away from the spirits," announced the Boston papers.

Appearing at Keith's, Handcuff Harry was once again the Hub's unparalleled occult performer. The *Boston Transcript*, the favored newspaper of Beacon Hill society, called him "Unconquerable Houdini," the "marvel of the century" to his audiences. Contrary to Margery's fear, he did not denounce her from the stage. Without mentioning the spirits, he presented the vaudeville feats that had made him famous. His hair had "grown a bit thin at the temples," his athletic frame "inclined to stoutness," but he had lost none of his verve. The escape artist performed the old East India Needle Mystery as cleverly as ever. He slithered through Metamorphosis with Bess, still limber at forty-four, even though she rarely shared the stage with him anymore. And for the main feature he demonstrated his excruciating straitjacket caper. "He bows and is gone," said the reporter. "He has lived up to his reputation."

A Drawn Battle

PSYCHIC EXPERTS FALL OUT OVER SÉANCES OF "MARGERY"
—*New York Evening Post*

MARGERY WILL CONTINUE TESTS
Medium Not Affected by Row Between Houdini and Bird, Which
Caused Latter's Resignation
—*Boston Post*

*U*nsurprisingly, there were two perspectives on the Charlesgate séances: Houdini's and Dr. Crandon's. Some tabloids reported that the Crandons were depressed after the sittings there, yet, by Roy's account, it was a triumphant ABC Club that gathered at Lime Street on the night after Margery's last encounter with Houdini. When Walter came through with his most cheerful whistle, he was "greeted with a recital of his wonderful achievements of the last three nights—namely, the discrediting of Houdini in the sight of the Committee." During the exchange, Walter revealed that although Houdini's box was fixed, the magician's ally, Prince—whose honesty few ever challenged—was guilty more of dimwittedness than malice. So spot-on was the ghost's imitation of Dr. Prince's querulous voice that even Aleck Cross, usually not responsive to séance hijinks, laughed heartily.

The tone in the room changed when Walter promised that if the magician lied on the stage, he would *"finish him."* The voice made clear why Houdini had responded so emotionally when sworn at for laying a plant on Margery. According to Walter, Houdini's parents had not been married when he was born; he had entered this world a bastard and would leave it, the ghost whispered, with a legacy as wretched as his birthright.

For the remainder of the séance, Walter and his friends rehashed how he had exposed Houdini's subterfuge. But where, a sitter asked, was the spirit last night, when the Charlesgate was dead quiet? Walter had been watching over his sister, he answered, but was unable to manifest given her depletion of ectoplasm.

The next day Dr. Crandon began disseminating his record of the events to interested parties in Boston, New York, and London. Aghast at Roy's report on Houdini's misconduct, many of them rallied around the psychic. "Surely the Committee will not stand for this," Sir Arthur complained to Bird, "and will protect a very self-sacrificing lady against such attempts upon her honor. I trust the matter will be most fully ventilated in the Press. It is a complete exposure—but not of the medium." Carrington was as outraged: "I never heard such terrible stuff in my life!" he wrote Dr. Crandon; "I would have given a lot to have been present at that sitting when H. wept!"

Their effusive support heartened Dr. Crandon—whose admiration for Doyle "merges into love," he told Sir Oliver Lodge. And just as Walter had urged, the Crandons prepared for another round of the test séances that were apparently not over.

Malcolm Bird, who had always sought a physical explanation for supernormal manifestations, claimed that Houdini's thick oaken box had only succeeded in temporarily cutting off the psychic current. But since she hadn't lived up to Bird's panegyrics, the *Scientific American* and its editor had some explaining to do. Though they had promised more reports on the candidate, the September issue, for the first time in twenty-six months, carried no psychic story of any kind. Instead, Bird explained in his column why they had pulled their latest article on Margery. He said that two of the judges (Houdini and Prince) had threatened to quit if the magazine continued to publicize her work before their verdict was delivered. With a scientist's disdain, Bird accused the scandal sheets of causing the misunderstandings and discord. At the same time, publisher Munn, as if to refute the rumors that he had banned Bird from the contest, announced his promotion from associate to managing editor of the *Scientific American*.

In a sense Bird was right; the newspaper coverage was so mercurial that headlines seemed written in quicksilver. Soon it came out that, aside from Houdini, the committee was not ready to dismiss the psychic whose manifestations had "stirred the scientific world." Her poor showing at the Charlesgate did not portend a negative verdict: if anything it was a hung jury. "All Boston and New York have been buzzing with the story of a *big row* in the committee"—which meant, to Houdini's displeasure, that MARGERY STILL HAS A CHANCE. To bolster her case, the candidate finally emerged from behind the veil to speak to reporters. Two days after Houdini made her dead brother disappear and seemed to dispatch her to the brimming ash can of discredited mediums, Margery presented her side of the story.

"It was not a fair test," she told the *Boston Traveller*. "Why, Harry Houdini himself admitted that a psychic rod couldn't be expected to pierce a thick wood panel." Like Bird and Doyle, Margery argued that Houdini's box was an insulator of the psychic current. And with every interview she gave, a new headline issued from the ether. MARGERY SCOFFS AT HOUDINI STATEMENT. The medium dismissed his claim that with proper control her phenomena were nonexistent—"That is untrue, at every one of a hundred sittings there has been perfect control"—and she was through remaining quiet while Bird and others defended her. "I have the greatest respect for Mr. Bird," she admitted to the *Boston Herald*. "He's a gentleman, he's my friend, but at least one member of the committee has not been acting like a gentleman."

The image of the obliging medium locked in Houdini's box made many feel sympathetic to her. One Boston paper observed that the Handcuff King had always "objected to the publicity accorded Mrs. Crandon." After her ordeal she was receiving even more attention. "I honestly want to keep my obligation to keep silent," Houdini wrote Prince, "but you must allow me to defend myself, please." Prince relayed his complaint to Munn, warning that Bird and Dr. Crandon were provoking him. "It is very unfair that criticism should be launched which affect him, while he is obliged to be silent for perhaps two weeks longer."

In an editorial on the Margery controversy called "The Quest Eternal," the *Hartford Courant* offered a prescient view: "What is evident is that the question remains unsettled." There were two views on Margery's phenomena: believers in the spirit life saw nothing to shake their faith in her, while those who denied it were calling her another pretender. "Again," predicted the *Courant*, "we see a drawn battle."

♦

Two weeks later the Crandons were in the newspapers for something other than séance research. At just before noon on September 8, Aleck Cross, the sweet and troubled British war veteran whom Roy employed as his secretary and librarian, was found unconscious in a doorway on Brimmer Street—just around the corner from the Crandons' house. It was at first unclear what had caused the deep wound in Aleck's forehead. By the time an ambulance rushed him to the hospital, he was dead. As it was unusual for a man to be discovered mortally wounded, perhaps bludgeoned, in a doorway in Beacon Hill, reporters had again arrived at Lime Street.

Dr. Crandon described the dead Englishman to the police and newsmen as a world adventurer who had served the Crown for three decades as a customs official. Yet he was so squeamish at séances that it was difficult for anyone to envision his swashbuckling past.* It was clear that he had an intense, boyish devotion to Margery, and that her phenomena changed his life. Recently, his wife had left him. She was in Canada when he died.

The details of Cross's itinerant life were related by Roy, who also told the police that Aleck had suffered several heart attacks while in his employ. The doctor believed he'd had an attack that afternoon, fell and gashed his head, then stumbled toward the doorway on Brimmer Street.

There was just one odd detail for the police to address. An unidentified neighbor had called to report an automobile crash near the spot where Aleck was found. The police investigators wondered if Cross, contrary to the doctor's statement, had been struck by the car. But no witnesses came forward and the inquiry was dropped.

When the Crandons held a séance on the evening of Aleck's death, Walter arrived and immediately said, *"You are very serious tonight."*

"Walter, I have just lost a dear friend," Roy responded. "I am asked to say something tomorrow at his grave. What shall I say?"

A short time later, Walter whispered one of his poems. In the amber light Roy recorded the ghost's elegy.

---

* Cross attended 198 séances at Lime Street.

You call it death—this seeming endless sleep;
We call it birth—the soul at last set free.
'Tis hampered not by time or space—
you weep.
Why weep at death. 'Tis immortality.

The next day Roy read Walter's poem at the funeral service for their cremated friend that was attended by members of the ABC Club and assorted lodgers from Aleck's rooming house.

Farewell, dear voyageur—'twill not be
long.
Your work is done—now may peace rest
with thee.
Your kindly thoughts and deeds—they
will live on.
This is not death—'tis immortality . . .

That night the ABC Club gathered to make contact with Aleck. When Walter came through, he was displeased to find his circle still dejected by their loss. He told them that any death should be celebrated; it was like a birthday, a *"promotion,"* not a tragedy. But the ghost could bring no uplifting message from Aleck, who would be *"delirious for some time."*

Two Gospels

Parson, there's not a harp among us, nor a white robe.
—WALTER

HOUDINI COMES TO DENVER TO KEEP GULLIBLES FROM
GOING CRAZY ON "SPOOKS"
—*Denver Post*

$\mathscr{A}$ medium is only as credible as her circle, and how curious it was, Houdini commented, that the "most marvelous manifestations occurred" when Bird and Carrington controlled the séances—yet when he took charge the dead stopped talking. As a voting member of the psychic board and a staunch believer in her phenomena, Carrington would make it impossible for Houdini to push through a blanket denunciation of Margery.

Consequently, the magician was determined to have him kicked off the jury. Born Hubert Lavington, Dr. Hereward Carrington was all pretense, Houdini claimed, when it came to his title, name, and scientific résumé. Margery's champion was a "shut-eye," he said, a third-rate illusionist who turned at least one blind eye to spookery. A prolific writer on occult phenomena, Carrington heralded certain psychics because the books that endorsed their work sold better than the ones—like Houdini's own *Magician Among the Spirits*—that exposed it, the master magician asserted.

Houdini charged that Carrington had purchased his doctorate for $75 from a bogus university in Iowa, and that his opportunistic relations with the Crandons had compromised the SciAm investigation. Dr. Crandon was offering Carrington money to fulfill his longtime ambition, Houdini added, which involved starting his own psychical research institute, while Margery tempted him with other favors. But Walter Prince *did* trust Carrington—who once held his present position at the ASPR; and anyway, he didn't have the power to grant Houdini's motion to remove him from the investigation committee. Only the *Scientific American* could do that, and Orson Munn was not going to expel another Margery supporter from the jury. Thus, the anticipated Margery decision stood in what Prince called a "comatose state," with the other committeemen sitting on the fence that separated Houdini and Carrington.

◆

CAN THE DEAD SPEAK TO THE LIVING? That fall Houdini was booked for another tour out west, in which he promised to answer the burning question. He wanted the committee to deliver its verdict on the Margery case before he left, so that he could include an exposé on her in his program. To his consternation that did not happen; Prince had promised the public further investigation and he was "opening the matter de novo."

DO SPIRITS RETURN? HOUDINI SAYS NO AND PROVES IT. One week before Halloween, Houdini was back in Denver—this time to warn about the bane of superstition. "I'm trying to regulate this spiritism flood," he told the press, "to keep half the people from going crazy on the subject of spooks, ghosts, goblins and eerie voices." The Great Houdini fervently believed in the hereafter—he was not, to be clear, speaking against Sir Arthur Conan Doyle's religion. But the spirits did not come back to rap tables, scratch messages on slates, and float lampshades across a dark parlor. "Doyle and Sir Oliver Lodge, and other big men, are leading a lot of folks to the bughouse," he alleged, "because they have befuddled themselves into believing that the dead communicate with the living."

Yet if the dead, in his experience, did not call from across the Styx, there was still a lot of noise in the spirit world. The following night, during his demonstration on the methods of false mediums, he caused "a bedlam," the *Denver Post* reported, when a former candidate for the *Scientific American* prize stood up and confronted him. The protester was the Rev. Josie Stewart, who claimed to have followed him all over the country. When she and her gaunt husband yelled objections to Houdini's anti-Spiritualist gospel, he offered the entire house receipts if the two would come onstage "and give me one message from the beyond." Undaunted, the reverend offered to "fight it out" with him the next day, before a fair-play audience. "Do it now!" voices in all parts of the house answered for him.

"She cannot come to the platform now!" shouted her husband—"her health is impaired!" Showing no sympathy, Houdini said he would only battle a woman when absolutely necessary, but the Rev. Josie Stewart was a criminal. "You stand convicted and I know it," he charged, his voice trembling, his hand pointed righteously at what he claimed were incriminating documents. "Furthermore, you are a follower of non-Godism. You cannot deny that you do not believe in God."

Drawing forth his trunks and spiritist equipment—slates, a cabinet, a séance table—and glaring from the stage lights, he offered to place them at the reverend's disposal if she would step up and summon her spirits. The medium repeated that she would only accept his challenge the following evening. Again the crowd demanded that she "do it now!" This time, though, the defiant couple sat down. "I think that disposes of the Stewart case," said Houdini. "They are unbelievers."

◆

While Houdini spoke in the West against the charlatans, Margery continued to conduct test séances in Boston. That fall Prince sat with the candidate on four occasions; McDougall was back in her circle; and Bird, though no longer representing the jury, returned several times to Beacon Hill. Due to their conflicting schedules and personalities, the investigators did not sit together. Having failed to reach a consensus on Margery, they attended her demonstrations individually, with the intention of arriving at their own independent conclusions—a state of affairs Bird lamented. "The committee is dead and doesn't know it," he said while blaming his replacement, Prince, for the disintegration of the jury.

As it happened, Prince was no closer to explaining Margery's ability to activate a bell placed beyond her reach. He wanted to see a repeat of the time she made it ring for him in clear light without her husband next to her. But the demand that she manifest in this way, without darkness, frustrated Dr. Crandon: "You write as if I were a stage manager who can turn on a show at any time and under whatever conditions you desire. Such is not the case," he admonished. When confronted with an intransigent investigator, Roy was apt to question his motives or competence. In his medical opinion,

Prince was showing signs of "a mild senile dementia." He had a systolic blood pressure over 200, and was given less than a year to live by Walter—about the same life span the spirit gave Houdini.

If the Crandons had trouble with Prince, they were buoyed by an apparent breakthrough with McDougall. The night before Halloween, Margery gave a sitting that included the English psychologist, Roy, and an inquisitive Episcopal minister, Elwood Worcester, who believed in New Thought, faith healing, auto-suggestion, and psychoanalysis—all of which he blended with Christian sacrament. Dr. Worcester tied Margery's ankles together, then roped her to McDougall for good measure. To his astonishment, the Victrola began to sputter as soon as the lights went out, and minutes later the bell box pealed. Roy turned up the red light. The bell rang while the puzzled cleric carried it around the room. It stopped on command then rang again. This time Worcester could see the spark on the contact plate: the connection had to be caused, he surmised, by an invisible force rather than hocus-pocus.

From there on, Worcester added psychical research to his metaphysical interests. Roy felt the real triumph, though, was in nudging the skeptical McDougall toward belief in the medium he had once doubted. "I think we have McDougall committed," he told Sir Arthur. With Carrington convinced and Comstock and McDougall evidently leaning toward a positive verdict, Margery was ringing her way to a clear majority on the jury. Dr. Crandon believed "they were on the verge of a real victory," so long as McDougall committed to a vote for Margery.

"I agree that the bell-box phenomena are very impressive but I cannot say outright that they have convinced me of their supernormal nature," the psychologist wrote Dr. Crandon. "My slow caution must seem excessive," he admitted. "But you must remember that for me this is my Rubicon." It was a crossing he was not yet ready to make, though the bell box rang all fall. A signal for Houdini that once again he was needed in Boston.

◆

The medium who was giving her life—literally, Mark Richardson later said—to psychic research, did not reserve her gifts solely for friends and scientists. "Almost overnight 10 Lime Street became the Mecca for pilgrims from all over the world," Richardson recalled. Two nights a week were reserved for the seekers, their names taken from a long waiting list, who were neither friends of the Crandons nor psychic investigators. They included ministers of all faiths, lawyers, engineers, businessmen, mechanics, and schoolteachers. Unlike the scientists, the lay circle sought to be spiritually enlightened. In addition to wanting to witness her famous physical effects, each new visitor "brought with him his full quota of pet questions as to life here and hereafter.

"Such extravagant hopes were to be blasted immediately," Richardson noted. Many sitters became convinced that Walter truly was a discarnate personality, but he was one spirit never eager to describe the life eternal. Language, he explained, was inadequate to convey a picture of his dimension. No disembodied being could describe their existence in a way that was understandable to the living. "As to conditions in the next world, Walter has told us little," Richardson admitted.

Walter only said that after dying he had lingered in a sleeplike state while reliving his earthly experience. He awoke after death to find himself with new senses and powers, and a psychic connection to his loved ones still in their bodies. While dismissing visions of angels, harps, and golden cities, he made it clear that disembodied life was unimaginably pleasant. Our physical perception was as crude and narrow as the vision of a frog in a well, he said. Not even mystics could know what it was like when *"the silver cord"* was broken. Above all, death was not to be feared. No medium who made the crossing in her psychic sleep ever wanted to return to the earth plane, he told the circle. It was even more difficult for Walter to come back, yet he could not leave them until he had developed the kid. He was like the signal and she the receiver. But *"conditions must be right in order to tune in successfully. If things go badly you don't throw away the radio."*

Sometimes Margery channeled an intruder that blocked Walter's otherwise strong signal. During a séance in October, Dr. Crandon became alarmed when ghastly snarls were heard from the floor of Psyche's cabinet. Minutes later Walter whistled a weak greeting. He said his force was low and that he wouldn't be able to do that much for them. After some perfunctory bell work, and poor prospects for anything else that evening, a conversation began between the ghost and the minister who wanted to know what it was like to cross over.

Walter told Dr. Worcester that he would find as many descriptions of the afterlife as there were discarnates to convey them. What was his? the minister persisted. Walter answered that after leaving his body, his impressions were very much of the earth plane. It was like waking up in a strange hotel, he whispered, after dreaming of himself in a box and his mother and sisters crying. He knew he was dead, but he wasn't ready to leave them. Was he happy to realize that he had survived the grave? Worcester asked. *"No,"* Walter replied. *"I was the first in my family over here."*

Margery stirred, as if to awaken from her trance, while Walter explained that at first he was *"homesick and lonesome."* He had wanted to finish out his life on Earth as other people do. It was more difficult, he said, for those who died suddenly. The ones with lingering illnesses drifted unconsciously to the next world and back, but he wasn't ready to leave the physical plane, and so he hadn't. Dr. Worcester wanted to know if he could see the sitters, as he had seen his family when they buried him. Walter answered that he perceived rather than saw them, and that, in any case, the physical world was as unreal as a movie; all earthly strivings were absurd—why did they think the kid laughed so much at these gatherings?

Then what should they be attending to on their plane? Worcester inquired. Your thoughts, the ghost responded. Thoughts were *"things,"* he whispered. *"Look out for them; they go on forever."* As Walter spoke, Roy, straining in the red light, recorded his statement. Suddenly the ghost chortled at his brother-in-law's stenographic frenzy. *"We have imported ten thousand dollars' worth of pens over here for his use when he gets here."* The sitters echoed his laughter. Walter then wished them *"Good night."* And when he was gone, his sister returned to them.

She Did That with Her Hair

BITTER PSYCHIC CONTROVERSY RAGES AROUND BOSTON MEDIUM
—*Springfield Union*

HOUDINI REPORT CALLS MARGERY'S "SPOOKS" BOGUS
—*New York Herald*

HUSBAND OF MARGERY ASSAILS PSYCHIC TESTS: HOUDINI IN HOT RETORT
—*Boston Herald*

DO SPIRITS RETURN? It appeared that the jury was no closer to answering the question when in October the *Scientific American* released its preliminary determination on the Boston medium. There was still no consensus as to whether Margery deserved the psychic prize. The only two judges who had made up their minds disagreed on whether her phenomena were supernormal. As a result, the Crandons were disappointed, Houdini frustrated, and most others unsatisfied with the ambiguous outcome of a seven-month investigation. No matter the lofty goals involved, many saw the psychic challenge as a match between Margery and Houdini—and an announced winner, and loser, had seemed imminent. Few were expecting a draw. After a fifteen-round match in Shelby, Montana, no one had raised the arms of both Jack Dempsey *and* Tommy Gibbons, declaring them co-victors simply because Dempsey had failed to deliver the knockout blow that was expected. The jury that decided the Miss America contest hadn't announced that, as some of them preferred the Mary Pickford type and others the Gibson Girl, they could not choose a winner from among the teenagers who paraded across the Garden Pier in Atlantic City. No dance marathon ever ended indeterminately, with the prize money pocketed by the owner of the dingy hall that sponsored the competition, because after forty-eight hours it was deemed too dangerous for the two couples still on their feet to continue to shuffle.

Hereward Carrington, at least, was ready to vote. "As the result of more than forty sittings with Margery I have arrived at the definite conclusion that genuine supernormal (physical) phenomena frequently occur at her séances," he reported. Walter Prince provisionally disagreed; Comstock too said that "rigid proof has not yet been proven." They both called for further testing in visible light, while the elusive McDougall could not be reached for his decision. Houdini, conversely, saw no reason for additional trials. "Everything which took place at the séances which I attended was a deliberate and conscious fraud," he asserted.

Aside from presenting the jury's preliminary findings, the *Scientific American* issued no statement of its own on the medium. Unlike the tendentious articles that Bird used to write, the new psychic editor, E. E. Free, flatly affirmed that the journal's duty was to pay the award if the committee directed it, but to otherwise keep quiet until the jury reached a final decision.

◆

Even confined in a box, Margery had unleashed more mischief than Pandora, Houdini believed. And with the expert opinions on record, his gag was off and he could publicly accuse her of deception. The day after the *Times* published the committee's report on the medium, he released an incendiary pamphlet—*Houdini Exposes the Tricks Used by the Boston Medium Margery*—a detailed and damning account of the five séances he'd had with her, complete with illustrations of her effects and diagrams of the alleged trickery behind them. The Hearst papers published his accounts in a series that revealed Margery as a deft and acrobatic medium. Under manual control, she frees her feet to ring the bell box, leans forward and uses her head to raise the séance table, then balances the megaphone like a dunce cap before sending it hurtling toward Houdini. Though no medium was more artful, Houdini claimed to have unveiled all her maneuvers. The supposedly solid spirit cabinet that she propelled across the room, tipped over, or demolished, was rigged to collapse, he charged. What's more, she had accomplices—Bird and Carrington—to help her in the dark, as well as a husband who had attempted to bribe him. When her confederates were absent, she had tried to smuggle an extendable ruler into her box, but he caught her red-handed with the bell-ringing object.

Released while he was lecturing on spirit fraud, Houdini's exposé cost him as much to publicize as the *Scientific American* was offering in prize money to the psychics. Soon he was giving popular exhibitions on how he unmasked Margery, while his tour wound slowly to Boston.

Spiritists at every stop turned out in defense of their medium. CAN THE DEAD SPEAK TO LIVING? After Houdini answered the question negatively while exposing Margery's methods at Orchestra Hall in Chicago, legions of her supporters staged a protest in the same auditorium: HOUDINI DRAWS WRATH OF 1,500 SPIRITUALISTS, the *Chicago Tribune* reported. "No man has the right to get on a platform and ridicule a religion," declared the president of the Illinois State Spiritualists' Association. The speaker went on to praise Bird and Carrington and then—after more haranguing of Houdini—attempted to give an exhibition of the kind of supernal force the magician was discrediting. Working with the psychic auras of volunteers from the audience, he healed one man's rheumatic pains while failing to cure two others of the nervous spasms that were their chief complaint that evening.

Houdini was galvanizing, as only he could, a psychic army of enemies— not to mention the disfavor of researchers who felt he was the rogue in his own narrative. "I have just got the loan of one of Houdini's pink pamphlets," wrote Robin J. Tillyard, an Australian biologist sympathetic to the Crandons. "It shows Houdini up pretty badly. One can only conclude that he saw in Margery a performer far superior to himself and, taking the bull by the horns, resolved to ruin her."

In defense of the medium, Dr. Crandon gave the *Boston Herald* his ninety or so transcripts of the séances for the SciAm judges—a veritable Book of Margery. These records, kept by Drs. Crandon and Richardson, had been signed at the conclusion of every séance by each judge—including Houdini after each of the five demonstrations that he witnessed. "A fact is a holy thing," Dr. Crandon told Stewart Griscom; and his reports indicated that under "perfect control" phenomena occurred. "The wonder is that there has been any semblance of success," Roy stated, "considering the atmosphere of distrust, criticism, and hatred that has been exhibited by the committee."

Though Dr. Crandon wanted to avoid "mud-slinging," one of the judges, whom he didn't name, had tried to plant a carpenter's ruler at the Charlesgate sitting, for the purpose of discrediting the medium. The doctor felt it was the duty, "as gentlemen," of all members of the committee to publicly denounce this investigator. For this reason, and because the judges had apparently forgotten the records they signed, Dr. Crandon suggested that Orson Munn rename his jury "The *Scientific American* committee for the prevention of psychic phenomena."

◆

While not the journal of the upper crust, the *Boston Herald* won its first Pulitzer in 1924. An old daily known for solid reporting, it was becoming the paper of record on the Margery mediumship—and by December most revelations in the case were first published in the *Herald*.

Having taken Dr. Crandon's statement, Griscom sought out Comstock and McDougall the next day, to determine where they stood on the controversy. The headline of the story of December 19, LOCAL MEN HOLD HOUDINI UNJUST TO MRS. CRANDON, made it clear that they sympathized with the psychic. The commission may not have been in unison when judging Margery's phenomena, but with the exception of Prince, it was of one voice in condemning Houdini as "prejudiced" and "unfair" to Margery.

At Harvard, Dr. McDougall described the experiments with the bell box that he and Elwood Worcester were conducting with Margery. "I am not prepared to revise all my ideas of the laws of nature because a bell rings a few times on a table in semi-darkness," McDougall clarified. But he was inclined to attribute Margery's work to psychic force, if the bell box continued to ring under experimental conditions and if other tests proved positive.

While sitting in his Harvard office, the professor slammed Houdini for asserting that he had saved a misguided committee from awarding the psychic prize to Margery. "I do not require Houdini to teach me something about which I probably know more than he does," McDougall snorted. Indeed, he announced that the Margery case would be decided by Prince, Comstock, and himself—"a definite statement of belief from any one of us would award the prize to the Crandons."

At the Charlesgate Hotel, where the Margery mediumship was supposed to have received its deathblow, Griscom interviewed Daniel Comstock, whom he found more supportive of Mrs. Crandon than in his statement for the *Scientific American.* The substantiation of a mental force was Comstock's mission, and he wanted to complete his experiments with the medium that was his conduit. He said that just as radio activity and our new knowledge of the atom had revolutionized physics, so would certain physical laws have to be refashioned—because psychic energy had been "proved beyond question."

Margery was just one of such cases, Comstock said, though she was by far "the most interesting and promising" medium that he knew of. He doubted that the spirits were behind her mysterious phenomena, but neither did he share Houdini's belief that she was a world-class conjurer. He recalled how when he placed one hand tightly over her mouth and nose, and the other over Dr. Crandon's, Walter's voice still spoke to him. "How or from where it came I don't know. But it came."

In addressing her recent failure to perform in his apartment, Comstock speculated that the séances were blanks because the atmosphere was explosive and hostile. He said that Houdini "appeared to be convinced in advance that the phenomena were fraudulent and always reasoned from that basis. For instance, in discussing a certain test he said to me, 'She did that with her hair'"—an accusation that Comstock found unlikely. While it was still not certain that Margery's manifestations were caused by psychic power, he said that he was willing to bet they were, and bet heavily.

It Was Some Party, Wasn't It?

When the light was extinguished,
She covered me warm,
And prayed to the angels
To keep me from harm—
To the queen of the angels
To shield me from harm.

—EDGAR ALLAN POE

*A*ny vindication for Margery when the Hub experts rebuked Houdini was as short-lived as a winning streak by the hapless Boston Braves. Before the ABC Club could revel with Walter over the good press the previous day, the *Herald* published another scoop—this time an interview with a man who knew Mina as intimately as Dr. Crandon, yet supported Houdini's contention that she was neither the Beacon Hill matron nor the bona fide medium she seemed to be.

Stewart Griscom was beginning to suspect that Margery's pleasing scent inevitably threw investigators off the right trail. The public deserved to know more about Mrs. Crandon, he said, because her background and experience should have a strong bearing on whether her psychic work was accepted as genuine. On December 19, Margery's past life was unveiled on the front page of the *Herald*—right next to a photograph of President and Mrs. Coolidge posing awkwardly in skis on a snowless White House lawn. Griscom had found and interviewed Mina's first husband, a Faneuil Hall grocer named Earl Rand. And the exposure of her common background—she had been married to a lowly shop owner on Tremont Street!—diminished the aura that had made her seem more trustworthy than less cultured psychics.

Earl Rand had been introduced to Mina Stinson in early 1909 at the Union Congregational Church, where she was employed as a secretary. She lived then with her mother, Jemima, and her older siblings, Clara and

Walter—who worked for the New Haven & Hartford Railroad. It did not take a long courtship to get her away from Clara's South End boarding-house, and by the following year she and Rand were husband and wife. The couple had a son, Alan Rand. They toiled together at the provision store not far from their home, but Earl recalled that they "enjoyed the hard climb."

The Rands lived together uneventfully until 1917—when, complain-ing of stomach pain and fearing appendicitis, Mina was admitted to the private Dorchester Hospital where Dr. Crandon was on staff. Not long after Mina's acquaintance with Roy, she and her husband began to fight. Following a violent disagreement she abruptly left him on Christmas Day. A few weeks later, in January 1918, she sued the "cruel and abusive" Rand for divorce and custody of their son. By the fall, she and her son had made the short but uncommon move from South Boston to Beacon Hill. She had wed Dr. Crandon—her surgeon, savior, and proud skipper of a yacht that carried her to waters that Rand considered out of her depth.

While many details, including her childhood in rural Ontario, were not included in the *Herald* article, enough was said to indicate that Margery's pedigree was acquired when she moved to Lime Street. More damaging was the statement her former husband made about her psychic work. Rand said that she had never displayed any clairvoyance when she was his wife. Margery the medium was a stranger to him; they hadn't spoken since their divorce. Yet he claimed there were no hard feelings between them—even though Roy had adopted his son and renamed him John Crandon. Earl had also remarried and the Crandons bought their produce from him; the grocer insisted he had no ax to grind. But from what he had heard from Mina's mother, with whom he still talked, it was Walter, rather than Houdini, who was the séance autocrat. The ghost had banished those from the circle, including Mina's sister, who doubted he was real. Jemima, how-ever, was always welcome—and at one recent gathering she heard Walter promise that Houdini would be dead within a year.

"What do you think of spirit manifestations?" the reporter inquired.

"Bunk," Earl Rand replied.

The next day reporters from other newspapers descended on the shop on Tremont Street. Once again Rand was asked what he thought about

Mina's psychic gifts. "Ridiculous, absolutely foolish," he declared. "While Margery was my wife she never had any spiritualistic powers. She took lessons on the cornet before we were married. She tried the cello and she could play a few pieces on the piano, but I never knew her to be able to talk with ghosts."

♦

The *Herald* conducted a parallel investigation into Dr. Crandon's past and uncovered material that also suggested deep wrinkles beneath the polished veneer. Like Mina, the doctor did not like to discuss his matrimonial history, and for good reason, Stewart Griscom believed. In the summer of 1904, six years after finishing medical school, Roy married Annie Lawton, a petite and diffident girl. Their union produced a daughter, if not a happy home. The doctor routinely came home late, and Annie suspected he was unfaithful rather than detained by hospital work. On their fourth anniversary, Roy said their marriage was all a mistake. He needed his freedom, he explained. The doctor urged her to take their daughter to Europe for an extended trip, and then to return and divorce him.

After many months, Annie did reluctantly sue him for divorce. On the witness stand in Reno, she said that while Dr. Crandon was wealthy from the sales of his medical books and other enterprises, his fortune was never what she sought. "I wanted the love and protection of a husband and not money," she quietly sobbed. Later she would marry one of Dr. Crandon's best friends and move to Palm Beach. With his marriage dissolved and his daughter far away, the doctor had his freedom. Three years later, he was ready nonetheless for another attempt at matrimony.

In December 1914, a Maryland belle named Lucy Armes—formerly married to a US Navy doctor from Alabama—exchanged vows with a distinguished Old Yankee. Lucy, who deferred to no male authority, could not have been more dissimilar to the first Mrs. Crandon. She had the temperament of her father, Col. George Armes—an impulsive hero of both the Civil and Indian Wars; and in the beginning Roy admired her dash and fiery convictions. She was an active suffragette and aspiring actress, pursuits that he supported. But regrettably, he found that Lucy's aristocratic charms faded with familiarity. She was relentlessly demanding, had a violent temper, and was even more insane, Roy's friends came to feel, than her volatile father. Cruelly inattentive to his compliant first wife, Dr. Crandon suffered at Lucy's hands.

One morning, a few months after their wedding, Roy was boarding the *Black Hawk* off the coast of Camden, Maine, when he noticed a small skiff drawing near. In it were Lucy and a strange man, returning from an all-night spree. After being taken on board Roy's schooner, Lucy flaunted her tryst to Edison Brown and other future members of the ABC Club. She had gone ashore the night before to attend a hotel dance, which, in this boondock, had ended far too early for her. So Lucy had joined a group of men, "live ones," on a motor trip to the top of a mountain she now pointed out. Shamelessly, she announced that she had returned to the hotel at four a.m.—and presumably spent the rest of the night with the local gentleman who had just rowed her, in his rumpled suit, back to Roy.

Dr. Crandon was no more constant or faithful. But the detachment he exhibited that could so depress Annie sent Lucy into a violent rage. One night, in their home at 60 Fenway, she punched him in the face and pulled his hair, saying that she was going to ruin him or, failing that, blind and shoot him. On another occasion, she attacked him in front of his friends—breaking his glasses and stomping, when he fell, on his hand. Two years into their marriage, Lucy had declared domestic war on Dr. Crandon, vowing to never provide him with what she said he wanted most: a male child.

According to court documents and old newspaper reports obtained by Griscom, the doctor, after suing Lucy for divorce, charged that she "abused and shamed him." One day Lucy showed up at the City Hospital and "uttered serious charges against him to the superintendent." She returned to their home at Fenway after midnight with three men she had picked up at a dance. As she removed her coat and lit a cigarette, one of her escorts, a Fred or Charlie, declared, "It was some party, wasn't it?" The party was just beginning. The three men remained at the Crandons' home until six in the morning, while Roy endured their carousing and liberties with his wife.

Even before Margery, Dr. Crandon had been featured in the newspapers for what became a scandalous divorce. In addition to his money, stocks, bonds, Maine cabin, and yacht, she wanted him to be her escort at least once a week; and she demanded an apology from him, in her presence, to Fred and Charlie.

Griscom had wondered why Roy, a highly regarded physician, was banned from City Hospital, where he had been an attending surgeon for more than twenty years. There were rumors, which he thought unfounded, that the doctor had been involved in a financial malfeasance of some kind; and whispers, which sounded more credible, of affairs with nurses. In truth, Roy was quietly dismissed because Lucy revealed that he was performing illegal abortions in a Catholic town.

That was why, during his divorce proceedings, Dr. Crandon happened to be working in the Dorchester Hospital when Mina Rand was admitted with acute stomach pain. Soon after examining his patient, he relieved her of the inflamed vestigial organ that was in danger of bursting and poisoning her.

Voodoo Priestess

Houdini is the opposition's last hope in condemning Spiritualism and
if he fails I don't know what they will do. I do hope that a National
worker gets him in every city he shows.
—A CORRESPONDENT FOR THE *National Spiritualist*

Death within a year will be Harry Houdini's punishment for
impugning the validity and honesty of Mrs. Le Roi G. Crandon.
—*Daily Mirror*

*T*he Great Houdini's campaign was like a maelstrom in spiritland. In
Portland, San Francisco, and Washington, DC, rackets disguised as spiritist churches were broken up. Not long after he lectured in Los Angeles,
the local police raided "seven purported psychic headquarters" and hauled
to court forty-six ministers and mediums, charging them with larceny by
"trick and device." What he never told audiences was that the legitimate
Spiritualist Church in Los Angeles had helped to drive out the rogues.

Occultists saw the local crackdowns as old-time witch hysteria. And
Massachusetts, where the Crandons were already beginning to feel per-
secuted, was where the magician appeared next. Launched on the Pacific
Coast, his anti-Spiritualist tour was going to end in a public exposure of
Margery that was booked at Boston's Symphony Hall. He had visited many
cities in 1924 and at each stop presented his renditions of her séances. "It
takes a flimflammer to catch a flimflammer," he said; upstanding men
trained to deal only with facts could not contend with a lady "whose stock
in trade is a bag of tricks."

But was she a magician or a witch? Just before Christmas, Houdini
seemed to want to demonize Margery when he told reporters that she was
trying to use the forces of black magic to bring about his death. Her threats
had been carried to him, he said, by "semi-public statements" she made "in
the name of evil spirits" against his life. Then he described for reporters the

satanic rituals he said she led. "A wax-doll image of me will be made," he claimed. "The doll will stand at the bedside of my enemy, who will prick it with pen-knife blades, while chanting certain curses characteristic of the black days of the Middle Ages."

Margery's supporters considered the charges purely an invention of Houdini's dark imagination; with each accusation of curses and covens, they heard the echo: *Burn the Wretches!* But Houdini had a way of witch-mongering while denying that his enemies had real supernatural power: he accused Margery of practicing voodoo yet dismissed her ability to harm him. "This Boston group can't even give me a pimple by sticking hat-pins through my photograph," he promised. What worried him was the credit his enemies would take should something grisly coincidentally happen to befall him. Psychics had predicted his death dozens of times, he pointed out, and one day they were sure to guess right. "Can you imagine what these worthy Boston witch-doctors will claim for their dooms brewed in tea-leaves if, by chance, I start to cross Fifth Avenue next December 21st, and don't get to the other side?" He dismissed all supernatural pretensions, whether to communicate with the spirits or to use spells to add him to the ranks of the departed.

"All talk by Houdini that spirits are plotting his death within a year is not only false but absurd," Margery retorted. "Why, I never heard of Black Magic. I regard his statements as a joke," she scoffed. Flashing a knowing smile to reporters, she suggested he was "only seeking publicity." Two days later Houdini arrived in Boston for the sole purpose of unmasking her before a local audience. "She is a fraud your honor," he said to Mayor Curley while depositing $10,000 in New York bonds in his hands. He explained that half of the deposit was to go to the mayor's favorite charity should Houdini fail to prove before an impartial committee of local newsmen, conjurers, and clergy that Margery was a cheat; the other half to Dr. McDougall—who had claimed to know more than Houdini about psychic deception—if the psychologist could reproduce any of the magician's own feats. Then, in front of a burgeoning crowd at City Hall, he did his famous needle act and other tricks.

Margery, on the other hand, had kept a low profile that December, but only because she was frequently out of town. The psychic had visited New

York earlier in the month and performed there in Orson Munn's Waldorf apartment. But she was in Manhattan for personal reasons rather than in pursuit of the publisher's endorsement.

For months Roy had been reaching out to friends in England, including the Doyles, who might be able to help him find another orphaned boy—of six to nine years old—whose parents were free of tuberculosis, syphilis, alcoholism, and insanity. One potential adoptee was found: a ten-year-old named Horace Newton, who lived in the National Children's Home and Orphanage in London.

Because Joseph DeWyckoff was a lawyer with connections in Washington, he helped to arrange the unorthodox adoption and accompanied young Horace on his passage to America. By the end of the year, the couple looked forward to the arrival of their new son, though Roy wondered if the Newton boy was young enough to mold into a Crandon.

When, on December 10, Horace and DeWyckoff arrived in New York, Margery was there to greet them as they debarked the *Aquitania*. Horace was a feisty but personable child, whom the new parents renamed Edward Winslow Crandon. But something went wrong. Ten days after the boy arrived, Margery brought him back to New York and returned him to England on the *Doric*. Horace—then Edward, now once again Horace—hadn't taken to Lime Street, preferring the orphanage.

Part VII

SPIRITS OF THE DEAD

⌗

Be silent in that solitude
Which is not loneliness—for then
The spirits of the dead, who stood
In life before thee, and their will
Shall overshadow thee; be still
—EDGAR ALLAN POE

Think of it a moment, you who doubt immortality! If Walter is a returned soul, consider what that is going to mean to the world. It will give positive proof that we, in our individuality, survive the grave.
—EDWARD COTTON, *Christian Register*

It is profoundly and sardonically humorous . . . with almost a Molière touch. It has mystery, veiled motivations, true tragedy, howling farce, and a pervading aura straight from *Alice in Wonderland*.
—STEWART GRISCOM, *Boston Herald*

Braves Curse

MRS LE ROY CRANDON
HARRY HOUDINI

Harry Houdini, magician and exposer of fake mediums, was skeptical that the curse of death, called down on his head by Margery (Mrs. Le Roy Crandon) would be effective.

Houdini displaying bonds he vowed to forfeit if he lost his challenge to Margery, Boston, 1924

1925: The Fading Light

The mercury had plummeted to the zero mark on the clear January morning when the Crandons walked down the Hill to where a shivering throng had gathered in Boston Common. They were there to witness what newspapers were calling the spectacle of the century—a sign of faith in the scientists who predicted it, since the event had yet to occur. In those same dailies were the warnings of the astrologers who feared it—at this time marriage and new business ventures were apparently not a good idea. Few really believed the expected eclipse was an omen, yet there was something primitive in the sight of thousands staring trancelike at the heavens. Vendors hawked smoky photographic plates and dark glasses through which to view the celestial effect, and it was eerie indeed, thought Margery, to see so many in the glasses usually worn by the blind beggars on Boylston Street. It seemed all of Boston had taken off work—spectators were jamming the roofs and esplanades. And the police were out in force; no one knew what lunacy was possible when the sun went out.

Even in 1925, there were distressed reactions to the kind of phenomenon that once caused clashing armies to abandon the field, and had won Columbus—when he predicted the darkening of the sun—the fealty of native tribes. Recently sects of Seventh Day Adventists had quit their jobs in preparation for the Second Coming and the end of human life. But for most of those who lived along the path—from Minnesota to Nantucket—where the eclipse could be observed, the prevailing mood was one of reverence and excitement. That morning fleets of airplanes and dirigibles took flight, as if to diminish some of the 92 million miles that separated man from the glowing orb about to disappear. Every type of scientific instrument was pointed to the sky, and radio signals were said to be exceptionally clear and crisp.

When it happened, the Man in the Street felt he had witnessed a "great show and right up to its advance notices." The Herald-Tribune *reported that*

New York was given "a thrill that no Broadway show could ever hand her, a sudden fearful impulse toward religious fervor no evangelist could ever stir within her people." Prisoners about to be arraigned in court were led outside to witness the kaleidoscopic effect. Upon hearing the eclipse described over the radio by an army pilot speeding through the air at five thousand feet, blind inmates at a Harlem sanitarium were stirred to a rapture, their imaginations more powerful than anything working eyes could see. In New Jersey a blind man, happening to stare up at the sunburst just before the sky went dark, was reported to have suffered excruciating pain and then, hours later, his sight was miraculously restored. "And yet," a Brooklyn street sweeper leaning on the handle of his shovel was heard to utter as he gazed skyward, "and yet there are people who say there is no God."

In Boston, the Crandons watched beams of light—rose, yellow, and orange-colored—dance around the sun. Almost no conversation was heard from the crowd peering from the steps, and the windows and verandas of the statehouse. There was only the sound of cameras clicking and awed outbursts as a white corona flared from the upper-right corner of the still-blazing disk. The wind suddenly shifted. The air grew appreciably colder, just as before the occurrence of spectral phenomena, thought Roy. "There she goes!" came a chorus of voices as the sun began to slowly vanish into what looked like a half-crescent moon. Struck by the fading light, the dome of the courthouse took on a greenish-gold color and the Common an unearthly bluish-green hue. In the daytime sky, Jupiter, Venus, and Mercury were observed. Dogs began to bark. Confused by the encroaching darkness, pigeons on the Old South Church on Boylston went to roost, heads tucked under their wings. And when the sun finally vanished altogether, Margery could not help but wonder if it might somehow get stuck, never to reappear, and they would live out their days in this ghostly, twilight world.

A Stormy Forum

For I have neither wit, nor words, nor worth,
Action, nor utterance, not the power of speech,
To stir men's blood: I only speak right on.
—WILLIAM SHAKESPEARE, *Julius Caesar*

*A*s Symphony Hall began to fill, there was much glancing around to see who was present for the ballyhooed event. Many spectators were dressed in overcoats and sweaters, others in formal evening attire; there were the Back Bay types, university men, Jews from Brookline. Some had the look of mystics, while a few of the more casual did crossword puzzles, as if to say what few others felt: that Harry Houdini's was just another lecture in the fancy hall—it was not as if he were going to make an elephant disappear that January 3 or free himself from some deadly snare. Yet Houdini considered this one of the most important evenings of his life, and he wanted the best in Boston, the Crandons' peers, to turn out. Conspicuously present, though never confused with the upper crust, was the blustery mayor, James Curley—waving from the first row with his wife and children. Next to them sat Anna Eva Fay, one of the most acclaimed psychics of the old vaudeville stage, and the only notable medium on good terms with Houdini, as she had admitted to him that she was a fake. Flanking the stage was the large event committee—the scores of newspapermen, ministers, and magicians whom the wizard and mayor had personally invited. But to Houdini's disappointment, two of the most well-known people in Boston did not attend: the Crandons were not going to dignify a spook burlesque, they said. Despite their absence, the crowd was excited for the show to begin. Several times applause broke out as impatient spectators called for the speaker. Finally, as the *Transcript* observed, "Houdini comes on, muscular, curly-haired, bowing, smiling, his tread resounding firmly on the boards."

As he came to the footlights the crowd expected a nifty preliminary trick. Instead the magician paused for a moment, as if the right words were more difficult to access than the hidden picks he used in his escape work. The audience did not really know this Houdini, who had no sleight of hand to open his act, no needles to swallow, no torture cell to be lowered into headfirst.

The speaker began by stressing that he was not there to attack anyone's faith. In his four circuits of the globe he had witnessed the most peculiar kinds of worship, none of which he found harmful, he claimed. He had seen a Hindu suspended by a hook that ran through his bare back and still remembered the serene expression on the martyr's face. He had watched devotees in India rolling through the streets—for none in this obscure sect were allowed to stand erect. He had met another mystic with fingernails grown through his hand, and saw nothing wrong in that ritual either. These beliefs did not threaten the public like the cult of spiritism did.

So far as the forum at Symphony Hall, he had no set speech to give. He told them that he would say what came to mind, and invited the audience to question and challenge him whenever they wished—which reminded him that he wanted to withdraw his own challenge to Dr. McDougall, with whom he had made amends. The Harvard psychologist was a gentleman and a valued colleague, he said, as the audience applauded news of their rapprochement. Houdini smiled broadly. They had always cheered him in this town.

"Perhaps some of you witnessed when I was engaged at Keith's Theatre and was hung up by my ankles and drawn up to the top of the building in a straitjacket and came down—well, the whole town of Boston whirled around me," Houdini recalled, "and Manager Larson stood there by me and I could not understand it. The town whirled around me. I said, 'I will be all right in a moment.' But my eye was the axis of the town."

His point was that spirit mediumship also distorted the senses, though he confessed that he himself had been seeking a genuine medium for thirty-five years. "If there is one, trot her out," he urged. A million dollars had been spent on psychic research over the years. Where was the proven psychic? "Trot her out!" When no medium came forward, Houdini invoked the great hopes of the past. He dimmed the lights to show stereopticon slides—for all such gatherings expected spooky photographs—of Mrs.

Crandon's predecessors: the raven-haired, blue-eyed Fox sisters, who had mystified millions when they produced the seminal spiritist effect—their galvanizing raps on tables and walls. Then came another type of phenomena, psychic slate writing, and its accompanying cult of swindlers. Houdini called a volunteer from the stage committee to demonstrate "a regulation spirit slate writing trick" of the kind made famous by Henry Slade. "I want you to watch me carefully, ladies and gentlemen, because if things are right, this will be a very extraordinary experiment—if things are right."

In preparation for the séance, Houdini asked the volunteer to hold a blank school slate on his head. Whereupon he called on "the best known spirit in the world today to give me a sign of his presence." When removed from the gentleman's head and presented to the committee, the slate magically contained the message *"My last photograph. Love to all, Walter"*—and a gruesome photograph of a dying Walter Stinson crushed between railroad cars. A pall fell over the audience. Houdini explained that it was "just one of those coincidences of fate" that he was able to obtain the picture. While the photograph was genuine, he said the slate manifestation showed "what can be accomplished by trickery." The magician who collected grisly pictures had somehow uncovered one of Walter's annihilation—an image even the Crandons didn't know existed. The committee was still gawking over it when he announced, "I think we had better have a Margery séance next."

◆

Seated near the stage, while keenly observing Houdini, was a man of many hats—none of which altered his donnish appearance. Eric Dingwall, curator of chastity belts and expert on ectoplasm, was a competent magician on good terms with the speaker. When Dingwall, perpetually lacking funds, had to withdraw from the Society of American Magicians because he could no longer afford the dues, Houdini had paid it from his own pocket. The two men were friends and colleagues. In London they had sat together with Eva C, whose phenomena both experts had dismissed. Yet as research officer of the English SPR, Dingwall's current mission was to start a new investigation of the Margery mediumship.

Because most SPR investigators did not endorse the spirit hypothesis—

the belief in the objective existence of ghosts like Walter—Sir Arthur Conan Doyle had abandoned the SPR; in particular he didn't trust Dingwall, whom he found as skeptical as any investigator in England. Still, Houdini was uneasy about where Dingwall stood on the Margery mediumship, for he had tried phoning him four times without receiving an answer. In a subsequent letter to Dingwall, he confessed to feeling slighted and wished to get to the bottom of a disturbing rumor he could not credit: that Dr. Crandon was paying the Englishman's traveling expenses.

"Everything is now ready for the exposé," Houdini announced. To simulate the séance darkness, he had just blindfolded two volunteers from the stage committee—and when he joined them in a circle, their feet controlling his feet, their hands his hands, they became the sitters and he Margery. To the delight of the crowd, Houdini, while entreating Walter to levitate the table, leaned his torso forward and raised it with his head—a maneuver he attributed to the Boston psychic. "That's exactly how she performed the stunt," he promised. "If it isn't, I lose $5,000." As the sitters were blind, Houdini described the brilliant lights zipping by them. Then he allowed one of them to verify, while still gripping the escape artist, that the spirit trumpet remained on the floor beside the sitter's leg. "Walter, pick up the megaphone," Houdini commanded. Instantly he deftly flipped the instrument onto his head, but told the volunteers it was "floating through the air." He asked a sitter in which direction he wanted it to fall: "To the right?" As the crowd roared, Houdini deposited it there.

Next came the bell box demonstration, the unveiling of Margery's most convincing scientific feat. To leave no room for mystery, Houdini showed how, with his hands and feet controlled, he could thrust himself toward the table and ring the bell box with his forehead. He rang the bell box while it was suspended on strings and far out of reach. He rang it inexplicably, from wherever he stood and whenever he pleased. He was able to ring it when audience members called for it. He could ring it while he, enacting what McDougall had done, carried it around the hall. But he did not expect the voice that called out: "Let me see that box!"

"What's that?" Houdini asked.

"Will you let me see that box!"

To Houdini's consternation, it was his friend Dingwall making the demand. The SPR officer suspected, rightly, that Houdini was using a trick bell box rather than the model that Comstock employed. In attempting to reveal another magician's trick, Dingwall was breaking the cardinal rule of the magic order in front of a full house at Symphony Hall! Houdini looked incensed. He had always been "extra kind to Eric Dingwall," thinking no less of him for collecting pornography. He had given him inside information on the Crandons, even kept him in good standing in SAM. Nonetheless, there he was, trying to embarrass Houdini as few magicians ever had—it was as if Dingwall had informed the audience that the irons from which the Handcuff King had just escaped were fixed.

"Well, Dingwall," Houdini responded, "you here and challenging me when you know that any secret I have in Spiritualism is yours simply for the asking? You ought to be ashamed of yourself. You know everything I do is trickery."

Turning to the audience, Houdini announced that Dingwall, a representative of the Crandons, was trying to subvert a fellow conjurer's work. Those who didn't find the challenge sporting began to hiss and jeer. "Dingwall, this is not cricket," Houdini stormed. Someone urged the Englishman to step onstage and speak, but Dingwall thought better of scrapping with the Wizard of Locks and Chains in front of his fans. "Kindly address your remarks to the lecturer," he snapped as he sat back down.

Houdini explained that while Dingwall had rebuffed him as a friend, he felt that he was an honest man. Unlike Carrington and Bird, he was sure the SPR agent would expose Margery if he ever caught her in fraud. Then he proceeded with the séance that Dingwall had disrupted, though the bell the researcher wanted to examine rang no more.

Following his clash with Dingwall, Houdini's assistant hauled out what they called Margery's black box—the very one "that finished her."

"This is the box that she objected to," Houdini claimed, pointing out the armholes for ventilation and other features that made it humane. Once again Dingwall suspected that this was not the actual device the SciAm judges had used, but he held his tongue while the magician climbed into the cage. Calling for more volunteers, Houdini asked them to hold his hands. "It will not be as nice as holding her hands," he quipped while demonstrating "exactly what she did."

The Great Houdini imitated how she rose up and tore the front off the cabinet, asserting that she had the battle scars to prove his account. "You will find the bruises where she lifted up her shoulders," he vowed. But there was nothing torturous about the box itself. "I slept in it one afternoon. That is how easy it is. She smuggled a ruler in with her." And when he caught her, she called him a vile name—she said his father was never married to his mother. "Culture!" Houdini snorted. He had better ethics and manners, his gesture suggested, than the upstanding Crandons.

For the finale, Houdini called again for one of his committee to come to center stage, but this time none were eager to be his sitter—one reporter pleading a sore throat, the six others declining. An audience member was thus selected to hold Houdini's hands and firmly plant his feet on the speaker's. With a nod to Anna Fay, Houdini proceeded with the séance. "Now, spirit fizzy fizzy. That is what I say when I ask the spirits to appear. Would you mind ringing the bell, spirits?" While the volunteer confirmed that he had control of Houdini, a bell and then a tambourine rang. The audience exploded, for they observed what the sitter could not: Houdini had withdrawn his feet, leaving the man to control his empty shoes while the escape artist clanged the instruments that were gripped in his bare toes. "This and the running patter of the séance chamber convulsed the spectators," a reporter wrote. "They were getting their show."

Houdini closed the program with an "open forum." Only then was it clear that he had many critics in the house. Could he explain, one lady inquired, how the Boston medium could manifest the voice of Walter when McDougall held her lips?

"I will answer that question by asking you one. Was Carrington or Bird at that séance? If they were, they did the talking."

Later, someone called Sir Arthur the best lecturer ever to speak on mediums and spirits in this town: "I will tell you one thing, you can't fill a house like Conan Doyle did twice!"

Always sensitive to his credentials as a scholar and speaker, Houdini responded with a gratuitous sneer at Sir Arthur's literary work. "Well, all right, if I am ever such a plagiarist as Conan Doyle, who pinched Edgar Allan Poe's plumes, I will fill all houses."

After further discussion, Houdini asked if there were any more comments concerning Margery. "Anything more you want to see?" A response from far back in the house registered the general mood in the hall.

"Do some more tricks."

◆

The next day John Crandon entered the newsstand where his parents bought their papers and made a surprising request. The boy wished to buy all the copies of the *Transcript* and the *Herald,* as he didn't want his mother to read about what Houdini had said about her at Symphony Hall. Yet the coverage, at least in the *Herald,* was not entirely unsympathetic to her. There was no doubt, a reporter affirmed, that many mediums were indeed as crooked as Houdini portrayed them, but "are there not certain men and women who have the ability to utilize natural forces at present unknown, incomprehensible, beyond their power to explain? There are more things in heaven and earth than are dreamt of even in the philosophy of Mr. Houdini."

Showman and Scientist

Those of us belonging to that portion of humanity which does
not subscribe to belief in the existence of spooks should be
grateful to Houdini, the handcuff king.
— *New York Herald Tribune*

He will be a wild donkey of a man, his hand against everyone
and everyone's hand against him.
— GENESIS 16:12

*T*he Handcuff King performs alone and rarely shares the stage. Walter
Prince was the only committeeman with whom Houdini felt allied—the
one investigator he had not belittled in the newspapers or clashed with over
the Crandon case. Yet Prince, who had objected to Bird's heralding the
Margery mediumship while it was still being investigated, was not going to
abide Houdini trying the case in a concert hall. Houdini knew only that
he and Prince were of the same skeptical mind. He was mortified the day
after the Symphony Hall exposé when he read what his colleague had to say
about it in the *New York Times*.

The headline announced that the other committeemen were challenging the "Houdini Story of Margery." They wondered why the magician,
if he had detected Margery in fraud, did not expose her at the Charlesgate séances rather than at Symphony Hall. And they excoriated him—in
a statement signed by Prince, McDougall, and Comstock—for offering
no credible proof to back his argument that Carrington and Bird were in
league with Margery.

While Houdini had expected such opposition from McDougall and
Comstock, Prince's slap surprised him, since he had only said and demonstrated onstage what he and the old sleuth conjectured privately. It was
plain as day, and Houdini thought his friend saw the truth as clearly: Margery had hoodwinked a jury enamored of her class, bewitching charm,

and beauty. To convince them she used sleight of hand more befitting a dime museum than the halls of MIT and Harvard. If Prince had been there when he gave his exposé, rather than relying on the stories of yellow journalists and Malcolm Bird, Houdini was sure the chairman would see there was more truth in his stage exhibition than any scientific report on Margery.

The row between Houdini and Prince began to mirror the falling-out between him and Sir Arthur—this time with Houdini the petulant child and Prince the exasperated father. "You have been banging everybody connected with the case all over the country," the senior investigator chided him. "If you will reconsider all that has occurred I think that you will understand why I find it a little amusing that you resent a little pat at the same time that you are walloping right and left."

No one, however, was going to keep Houdini from performing what he considered his magnum opus as both a psychic detective and entertainer. His brother Bill had just died of tuberculosis and once again the magician had failed in his attempt to make contact with the spirit of a loved one. He was impassioned when he presented his Margery exhibition to packed halls in Brooklyn and Manhattan. "Houdini is the greatest showman in vaudeville today, and a tremendous draw," *Variety* marveled. "His latest act surpasses anything he has ever attempted before on account of the world-wide interest in spiritualism."

It was the same show Houdini had presented at Symphony Hall, with a few new flourishes and disclosures, such as his announcement that Malcolm Bird's relationship with Margery had just cost him his job as managing editor of the *Scientific American*. Later, though, from his office in the Woolworth tower, Orson Munn refuted everything Houdini had said about Bird at the Hippodrome. Bird had resigned, Munn attested, to attend to his "own personal business." The editor had left for a tour to promote his new book, *My Psychic Adventures*.

When the psychic challenge was first proposed by the *Scientific American* staff, Orson Munn had anticipated a popular and important inquiry; now he feared that the contest bearing the name of his journal might forever tarnish it. The investigation had turned into a Frankenstein's monster. Conceived in Munn's offices by journalists and scientists, the monster was running amok when it was never meant to leave the *Scientific American* library. In large part Prince blamed Houdini for sensationalizing the investigation. He recommended that Munn remove him from the committee while it still had some semblance of credibility.

But Houdini was now the publicly accepted voice of reason on this subject—the expert in discerning the nebulous boundary between magic and psychic manifestations. Besides, for all Houdini's self-aggrandizing antics, Munn suspected he was right, overall, about Margery. Thus he wrote the wizard a reprimand, not a pink slip. "I am not very favorable to all this controversial newspaper notoriety that is being given to this case," Munn told him. It was time for Houdini to behave, the publisher warned, like he was a member of a "truly scientific investigating body."

Rebuked by Munn, Houdini was praised in other places. Reporters noted that roles had a way of becoming reversed when magicians, professors, and mediums mixed. Houdini was now the critic, the deductive thinker, while Doyle, and even some scientists, were promoters of magic and wonder. The *Herald Tribune* called Houdini a showman with a scientist's devotion to the truth. "The dragon with which he is engaged dwells in the slough of human ignorance," observed the newspaper that shared his disdain for "the jugglery of Margery."

With Houdini heeding no more calls for restraint—he had just called Margery a "very cheap fraud"—Sir Arthur took up "the defense of the honor of a most estimable lady." Like a commander behind the lines, he had been kept apprised, by Roy, on each test séance for the committee. And in late January, he delivered to the *Boston Herald* an explosive article that he hoped would set the record straight on who the crook was.

Sir Arthur described in detail what Bird and the Crandons had never explicitly told the newspapers: how they believed Houdini had tried to sabotage the Charlesgate séances and frame the medium, and how he had cowered before the spirit who revealed his perfidy. In presenting the Crandons' version of the story, he also appealed to racial prejudices when he criticized this committee of "American gentlemen" for allowing "a man with entirely different standards to make this outrageous attack."

Houdini's response was to threaten to sue his old friend for slander. Sir Arthur had suggested that Houdini was bribed to ruin Margery, and as supporting evidence he quoted what Walter had said at the Charlesgate: *"Houdini, how much are they paying you to stop the phenomena?"* While Houdini claimed to present proof in his unmasking of Margery, Sir Arthur offered the statement of a phantom! The magician was further irked by how Doyle persisted in exaggerating Mrs. Crandon's refinement. "The truth of the whole matter," Houdini retorted, "is that Margery, in my belief, is a social climber."

As always there were two stories, both well publicized, of the same incidents between Houdini and Margery. There were also two grand auditoriums in Boston—Symphony Hall had featured Houdini, while the other, Jordan Hall, was reserved by the Crandons.

A Living Demonstration

It is a truth that spirits commune with one another while one is in the
body and the other in the higher sphere . . . and this truth will ere long
present itself in the form of a living demonstration.
—ANDREW JACKSON DAVIS, *Divine Revelations* (1847)

MARGERY WILL GIVE PUBLIC EXHIBITION
Noted Boston Medium Hopes Test Will Silence Critics
Who Doubt Her Power
—*New York Evening Journal* (1925)

A few days after Houdini's Symphony Hall exposé, the very foun-
dations of Boston were shaken by a subterranean force that sent people
rushing "madly into the streets." Houses in Beacon Hill and other districts
swayed and shuddered. Jolted by the convulsions, men preparing for work
cut themselves shaving. Clocks stopped. Fire alarms went off, though there
were no fires. Pictures fell in the homes hit by the tremors. Parlor furniture
rocked back and forth. Windows shattered.

It was an earthquake, Roy had immediately realized, and though
10 Lime Street would not cave in like some flimsy spirit cabinet, he had
never heard of the phenomenon occurring in New England. While causing little significant damage, the quake seemed weird and foreboding—
particularly since Sir Arthur had warned the Crandons of a cataclysm in
1925. *"Much has to be swept away with the rubbish of humanity,"* Jean's spirit
control had told him. *"Earthquake!"* Walter was known to call out just
before Margery's cabinet began to tremble. Many Spiritualists believed—if
not necessarily in the apocalyptic sense—that something earthshaking was
about to happen.

The Doyles anticipated a mediumistic demonstration that would draw
the world to Spiritualism. And while mass displays were more Houdini's

game, Margery seemed ready to present her work on a larger stage. In response to his exposé in Boston, the Crandons had rented out the elegant 1,000-seat Jordan Hall, one block from Symphony Hall, for the purpose of giving a public exhibition of her work. As a Boston newspaper announced, "Margery, the most talked of medium in America, has accepted the challenge of Harry Houdini, king of magic, for calling her a fraud."

♦

While traveling years earlier in Germany, Houdini wrote a Boston friend that he noticed how whenever a wrestler came along who "could actually throw the champion, someone else would step up in the employ of the champion and a great big controversy would be started." What he meant was that Margery, the prizeworthy medium, was dodging him in favor of Eric Dingwall, a lesser challenge, and the instigator of her public forum.

With the *Scientific American* committee in disarray, two British investigators, Dingwall and McDougall, began testing Margery together in early 1925. But Houdini feared that the SPR agent was already in her corner. In a letter to his Brahmin friend Robert Gould Shaw, he claimed that Dingwall was being subsidized by Dr. Crandon. He noted that when the SPR financed Dingwall's visits to America, he ate cheap meals and worked out of shoddy hotel rooms. This trip he had stayed at the Algonquin when arriving in New York, and so Houdini smelled bribery. He was certain that money, rather than magic, harnessed the forces of nature at 10 Lime Street.

Margery herself saw something direct, not venal, in her new English guest. "The first thing he told me was to take off my clothes," she admitted later. No clothing meant no impediment to the secretion of ectoplasm and, proudly uninhibited, she felt that any séance nudity was all for science. When Dingwall had sat with her in London two years earlier, she dazzled him with table effects but produced no visual manifestations. As with any developing medium her program was changing.

Not only had Dingwall arrived auspiciously by challenging her rival before a hall of thousands, he had personally inspired this new phase in her mediumship. "I rejoice that you are now in charge of the Crandon phenomena," Lodge wrote Dingwall. "I am very glad that they are now in reasonable and expert hands . . . The development is evidently going to be of importance in the whole history of the subject."

Being that he preferred the English investigators, Dr. Crandon was just as hopeful. He felt that Dingwall, who had spent eight years at Cambridge, was the perfect alternative to Houdini. As McDougall pointed out, Dingwall, "no mere academic scientist," was a member of the English Inner Magic Circle that was "the most select of its kind perhaps in the world." This investigator knew a ghost from a costume of fluorescent cheesecloth: he had discovered and edited *Revelations of a Spirit Medium,* the definitive guide to a false medium's methods.

And it was clear that Dingwall enjoyed working with Margery. "She is a highly intelligent and charming young woman," he would write in his SPR report, "exceedingly good natured and possessed of a fund of humour and courage which make her an ideal subject for investigation." The ease with which they got along made him feel that he, one year younger than she and married, was also pleasing to her. He believed that he was smart enough to be careful—everyone knew what Houdini said about her relations with Bird and Carrington. But the tests carried out by Dingwall, McDougall, and Reverend Worcester were intensive and intimate. Often the circle consisted only of the three investigators, Dr. Crandon, and the scantily clad medium. Dingwall had wanted her to wear the black tights that he said prevented fraudulent mediums from manifesting sham substances from their most accessible storehouses. Roy objected that they would also stanch the flow of real ectoplasm. Their compromise had Margery wearing only her robe and silk stockings, along with the luminous bands Dingwall attached to her wrists, ankles, and forehead as well as Roy's cuffs, so that the investigators could spot any suspicious movements in the dark room.

The new program suited the Crandons. "We still keep our fingers crossed but Dingwall seems to be alright," Roy wrote Sir Arthur. It was refreshing to them that Dingwall operated by the hypothesis that Margery's work was genuine until proven otherwise, for open minds were the generators that powered Margery's effects. As always, she was at her best when the circle was sympathetic. On the heels of Houdini's exposé, the Crandons felt redeemed. Encouraged by Dingwall's enthusiasm for the "marvelous crescendo" that Walter produced, Roy speculated that the ghost might "be the means of bringing together the spiritualists and the S.P.R."

Margery appeared ill and peculiarly depressed, though, when the investigators gathered on January 1 to begin the new series of test séances. Having never seen her so dispirited, Dingwall was sure a blank sitting was in order. To his surprise, she produced the same striking table manifestations that he had witnessed the previous winter in London. At the demonstration the following evening (Dingwall would sit with Margery virtually every night for the next six weeks), a ukulele rose from the table and twanged in the air; and what the Crandons called "the Houdini handkerchief"—a black cloth with a grotesque face luminously painted on it—fluttered magically across the table that tipped then levitated. The following evening, Dingwall sat with Margery at the home of two of the most respected members of her circle: the Harvard benefactor Augustus Hemenway and his wife, Harriet—notable protector of birds and their habitats. This time the SPR officer was allowed to grasp a floating tambourine, which Walter then pulled and twisted in any direction the scientist requested. Dingwall said he'd wanted to try this experiment "in many places all over the world," and so he had, in Harriet's Audubon sanctuary.

But Dingwall was not content to study effects that Margery had produced before. While he had brought his own bell-box device, which she rang convincingly, his ambition lay in observing the ectoplasm that caused these things to happen. Dingwall wanted to see the spectral hands with which Walter played the tambourine and pulled the hair of sitters. He needed to touch the fleeting matter that formed into the psychic terminals thought to hold tables aloft and obliterate cabinets. It was the "appearance of living, mobile substance emerging from the body of the medium," and the spectral limbs and forms manifesting from that secretion, that he wished to study. The mechanism behind the psychic effects was, in his view, the key to the mystery. As accommodating a medium as she was a hostess, Margery therefore changed her program. And that first month of 1925 she began to show Dingwall, and then the world, her first proofs of ectoplasm.

A Lime Street séance on the evening of January 6 began with the slight lift of a glowing ring that Dingwall provided Walter to play with. When the ghost told him to place his hand palm upward on the table, he felt something cold and clammy brush the nail of his middle finger. As the sensations spread to his other fingers and the rest of his hand, he started at the realization that an invisible being was touching him. "The substance resembled a cold, damp tongue," Dingwall recorded, "which sometimes appeared to thicken at the end and exert pressure." When McDougall put his hand across the table, something slimy flopped on it three or four times. Then Reverend Worcester, the most prosaic in his observations, was touched by what felt like a piece of cold raw beef, and with each contact he heard a beastly sound. Later Walter asked for a luminous plaque so that the men could observe the materialization of a black mass that formed shapes variously described as fins, claws, or prehensile terminals that slithered across the table. This "teleplasm," as they called it, moved toward a basket and slapped it away—then levitated the plaque with the basket precariously balanced on it. The shadowy claws glided toward Margery's lap—or more precisely to "an opening in the anatomy"—from which they were believed to emanate. When the force was low, they appeared to recede back inside her.

Walter explained that she had given birth to the teleplasm. In subsequent experiments the matter that emerged from Margery's vagina formed into a spectral hand—sometimes two, with one molding the other—connected by a placenta cord to her navel. With each flash of red light, Will Conant photographed the phenomena. Dingwall was so impressed that he urged, as a rejoinder to Houdini, the public demonstration that the Crandons scheduled for Jordan Hall. "Nothing can exceed Dingwall's enthusiasm for the case," Dr. Crandon informed Sir Arthur. "He is belligerent about it. He wants to proclaim it to the world." Soon there were other "great developments" to convey to Windlesham. Roy believed 1925 was to be the year when the real experts prevailed over the rabble-rousing Jew on the committee. Orson Munn was disgusted with his jury of experts, wrote Roy. "He hopes that now, since he cannot dissolve the Committee legally, that the white men in it, namely McDougall, Comstock and Carrington will resign. Munn will then appoint a new Committee of McDougall, Worcester and Dingwall, and ask them to decide the case, with award if deserved . . . You can readily see that at this moment, it looks as if the sun were coming out."

While Roy saw bright days ahead for Margery, Dingwall said the darkness necessary for her manifestations was the greatest obstacle to studying them. Unable to exist in light, the psychic structures were verified by touch and brief observation during the red flashes that Walter never seemed to allow when Dingwall most wanted them. The photographs usually captured the solid product when the proofs lay more, he still stressed, in the means of their development. Fully formed hands were not thought to pop out of the medium's womb as though from a spawning assembly line; rather, they materialized from her ectoplasm. The pictures showed thick globs oozing from Margery's ear, her mouth, nose, and genitals, or captured the shadowy terminals that supposedly formed from the discharge. But Dingwall was not able to witness or capture what he considered the real magic: the actual transformation of that substance into the psychic rods that moved objects.

On the other hand, it frustrated Dr. Crandon when researchers expected an immaterial process to be more discernible than physical forces that, though invisible, were accepted as real because of observed chemical effects and reactions. He realized that what Einstein had done with Brownian motion—used it to prove that atoms and molecules exist—was considerably more than could be expected in the psychic field from Dingwall, an anthropologist by training, and a couple of Boston psychologists. So when challenged on the elusiveness, or just plain absurdity, of certain teleplasmic effects, Roy was known to respond, "You didn't make the Universe; you must accept it." European researchers like Charles Richet *had* shown, to Dr. Crandon's satisfaction, that ectoplasm was real stuff. And he consoled himself that at least Dingwall's knowledge of magic, physics, and the female anatomy was superior to that of Professor McDougall, who was telling colleagues that Margery's vagina might be a storage place for spirit hands and fake teleplasm.

◆

Clearly under strain, Margery was ill again and worried about her forthcoming debut at Jordan Hall. She needed a rest, Dingwall suggested to Walter. But the answer from the spirit was a firm *"No."* They had to sit every night, he said, so that he could *"practice."* Nothing he did would harm the kid, he assured the scientist. *"Pay no attention to her,"* he announced one evening, *"let her groan. She really hasn't any pain. Blow your nose, Kid . . . Don't ask her how she feels."*

Both Roy and Walter denied that the medium was overworked. On the contrary, Roy remarked, she often emerged from her trances rejuvenated while her sitters were the ones exhausted. Reassured by the doctor, Dingwall let the matter go, though he had doubts that she would go through with the public exhibition.

At the test séance of January 9, speaking of the *"great night"* approaching, Walter instructed the circle as to how he wanted his sister to be controlled at Jordan Hall. Dingwall was to have one leg, he said; Roy the other; *"Dr. McDougall may have a wing,"* the ghost cracked, and *"Dr. Worcester may hold her nose if he feels neglected."* The joke produced barely a chuckle. Walter was working with a circle of four serious men—the doctor, the alienist, the anthropologist, the minister—and his phenomena were never more lurid. His materializations were like the severed appendages that live on in ghost stories while the rest of the body decays in a catacomb.

As soon as Margery passed into trance, a rustling was heard from her lap. Walter instructed Dingwall to run his hand up her stocking until he reached her thigh. But the spirit found Dingwall clumsy: *"Your hand is caught in the lining of the bathrobe, follow the stocking."* After trying this, Dingwall found an ice-cold, knobby mass on Margery's skin. Then another globule was found on the table, connected by a rough placental cord with shiny rings that Dingwall followed to her abdomen. Against the light of the plaque, little fingers, as if amputated, suddenly grew out of the form on the table—some slowly, some quickly. The fingerlike projections lifted a luminous ring "and waved it about with great freedom." The fingers on the mass vanished as it became more amorphous—its movements "sometimes violent, sometimes stealthy." Yet the teleplasm shook hands with Dingwall and McDougall. They were later told to wake Psyche by gradual exposures to red light. By midnight the séance was over.

The spirit hands were the first step to the full materializations Walter promised but had still not delivered. As the experiments continued, though, it became harder to ignore his sister's physical reactions. After one sitting she suffered nausea and vomiting. Following another she was weighed and found to have somehow lost four pounds during the experiment. Once she complained of "pain, headache, soreness all over." A séance was canceled when Mrs. Hemenway, while conducting an anatomical search of the medium, discovered that her right ear was bleeding. More often Margery was upbeat—inane when others were serious—and apparently as perplexed as the scientists by what her body was producing. Her ectoplasm continued to take on different appearances and was at various times said to look like the back of an armadillo, a pancake, a starfish, a huge knobby potato—pinkish-gray in color, elongated tuberosities, a membrane filled with a semifluid substance, and the different organs of an animal. The developed forms were described as a pinkish-white appendage and shriveled forearm, detached fingers, a small human skull, and the hand of a child.

All Eyes Were on Boston

Thus I pacified Psyche and kissed her,
And tempted her out of her gloom—
And conquered her scruples and gloom;
And we passed to the end of the vista,
But were stopped by the door of a tomb—
By the door a legended tomb.

—EDGAR ALLAN POE

The baby is born. And it's a hand," Walter announced. After the séance, Dr. Crandon spoke of the materializations with awe, as though he had both planted the seed for these effects and delivered the teleplasm. He had planted *something* within Margery, Houdini conjectured, but as the only committeeman who was persona non grata at Lime Street, he could not touch Walter's clammy hands or witness the production of ectoplasm. And since his colleagues had also ostracized him—even denying him séance reports—he turned to a network of sleuths, journalists, and society friends for information on the Crandons.

One important source was Quincy Kilby, treasurer and historian of the Boston Theater, and an acquaintance of the Crandons. When Margery first attracted notice as a pseudonymous medium, it was Kilby who had informed Houdini of her true identity. Months before the *Herald* revealed Margery's obscure roots, Kilby suspected she was not really of society. Her vaguely rural accent had never been heard, he was certain, in a Seven Sisters dormitory. Particularly after a couple of highballs there was sometimes a coarseness to Margery—her hands were not soft like a Gold Coast lady's, and Kilby sensed she was not afraid to get them dirty. Even her ectoplasm was not the fine, diaphanous stuff that one expected, though Dingwall was still keen for a public display of that sought-after substance.

"Nothing surprises me about Margery," Houdini wrote Kilby. "A woman who will drag her dead brother from the grave and exploit him before the public as a means of gaining social prominence would do anything." However gregarious she seemed, and no matter how erudite her circle, Houdini believed something wicked was fomenting at 10 Lime Street—a plot more insidious, given the influence of her patrons and zeal of her followers. "I have just received warning letters," he informed Kilby, "of what Margery and the Spiritualists are going to do to me."

Houdini feared that his legacy would be tarnished if he should die tomorrow and Margery continue to flaunt her powers. Even his provocative pamphlet had not revealed the darker details, he hinted, behind their encounter, and he did not want his version of events to be lost, or distorted after his death by mediums who claimed to channel his own disembodied spirit. "I am going to write the real inside of my experiences in Boston so that some day the truth will eventually be known," Houdini informed his friend Shaw, the Harvard collector.

In the field of mediumistic research, where matters may play out beyond the grave, Houdini knew his case could be won or lost posthumously. So he made photostatic copies of important documents concerning the Margery case, including a copy of Bird's aborted article on the medium—the one that allegedly proved the journal was about to endorse her—and sent them to his brother Hardeen, "in case anything should happen to me."

Of more immediate concern was what the Crandons planned to unveil at Jordan Hall. On January 19, twelve days before Margery's public séance, Houdini wrote Kilby three times, pressing him for information on her "new routine of manifestations." The uncertainty was tormenting him. A rival mystifier had rented a hall for the express purpose, he believed, of embarrassing him. Not even his stage rival, Thurston the Great, would have attempted it. When Houdini had mysteriously produced the photograph of Walter crushed to death by the railroad car, the witnesses onstage were astonished. It would be considered a far superior feat, though, for Margery to summon her dead brother—his voice and some aspect of his form—back from the void, so that he might perform a few uncanny effects for a hushed audience.

As a matter of fact, it was a restrained and select crowd that gathered in Jordan Hall on the last evening of January. While less than the 3,000 that had seen Houdini in a larger auditorium, Margery's was a fine turnout,

Stewart Griscom noted. Thirty minutes before showtime he could spot only a few vacant seats in the rear balcony. Yet the event wasn't open to the general public; sensation seekers and even some with press credentials were turned away. Most in attendance were sympathetic to the Crandons. In a minor flap, Dr. McDougall, the host of the affair, was denied admission until he could prove his identity. By Roy's design, no intruders—the Houdinis and Joseph Rinns of this world—were going to be allowed to disturb the proceedings. Instead, the Crandons had invited the Boston members of the ASPR, the medical faculties of Tufts and Harvard, and a good portion of the teaching staff at MIT. An inspection of the audience made it clear that most of those invitees had accepted. But where were the Crandons?

The evening began with McDougall announcing his gratitude to Eric Dingwall for coming to America to test Margery. McDougall affirmed that Boston had always been "the home of new things, the very fountainhead of new religions, of new cults, new methods of healing, new wonders of all sorts." Ultimately it had produced Margery, he said, and with her rise "the very eyes of the world have been centered on Boston." Griscom's own eyes shifted to Dingwall as the speaker turned the stage over to the SPR investigator. Dingwall was the most qualified man in the world to determine the cause of Margery's phenomena, Dr. McDougall declared.

And tonight it would be his show, in lieu of the star medium. Days earlier, Griscom had surprised Houdini with gratifying news: the Crandons were not going to be in attendance at their own demonstration. Margery had gotten cold feet. Or rather, the Crandons decided they were playing into Houdini's hands by trying to answer his exposé with a public séance. "They said they were going to show me up and denounce me by having the medium present her manifestations in front of an audience and all it turned out to be was a lecture by Dingwall," Houdini gloated.

Dingwall actually gave what the *Herald* described as a vivid account of the phenomena he witnessed at Lime Street and a stinging assessment of how Houdini and his colleagues had mishandled Margery. To McDougall's embarrassment, Dingwall accused the *Scientific American* of giving psychic research an "evil odor"—and of treating the Margery candidacy like "a burlesque puzzle or vaudeville show." He blamed the row chiefly on the entertainer "whose knowledge of the art of self-liberation is as profound as his ignorance of the method of scientific investigation." But Dingwall questioned the competence of *all* the judges at the Charlesgate séances. He could not understand why the ruler controversy wasn't settled by simply dusting the suspicious instrument for fingerprints. He encouraged Margery to come to London so that her effects could be examined in a less antagonistic environment and with more advanced equipment. The English SPR was less fractious and publicity-minded, he suggested, than Orson Munn's hung jury.

Later he called for the lights to be dimmed, as if the spirits were to be summoned after all. Just like Sir Arthur's lectures, the highlight of the evening was the proofs he projected. Unlike Doyle's slides, however, these "pictures were not of shadowy vapors or mist-like forms, but were of solid masses, strange things which revealed themselves to the eye of the camera." Clearly they issued from Margery's body, and her flood of ectoplasm looked almost too weird, Griscom thought, to be invented. But without a live séance the event lacked the intended impact. The circumspect Dingwall was not a powerful orator like Sir Arthur. When he responded to questions, his voice failed to carry. "Louder!" a woman next to Griscom shouted. The researcher walked forward, more into the stage light, and with a strained effort raised his voice. Griscom felt that he was still not loud enough; he was supposed to be presenting the case to a larger audience than this hall of Margery partisans.

From what Walter Prince gathered from the newspapers, Dingwall's presentation, despite its coldly scientific tone, was a thinly disguised tribute to Margery—another glowing feather for her to wear in her silk headband. With Houdini trying her daily before thousands at the Hippodrome, Dingwall had defended her in a dignified and widely covered forum. This time, Prince mused, her savior was the SPR representative, yet ever since discovering her spiritist powers, the right advocate—Doyle, Bird, Carrington—entered Margery's life, as if each materialized at the opportune time in her development. In response to Houdini's charges, Bird, who wrote "rhapsodically of her personality and charm," was praising Margery's work in auditoriums throughout the country. Unlike any other medium, she inspired chivalrous gestures among otherwise hard-boiled journalists, conjurers, and researchers. It *was* a kind of magic, Prince joked—though not the kind available to male mediums or shrews like Palladino.

By this time Dr. Crandon anticipated that Margery's gifts would be endorsed by Dingwall and the English SPR—an investigative body that he deemed superior to Prince's haphazardly constituted SciAm committee. The jury had tested Margery for more than a year and the Crandons were tired, Roy told Prince, of its endless infighting and deliberations. In favoring Dingwall's investigation, the doctor treated Prince and the New York experts like jilted lovers. Of Prince's group only the Englishman McDougall was now allowed to test Margery. When Prince wrote Roy to try to arrange another official jury sitting, he answered that she was tied up with Dingwall's investigation until February 14, when the SPR officer would return to London. More pointedly, he told Prince that if the committee did not disavow Houdini's verdict and ban him from further investigation, there would be no more séances for the judges.

Whatever wonders Margery was showing McDougall and Dingwall in private, there seemed little likelihood for further SciAm tests that winter. There was no point, Munn decided, in deferring a Margery decision if the Crandons were not going to cooperate—especially as there was only one judge, McDougall, who had not already submitted an opinion on the medium. Even now the psychologist wanted more time to test her. But at Prince's behest, McDougall finally agreed to vote on whether her powers were genuine. Her hopes for the psychic prize lay in the hands of the judge who had so warmed to her that he presided over the Jordan Hall exhibition. Three weeks earlier, McDougall had praised her work in a letter to Roy, calling it a "remarkable and outstanding case of mediumship." He had been the first committeeman to investigate Margery, and his would be the last word in the contest.

The Unkindest Cut of All

*T*he story in the *Boston Herald* shocked Mrs. Crandon. "The famous Margery case is over so far as the *Scientific American* Psychic Investigation is concerned." No one on the committee had bothered to call her with the decision, yet on February 12, 1925, a negative verdict was delivered. She had failed to convince four of the five judges that her mediumship was authentic. There would be no award for the Boston medium, nor further investigation of the case by the *Scientific American*. In the end she had been rejected almost as brusquely as the other candidates. Because three of the judges had had no sittings with Margery since their previous determinations, only two were heard from—jointly, Prince and McDougall announced that they had "observed no phenomena of which we can assert that they could not have been produced by normal means."

Prince said in his individual statement that the séance conditions the Crandons insisted on were "embarrassing and suspicious." While at first less severe, McDougall charged that her mediumship might have been a hoax Roy concocted to show the gullibility of scientists. Shortly after the announcement Margery underwent a sinus operation where she endured the jabs of "wires and long pointed knives." But since she liked McDougall, his "was the unkindest cut of all. I wonder if he really means what he says?" she wrote Dingwall.

The postmortem was repugnant to the Crandons. In his brief statement Prince spoke of the unusual private séance he'd had with Margery and how he suspected she hadn't actually rung the bell box he controlled in his lap. Rather, he believed she rang one she concealed, then and at other times, between her knees and in her undergarments. McDougall went even farther up the medium's dress in revealing her supposed methods. In his report that ran in the *Boston Transcript* and later in the *Scientific American,* he suggested that she concealed fake ectoplasmic hands within "one particular opening in her anatomy." Privately, he said that Dr. Crandon had surgically expanded Margery's "most convenient storehouse."* So whether she was in bed with her researchers, as Houdini attested, or packing objects in her vagina, the suspicions of some of the jury members were clear: Mina Crandon was a loose woman.

Often the mass she produced had an inert and grisly quality that smelled to McDougall like something from a butcher's shop. Suspecting that the teleplasm was composed of animal organs, he had taken photographs of it to a Harvard physiologist and a zoologist, both of whom confirmed that the masses contained what appeared to be the cartilaginous rings of an animal's trachea. McDougall concluded that Walter's hands were molded "of the lung of some animal." He alleged that Dr. Crandon surgically manipulated the meaty tissue into the forms that Margery hid in her anatomy. The ectoplasmic effects that had amazed Dingwall, and the photographs that had awed the professors at Jordan Hall, were conversely what "clinched the decision" for William McDougall.

Admittedly, some of her work still puzzled him, but in general the more stringent the control, the fewer the manifestations. "The ectoplasm exhibited abundant and most intriguing movements," but only when her husband controlled her right hand and only with the lights dimmed. McDougall dismissed the evidentiary value of Walter's disembodied voice—one that reportedly emanated from all kinds of places and directions—when he said he never sensed it coming from any source other than the psychic. His judgments were a far cry from weeks earlier, when he'd praised the Margery mediumship. In a mea culpa, McDougall conceded that in his recent letter to Roy, "I stated my openness of mind towards the phenomena too strongly." He publicly apologized as well for presiding over the Jordan Hall demonstration. In hindsight he realized that it looked odd to host a defense of the medium just before condemning her, but he did it, he claimed, out of obligation to Dingwall. He concluded that the mediumship, however

---

* He once also wondered if Dr. Crandon had inserted some sort of refrigeration device within her vagina, to give the ectoplasm its cold texture.

remarkable, was "an extreme case of double personality" that ought to fall within the field of abnormal psychology.

Publicly, Margery appeared unruffled in defeat. "The decision does not bother me at all," she told a Boston newspaper. "And I can certainly say I am neither discouraged or disappointed . . . Any further statement must come from my husband. It is up to him to do all the talking." Privately, though, she was crestfallen. "Needless to say I am quite discouraged," she admitted to Dingwall. "McDougall's blast quite froze the kindness within me."

All of Margery's vital force, be it psychic or physical, had been engaged for endless months in the pursuit of this one goal—to win the endorsement of the committee of experts. Even if she were only a tireless producer of phony effects, as Houdini insisted, she was no less distressed at having been rejected by the judges of the contest that made her a celebrity. She was the queen of psychical research, and Malcolm Bird the queen maker. His reports still lauded her psychic gifts, while McDougall's indicted her as just another delusive miracle worker—the latest ingenious quack or false Spiritualist messiah. Though Hereward Carrington's support hadn't wavered, the two scientists Roy thought were on the verge of crossing the Rubicon, Comstock and McDougall, had turned away.

But like Pandora's box, it was easier to open the Margery case than to close it. Voices on two planes immediately challenged the verdict: *"McDougall couldn't do any better without changing the philosophy of a life-time,"* Walter whispered to his circle. *"Tell him the kid carries equipment in her insides of a little ice-box, a pair of bellows, and six lungs with bones in them. She chews liver for a cud. She has insides as big as a cow."*

At the Boston City Club, Malcolm Bird held up copies of séance reports, bearing McDougall's signature, which contradicted the psychologist's statements that Margery never manifested under perfect control and in red light. "I'm afraid," said Bird, "he has a bad memory." By this time, though, Roy's hopes, and emphatic missives, were directed toward England. He had turned the case over to Dingwall, "the research officer of the parent of all psychical societies—the supreme court of appeal." Roy promised that Dingwall would "find the gateway to a high place in psychic research" through his work with Margery. In her own inimitable way, she too cajoled him. "We have never had anyone here we missed more," she wrote Dingwall; for he was "the one and only investigator in the world," and she needed his "cheery smile." None of the others could compare, Margery hinted, to the scientist who directed the study of her ectoplasm, and replaced constrictive methods of control with the glowing bands she wore like haloes in the séance.

◆

Astonishingly, after what had appeared to be the decisive case in his contest, Orson Munn said the hunt was on for another psychic candidate. An editorial in the *Times* called the endeavor futile. The *Scientific American* was not going to find another contestant with credentials like Margery's. "She was educated; she had never sought to exhibit her powers for hire and she had no history of association with mediums or magicians who might teach her the tricks of mystification." Mrs. Crandon was the one true candidate—and yet after many months and scores of trials, the committee determined that not a single of her observed effects was genuinely psychic. "Margery," the *Times* opined, "might have won a peace prize with much less effort." The verdict was considered "rather unsatisfactory," after so much of the experts' time and Munn's money.

Whatever the cost, Margery's critics felt that science had won an important victory. For them an occult revival spelled the end of the period of rationalism that had begun not so long ago, when scientists like Newton and Descartes demystified the laws of nature. Not everyone saw the debunking of mediums as a sign of progress, however. The *Baltimore Sun* observed that if Mrs. Crandon had been found genuine, the award would have signaled a discovery "far transcending any miracle of science, far more revolutionary in its effect upon thought and life than any material wonders." Yet the "long cherished human hope" remained "deferred, and Margery of Boston joins the far-flung line of unconvincing charlatans."

Soon it was clear that the obituary for Margery's psychic career, and the eulogy for the spiritist movement, had been written prematurely. Among the ASPR directorate were steadfast believers in her mediumship, and the *Scientific American* verdict caused a dispute that divided the entire sphere of psychical research according to one's attitude toward Margery. The schism began when Walter Prince was demoted by Frederick Edwards, president of the ASPR, for what he thought was prejudiced and poor handling of the Margery case.

A Spiritualist, a Detroit clergyman, Edwards was not comfortable overseeing researchers like Prince and McDougall, who were openly skeptical toward his movement.* So when Edwards, allied with Mark Richardson and other Margery supporters, won a power struggle within the organization, the ASPR hired a new investigator of physical mediums. To Prince's consternation, Malcolm Bird—"a man whose journalistic methods were distasteful to every member of the *Scientific American* Committee"—was given his former position: research officer of the ASPR, the traditional function of the most respected ghost hunter in America.

The organization that was supposed to solve the enduring mystery of psychic phenomena was now, warned Prince, in Dr. Crandon's deep pockets. In consequence, Prince, along with Houdini and McDougall, quit the ASPR. The aging investigator promptly formed a Boston Society for Psychical Research, and brought in Hub investigators who repudiated the Margery mediumship. Meanwhile, Bird, the young turk, was returning to Lime Street—despite a letter he'd received from Roy's sister, Laura, warning that Margery was on the verge of a breakdown: "Mrs. C is reaching her limit nervously—& the goose who lays the golden eggs is going to be killed unless there is some let up somewhere. She is threatening not to sit at all for any of you anymore. Rather than this happen, I would suggest that when you go up you stay at a hotel."

Brushing off Laura's concern, Bird did stay and sit with Margery, and he found the medium in good form—only one night was there any sign of turmoil. A sitting was winding down that April when suddenly Walter's whisper came through forebodingly. *"Good night, I've got to go now, quick."* Moments later Bird and the other sitters felt the entire house shake as Boston was hit by another earthquake.

---

* When McDougall was president of the ASPR he tried to bring more conventional scientists into the organization. The psychic board had resisted and eventually replaced him in 1923 with Edwards.

The Craziest Road of All

Oh the road to En-dor is the oldest road
And the craziest road of all!
Straight it runs to the Witch's abode,
As it did in the days of Saul,
And nothing has changed of the sorrow in store
For such as go down on the road to En-dor!
—RUDYARD KIPLING

*P*assing shadowy gaslit lanes and brick homes of Federal and Georgian style, it struck the reporter that the Crandons' neighborhood looked unchanged since the days of witch trials. "The house," he wrote of 10 Lime Street, "stands hardly a stone's throw from that spot on Boston Common where the colonial rulers built their gallows and executed their witches. Indeed, I do not see how a phantom can possibly make its way to Margery's house without rousing the ghosts of those old witch hunters, who, with faggot and Scripture, pursued through this very neighborhood many an ancient medium."

The visitor, John T. Flynn, was not the usual ghost-chasing scribe; no unshaven hack with a slouch hat, he was a gentlemanly reporter who saw more to worry about in trade unions than supposed witch covens. If anything, he found Margery to be a good witch—a patroness of wisdom—whose library held the enlightened works of Hume, Thoreau, and Emerson. Quickly becoming one of the couple's favorite newsmen, Flynn would write a long and sympathetic portrait of Margery: "The Witch of Beacon Hill," for *Collier's*. In the most eloquent interview she ever gave, the medium communicated volubly with Flynn. "She seemed to enjoy answering my questions," he reported, "and telling me of her tormentors."

Her greatest antagonist remained the magician who had associated her with darker witchcraft. Her notoriety was partially due to Houdini's popular exposés, yet he believed she wouldn't lose her mystique until the word "fraud" was indelibly stamped next to her name. When the committee denied her the psychic prize without exposing her as a cheat, as he had urged, it had not diminished the Margery craze. Months later, at the International Spiritualist Congress in Paris, a near riot occurred when thousands of citizens, a throng too large for the auditorium, clamored to see Doyle's lantern slides of her ectoplasm. In London, Dingwall continued to trumpet her as "the medium of modern times." Meanwhile, in Boston, just after Dingwall left, a new group of scholarly investigators sought to test her. "It was strange to find the intellectual university of Harvard in the throes of a mental, if not a moral, revolution because of one woman," noted Robin Tillyard, the Australian entomologist sympathetic to the Crandons.

Harry Houdini, among others, petitioned Harvard's president, Abbott Lowell, to forbid Margery from being tested again at his "wonderful institution." But in May the medium's chief nemesis kept her topical by bringing his spook act back to Boston. Oddly, after Houdini's run at Keith's was over, a disturbance there made it seem as if Walter still haunted the theater. During performances iron pellets, deliberately launched, fell onto the orchestra, wounding a number of terrified spectators. For a subsequent show "the police distributed forty plain-clothes men throughout the audience with the view of detecting the criminal," Dr. Crandon wrote Dingwall. Again the missiles struck with no culprit visible. A reporter for the Associated Press phoned Margery to tell her the police had just about "come to the conclusion that it is the spirits who are doing it." Did they really think, she gasped, that she was responsible for the mischief there?

Witches were no longer held accountable for the darkening of the sun and shaking of the earth, or mysteries like that at Keith's. Yet Margery would soon face what she joked was as bad as a witch trial: another Harvard inquiry. Her case hadn't been solved to everyone's satisfaction. Even Walter Prince, who doubted her supernormal gifts, recognized that there was something extraordinary about this medium. "Margery," he told Dingwall, "has developed a technique which is very remarkable, but we have to put up with the fact that there are remarkable people in the world and even geniuses of which she may be one." Even so, her riding companion, Kitty

Brown, failed to see anything devious about her. "If they knew how dumb you really were," she remarked, "no one would accuse you of such things."

◆

In her *Collier's* interview, Mrs. Crandon recalled the amusement-seeking visit she and Kitty once made to the spirit medium who reunited her with her dead brother. Goodness, was it only three years since they rode toward that first psychic adventure? Since then she had been imbued with a gift, but also a stigma she hoped to erase.

"You want to know what it feels like to be a witch," Margery told John Flynn. "You know that's what they would have called me in Boston 150 years ago. And they would have hauled me before the General Court and executed me for consorting with the devil. But now they send committees of professors from Harvard to study me. That represents some progress, doesn't it?"

Rather than spiritualize her powers, she said they sometimes felt "a little creepy." She recalled, for instance, the time at a neighborhood teahouse when the table she shared with a Beacon Hill matron began to sway, tilt, and reverberate. The distraught lady summoned a waitress and proceeded to rebuke her for the rocking table. Mortified, Mina fled the place rather than admit she was to blame.

She had no explanation for such phenomena, but neither, in her view, did the so-called experts—the grave and supercilious investigators who seemed to her "so very little and so very futile." Most of the scientists who came to study her were "terribly at sea about this whole business of psychic research and do not know how to approach it. I do not know myself . . ." she admitted, "but they seem quite helpless."

All of them? asked Flynn.

Well, not all of them. She recalled how one younger but experienced investigator (Carrington?) told her, " 'My dear Psyche, do you know what is going to happen to you? You will lose your mind and that quite soon.' "

"There is a pleasant prospect for you!" Margery exclaimed to Flynn. She denied being afraid, however. Her work, she realized, could not be established "without much misunderstanding and pain." And she hoped that despite the controversy and religious unrest, the earnest men and women probing about in the darkness might yet find their proofs.

"How does it all feel?" she summed up. "Well, I am sure I am a good deal sobered by it. I look at my cello, standing in the corner of the music-room. It never comes out of its green hood anymore. Somehow, I do not find myself moving around in the dance as joyously as I once did."

Houdini Won't Talk No More

Hearken not to your prophets and diviners, and dreamers, and
soothsayers and sorcerers.

—JEREMIAH 27:9

*W*alter arrived in the Crandons' séance room and immediately began
to perform. While singing in a whisper he tapped the megaphone on the
table to the beat of "It Ain't Gonna' Rain No More."

> *Oh Houdini won't talk no more, no more.*
> *He ain't goin' to talk no more.*
> *What in the hell will the newspapers do,*
> *When Houdini won't talk no more.*

In Houdini's parlor a dark-haired woman with a long Mediterranean
nose—who might have been a salesclerk or usher at the Hippodrome—
closed her eyes as he directed. Moments later she heard an eerie clicking
noise pervading the room, sometimes close to her then receding. Houdini
had only been tapping two coins together next to her ear, and never moved
them, he later told her. He wanted to simulate the conditions of the séance
and demonstrate how a sitter's imagination shaped the phenomena. So began
Rose Mackenberg's training as a detective in what he called "my own secret
service"—the small but ubiquitous force he led against the spook racket.

> *Houdini won't write no more, no more,*
> *Houdini won't write no more.*
> *He writ' so much that his arm got sore,*
> *Houdini won't write no more.*

"Sometimes I wonder," Houdini told a Jewish magazine, "whether I am
truly a reincarnation of some old magician because magic never did seem

a mystery to me." Just as Sir Arthur had decided his true calling was religion rather than detective fiction, so Houdini had the nagging sense that his legacy would be connected to his campaign against false mediumship. And the newspapers and magazines that were his weathervane seemed to support his ambitions. "It may be indeed that Houdini has appeared at a crucial moment in the history of spiritualism and that he is destined to play an important role," wrote Edmund Wilson in the *New Republic;* for "in a committee of scientists on which Houdini sits, it is Houdini who is the scientist."

It was astounding how much authority was bestowed on a magician. When the Great Houdini presented his medium-debunking routine daily at two New York theaters, he was escorted—from the Albee in Brooklyn to the Hippodrome in Manhattan—by a convoy of motorcycle policemen that stopped and diverted traffic, as if he were a dignitary delivering an important message to the masses rather than, as his rivals said, using the Margery controversy for his own profit and self-aggrandizement. Not only psychics begrudged him these privileges. "Every magacian [*sic*] in this country would like to see Houdini BEAT in the Scientific American Psychic Prize," wrote Robert Gysel, an Ohio conjurer and medium baiter. His downfall was assured if the spirits had any say in it—*"The waters are black for Houdini,"* wailed a disembodied voice through the trumpet. *"Houdini is doomed, doomed, doomed,"* warned the spirit whom Jean Doyle channeled.

> *Oh Houdini won't talk no more, no more,*
> *Oh what will Pop McDougall do*
> *If Houdini won't talk no more.*

Technically the *Scientific American* contest remained active. The search for a new candidate found Harry Houdini in Philadelphia, interviewing a woman named Sarah Mourer—who wore her white hair in a bob, seemed "fairly intelligent," and talked incessantly before demonstrating the powers she thought prize-worthy. She claimed to make clocks stop, but displayed none of Margery's flair or mystery. The medium simply grabbed a clock from the mantel then shook it violently until it stopped ticking. She had another gift, she boasted, for foreseeing the outcome of fishing expeditions—"You are going to catch three fish and one is a flounder," she told the magician who had no plans to fish for anything. Then she put her hands on his head and claimed to cure him instantly of nearsightedness he didn't have. "There is something gone wrong with the lady," Houdini reported to Orson Munn. As it turned out, she was the last clairvoyant he investigated for the *Scientific American*.

> *Oh Houdini won't talk no more, no more.*
> *He ain't goin' to talk no more.*
> *What in the hell will the newspapers do,*
> *When Houdini won't talk no more.*

Anyone who dabbled long enough with the spirits might have hallucinations, Houdini attested. While in his study late at night he half-joked that he saw forms go by and heard voices. Immersed in the study of witchcraft and psychics, all roads for him led to Endor. By this time he had stopped making movies: his last cinematic effort was an attempt to import the Swedish film *The Witch* to America. He wrote now on only one subject. "Am busy on a pamphlet against the spiritualists making use of the Bible and am showing the Witch of Endor in modern light," he notified his friends and colleagues.

Though wary of a theological fight, Houdini was certain he had Scripture and the clerics of a Christian nation on his side. Like Saul in the Bible, he was trying to rid a land of heretical necromancers while still seeking that one genuine medium—his own Witch of Endor—to do the very thing he was condemning. For all the bad blood between him and the Spiritualists, he still considered himself a sincere seeker of spirit contact. "Well, Mama, I have not heard," he would say at his mother's graveside after yet another phony séance.

> *He writ' so much that his arm got sore,*
> *Houdini won't write no more.*

Even if no city was truly plagued by spirit crime, Houdini channeled a wider impulse to purge the republic of something insidious. Whether the villains were members of political or superstitious cults—the country threatened by Anarchists or occultists in the red-light districts—many feared that a movement hatched in clandestine dens was encroaching on Main Street. HOUDINI'S WITCH HUNT, the headline blared, BRINGS OUT THE FAITHFUL.

While he saw vile felonies in what the law called misdemeanors—taking money on false pretenses—he *had* successfully provoked a crackdown on the spirit racket. Cloaked in the myriad disguises he used to infiltrate séances, Houdini was to the spook crooks a shape-shifting bogeyman—all it took were rumors that he was in town to send them undercover. At the New York Police Academy, he taught cadet detectives "How to Catch Fake Spiritualists." The slickest of them all, he told them, was Margery, who would have made $5 million had he not unmasked her. He went to incredible lengths to obstruct her and other notorious psychics, and even went as far as petitioning President Coolidge to support a bill that would outlaw fortune-telling and mediumship for hire. He had obtained the business records of an old Spiritualist journal, *Banner of Light,* to inspect its legal papers, IRS forms, bank deposits, and lists of benefactors. He wanted to know how his enemies operated. Though he found no signs of malfeasance at the defunct magazine, no stone was left unturned. He acquired all manner of other, darker material, including a copy of the spook racket's infamous "sucker list," which provided detailed information on those who frequented séances. In reaction, his enemies called him a drunkard, a drug addict, a keeper of harems, an agent of the pope, the Antichrist; "they are panning the hell out of me," he noted. To American mediums he was the barbarian at the gates, seizing spiritist plunder—and if Summerland were razed, only the tombstones would be left standing.

"Getting ready for my forthcoming season and battle with the spiritualists," Houdini wrote a friend. His strategy was to send a member of his attractive corps of investigators—that included his young niece, Julia Sawyer, and showgirls from his magic ensemble—to the vicinity he toured. There they posed as easy marks for the swindlers to prey on. Houdini's most effective agent, Rose Mackenberg, would devote twenty years of her life to running fake mediums out of US cities. Even before he had trained her, Rose was an experienced private investigator who had worked on gambling, blackmail, and murder cases. But she came to find spooks who suckered the bereaved "the most vicious criminals in America." Camouflaging her sharp eyes behind Buster Keaton–esque shell-rim glasses, she called herself Francis Raud (F. Raud) while posing as a jealous wife, nervous schoolteacher, factory girl, naïve servant, or small-town widow. For Houdini, she would investigate over three hundred mediums, each time calling in the wizard to lay the trap once she determined that they were crooked.

So convincing was his favorite disguise—a feeble and bereaved husband or father—that no psychic suspected the harmless old mark might be their nemesis. Posing as the "old man's" fellow sitters were the reporters and detectives or county prosecutors who performed their respective duties after he revealed the frauds cheating their customers. The attendant publicity led to the purges that Houdini wanted. Twenty-two spooks were arrested in a crackdown in Cleveland after one of his séance capers. EXPOSÉ IS DRIVING MEDIUMS TO COVER, ran the typical headline.

> *What in the hell will the newspapers do,*
> *When Houdini won't talk no more.*

The scourge of crooked mediums did not use all of the ammunition that Mackenberg supplied him. For all the "sex attacks" she repulsed in the séance parlors and the advances Houdini claimed to rebuff from Margery, he did not like to publicly discuss the lewdness some saw in the Shadowland. "One of the tenets to which they are drawn is free love," declared one Boston pastor. "The only safe thing for Christians to say of Spiritualism is get thee behind me, Satan."

Having been ordained many times as a Spiritualist minister, Rose had endured "purification healings," which involved a male psychic getting "the proper vibrations," by the laying of his hands upon her breasts and thighs. Houdini urged her to carry a gun into the séance. It wasn't safe for a woman there, echoed Robert Gysel, who had even worse things to say about what went on in spiritistic rituals. In Chicago a male medium— who for $25 was offering to help women and young girls develop their psychic abilities—conducted a ceremony where the girl took his penis into her mouth and drew the semen from it, so that she could absorb the "wonderful power," Gysel reported. The spirit fakers, he wrote, were "positively worse than animals."

Most of the grifters Houdini encountered were more interested in fleecing than violating their victims, yet none seemed capable of the ingenuity that he attributed to Margery. At one sitting a well-known professional medium channeled a sitter's drowned relative, who was heard to scream "Help!" as the sea choked him. Shining his trusted flashlight at that moment, Houdini unveiled the psychic blowing a straw into a bowl of water.

In the disguise Houdini favored of white whiskers and hump, tousled hair, and a hand raised to his ear whenever the mediums spoke, he looked the part of the half-demented fogey any spook could fool six ways from Sunday. After the lights were dimmed for a Cleveland séance led by George Renner—a medium of forty years' good standing—the "old man" crawled around on the floor smearing with lampblack the instruments the spirits were supposed to enchant. When discarnate voices were later heard through the trumpet and the guitar began to levitate, Houdini shone his pocket flashlight to reveal the medium tarred with the soot he had planted. "Mr. Renner," he declared, "you are a fraud."

In every city he toured Houdini proved it was the ghost talkers, not the spirits, who spoke through megaphones, and it was the medium's hands, rather than spectral force, that manipulated the floating instruments. At a Harlem séance, his flashlight caught the popular Mrs. Cecil Cook with her mouth on the trumpet, rather than the lips of her spirit controls— Snowdrop, Chief, and Bright Eyes. "What is that?! What is that?!" cried Mrs. Cook. "Why that is the old man," her minions warned. "I'm killed! I'm killed!" wailed the medium who had been struck down, her sitters feared, by the sudden violence to her ectoplasm.

"I am Houdini," announced the geriatric, raising his cane as the Spiritualists rushed him. They were stopped by the undercover policemen who dragged Mrs. Cook to her arraignment. When testifying in court against occultists like Mrs. Cook, Houdini chimed, "I had ready in my pocket all the allusions in the Bible against witches, familiar spirits and when the defendant's lawyer pulled a pro I replied with an anti." He sounded increasingly like a wizard on a religious crusade. On a Worcester stage he unfurled a long, bound-together scroll of various fake church charters Rose Mackenberg had obtained from false spiritists. "I drove out the fakes in California," he promised, "and I intend to drive them out of Massachusetts."

The Blooded Reporter

Oh there is a great medium named Marge,
Who will give you a show without charge,
There is no need to pay,
Excepting to say:
"You're the wonderf'lest medium at large."

Her man is a sawyer of bones,
And cuts a swell figure, he owns:
But his work with the knife
Has infected his life,
For he's "cutting up" lots besides bones.

—PUSSYFOOT, A PSEUDONYMOUS PSYCHIC INVESTIGATOR

*T*asteful as the dinners were at 10 Lime Street, something unsavory was being served up before the red lights in Roy's den were dimmed, one well-placed reporter believed. Stewart Griscom was there when the doctor passed around photographs of ectoplasm emerging from his wife's vagina while probing hands reached between her thighs. Later he couldn't help but feel there was more than science to this affair—"A morbid or abnormal strain of sexuality which pervades the case is one of its salient, and perhaps its most significant, features," he wrote the ASPR.

While aware that a spy was in their midst, the Crandons never suspected that the *Boston Herald* reporter was Houdini's eyes and ears. It was Griscom who told him that Margery would be a no-show at Jordan Hall. And whenever she performed at home, Houdini seemed to be watching—he was mimicking on vaudeville many of her latest ectoplasmic feats. The Crandons also didn't realize, as the *Herald* pieces often carried no byline, how involved Griscom had been in unearthing Mina's past. Blind to his intentions, the Lime Street hostess liked and trusted him; for he was a gentleman reporter, like John Flynn, who did not appear to have a taste for salacious stories and contraband drinks. He gave Margery reason to feel he was sympathetic to her—even her friend. Maybe that was why Walter liked having him in the séance room. *"If you don't come back, I won't,"* the voice whispered in Griscom's ear.

In his reporting Griscom seemed as enamored of the ghost. Walter's invisible presence, he wrote, "is vivid, sharply defined and unforgettable. His moods are swift and evanescent. By turns he is gay, impudent, ironic, ribald, but always witty, with a gamin-like ability for a quick retort or a cutting phrase." But the newsman wished to acquaint himself with the lady more than her spirit control, as that was the key, he believed, to understanding what was going on in her house. Though Margery fleeced no superstitious widows or grieving financiers of their savings or stocks, and was of a social rank that set her apart from the mediums who advertised sketchily in newspapers and led séances in a subterranean church, there was an unseemly side, Griscom felt, to these martyrs to psychical research. The talk of wild parties, the bacchanals at Lime Street, he thought was largely myth. Nevertheless, he was wary of Margery's friends, whom he found less credible than McDougall, Houdini, and Prince—the prudes who drank less of Roy's wine and never slept under his roof.

His sense was that Margery's gaiety gave a false impression—10 Lime Street was not really a happy place. According to an investigator in the new Harvard group, Dr. Crandon—characterized as a libertine who ultimately tired of and disposed of his wives—had given the present Mrs. Crandon reason to feel "that her position is none too safe. She has gone up the ladder in marrying him and may be really in love with him." Yet when her phenomena ended, so would her marriage, the source conjectured; for at the end of the day, the Crandons were "two oversexed people matched together with little else in common."

Griscom never stayed overnight at Lime Street, but he suspected that more than the ghosts there went bump in the night. Again, though, he didn't believe every whisper and innuendo. A few of the bookish investigators appeared to take pride in being linked romantically to the glamorous medium—in being perceived as the Don Juans they were not. For her part, Margery seemed to delight in her aphrodisiacal power over the scientists—

these supposedly incorruptible professionals—and she was the source for some of the rumors surrounding her love life.

One of the new Harvard investigators, Grant Code, was smitten with the clairvoyant practically as soon as he entered her house. Like others who had studied her, Code was both an intellectual—an English professor at Harvard—and amateur conjurer, and again like many psychic investigators, he had a troubled personal life. He was a free-lover, Margery learned, whose wife had tested the arrangement by running off with his psychotherapist. Perhaps accordingly, Code had a tendency to give confessionals—to Margery and Griscom—while also eliciting them from others familiar with the case. Bird confided to Code that relations were so strained between Margery and Roy during the later stages of the psychic contest that "Crandon would only be decent to her after a good séance." Disconsolate, the medium would then seek attention elsewhere and "was making advances to every man in sight"—beginning, Bird hinted, with himself.

Undoubtedly Bird did not have to be coaxed. At one sitting Walter got him to admit that touching Margery's ectoplasm was like "feeling a woman's breast." At a séance the previous July, Houdini said he caught Bird groping underneath her dress. In fact, he told Code that his detectives had provided him with photographic evidence of Margery's trysts, including her affair with Carrington. Most of the committeemen felt she made flagrant advances: Houdini said she tried to vamp him in and out of the séance room; McDougall suggested she'd done more than bat her catlike eyes his way; even Prince, whom the Crandons regarded as a crotchety old puritan, believed she had offered her lithe body to him—as if she were the sacred prostitute who could rekindle both his libido and faith. When he showed no interest, she cried, "O you are a wooden man," or so he claimed. While none of this was publicly stated, the seduction factor was central to Houdini's campaign. "Read between the lines," he told a friend, "and you will see I accused Margery of using sex charm and it has been authenticated"—as in a scathing pamphlet he published anonymously, where Bird and Carrington help her cheat in return for hooch, sweets, and a warm bed.

◆

Houdini's joint investigation with the *Herald* had begun in January, when two of its reporters, Griscom and A. J. Gordon, approached him for information on Eric Dingwall, whose Margery inquiry was being financed by Augustus Hemenway—the venerable Boston philanthropist and friend of the Crandons. Eager to help the Boston newsmen, Houdini sent them copies of all his correspondences with Dingwall. The British investigator was "a low salaried man," he told them, who came ambitiously to the land of jazz. "Never having been in fast company, never having tasted the luxuries of life before, he now being *used* imagines himself important—and you know no one is important until they are dead."

A night owl as well as an early riser, Houdini gave Griscom his home phone number—Monument 8260—and told him to call anytime after midnight. The magician also had a request to make, as he was no longer on civil terms with Margery: "By the way, I have been told that she has changed all of her tricks. Can you find out what she is now doing?"

As the only reporter with an open pass to Lime Street, Griscom was an effective spy. And Walter, who knew all, somehow never caught on to him. Considering himself "blooded" after his first sitting with the medium, Griscom gave Houdini an account, including diagrams, of all he experienced the June night he was initiated. "The customary bag of tricks" included the rising basket and streaking disks; the bell that rang at Walter's command—whether positioned on the table or when Griscom carried it about the den; the ectoplasmic hands that stroked his head and leg, untied his shoes, and pulled the hairpin from his wife's bob; the spirit trumpet that floated erratically about the room—and through which Walter at one point issued threats: "*It's all over with Houdini,*" the phantom hissed. "He's done for," echoed Dr. Crandon. All this while Margery sat groaning in her kimono, holding Griscom's hand.

Lovers were less intimate, Griscom felt, while caressing each other in a parked roadster after a dance. Many a sitter before him had grasped Margery's hand and attained such close proximity to her—leg-to-leg, foot-on-foot, at times her head falling reflexively to their shoulders—that the arrangement would have afforded them opportunities for a sepulchral petting party. Yet when Griscom asked the Crandons their opinion of some of the investigators, he found them to be correct and candid. Margery described Prince as the most honest man she had ever known—"He's an ass," she added, "but he's absolutely reliable." At this, the reporter had to suppress a laugh, given how Prince privately maligned them. She said Bird was honorable too, which somewhat weakened her assessment of Prince, Griscom decided. Carrington she called "a real man," which again had a double meaning for the reporter who knew of their romance.

As if gauging his loyalty to Margery, the Crandons then wished to know what Griscom thought of Houdini. To their surprise, he admitted to liking him very much both as a person and an investigator. As unexpectedly, Margery cried: "I like and respect Houdini's attitude much more than most of the others. At least he's not afraid to say where he stands." She all but admitted an attraction to her rival, but more amusing to Griscom was that the Crandons had become fond of two reporters who had nothing but disdain for their cause. "Talking about laughs," Griscom chortled to Houdini, "Crandon handed me one yesterday when he told a man on the *Herald*—who's wife, God help her, is a patient—that he liked Gordon and me, and that we had treated him more fairly than any other newspapermen. Walter evidently has failed to tip him off about our exposé of Margery's past." Griscom did find the couple brilliant, though. "You'll have to admit that they are damn clever magicians. You should get them in your show."

Testifying to Margery's cleverness, Griscom had no explanation, even after conferring with Houdini, for how she pulled off the manifestations at his recent sitting. They had coated the medium's hair with luminous paint so that she could not surreptitiously use her head, as Houdini promised she would, to raise tables and hurl trumpets through the air. But it was Margery's mouth that was of more interest to Griscom. Walter used many of the same expressions, and seemed cognizant of the same information as the medium. When the spirit's voice manifested from the far side of her cabinet, the reporter thought he detected a faint hiss from where the glowing locks indicated her mouth was located—as if, he suggested to Houdini, she spoke through the mouthpiece of a tube that projected her brother's whisper. One of the charter members of the ABC Club, Frederick Adler, was supposed to be a mechanical expert—so maybe he had rigged a contraption, offered Griscom, that created some of her telephonic effects. As for the slimy spirit hand that had teased him and his wife, it was a gloved human hand or foot, the reporters agreed—but Griscom doubted it was Margery's. Her hands were too well controlled, he insisted, to reach Mrs. Griscom, and the removal of pins from his wife's hair was too delicate an operation for even a conjurer's toes.

Having suggested that she had a confederate, Griscom as quickly talked himself out of it. The séance he witnessed had been a dress rehearsal, he told Houdini, for Margery's performance for the new Harvard group. "It would have been possible," Griscom speculated, "for Margery to have brought in a boy under her long kimono at the home séance." Later, however, she reproduced the same effects for the investigators at the Harvard laboratory, where the smuggling of any accomplice, no matter how small, would have been impossible. Admittedly, Griscom had not solved the mystery. But new developments made all talk of séance hijinks inconsequential. The spirit world had always abounded with rascals guilty of common swindles and misdemeanors. Few, though, were ever accused of the supposed sins for which Dr. Crandon was now being investigated.

Lost Boys

And oh! of all tortures that torture the worst
Has abated—the terrible Torture of thirst
For the naphthaline river of Passions accurst:
I have drunk of a water that quenches all thirst.

—EDGAR ALLAN POE

*E*ver since Medea slew her babes, witches have been portrayed as menacing to children. When Sir Arthur was a schoolboy at Stonyhurst, in the heart of England's witch country, he and his peers pretended to flee the hags said to haunt Pendle Hill—and it was feared that if a witch should ever snatch a boy, he might wind up roasted on a spit or boiled in a cauldron. His bones the grist for spells, his blood the sustenance for demons. But Sir Arthur had long ago renounced his Catholic education and the Church's bias against occultism. More than witches, he feared the traditional enemies of spiritism; so he smelled a papist plot when Dr. Crandon confessed to being the target of an investigation into missing children.

"A highly incredible story which persists is that a boy who was in his family some weeks mysteriously disappeared," Walter Prince disclosed. "He claims that the boy is now in his home in England, but still official letters of inquiry and demand are received from that country. This is no mere rumor, for I was shown some of the original letters." Unwisely, Margery had confided to Prince that the Secret Service—the real agency, as opposed to Houdini's people—was investigating her husband. "Doctor Crandon, she tells me, was threatened with arrest at one time. It is very mysterious."

The charges were appalling. Someone had informed the authorities that Roy was bringing over British orphans—potential Crandons who were not making it back to England after he found them unsuitable for adoption. Seeking recourse, Dr. Crandon presented Sir Arthur with "a little problem for Sherlock Holmes." The Secret Service Department in Washington was told, he wrote, "that I had first and last sixteen boys in my house for ostensible adoption, and that they had all disappeared." Of most concern was the case of Horace Newton, the orphan whom Joseph DeWyckoff had delivered to Margery the previous December. A Member of Parliament in London had contacted the White Star Line to determine whether the boy had returned, as the Crandons attested, on the *Doric*. Meanwhile, agents from Washington were conducting an investigation in Boston.

"The U.S. inspectors have been up to see me regarding the boys," the *Herald*'s A. J. Gordon alerted Houdini. "Have you heard anything more from England on the matter?" In response, Houdini sent the *Herald* the initial findings of the British inquiry; no one was going to be arresting the doctor just yet—the most recent of the lost boys, Horace Newton, whom Roy had gone to such lengths to bring over, had indeed been returned to England. As Roy explained to the inspectors, Mrs. Crandon had put young Newton on the *Doric* on December 20 for his return passage. Undeniably she had: Horace Newton was on the ship's manifest. Moreover, he was the sort of spunky child—a quality that hadn't endeared him to Dr. Crandon—whom people distinctly remembered. The ship's doctor, a friend of Roy's, recalled him as being "very popular with everyone, on his return voyage." But there appeared to be other boys who might have made a one-way trip from England to Beacon Hill. "I am not clear how many boys have gone across. You will let me have the facts," Doyle advised.

While Holmes sought to clear the Crandons, Houdini's own investigation hadn't doused his suspicions of them. "Gordon wants me to ask you . . . what are you doing to find out about that boy in New Jersey," Griscom wrote Houdini. The remains of a vagrant teenager had reportedly been found in the general vicinity of DeWyckoff's two hundred acres; indications were that one of the missing boys had also wound up in New Jersey—and any mention of DeWyckoff only added, by dint of his past, to the pall over the investigation.

Though DeWyckoff had influential friends in Washington, Griscom discovered that he hadn't always been the venerable citizen—the Russian Horatio Alger—that his wealth and connections suggested. As a young lawyer, DeWyckoff had fled Chicago after being indicted for pilfering thousands of dollars that had been willed to one of his clients. In another incident he was arrested and charged with grand larceny in Florida.

Houdini didn't believe that villains change their stripes, least of all because of some spiritist epiphany. Yet the magnate whom the *Boston Globe* once called a "Russian fugitive," for defrauding four different parties, was the individual whom Dr. Crandon had entrusted with the Newton adoption. It was DeWyckoff who had accompanied the orphan from England—as if he, an aging immigrant, could assure the new one of a bright life with the Crandons.

For Griscom, the Margery case had become more of an inquiry into the pathology of Dr. Crandon. "I find that many of those who have known Crandon best and longest," he wrote Houdini, "believe he is insane, at least on this one subject." He had heard, for instance, that after one scientist tried to reach for Margery's ectoplasm without permission, the doctor warned: "If he had carried out his test, he would never have left the house alive." While Dr. Crandon had no reputation for violence, whispers persisted that he was preying on children. The investigations went nowhere, though, and the *Herald* reported nothing on the missing boys.

In the course of Sir Arthur's opposing inquiry, as to who was conspiring against the Crandons, he had managed to determine the identity of the MP causing such a flap in London; it was Harry Day, a relatively new hand at politics. Sir Arthur warned Day not "to act as the unconscious agent of any personal enemy." He demanded to know who had persuaded him to call for an investigation into the Newton adoption. Dr. Crandon believed that only William McDougall wielded the influence to draw an MP into the affair. Doyle, meanwhile, still felt the Catholic Church was after the Crandons. They were both mistaken. The former impresario of "Harry Day's Crystal Cabaret," Day was Houdini's close friend and theatrical agent in Britain.

Were this one of Houdini's action movies, no doubt the Svengali-like Roy, and his strong arm, DeWyckoff, would be child traffickers foiled at the end of the third reel by Haldane of the Secret Service. Houdini had already called Margery a voodoo sorceress, and was now collecting articles attesting to the discovery of human bones in the New Jersey cellar of a "Voodoo Witch Doctor." Bedeviling children is a charge for which many an eccentric woman, a supposed witch, has stood trial. Margery's only immediate summons, however, was to Harvard.

To Hell with Harvard

*T*he Margery mediumship was still attracting serious scientific interest, with Harvard professors more interested in the case than agents of the Secret Service. The original questions were still unresolved in the eyes of many psychic researchers. Although the *Scientific American* had rendered a decision of "supernormality not proved," some of the judges had called for further testing. Because the committee's verdict had not settled the controversy, a new team assembled to investigate Margery.

Hudson Hoagland, a graduate psychology student and protégé of Mc-Dougall, had a zealous interest in the case: he intended to write his Harvard dissertation on Margery's phenomena, should he find her work convincing. Like many of his predecessors, Hoagland was impressed with the earnestness of Dr. Crandon. But after he and his colleagues had several sittings with Margery, and were showered with an array of Walter's effects, they made some rather frank criticisms: primarily that it was futile for the doctor to try to convince the scientific world of anything as long as he insisted on holding the gatherings at Lime Street and on imposing his conditions. They suggested that Margery be brought to the Harvard Psychology Laboratory for further experiments. Finding their argument persuasive, Roy agreed to what became known as the Second Harvard Investigation—the enterprise that Hoagland hoped would offer more conclusiveness than the *Scientific American* inquiry.

A far cry from the established experts Munn and Bird had assembled, these young investigators were a hodgepodge of graduate psychology, English, and poetry students, including the admiring Grant Code—whose goodwill made the Crandons feel more comfortable than they had felt at the Charlesgate tests.* Yet once word got out that Margery had consented

---

* The Harvard group consisted of Hudson Hoagland, Grant Code, Foster Damon, Robert Hillyer, and John Marshall.

to a thorough examination on their side of the Charles, some of Harvard's most respected scientists wanted to join the undertaking. To shield the school from involvement in another Margery controversy, the professors called themselves observers rather than committee members.* They felt they had to be more careful than their students; if they were married to their academic specialties—mathematics, astronomy, and biology—then psychic research was where they sought illicit excitement.

The press was not informed that once again Walter and scientists were tangling. The Harvard investigation of the Crandons was sub rosa—only Griscom and his colleagues were aware of it, and they respected the news blackout. It remained to be seen, however, whether one dark room was like any other. In crossing the Charles, the Crandons had entered an environment less hospitable to a spook show and more conducive to a controlled experiment. The séance laboratory was a small square room on the third floor of Emerson Hall, where fraud was deemed "impossible." It had no windows and the only door was to be kept locked during sittings—any intrusions would have to come from the spirits, not lightfooted accomplices. The meager room—one that Walter would liken to *the Charlestown jail*"—could accommodate only a table and chairs, a cloth spirit cabinet, a Victrola, and the usual playthings for Walter. To protect against deception researchers sent a mild electric current through the circle gathered there—so that if anyone were to release their hands it would instantly break the circuit and sound an alarm. The luminous bands that Dingwall had introduced were also attached to the medium's head, arms, and legs, as well as her husband's. Layers of humane control, rather than Houdini's box, were used for this trial.

As the tests commenced on the evening of May 19, 1925, the circle was literally charged with energy. On a Windsor chair sat Margery, restrained by the usual hand and foot control, monitored by an electrical apparatus,

---

* Among the notable witnesses present at various séance tests, though never as an entire body, were the Harvard psychologist Edwin Boring, Dr. S. B. Wolbach of the medical school, and the astronomer Harlow Shapley. The physicist E. B. Wilson was MIT's observer; Professor W. J. V. Osterhout represented the Rockefeller Institute; and the ASPR's Malcolm Bird attended one of the Harvard test séances.

wrapped in gleaming bracelets, and surrounded by those who, for the most part, doubted her. Within minutes Walter arrived with his typical defiance. After hearing his lively whistle, Roy was confident that the spirit would not forsake his kid sister. *"To hell with Harvard,"* the voice jeered—and within minutes the researchers noted cool breezes and "inexplicable noises and movements." One of Walter's illuminated round toys, which he called *"a doughnut,"* was propelled around the room then flopped on the table next to Hoagland. Did they really think their electric current could impede psychic force? Margery, now in trance, was more powerful in her sleep, Walter's activity suggested, than their feeble apparatus. Together, brother and sister performed many of their best numbers: the bell box rang; the lambent megaphone floated; the ghost yanked Hoagland by his forelock.

The atmosphere was so hot and draining that Margery could give only one of her two weekly demonstrations at Emerson Hall, with the other conducted at Hoagland's apartment in West Cambridge. But after six sittings the team was impressed by her work at both locations. At various times Walter used his phantom limb to raise a white basket loaded with metal weights, while a corresponding increase in Margery's weight was registered. He liked to rap the sitters with his clammy hands, untie their shoes, and send tremors through the table while crying, *"Earthquake!"* His most discussed feat, though, was the game of checkers he played with the astronomer Shapley. Both the living and the dead man moved painted electrodes across a glowing coordinate board until Walter outmaneuvered his opponent and whispered, *"Checkmate!"*

Walter was never more outrageous. The Harvard students were most entertained when the spirit led them in a song that parodied his old nemesis, who had said Margery's ectoplasm smelled like liver, and whose office was just down the hallway.

> *Shall we gather at Old Harvard,*
> *Shall we go to all the bother*
> *For McDougall?*
> *Shall we gather at the river?*
> *Shall we eat a pound of liver*
> *For McDougall?*

During Walter's manifestations, the investigators noticed spirit lights, unexplained luminosities that gathered around the medium's legs. Professor Shapley, who observed this and the rest of Margery's repertoire, affirmed that "there was no evidence of trickery" or "suspicious actions on the part of anyone in the circle." Whether one believed her feats were psychic or clever spookery, Margery had lived up to her billing. "The whole thing," wrote Hoagland, "was extremely baffling." Thus, at the seventh test séance, on June 29, "the nervous tension of the sitters was at a high pitch" in Hoagland's apartment at 18 Traill Street.

"Some of the group believe that the true story of the final nights will never authoritatively be told in full," Griscom later wrote. What is known is that the medium subjected herself to the customary nude search. Afterward the circle formed and Walter arrived with abundant energy. Using his teleplasmic arm, the ghost rang the bell box repeatedly, then lifted a luminous spool with weights attached to it—once levitating a six-pound bundle five feet from the ground. Minutes later, Grant Code saw shining on the floor the control bracelet that belonged on Margery's ankle. Yet when he announced into the Dictaphone that her leg was effectively free of control, Walter denied it. *"No it isn't,"* said the ghost as the band suddenly disappeared. *"I can hide it any time I want to."*

If Margery were indeed cheating, she recovered wonderfully. The band was now clearly back on her foot, though slightly elongated. Hoagland saw this as proof of how effortlessly she could manipulate it. But she hadn't actually been caught faking phenomena. Perhaps it was only that the bracelets were too large, as she later claimed, for her slender ankles.* In any case, her performance went on as if nothing suspicious had happened. Then, at a little before eleven p.m., Hoagland sensed the case for Walter's existence unraveling.

The spirit hand took on at least three different amorphous forms, but it had stubby "finger-like processes" and felt suspiciously like a heel to one

---

* According to the official minutes of the sitting, Margery had complained just before the demonstration began that the control bands were too loose; she had attempted to tighten them with pins.

outside observer present that evening—a Dr. Wolcott, who was grazed by it. This visiting scientist from Minnesota, who told Walter from the beginning that he didn't believe in him, had been engaged all that evening in a battle of wits with the goblin. Believing that any spirit should have the "gift of tongues," Wolcott tried to address Walter in Japanese. When the voice answered with a cuckooing noise, the room erupted in laughter. Wolcott lost these contests, yet there was one crude ghost-busting tactic he dared not attempt. As *Time* magazine would report, "none of those present employed the obvious investigatory stratagem of seizing the ghostly arm and calling for lights." It was understood that only with Walter's permission could a sitter touch the teleplasm. And so Wolcott did not exactly break the cardinal rule when Walter's spirit hand waved the doughnut tantalizingly in front of his face. Instead, he blew hard on it.

Enraged when the doughnut fell onto the table, Walter reclaimed the object and passed it repeatedly by Wolcott, daring him to blow it out of his terminal again. The professor tried to and failed—but if the phenomena were really fake, then Margery, supposedly unconscious in her trance, had just made a careless misstep. Waving the doughnut over the incandescent coordinate board, she gave Hoagland the sustained glimpse of the spectral hand that he had been waiting for since the tests started.

What held the doughnut, he discerned by its silhouette, was a human foot.[*]

Without mentioning what he had observed, Hoagland received Walter's permission to make a Plasticine impression of his teleplasm. *"What's this damn stuff—glue?"* the ghost asked while dipping his immaterial hand into the compound that formed a cast of it. When the lights were turned up, Margery's leg bracelets looked to be in place, even though they had slipped from her ankles to her heels. A heavy rain began. The séance was over. But the Crandons had no idea how much activity began as they motored away from Traill Street.

---

[*] Hoagland's observation was not recorded in the signed minutes but inserted as an addendum after the sitting was over—a practice that Dr. Crandon, who believed no witness statements should be allowed after the fact, had prohibited.

Upon examining the impression of Walter's "hand," the scientists saw that it had the whorls and skin marks consistent with a hominal foot. Grant Code said this explained everything. The proof was in the magic. Although shabbily attired in his typically mismatched coat and trousers that hung low over canvas sneakers, he was an adept conjurer and something of an acrobat. While Hoagland and Foster Damon held his hands, he showed how he could use his toes to obscure or displace the leg bands, or even create the illusion that the bracelet on the floor was still on his leg. With his freed right foot he rang the bell boxes, raised the glowing doughnut, levitated the basket with the weights, pulled hair, undid shoes, and produced with his clothes and feet various silhouetted shapes—which resembled Walter's terminals and shapeless forms—against the coordinate board. All the while he imitated Margery's deep moans and quavering. The researcher who adored Mrs. Crandon was destroying her case at Harvard.

As if that weren't enough, Margery had evidently made another blunder. While leaving the house she had dropped one of her séance slippers in Hoagland's yard. The next morning the psychologist found it soaked and mauled by his dog. Under a microscope he deduced that the lint from the slipper matched perfectly the samples taken from the cast of Walter's teleplasmic hand. By now Hoagland believed he had all he needed—the concrete evidence Houdini had never produced—to support his determination that Margery's manifestations were most certainly of this world.

The Harvard team decided to allow the medium one more chance—only, not the same chance as before. Having determined that Walter was powerless with his sister's legs subdued, the committee decided to secure them with surgeons' plaster during her final sitting at Emerson Hall. To their surprise, Margery found the severe restraint agreeable. Chiding the scientists for their inadequate control the night before, she was in good humor while they plastered her. Patiently she waited as the electric circuit was sent through the circle. Dr. Crandon was moved to the opposite side of the table; only the investigators were allowed to touch her arms and legs. Code, who had revealed her methods, was on her right this time. All awaited the expected blank séance.

Minutes later Walter came through, unashamedly admitting that the ankle band was off the previous night. He had not wanted to reveal this gaffe to Wolcott, he said, since it wasn't his sister's fault. To everyone's shock he then announced that he was there when Code performed his post-séance exhibition and that they were all wrong in their judgments. Before Hoagland had absorbed this revelation—how could Walter know about what had happened after the Crandons left his house?—the spirit wrought his marvels.

That night all the phenomena reoccurred—the bell box rang, the objects floated by, the clammy terminals caressed the observers—only this time the spirit hand materialized with "long cordlike structures" clearly incongruous with a human foot. When the tentacle grasped Professor Shapley's wrist, Walter asked if it still struck him as a human heel. The professor replied that the slimy teleplasm felt more like "the heel of an eel."

Hoagland had no explanation. "Teleplasmic Arms Puzzle Scientists," the *Times* would report when the press gag was lifted. The Harvard group formally admitted that what they witnessed on June 30 could not have been caused by Margery's feet. "Through the scintillating skill of his attack," Walter had reversed all of Hoagland's and his colleagues' expectations. The chief investigator was put in the embarrassing position of having to admit on record that his team's suspicions of legerdemain were unfounded. He still believed that Margery's phenomena had a natural cause, but with the inquiry over, he had failed to determine it.

It was then that Grant Code dropped his bombshell. Two days after the last Harvard séance he told the committee that he could explain how the effects on June 30 were possible. Their expert conjurer, who had been given control of Margery's right arm for that final demonstration, admitted that he had deliberately released the medium. He did so, he said, because something "dangerous" would have happened if he hadn't.

Like so much that had occurred in the Margery case, his story seemed both absurd and plausible. Code confessed that a few hours before the final séance, he had visited Lime Street with the intention of preventing a disaster. If there was one truth of which he was "thoroughly convinced," he told Margery, it was that she and Dr. Crandon were sincere in their belief in Walter. However, she was about to be exposed, he said, as her methods had been found out and Code himself had duplicated them. He knew she wasn't consciously cheating. Rather, he offered, Roy was hypnotizing her and then impelling her to perform through autosuggestion. In Code's view, Roy was just as oblivious to what was actually happening: he genuinely, and perhaps desperately, believed in Margery's supernormal power. If she gave a blank séance, or was caught in trickery, Roy would think she had "deceived him and made a public fool of him." Code felt there was "every chance of a dangerous mental and domestic crisis," should this happen.

So he offered to help her.

According to Code, Margery was frightened and confused by his accusations. "I'll give you my word of honor that I have never done these things," she said in reaction to his explanation of the foot-induced phenomena. She denied as emphatically the theory of automatism, as it meant, she felt, that there was something wrong with her. Code persisted that the music, the dialogue of Dr. Crandon, indeed every aspect of the séance ritual had been instrumental in lulling her into the hypnotic state that caused her to fake phenomena. "Her reaction," as he reported it, "was increasing conviction and fear." She said she was willing to do whatever he advised. Oddly enough, Code, who claimed to no longer believe in the ghost, replied that "it would be dangerous to do anything without consulting Walter." Hence, he and the medium retired to Roy's den for a private séance.

While darkening the room, Code told her that Walter had never failed to come through in an emergency and surely, at this desperate time, he would materialize and advise her on the best course of action. He then sat beside her and held her hands. Trying to relax her, he lowered his voice and gossiped about the men she was to perform for that evening. Suddenly, Margery had a convulsion and freed one of her hands. Code did not attempt to restrain her. Moments later she slipped into trance and Walter's voice, through her lips, was heard as if thrown against the cabinet then reflected so that "the exact position of the sound was very deceptive to the ear."

"What's the matter, Code?" asked Walter. There was a lot the matter, Code answered; the committee was fairly certain "that the whole business is trickery, and if there is a blank to-night they will be sure. I'm afraid there will be some sort of a blow up that will have a bad effect on everybody. I'm

very fond of you and Roy and the Psychic and I don't want anything to happen that will hurt them."

"I never tricked you, Code."

"I know. But I thought it was best to tell you about things in advance and let you see how serious the situation is."

"Whew!... What do you want me to do, Code?"

The investigator demanded that Walter come through strong that night, and with teleplasm. A blank séance or any change in the phenomena would give the Harvard team all it needed to announce a negative finding. Code offered to assist in any way possible: he would manifest himself if Walter wanted.

"No, don't you do anything," the ghost whispered.

By Code's account, Walter asked him only to relax control of the medium at the séance that evening, *"and let her hand move a little."*

"All right, Walter. I've got that. Anything else?"

"Don't let it be a blank, Code."

"You can count on me, Walter."

After Code received Walter's assurances that Dr. Crandon would not be informed of their predicament and plan, the spirit returned for a few hours to his indigenous dimension, leaving his sister in the hands of the English student who seemed torn between wanting to expose and save her. Still vexed by Code's visit, Margery emerged from trance complaining of a pain in the neck. At which point her guest begged her to lie down for a while.

Code's admission was enough for Hoagland, who accepted that his disturbed colleague had helped Margery circumvent both the physical and electric control during her last display for the investigators. These last pieces to the Margery puzzle fit perfectly with the observations of the sitters at the final Harvard gathering, who noticed that Margery's right arm appeared to move slightly every time Walter's hand performed a task. Having had her foot techniques discovered, she pulled another trick, they deduced, from her bag of wonders. The last Plasticine cast of Walter's hand was imprinted with long tentacles, as well as small chainlike structures that the investigators believed were responsible for its mechanics. But how had Margery gotten the fake teleplasm into the secured laboratory? Again Code had the answer. He told the committee that at the final sitting he saw her remove three artificial objects, one of which looked like a baby's amputated hand, from between her legs.

With this, the most shocking of Code's statements, the Harvard group closed its case on Margery, thereupon ending the university's two-year association with the clairvoyant. As a way of delivering what he considered the definitive verdict on Margery, Hoagland agreed to write up his findings for the *Atlantic Monthly*. He took his time, though, and for three months the Crandons heard nothing from across the Charles. They were mortified when Stewart Griscom finally informed them that Grant Code, of all researchers, had provided evidence against them. After an intense conversation, the reporter persuaded Dr. Crandon to show him the Harvard séance reports. "My purpose in this was twofold," Griscom wrote Houdini: "first to get a scoop for the *Herald,* which we certainly did; and second to create such a stink that all the scientists on the committee would be forced to talk in self defense."

Griscom's plot worked to perfection. As much as Roy had detested the *Scientific American* carnival, the once secretive Harvard investigation ultimately played out as sensationally and before the same national audience. Scooping the *Atlantic*, Griscom reported that while the Harvard team believed the Crandons acted in "good faith," Margery's effects were natural in origin. Delicately, and to Griscom's mind unsatisfactorily, the committee tried to resolve the paradox of calling the medium both sincere and fake by theorizing that she operated under hypnosis, or was in a state of unconscious automatism during her séances. As a result, "there was immediately hell to pay at Harvard," Griscom told Houdini, for the senior scientists now felt their names were attached to a misleading report that, because Hoagland did not want to shame the Crandons, made no mention of conscious trickery. Was the medium in the hypnotic state, they privately scoffed, when she packed artificial hands into her vagina?

As Halloween approached, the professors and most of the official Harvard group told Griscom that the effects were unquestionably legerdemain. With the exception of Code, all of them believed she knew what she was doing. In truth, Dr. Crandon was the one who they felt had a double personality—

"He believes in the phenomena at the same time that he is helping to use trickery, they say. Of Margery the case is different, and not one of them, except Code, feels that she is sincere," Griscom informed Houdini.

Margery did still have a sympathetic newsman, though, in John T. Flynn, who would soon publish the glowing portrait of her for *Collier's*. After interviewing Code, Flynn told the Crandons that the first six sittings had made "a profound impression on the Harvard group and that they were on the verge of bringing in a favorable verdict." Even after ruling against her, Code was inclined to view some of her phenomena as genuine.

Code's was the dilemma of a number of Margery's admirers. Having become attached to the medium, they couldn't reconcile their adulation of her with subsequent signs of deception. Code was aghast that the committee used his private deductions to turn what he felt was a gray case into a black-and-white one: the scientists had ignored some inexplicable effects, he protested, "in order to make the case blacker against the Crandons." He felt he knew Margery's heart, if not her mind; and writing her, he said that she was "no fraudulent lady but a fine woman whom I believe to be honest." He told a fellow investigator that "the tricks are far from being the whole of the mediumship."

Grant Code had always struck Margery as nervous, dramatic, and forlorn, and she was sympathetic to his emotional plight—his failures as a writer of fiction, his wife running off. It was true that he fought to prevent the Harvard group from charging her with fraud, yet he had debunked her. And if he were indeed a free-lover, as Margery confided to Griscom, then he did not understand that her love, or at least affection, came at a cost, since his reputation was also vulnerable.

Margery revealed to Griscom how Code came to her house and cried bitterly. She showed him Code's letters to her, which the reporter told Houdini were "affectionate, wild, hysterical and almost insane." More damagingly, Roy portrayed him to his colleagues as a degenerate. Code understood that Margery's effects had stirred "a profound religious faith" in Dr. Crandon, so he shouldn't have been surprised when he was accused of violating the medium. It was not just that she had spurned Code's advances, Dr. Crandon also charged that the young investigator tried to rape her.* After all that, Roy threatened, as he had other investigators, to sue Code for libel. Upon hearing this, Code's colleague Foster Damon laughed and told his fellow researcher that "the faces of an Irish jury in Boston would be quite a sight when it slowly dawned on them where she keeps her apparatus."

The dispute pitted the Harvard group against the ASPR when Malcolm Bird came with his sharp pen to the medium's defense. In the ASPR journal that he edited, Bird called the Harvard investigators "a group of excessively young men," who were comically ignorant, he implied, of the physiology of their female subject—and the true proportions of any woman's vagina. Their theory of anatomic concealment was "stretched far past the breaking point," he contended. Was it any wonder they were poets, medievalists, and aspiring psychologists rather than medical students? "Mr. Hoagland and his collaborators from the Department of English, are under an obvious and severe misunderstanding as to the size, shape, and other dominant characteristics of the anatomical storehouse which it is customary to mention under the gentle euphemism 'within the medium's body.'"

Dr. Crandon offered another defense against the Harvard charges. The séance minutes indicated that Margery had been menstruating on the night she was supposed to have removed objects from her vagina and placed them on the table. Yet no blood was on the hands of investigators who had touched the ectoplasm, nor on the table. Dr. Crandon was using that as evidence, wrote Griscom, "that Margery could not have been faking." The absence of blood proved her innocence.

---

* "Mrs. Crandon flatters herself as she did when she tried to vamp Houdini!" Code said in his defense.

Such Damn Fools

MARGERY RIDICULES HARVARD GROUP FOR "TRICKERY" CHARGES
SAVED THEIR FACES BY SHIFT, SHE HINTS
—*Boston Herald,* OCTOBER 24, 1925

*I*n the end Fair Harvard had not lived up to its name, rued Margery. The university investigators hid behind the Harvard gates when they denounced her: her detractors would not put their names behind their statements to the press; and Grant Code was somewhere in Delaware where reporters couldn't find him. The whole affair, she said, was wasteful and dishonorable.

The medium was puzzled and amused, she told Stewart Griscom, by the scientists who had appeared to be impressed by her effects yet concluded on the basis of what she felt was shoddy evidence—a fallen bracelet and slipper!—that over the course of eight test séances she had successfully bamboozled them with nothing but her right foot. In none of the séance minutes the scientists had signed, which she now turned over to Griscom, did they mention any suspicion of sleight of hand. They had decided to reconsider their own observations because "Fair Harvard" would have been put in a queer position, she maintained, had the committee of ambitious students and their mentors admitted they were at a loss to explain what they had witnessed. Concerning Code's claim that in a private séance she had plotted more deception, she stated—and both she and her maid would give affidavits refuting him—that no such session occurred. In her view she had been convicted on the word of an unstable admirer whom she confessed off the record to throwing over. This was what came of entrusting her case to prejudiced amateurs. "Seriously, all I ask on behalf of myself and this subject is fair play," she declared.

In the two days that Griscom had just spent with Mrs. Crandon, she also expressed something not evident in the bluster of her official statement. During his "many interesting talks with Margery," she seemed most distraught at how Houdini would react to what appeared to be the end of her mediumship. "Just think how Houdini will shout," she predicted. "He will say that he discovered in one sitting what it took the Harvard crowd eight sittings to find out."

As it turned out, she knew only too well the ways of Houdini, who boasted to Walter Lippmann that the Harvard group had "accomplished in half a year what I did in one night." Undeniably, the young investigators had upheld his claims. But the one thing puzzling Houdini was how Griscom had won Margery's confidence, given that he was doing his utmost to discredit her. To that Griscom answered: "Although she has never actually confessed, when we are alone it is tacitly admitted between us that the mediumship is all trickery. I think she respects me on exactly the same grounds that she does you, because we weren't taken in by her."

Griscom sensed that Margery would finally come clean if only "Crandon did not firmly believe. She knows that it would end all their relations and she doesn't dare to do it. She and I had a private conference the other afternoon and I advised her to admit it was all a hoax. She smiled broadly and asked how she could when it wasn't true. Then she said, with a grin, 'Aren't people such damn fools. Such damn fools. The investigators most of all.' "

♦

The front-page muse was not expected to be featured there much longer. "This verdict, I think, will kill the Margery phenomena with the great majority of intelligent people," Griscom wrote Houdini. "This has been a triumph for you, for the *Herald* and for me," the reporter gloated after his final Margery story. "I am rather pleased with myself for being the first to print the finding that she was fraudulent. At the same time I am sorry for Dr. Crandon and rather admire her for her sheer nerve, for her wit and for the good sportsmanship she has shown when shown up. Remember she has the doctor still to fool."

Not everyone agreed that the Harvard finding spelled the end of the Margery mediumship. *Life* magazine called Hoagland's investigation "an inquiry into anatomy by butchers seeking not so much knowledge as meat." In the eyes of some of the intelligent people to whom Griscom referred, Dr. Crandon was entirely more rational and trustworthy than the graduate student whom the Hon. Everard Feilding, one of the SPR's most influential officials, found "pathologically peculiar." It was really too late, though, to impeach Code and other witnesses. The precocious Harvard investigators—the psychology students, the Harvard aesthete, the literary toe dancer—had already made their case. And unlike the *Scientific American* committee, they were interested in exploring the motivations behind what they saw as a grotesque hoax from the beginning. In a private response to Feilding, Hoagland presented what many regarded as the definitive portrait of the Crandons.

"Dr. Crandon, is a man who has never learned to play," Hoagland wrote. "He takes everything very seriously. Mrs. Crandon on the other hand is extremely fun loving." Her penchant for mischief and Roy's maniacal drive merged dangerously when "Dr. Crandon took up spiritualism as a violent hobby and Mrs. Crandon played it for all it was worth . . . As long as Mrs. Crandon could fool her husband at all, and I think that in his present state of mind she may still, he is willing to do anything to convince others of his claims. He is able to pose as a martyr to science likening himself to Galileo. A half million uncritical spiritualists in the country regard Margery as a sort of Messiah.

"It would be quite impossible to imagine one's having faith in a fraud in which one is an active confederate, however in certain pathological cases such inconsistencies are not uncommon," Hoagland concluded. In his view, Dr. Crandon had become aware that only Margery's spook tricks, not genuine clairvoyance, would advance the mediumship. But by this time Roy, his friends, and some of the scientists were possessed by what H. L. Mencken saw as often among atheists as spiritist drones: "the irresistible and perhaps pathological impulse to believe and cherish the incredible."

As Grant Code put it, "The doctor was crazy enough to believe his own tricks, and honest enough to devote himself and his wife as living sacrifices to their own dishonesty." While Roy had morbid fears that drew him to Spiritualism, he had buried doubts about Margery that only scientific validation could assuage. As far as Harvard was concerned, the ghost was only a clever invention.

"Walter's a genius and I guess I told you I boohooed like a baby, when I just couldn't believe in him anymore," Code wrote Margery. "I wish Dr. C. could believe me and trust me, but I'm afraid he doesn't and I don't blame him much. He's had some pretty raw deals from investigators so it's natural that he should mistrust the breed."

Code's final letter to the medium expressed how devastating it was to be cast out by the Crandons. He lamented that he would never again hear Walter whisper, *"Here comes the works"* or *"Hello, Code."* But perhaps Walter might not be long for this world anyway. Goodbye, Walter, he closed. Goodbye, Kid. Goodbye, Dr. C. Goodbye, 10 Lime Street.

Part VIII

HOW DEATH DEALS ITS CARDS

⌘

Personally, I now doubt if there is any physical medium in existence,
for Margery was recognized as the best.
—PROFESSOR HARLOW SHAPLEY

The "Margery" mediumship which aroused Boston last winter is
proving equally disturbing in England and France, where eminent
parliamentarians, scientists, and physicists are debating it.
—*Christian Register*

Dr. and Mrs. Crandon

Houdini demonstrates a fraud medium's use of spirit trumpets, 1925

1926: The End of Magic

*T*he heyday of magic appeared to be over. "Visits of magicians to this city have become not unlike the reputed calls of angels," observed the New York *Sun*. "They are rarer even in vaudeville than they formerly were. Some of the practitioners of what used to be called the black art are quite as expert as their predecessors, but there is not the same degree of interest that once existed." Only Houdini and Thurston, King of Cards, were known to still draw turnouts. But Houdini was now performimg the kind of old-time conjury that was supposed to be Thurston's forte. And his show was a triumph on Broadway.

While Houdini's life had many pinnacles, his present engagement at the Forty-fourth Street Shubert Theatre was the high point, he said, of his life as an entertainer. His show *HOUDINI* played near productions of Eugene O'Neill, Noel Coward, and Shakespeare. His profitable run countered the views that stage magic was antiquated. The Great Houdini blended the old sleight of hand and spookery with showgirls and electric phosphorescence. The "Radio of 1950" was a huge cabinet with glowing meters and spinning dials that Houdini revealed to be empty inside but for some tubes and wiring. When he turned a knob and blasted jazz, a beauty in silver lace emerged dancing while the crowd roared to the Charleston.

The *Sun* reported, perhaps unfairly, that *HOUDINI*'s popularity was due to the part of the show where he unveiled Margery's charlatanism. Whatever the reason, the magician had never seemed more fluid and commanding. Praising his vitality onstage, even after suffering a broken ankle late in the run, *Billboard* belittled what Margery had prophesied: that he would die in December of 1925. When the appointed time came all he suffered was a minor fracture. "Margery's crystal," it was noted, "seems to be a bit misty."

Philadelphia

*A*fter Margery was given the gate by the Harvard boys, her elder and more steadfast admirers attempted to restore her honor. In February they—Mark Richardson; Dr. Crandon; three other illustrious Harvard alums;* and Joseph DeWyckoff, the one author who did not attend the university—put out a booklet, *Margery Harvard Veritas*, which rebutted the Harvard group's charges. Their record of events was distributed to virtually every university-employed psychologist and physicist in the world; to all the major libraries; to everyone employed at the ASPR; and to each professor and administrator at Harvard.

At the same time, Malcolm Bird swooped across the continent—deriding Houdini and the Margery bashers while promoting his own new book on her mediumship. From platforms lacking Broadway panache, Bird spoke in Boston, Memphis, Salt Lake City, Richmond, and Winnipeg. He appeared at Rotary Club luncheons, Women's Club events, Kiwanis Club forums, university auditoriums, and YMCAs and YMHAs. He made his case at engineers' clubs, physicians' clubs, and before the social elite as well as the local Spiritualist chapters. No one was more active, and few more passionate, in defending Margery. After his New York run, Houdini made the counterargument at some of the same types of associations, as well as in churches and on vaudeville. And ultimately, as if the spirits ordained it, they engaged each other in February at the Broad Street Theater in Philadelphia.

While Bird disparaged his competence and character, Houdini sat quietly in his box. Watching stoically, he seemed to take the attack in the same way he was said to let any challenger take their best shot at his midsection.

---

* Alfred W. Martin, Charles S. Hill, and S. Ralph Harlow.

Arguing that Houdini was a liar and an ignoramus, Bird recounted the most violent of Margery's phenomena—the spirit cabinet she shattered in the magician's presence. He described how the screws were forced out of the structure rather than unscrewed—and there was sawdust on the floor and sheer puzzlement in Houdini's eyes. Margery could not have accomplished this, Bird insisted, with her legs and her shoulders. "Mr. Houdini agrees with me because he says it couldn't have happened unless I did it, and I didn't do it, so there you are."

When it was his turn to address the audience, Houdini leaped fiercely onto the stage. Speaking from the gut, his rejoinder came out in a torrent of emotion. In only a few minutes he called Bird "a liar," "a contemptible liar," "a dirty liar," and "the man who lies." He condemned him as a betrayer of Orson Munn and an embarrassment to the *Scientific American*—a journalist whose reports on Margery were silly rot, and an author whose book on the medium was filled with more bunk than Baron Munchausen. By this time the mood in the house resembled a prizefight, yet the divide did not completely fall along expected lines. One Spiritualist who had met Dr. Crandon and felt misgivings on first sight had the same impression that evening about the ASPR officer. "The minute I saw and heard Bird, I felt distrust," she said. "He had eloquence, but not the truth that would have made him convincing. Houdini, without eloquence or command of speech, seemed to me to be trying, incoherently and hopelessly, to express truth."

Chicago/Washington

*T*he next city the Great Houdini played was Chicago, which was bad news for the many fraud mediums prospering there. For the eight weeks that his shows ran, he fought it out with the Midwest spooks; even though a supposed matriarch of the Spiritualist movement, Annie Benninghofen, came over to his side. At the Sherman Hotel he presented Mrs. Benninghofen to the newspapermen who had gathered to watch her reveal her secrets. Following a slick séance display, some were touched when the medium admitted her deceptions while denying her sins.

"I really believed in spiritualism all the time I was practicing it," the psychic quietly explained, "but I thought I was justified in helping the spirits out. They couldn't float a trumpet around the room. I did it for them. They couldn't speak, so I spoke for them. I thought I was justified in trickery because through trickery I could get more converts to what I thought was a good and beautiful religion."

Armed with Mrs. Benninghofen's affidavits, Houdini moved on to Washington, DC, for the defining moment in his crusade. With the Capitol as his stage, he would throw his support behind a fortune-telling bill sponsored by Congressman Sol Bloom that would effectively outlaw mediumship for profit as well as all forms of divination for hire.[*] In reaction to the impending vote, the ghost talkers came to Washington—MEDIUMS JAM CAPITOL, the headline flashed—to protest this threat to their religion and livelihood. Bloom had produced the anti-clairvoyant legislation, but the press considered Houdini the "motive energy behind the bill"—and the psychics were there, as he hoped, to defy him.

---

[*] Houdini would speak before House and Senate subcommittees in February and April.

It looked like an out-of-season Halloween celebration, with so many spooks walking the marble halls. During the sessions spirit mediums and fortune-tellers sat on the floor, hung from the windows, and huddled outside the door to the committee room. What transpired were the most bizarre and volatile hearings anyone could recall in the capital; the effort to keep Houdini and the spiritists apart so overwhelmed Bloom that at one point he fainted. Invigorated by the melee, the magician unrolled long scrolls compiled by Rose Mackenberg that he said contained evidence against the mediums debating him. When they called him a liar, he slammed $10,000 on the committee table and challenged any of them to perform a single feat that he could not unmask as flimflam. There were no takers. "Tell me the name my mother called me when I was born?" he cried. There was no answer. No spirit raps were manifested in the Capitol Building, only the raps of a gavel on sounding block. No disembodied voices came through, only the cries of "Infidel!" "Traducer!" as the chairman called for order.

In their defense, the mediums claimed that Spiritualism was backed by the Bible—and that when Houdini attacked prophets and seeresses he was condemning a religion. "How can you call it *religion*," Houdini mocked, "when you get men and women in a room together and feel each other's hands and bodies."

The exchanges became so heated that the police were later called to separate Houdini from his psychic opponents. Even some on the subcommittee were not clear as to why a conjurer, of all people, should object so harshly to the work of fellow occultists. "Would you be so cruel as to deprive a young country fellow of the pleasure of getting a picture of his sweetheart, or being told he is 'going on a long journey,' and all that frivolous stuff?" Congressman Gilbert asked Houdini. Also wary of the bill was Congressman McLeod, who wished to know how Spiritualism could be "such an outrageous fake and fraud," if it was advocated by "such men as Conan Doyle, who is an outstanding authority?"

"He is one of the greatest dupes, outside of Sir Oliver Lodge," answered the magician whom the psychics called "a Judas."

"In the beginning, 3,000 years ago, or 2,000, Judas betrayed Christ," an aggrieved medium testified, "he was a Jew and I want to say that this bill is being put through by two—well you can use your opinion." The witness warned that if lawmakers passed the legislation they would be reenacting the religious persecution of the Romans—a statement applauded by many in the chamber. Reporters noted something atavistic to these hearings—as if Roman senators were deciding whether street oracles should be allowed to prophesy in the shadow of the Forum. It was only when Houdini demonstrated spook tricks that the assembly was brought "back into twentieth century sunshine."

As Houdini saw it, he performed his tricks with spirit trumpets and slates so convincingly that both the lawmakers and the mediums believed he was psychic. The bill was ultimately rejected, he said, because the subcommittee had been taken in by his own phony manifestations. Actually, the politicians decided that any measure against professional mediums and soothsayers was not only unconstitutional but unnecessary. "We are making ourselves ridiculous with this bill," complained Congressman Gilbert. Unbowed, Houdini intended to continue his campaign. He didn't know that the curtain on his life of mystery was closing.

New York

*A*t just after noon on August 5, Houdini was put into his casket. He wore a watch with a radium dial and next to him was a battery-powered telephone so that he could communicate from the coffin. Sealed inside, he was lowered beneath the surface of the Shelton Hotel pool in Manhattan. An unparalleled demonstration began. Houdini was attempting to prove that he could rise from a watery grave after having been submerged for more than an hour.

The Great Houdini had had showdowns with Margery, Bird, and the Spiritualists en masse when he confronted them in Washington. This time he was dealing with another of his nemeses, Hereward Carrington, who had always avoided the Margery séances that Houdini attended. Dr. Carrington was promoting the work of an Italo-Egyptian fakir named Rahman Bey, who mystified New York audiences that summer. On the stage of the Selwyn Theatre, Bey punctured his cheeks and breasts with hatpins, then slashed the folds of his neck with a dagger. He showed physicians how he could increase the pulse rate of one wrist while simultaneously slowing down the other. Dr. Carrington, his manager, said that Bey had an "almost unlimited ascendancy over the body." The fakir hypnotized animals and psychically read the thoughts of volunteers from the house. And in his most remarkable feat, he was encased in an airtight coffin that rested at the bottom of the Dalton Hotel pool for one hour. He emerged from it Houdini-like: happy and triumphant.

For Houdini this was an old act in the days of Evatima Tardo, probably even old when the pyramids were erected. There was as much Eastern hypnosis in Bey's work, he told Walter Lippmann, as there was a lack of liquor in America. The problem, he explained, was that since Carrington had not attributed his performer's work to supernaturalism, Houdini was bound by the ethics of the magic profession not to reveal Bey's circus methods.

The only thing to do, Houdini decided, was surpass him. At fifty-two, he was twice Bey's age. He carried twenty pounds more weight than he had during his prime. He had high blood pressure and was phasing out his more acrobatic escapes. But Houdini never ducked a challenger. And so, after weeks of arduous training, he was put in a coffin and lowered into the pool at the Hotel Shelton.

Designed like an Ottoman bath, with a high gallery and ornate tiles, it was the right setting for a display of sorcery. Houdini had emphasized, however, that the feat required no spiritistic power or mastery of Eastern mysteries. The telephone wasn't there for the dead to speak to the living, but so that he could call for help if he felt himself losing consciousness. For decades Houdini had relied on his uncanny dexterity and athleticism, yet he knew that to match Rahman Bey he would have to achieve a preternatural state of motionlessness and inner quiet.

Six swimmers held the coffin underwater by stepping on it. Whenever one of them slipped and the coffin bobbed, it was agony for the escape artist inside. It was a struggle to control his breath and sustain the depleting oxygen in the coffin. Physicians said it would be impossible for him to endure more than fifteen minutes underwater. He remained there far longer, while the reporters, in their straw skimmers, quietly counted the minutes. There was a pall over this demonstration. Houdini's intention was not to entertain or escape—the goal was survival.

After ninety minutes, Houdini had shattered Rahman Bey's record by half an hour. Within the sweltering box he was panting and disoriented. His lungs burned. His saliva tasted like metal. He saw yellow flashes and felt agitated. Finally, he called for the casket to be raised. There were no shackles to be held up, no bows to take. Houdini never felt such relief, though, as when they pried the lid off the coffin. The onlookers applauded while doctors received him like an emergency patient. His pulse was racing. His systolic blood pressure had soared, his diastolic had plummeted dangerously. He was bathed in sweat, his face "deathly white." He was smiling broadly. Carrington was saying that Houdini must have had oxygen pumped through the telephone line; otherwise the achievement was impossible. No one was listening to him. The invitation-only audience, mostly newspapermen, gathered around the escape artist, their pens at the ready. But he had little to say after this, his final resurrection.

Boston

*B*ack in May, while Houdini battled the psychics on Capitol Hill, the Boston newspapers were reporting on another proceeding—in which MRS. CRANDON GOES TO COURT. This incident had nothing to do with the spirits; rather, Margery's penchant for speed had gotten her into trouble, as Roy had feared it would, when she drove so recklessly that a police sergeant alleged that he and his patrol car were almost knocked off a suburban hill. Found guilty by a Woburn judge, she received only a fine in the end, a slap on the wrist. Another verdict that came down that summer had a greater influence on her life.

In June, Eric Dingwall officially weighed in on the Margery mediumship. In his highly anticipated report, he called her phenomena "the most remarkable hitherto recorded." Praising her dedication and personal traits, he emphasized that he had never detected her in fraud. At length, he described her brilliant effects when he sat with her during the winter of 1925. He presented a convincing case that the mediumship was genuine.

He then tore apart his own argument.

While admitting that he had been of the provisional opinion that her work was authentic, he stated, "I no longer hold this view, and admit my change of mind." About halfway through his two-month series of test séances, he began, so he now claimed, to have his doubts. Flashing through his mind, like scenes in a movie reel, were impressions that the medium's phenomena were contrived and her ectoplasm fake.

When Walter had laughed at the same time a camera flashed, Dingwall saw the corner of the medium's mouth fall, as if pulled by a string. He realized then that the ghost's distinctive cackle came from the kid. He had noticed that jerks of her shiny headband coincided with some of Walter's effects. So he wondered whether Houdini might be right about her making ingenious use of her mouth or head. While he could not explain much of her work, he observed that the teleplasm "which flapped about so gamely when hands were available would cease their gambols when those hands were controlled." He also saw an incriminating pattern to when light fell on the spirit hands. Walter would never allow red light while the ectoplasm was forming. Dingwall found it suspicious that he could only view the finished product, the teleplasmic mass, but not the means by which it sprang from the medium's lap. On one occasion, while he was touching the manifestation, Margery had turned quickly away, pulling the appendage with her, and he heard it crumble like an inflatable bag.

Ultimately, it was the quality of that teleplasm, particularly during the final séances he witnessed, that troubled him the most. He began to feel that Elwood Worcester and William McDougall were right: the stuff was inert, flaccid, and felt like some part of an animal that a butcher might throw out. Dingwall wondered if his colleagues were also correct in thinking that Dr. Crandon, a skilled surgeon, had sewn together the clammy material that was stored inside the psychic. He could not conceive that such shriveled pulp was the substance of eternal life. In conclusion, Dingwall said he could not support the hypothesis of either authenticity or fraud. He had changed direction—as if he saw where the mediumship was headed and did not want to be a passenger when it crashed.

Malcolm Bird, still chief investigator for the ASPR, the organization that was sister to the British one dominated by Dingwall, decided that the Englishman's doubts about Margery, echoed as they were by Houdini and Harvard, had to be answered once and for all by unbiased experts. Appearing before the powers at the ASPR, Bird urged them "either to abandon the task of proving here and now, to the man in the street, whether the mediumship was valid or not, or for it to seek a new agency through which to attempt this proof." Recognizing that he was perceived as pro-Margery, Bird recommended that the society hire a second research officer to test the psychic.

Henry C. McComas, a respected Princeton psychologist, was thus brought in to fill the shoes of Walter Prince. And he was present at the Lime Street séances in September 1926—where, in honor of the International Philosophical Congress at Harvard, Margery dazzled some of the great minds that came to Boston for the event. Surprisingly, McComas wanted to apprise her rival of her return to form. When the sitting ended, he and Edison Brown of the ABC Club drove to the Majestic Theater—where Houdini had just performed. Shirtless and still flushed from a climactic escape, Houdini sat in his dressing room, listening to McComas describe how Margery had levitated a basket though her hands, feet, and head were thickly fastened. "Never," recalled McComas, would "he forget the scorn" with which Houdini replied to the description of what they had just witnessed. "You say, you *saw*," snapped Houdini. "Why you didn't see anything. What do you see now?"

The magician took a half-dollar and slapped it between his palms. It vanished. As he was stripped to the waist, his guests had no idea where it went. He refused when asked to repeat the effect. The visitors then made a challenge they were sure he would accept—they wanted him to come to Beacon Hill and reproduce Margery's phenomena under the same stringent control to which she had just been subjected. Almost without conditions, Houdini agreed, his eyes brightening as he envisioned his return to Lime Street. Since Margery was to hold another séance the next evening, he made suggestions for her control. He vowed that on the following day, that Sunday, they could wire him in her new glass cage and he would reproduce her entire routine.

At her Saturday séance Margery agreed to the proposal. After being searched she sat nonchalantly as they bound her to her cabinet. Psychic investigators had imaginations like hangmen, she joked. Braided steel picture wire was lashed to her wrists and ankles; surgeon's tape and plaster were wrapped and laid around her waist, so that it covered the tops of her bloomers, and then around her thighs, so that the bottom openings were also sealed. Only then could the men be reasonably certain that no fake ectoplasm would escape that suspect region. In the previous investigations, Margery had been accused of making skillful use of her mouth and head, which was why they padlocked her in a dog collar attached to the back of the glass booth. Luminous pins were inserted into her clothing and affixed to her hands and feet so that her form could be seen in the dark. McComas then explored her mouth with his forefinger, as Houdini had directed.

After all that, Margery, in one of the last of her storied exhibitions, produced some of her best effects—the quaking of furniture, cold gusts, the crashing of objects, and the jingle of the bell box—the highlight being the flight of a glowing basket along a shelf and into darkness. While Walter whistled and Margery gasped, the basket later rose from the table and then slowly ejected a luminous doughnut that proceeded to follow it on its trajectory above the psychic's head. Minutes later the basket crashed, then began banging against the glass cabinet, which threatened to shatter. When the violence ceased, Walter, saying that his force was low, soon left.

Following the sitting, McComas went directly to Adams House at Harvard to consult Houdini. Once again the escape artist spoke of "malobservation," protesting that the experience would be entirely different before his own eyes. "She can do her stuff in my presence," he promised, "and I will go right in and duplicate them, or if you wish, I will stop her from doing anything by having her controlled properly." Yet the more he talked, McComas detected wariness behind his bravado. "The lady is subtle," Houdini added, "and changes her methods like any dexterous sleight of hand performer." Her latest effects he could not readily explain. He wanted time to think them over.

Now the magician made new demands, insisting that he would only show up later in the week and with a committee of witnesses. When he said that Margery was using confederates, McComas wondered if he was going to enlist some of his own in order to reproduce her program. Whatever his new plan, Houdini was asking for "ample time" to prepare for Margery.

On Sunday, McComas relayed that message to Dr. Crandon. So Houdini was getting cold feet? the doctor remarked. He was expected *that day,* and *alone,* at Lime Street. He had failed to appear, which Roy considered a major victory for Walter and Margery.

Back went McComas to Houdini's hotel, where for two hours they discussed new terms for the challenge. This time Houdini wrote Dr. Crandon directly, telling him to expect his arrival before he left Boston.

The doctor replied that, as the only value in Houdini's visit "would be because it would afford some amusement to watch your attempts to duplicate these phenomena and since this you very wisely decline to do, there seems no other compelling reason for your coming again to Lime Street."

For the rest of his days, Dr. Crandon would claim that Houdini, who left Boston a few days later, had ducked a final showdown with Margery—a charge the magician would not be able to answer.

Montreal/Detroit

*H*oudini anticipated that his days were numbered—at least according to Fulton Oursler, impresario of the MacFadden publishing empire and the magician's medium-busting ally. Oursler recalled that before Houdini left New York for Boston he said that he was "marked for death" by spirit circles everywhere. Other signs indicated that Houdini did not consider himself in any more danger than usual. The last summer of his life had been, if anything, unusually tranquil. He had been away from the stage, working on his book on witchcraft and planning the next phase of his career—in which he intended to teach a curriculum of magic at Columbia University. After his next circuit he wanted to attend Columbia himself, as a student, to sharpen his English and other skills necessary to becoming a professor there.

It was during his fall tour that he experienced a series of misfortunes. Nothing untoward, other than Margery's resurgence, had occurred in Boston. But in Providence Bess came down with ptomaine poisoning. After staying up all night with her, Houdini broke his ankle while performing the Water Torture Cell in Albany. A few days later, yielding nothing to his injury, he arrived in Montreal, where excited crowds turned out for his performances at the Princess Theatre and lecture at the McGill student union. Among those cheering at the university was an arts junior named Samuel Smilovitz, who had come to sketch Houdini lecturing on the era's Great Delusion.

Smilovitz's expectations did not match his first glimpse of the magician limping to the lectern. Was this really the Handcuff King, he wondered, who had "filled half a world with awe and admiration"? Houdini looked unwell, "with a drawn face and dark shadows under tired eyes." Yet when he began to speak Smilovitz's first impression faded. Once Houdini had absorbed the energy of the audience, he seemed to glow with intensity. His gray eyes flashed as he leaped boldly into his subject; Smilovitz noted that the crowd could feel his urgent power, "sensitized mind," and vitality.

But the magician was no superman. What most people lacked was the ability to *see*, he told the students. If only people would educate their eyes and minds, they would easily see through practically every one of his "miracles," as well, he said, as those of psychics like Margery, whose one true power was her sexual charm. "Margery handed out applesauce to the investigators," he asserted. "I know this because I have walked through apple orchards myself." While he had resisted that fruit, she was only one of many enemies. "If I should die tonight," he declared, "the spiritualistic mediums would hold a national holiday."

As Smilovitz sketched, another figure in the crowd took notes while watching the magician who spoke for science and reason. Penetrating and curious, Jocelyn Gordon Whitehead was keen to get to the bottom of things. He had a fetish for detail and hidden meanings. When reading the newspapers at home, Whitehead always kept a dictionary on one side of the table and an atlas on the other. Six-foot-two with a muscular build, he didn't look like a scholar, and at thirty-one years old, he didn't appear to be a freshman, though officially he was one. Even at first glance there was something vaguely misplaced about Whitehead. It isn't known why he started college in his thirties. He claimed to be studying religion; at other times it was medicine or engineering. He studied boxing too, and had a right hand like a sledgehammer to prove it. A loner, Whitehead withdrew to his own world after applauding Houdini's presentation. Meanwhile, two of Smilovitz's fraternity brothers tried to get the star to sign the sketch portrait after his magic show that night at the Princess Theatre. Their efforts were rewarded when he received the students in his dressing room and autographed the picture. Then he gave them a message for the artist—would Smilovitz be so kind as to come to the venue the next morning and make another drawing?

Delighted by Houdini's interest, Smilovitz arrived with another student, Jack Price, and waited with other fans outside the theater. When Houdini walked in, accompanied by a nurse, he was surrounded by petitioners. Amid the fuss, Smilovitz heard the nurse impatiently urge him to go inside and eat. Replying that he wasn't hungry but could always get something, Houdini materialized a hot dog from the lapel of one of his fans. While the others applauded, Smilovitz produced his sketch and introduced himself.

A short time later, Smilovitz was again drawing the legend, this time as he sat in repose on a sofa in his dressing room. Houdini was relaxed, "in the best of spirits" and a thrill to be with, Smilovitz remembered. When he read his mail he had a way of flicking envelopes open, the artist noticed, with panache and dexterity. Smilovitz realized, though, that his initial impression of Houdini's infirmity was accurate. The magician apologized for having to recline. He said he was not in the best of health and had "to take things easy." At close quarters Smilovitz could see the weariness in his subject's eyes and the mouth that twitched nervously.

The Great Houdini regaled the boys with tales of his stunts, telling them that his recent feat at the Shelton Hotel was no miracle. In the casket he had only achieved a state of remarkable stillness: it was as if his heart had stopped beating and he was no longer breathing.

While Houdini was holding forth and Smilovitz drawing him, there was a knock on the dressing-room door and Whitehead—who appeared to already know their host—was admitted. Whitehead was wearing a blue gabardine suit that looked a size too small for him. He carried with him three books, one of which the magician had apparently loaned him. There was something forced about the visitor, if not his entrance. Whitehead spoke with an exaggerated Oxford accent. His face was ruddy, his hair thin; he spoke softly, but to Smilovitz's irritation he spoke too often. After sitting down, he began to dominate the conversation with Houdini.

Soon the two began an intriguing contest. Houdini claimed to be able to unravel the mystery in any detective story after hearing only a few sentences read to him. Whitehead had brought with him a pulp serial and, after reading a few excerpts, Houdini successfully divined the gist of the stories. While the students complimented him, Houdini flashed a wide smile. Then the conversation turned, as Whitehead directed it, to a loftier book—one on which Houdini did not like to offer commentary.

"What is your opinion of the miracles in the Bible?" asked the divinity student. This was just the sort of question that made Houdini uncomfortable. He said he would prefer not to answer, but he wondered how his own stunts would have been received in Biblical times. Would they too have been perceived as miracles?

Whitehead looked affronted by the statement. He again changed the subject, this time to Houdini's famed invincibility. As if out of nowhere, he asked, "Is it true, Mr. Houdini, that you can resist the hardest blows struck to the abdomen?"

Houdini sidestepped the question, calling attention instead to his iron forearms and back muscles. "Feel them," he invited.

After the students touched his physique and expressed admiration, Whitehead repeated his question. Was it true, he persisted, that he could take any blow to the stomach? Houdini seemed to want to demur, but Whitehead wouldn't let him. "Would you mind if I delivered a few blows to your abdomen?" Houdini nodded his assent. He still lay supine, though, and had not braced himself when Whitehead suddenly attacked with "four or five ferocious blows to his lower abdomen."

"Are you mad?" cried Price, "what are you doing?" Houdini stopped the assault with a wry smile and an arresting gesture of his hand. "That will do," he said. Although the visitors were disturbed by the sudden violence, nothing had seemed immediately wrong with Houdini. He sat back down and Smilovitz finished the portrait.

♦

In his affidavit, Whitehead would claim that Houdini had given him a copy of the November issue of the *Scientific American,* calling his attention to an article titled "How Death Deals Its Cards: Death in a Thousand Shapes Is Knocking Eternally at Everyman's Door." Certainly it was knocking at Houdini's, who was wrong to assume that Whitehead was just another devoted fan. Whitehead is a mystery. It is known that he dropped out of school a few months after Houdini left Montreal. He then disappeared, becoming as elusive as a fugitive. He was arrested once for shoplifting—for stealing books on boxing and palmistry. Much later he wound up residing in a dank apartment with magazines and other reading material stacked to the ceiling, his only company two eccentric women who were drawn to mystical arts like numerology and the "Science of Being." By that time

Whitehead subsisted on disability payments he received for a head injury suffered while working as a day laborer on a construction site. He had a plate in his skull and the memory of a violent incident he almost never spoke of. The once formidable Whitehead would die of malnutrition, having revealed to practically no one that he had killed the Great Houdini.

♦

Sometime after Whitehead left his dressing room, Houdini told his niece, Julia, that due to a "misunderstanding of his remarks," a student had assaulted him before he could stand up and prepare for it. He complained of stomach pain but tried not to let the condition affect him. Believing himself able to transcend any malady, Houdini performed that night— even though he was too weak to undress himself afterward. On the train to Detroit, his next engagement, his pain became so intense that Bess insisted a wire be sent for a doctor to meet them upon their arrival.

Though the physician diagnosed appendicitis, Houdini refused to cancel his bookings. He gave his show that night with a 104-degree temperature. But he was sluggish and hoarse and could not pull off the entirety of his routine. Collapsing after the first act, he was revived, then fainted again after the final curtain. Back at the hotel, a hysterical Bess summoned a young surgeon, Dr. Charles Kennedy, who arrived at three in the morning. When told of the blows Houdini had received, Dr. Kennedy pleaded with him to enter a hospital. He still refused. It took a call from his New York physician to persuade him.

Examining him at Grace Hospital, the surgeons determined that Houdini had peritonitis. The punches, they said, had burst his appendix. They gave him twenty-four hours to live. But the doctors had not taken into account the preternatural strength of their patient. For six days Houdini hung on while enduring two operations. The pain was excruciating. His bowels were paralyzed, yet no one heard him complain. He was polite, ever-smiling, and upbeat with his attendants and with the family members who had rushed to his bedside. He felt that he would recover and be back onstage shortly. His dire condition was no secret, however. The nation hung on press releases from the hospital and there was great hope when a miracle serum brought his temperature down to normal. But it was a medical chimera, like false hope from a spirit medium.

In one of their bedside conversations, Houdini told Dr. Kennedy that he wished he had been a surgeon. "You actually do things for people. I, in almost every respect, am a fake," he lamented. During other exchanges he talked about his boyhood in Appleton. When he said he had a yen for Farmer's Chop Suey, a Jewish dish from his childhood, Doctor Kennedy went to a delicatessen across the street and returned with the meal, which appeared to comfort him. Houdini was not quiet on his deathbed. He spoke often of Spiritualism and the victory his death would be for the movement.

Finally he told his brother Dash that he couldn't fight anymore. A short time later he uttered the name Robert Ingersoll. They were strange final words, since he had never known the great orator who died a quarter century earlier. But Ingersoll, "The Great Agnostic," had preached against the bane of religion—he equated Christianity with superstition, as Houdini had Spiritualism. They were the two most famous skeptics of their respective generations, and in the magician's death throes, the name Ingersoll came to him.

It had been a sunny day, yet Dash recalled that just as Houdini closed his eyes, "the heavens clouded over and it poured rain like I have never seen it pour before." Houdini was declared dead at 1:26 p.m. on Halloween, 1926. Even the date of his passing had linked him to the spirits, and some found it poetic justice that on the day the dead return to Earth, he left it.

A Grim Halloween

$\mathcal{A}$t the Lime Street séance that Halloween, Walter arrived whistling in a minor key—then the spirit communicated that Houdini's crossing would not be easy, for the wizard was still *"much confused and resistant to the idea of death."* Without gloating over Houdini's passing, Walter indicated that he would have one more encounter with him. *"I am not sure but that I will have something to do with Houdini and his admission."*

Dr. Crandon observed that Walter had prophesied Houdini's death innumerable times over the last year by saying, *"Give Houdini my love and tell him I will see him soon."* The sitters wanted to know whether or not Walter had caused the tragedy.

"Look out don't get superstitious," the ghost cautioned. Spirits had *"nothing to do with a human death,"* he told them, *"but sometimes we can see a little farther ahead than you can."* As if to prove it, Walter made a prescient statement concerning the future of psychic research—promising that the field *"would have moved faster if Houdini could have lived to advertise it."*

If Walter now sounded less vindictive, there was a sense from Margery partisans that a higher justice had been meted out. "Well, Walter has GOT Houdini, and I hope Houdini is enjoying it. His 'sainted Mother' will have something to howl about now," wrote Robin Tillyard. In a letter to Dr. Crandon, the scientist speculated that Whitehead had been operating under Walter's psychic influence when he assaulted Houdini. In Boston, Joseph DeWyckoff expressed satisfaction that the magician he likened to a "Jew renegade" had entered the fourth dimension; it was an "eye for an eye," he told Dr. Crandon.

That attitude was not expressed by Margery herself, who seemed genuinely saddened by Houdini's passing. In a statement to the press she praised Houdini's virility, determination, and physical courage, and said that she had enjoyed entertaining him in her home, though "at other times and places we have had our differences."

For Margery, Houdini had been a man of action among old fussbudgets and callow graduate students. "He had sat with us four times," she remembered, "and his behavior here was a pleasant contrast to that of certain men high in academic circles." Surprisingly to some of the reporters, Margery portrayed his death as a "serious loss" to psychic science, since wherever he went he created an interest in spirit mediumship. Still, the newspapermen would not let go of their rivalry. When asked if she had "willed" his death, she declined to comment and ended the interview.

Will Houdini Return?

*T*he Great Houdini's death "was most certainly decreed from the other side," Sir Arthur Conan Doyle believed. If that were so, the police could not investigate a spectral curse or warning, but Dr. A. A. Roback, the first Harvard psychologist ever to sit with Margery, wondered if the Spiritualist movement had "gotten rid of its most formidable foe" with the elimination of Houdini. No one found out whether Whitehead was acting out of impulse or some perceived higher calling when he assaulted him. There was no police inquiry. What voices, if any, the divinity student heard were never determined. Sir Arthur, however, knew what he had heard from *his* spirit guide just before the tragedy. *"Houdini is doomed, doomed, doomed,"* Pheneas had warned. And the next day the conjurer was fatally assaulted.

Sometime before that, Sir Arthur told Dr. Crandon that Houdini had a "pay-day coming soon." But despite the premonitions, Sir Arthur seemed shaken and perplexed by the tragedy. "His death is a great shock and a deep mystery to me," he told the newspapers. "He was a teetotaler, did not smoke, and was one of the cleanest living men I have ever known. I greatly admired him, and cannot understand how the end came for one so youthful. We were great friends. He told me much in confidence, but never secrets regarding his tricks. How he did them, I do not know. We agreed upon everything excepting spiritualism."

In truth, they had not been friends for some time. Houdini and Sir Arthur had fought a proxy war on Lime Street. When the spirits warned of the approaching tragedy, Sir Arthur hadn't tried to get through to his former friend, "for he would only have mocked at them, and us, if we had sent them on," he wrote Bess Houdini.

While searching for answers to the Houdini enigma, Sir Arthur began to communicate with his widow. And Bess, touched by Sir Arthur's expressions of grief, tried to make a final peace between him and Houdini. Her husband, she told Doyle, had admired him immensely and "would have been the happiest man in the world had he been able to agree with your views on spiritism."

Sir Arthur believed her. But then he had always seen Houdini as essentially a fallen hero. His crusade "was a general wild attack upon all that we hold dear," Doyle wrote Bess, "but beyond all that, I can see quite a different person—a loving husband, a good friend, a man full of sweet impulses. I have never met anyone who left so mixed an impression upon my mind."

Sir Arthur hoped that in death—just as Kingsley had apologized in the next life for his prior skepticism toward Spiritualism—Houdini would make amends for his destructive wrongheadedness. Practically as soon as the magician was lowered into the ground, in the same coffin in which he had performed the Shelton pool miracle, Sir Arthur hoped to hear from him.

Bess desperately wanted her own reunion with Houdini. His death sent her into a prolonged period of despair—and she sought solace in séances and alcohol. When in the doldrums she prayed for a communication, she told Sir Arthur. On one such occasion there was a crashing report caused, she said, by a mirror spontaneously shattering. She took it as a sign from her dead husband. On his deathbed he had vowed to try to return to her, and Doyle assured her that they'd hear from him. But with no message as yet, Bess reconciled herself to the more traditional ways of communion. "When next I go to my dear one's last resting place," she wrote Sir Arthur, "I will place a flower for you."

◆

For all his kindness, Bess wanted to send Sir Arthur some of the prized books from Houdini's massive collection on Spiritualism. This gift he refused. He was working on a long piece on Houdini that chronicled his machinations against Margery. In many ways the article turned into a panegyric, where Sir Arthur commended him as "exceedingly lovable," "charitable," "the bravest man of his generation." He didn't want the world to think he had softened his case against Houdini because of any gifts from his widow. Yet Bess insisted that Sir Arthur accept a certain item that Houdini had always wanted him to have. It was the one marked "Not to be sold at any price": a diary of sketches by an obscure Victorian artist.

The Gift

*I*n Charles Doyle's sketch of a midnight hunt, the moon reflects off a bog while hounds pursue their demon-faced feline quarry. Devoutly Catholic, Charles drew an angel over the hellish setting. The winged cat leaps away from her light. A white horse rears, almost throwing its rider. Sir Arthur believed his father was a medium who channeled his occult visions onto canvas. Unfortunately, like many with the Gift, Charles Doyle's downfall was alcoholism. He had a nervous tremor in his hands, which young Arthur had noticed whenever he held a fork or brush, or while scaling fish he caught for dinner. When Arthur grew up to become a doctor, and saw patients with the same affliction, he could not help but think of delirium tremens as the symptom of a soul about to crumble.

There was something of the windblown to Charles Doyle, due less to his gaunt appearance and reedlike frame than an unusually ethereal nature. "His thoughts were always in the clouds," Sir Arthur recalled, "and he had no appreciation of the realities of life." In a self-portrait from the book Bess sent, Charles drew himself as a wisp of a man, caught in the talons of a massive raven—all but defenseless against the monsters he imagined.

So magical and macabre was the work of Charles Doyle, who drew and painted ghosts and faeries, that the fear among his drinking cronies, when he disappeared during Arthur's childhood, was that the struggling artist, reduced to bartering his sketches for burgundy wine, had gazed into the dark well once too often. It was whispered that he was incarcerated for a violent crime, or in the netherworld that was his subject.

In reality, Charles had become the living skeleton in the Doyles' family closet. In a society where patrimony was everything, Sir Arthur revealed to no one the truth behind Charles's disappearance—that he was confined to a mental asylum. Turning away from his father, Sir Arthur rejected his mysticism. He became an agnostic doctor and then the creator of Sherlock

Holmes, who personified deductive thinking. Yet just after Charles died alone in the asylum, Sir Arthur killed off Holmes and joined the Society for Psychical Research. Ultimately, for both father and son, it was the invisible world that beckoned.

In the sketch book Sir Arthur received were many classic examples of his father's work—where helpless men are spirited away by mammoth birds or lured to God-knew-where by winged sirens. One picture was particularly meaningful to Sir Arthur. It was of dead soldiers lying in a field, the light of their souls ascending in unison to heaven. Putting the book aside, Sir Arthur looked out for a moment at the misty Sussex downs. He had no doubt that Houdini had delivered the book and silently he thanked him. Let anyone try to disprove the presence at this moment of the magician by his side.

Part IX

THE SHADOW OF A DREAM

⌗

I seem'd to move among a world of ghosts,
And feel myself the shadow of a dream.
—ALFRED, LORD TENNYSON

But Mina—ah, there was a heartbreaker for you. A natural blond with
the most devilish blue eyes I ever saw in my life. And there was pure
enchantment in her voice, no other way to describe it. I understand that
she went to pieces rather badly before she died and all the loveliness and
the laughter were no more. It was quite a tragedy.
—WILLIAM LINDSAY GRESHAM,
QUOTING A FRIEND WHO KNEW MARGERY

Harry Houdini and Margery,
Lime Street, July 1924

The Last Dance

The manifestations of the séance room are
childish entertainment, unless true.
—DR. LE ROI CRANDON

*M*argery was "almost as hard to bury as the League of Nations," *Life* magazine reported. Even now she represented what newspapers called an "unconquerable hope." Houdini had only been gone a few weeks before the Crandons took their case, via a national lecture tour, directly to the man in the street. In Buffalo, Cincinnati, Chicago, Denver, and on the Pacific coast, among other places, the doctor made a case that still resonated. The highlight of the tour came in Canada where, according to one Christian pastor, Roy enlightened "the finest audience ever seen in Winnipeg." During their visit Margery's phenomena were declared "absolutely genuine" by T. G. Hamilton, Canada's most respected conductor of psychic research. Yet this campaign, far from the eastern hubs of journalism and science, was like winning a string of provincial victories while the Mecca of psychical research was burning.

Back in Boston, the Crandons were on the verge of disgrace. In 1927, Dr. Crandon was censured by the *Boston Medical and Surgical Journal* for his occult activities. This was also the year that Henry McComas released the results of his ASPR-sponsored study of Margery, concluding, to the chagrin of those who had hired him, that her "mediumship is a clever and entertaining performance but is unworthy of serious consideration by your Society." If that were not enough, a McDougall protégé, Dr. Joseph Rhine—while on his way to becoming America's preeminent psychic scientist—called the Margery mediumship "base and brazen trickery." A botanist who had decided that psychical research, rather than the study of plants, brought him closer to the elemental mysteries of life, Rhine had gone to Lime Street with a religious sense of mission, but said he had encountered there only flirtation and mischief. A former Marine sergeant and national champion sharpshooter, Rhine now seemed intent on killing the mediumship—and accused Margery, after the only Crandon séance he attended, "of kissing and embracing" the researchers. "It is evidently of very great advantage to a medium, especially if fraudulent," said Rhine, "to be personally attractive; it aids the fly catching business."

Following his report came another journalistic frenzy. I KISSED A WOMAN, NOT MEN, Margery responded in the headline. "That's all poppycock," she objected. "My husband attends all my séances and I would have to be very rash to go around kissing." Swiftly, the usual champions came to her defense—"J. B. RHINE IS A MONUMENTAL ASS!" advertised Sir Arthur in a Boston newspaper—while her most vehement critics, Prince and Rhine, continued, she felt, to persecute her. It was not just their whispering about Roy's supposed affairs with nurses or Margery's with researchers. Prince was still spreading that most lurid rumor—that the bones of an English youth "were buried beneath the cellar floor at Lime Street."

Even with Houdini in the grave, there was no letup in the hostilities. "We are having a great battle here," declared the doctor who had never seemed more devilish to his enemies. "A nasty bastard, rotten to the core," Hudson Hoagland would say of Roy. Few, however, had anything as severe to mention about Margery's nature. One of Walter Prince's fondest memories was of her stopping by his home to bring him, an abstinent minister, a peace offering of homemade doughnuts and contraband scotch. And George Hyslop, perhaps the only Crandon critic at the ASPR, said that "if I should call on Margery today, she would receive me just as sweetly as ever."

Until the end her door remained open to ASPR scientists, though hers was now considered a "house of ill fame" by many of the Crandons' peers. When Robin Tillyard visited New England, he was told by one Harvard professor that 10 Lime Street "was a thoroughly bad place, that his honor would be stained forever" if he set foot inside the door, as would that of any decent man or woman—and that Margery was a kind of mystical prostitute, the reincarnation of Mary Magdalene. Despite her stigma, the ghost hunters still came to Beacon Hill—and returning for another go-round with Margery, Eric Dingwall almost died there. A heart condition exacerbated by thyroid trouble reportedly convinced two emergency-room doctors that they had lost him. Dr. Crandon, who took over the case, alleviated his symptoms. Dingwall was then brought back to Lime Street, where Margery nursed him to good health. "Never again, I am sure," noted one investigator, "would Dingwall countenance evil tales of the Crandons."

For the rest of the decade, Margery's star, while it still shone brightly at the ASPR, progressively faded with the jazz era. Befittingly, the Crandons tried to revive her career in the place where the broader scientific interest in her work began. In December 1929, the last month of the last year of the decade, they visited England, where six years earlier Dingwall and Doyle had heralded the nascent mediumship, and where she was now called "the short-skirted medium." This time the Crandons had a rough passage on the *Mauretania,* were besieged by reporters upon their arrival, and had no time to recover. Margery had agreed to perform the next day for Sir Oliver Lodge, at his home in Normanton House—just a few minutes by car from Stonehenge. The séance in Lodge's bedroom included a small circle of Roy, Sir Oliver, his daughter, his secretary, and his chauffeur. For the occasion Margery wore black silk knickers and a sleeveless red velvet kimono. The usual effects followed. The table was flung about. The basket rose, and when Sir Oliver tossed objects into it, Walter spontaneously identified them. Ghostly thumbprints that Walter claimed were those of Sir Oliver's dead son, Raymond, materialized. When Roy was asked to leave the room, the telekinesis continued. "You are a wonder, Walter!" exclaimed Sir Oliver. "It's a long time since I saw things move about like this, though I have seen the phenomenon long ago."

After a long dinner, Sir Oliver, still sprightly at seventy-eight, insisted on dancing for several hours. His preferred tune was the popular "Button Up Your Overcoat." Ten years earlier, the only time Lodge visited the States, he had inspired a séance craze, as well as Roy's own interest in Spiritualism. Sir Oliver was still the most respected psychic scientist in the world. And Margery had saved him the last dance of the era.

1930: A Troubled Spirit

Far safer, of a midnight meeting
External ghost,
Than an interior confronting
That whiter host.

—EMILY DICKINSON

*S*piritualism, as it turned out, had more appeal for the bereaved than the bankrupt. By 1930, in the wake of Wall Street's crash, public interest in the Quest Eternal was waning. In that year William McDougall and Joseph Rhine founded the Parapsychology Laboratory at Duke University, effectively taking psychic research out of the séance room. Rhine's experience with Margery had contributed to his mistrust of any case that savored of ghosts and spirits. The reign of the physical medium was over as far as he was concerned. His interest was in parapsychology—a term he and McDougall coined—quantifiable mental phenomena. And where Rhine led, much of the rest of the psychic research community followed.

The year 1930 was also the year that the apostle of the Spiritualist revival left his body. Having collapsed clutching his heart after a walk in his rose garden, Sir Arthur Conan Doyle, already infirm, was confined to his bed that summer. He told his family that he did not want to die there. In his last days, Jean and the children helped him into a basket chair, where he could look out on his beloved Sussex woodland. On July 7, he died with his family beside him. His last words, to Jean, were "You are wonderful."

Because he had believed that the death day is the true birthday, his funeral, as he had intended, wasn't mournful. The burial took place in the rose garden at Windlesham in an atmosphere that suggested bon voyage rather than ashes to ashes. Almost no one wore black. Light colors and summer dress were the decorum. Only a few in attendance cried. A Spiritualist minister presided. Jean brought a red rose to her lips and dropped it into the coffin. Days later, thousands gathered at the Royal Albert Hall for a memorial. While friends and dignitaries paid tribute to Sir Arthur, Jean sat onstage beside an empty chair. "He is there!" cried an excited medium.

Many of the influences that had led to the Great Spirit Hunt—the contest that Sir Arthur had inspired—were distinctive to the twenties. By 1930 the contest vogue was over. The Miss America pageant had been suspended after the crash of '29. The dance marathons had lost popularity. The Ouija and séance were no longer a rage: attention had turned from eternal to more immediate survival.

Even the luminaries of the jazz era seemed diminished. Jack Dempsey had lost not only the millions he had made as a prizefighter but the strength to recoup them. In August, beleaguered by scandal, Sister Aimee suffered a physical and mental breakdown. For almost a year the gaudy evangelist was silent. While still prodigious, Babe Ruth was embarrassed to be pulled late in baseball games. He was no longer fleet enough to cover the outfield.

◆

The year 1930 was also the year Malcolm Bird vanished. When one night he brought an "immoral woman" back to Lime Street, the Crandons turned him away. He became angry and made insulting remarks about their own sexual habits, yet there was a deeper friction between them. Bird was preparing a new volume on the Margery case for the ASPR journal—and this time it would not be entirely positive. For years Bird had prepared for a possible fallout with the Crandons. He had kept a blank check Margery had written him, to use as ammunition against them. He had made note of his discovery of a piece of yarn attached to the scales that were supposed to have been activated by Walter's invisible agency. The observations of Keating and Carrington, who thought they had seen luminous paint daubed on the soles of Margery's stockings, were also in his possession. While Bird still believed Mrs. Crandon to be an authentic medium, he alleged that she sometimes resorted to trickery when under pressure to manifest. He had recently gone before the trustees of the ASPR to inform them that before Margery's final showdown with Houdini, "she sought a private interview with me and tried to get me to agree, in the event that phenomena did not occur, that I would ring the bell-box myself, or produce something else that might pass as activity by Walter."

To the trustees' ears this was blasphemy. Most physical mediums were thought to cheat when under duress, but Bird had always portrayed Margery as the exception. Even now his descriptions of her proofs dwarfed his negative observations—only some of the phenomena may have been "normally produced," he asserted.

"Well, if he admits half a ghost, that's as good as a whole ghost," Walter answered. But the ASPR was not so cavalier. They refused to let Bird publish his report. They made it appear that his "frequent trips to Boston were the cloak for a series of illicit amours."

And then, in December, they fired him.

There would literally have been no Margery were it not for Malcolm Bird, who publicized her work and named her. As an ASPR officer he had presented the case for her mediumship before more than two hundred audiences—from Chicago to the Sorbonne. However, the powers at the society were themselves Spiritualists—Mark Richardson, Joseph DeWyckoff, William H. Button—who tolerated no reproof of Margery. The society's mission was to further develop her phenomena. And though Bird had been her stalwart advocate, he had never embraced Spiritualism. Sensing that Margery was, over time, resorting more to trickery, he had wanted to protect himself when the crash came. Now an aggrieved Bird crossed enemy lines and attempted to publish his report with Walter Prince's Boston Society. To his surprise, Prince demurred. The new policy of the BSPR was simply to ignore Margery.

Bird exited the stage quietly, his subsequent activities a mystery. Two years later Prince visited him without coming away with any notion as to how he occupied himself. "Really, and peculiarly, I have not the least idea what Bird has been doing," he remarked. Prince's secretary, Eleanor Hoffman, suggested that he became involved in bootlegging. An important player in the spirit hunt, he seemed to disappear with the fading force of Spiritualism.

◆

"Backward—turn backward, O Time, in your flight. Give us a séance, just for one night. I am so weary of teaching such rot: The stuff I am teaching convinces me not." In a poem that Margery had penned through automatic writing, supposedly conceived by Walter's mind, the professors and scientists who had been drawn to mediumistic research, only to turn away from it when his sister was discredited, would find their other endeavors mundane, the spirit promised, their futures unsatisfying.

Perhaps no one had been as prominently employed on the front lines of psychic science, only to abruptly abandon the field, as J. Malcolm Bird. But with his reputation besmirched, he never returned to the former professions, academia and journalism, that had brought him success. In many respects Bird withdrew from both the material and the psychic world. He had a small life income from the estate of his half-sister. Whatever else he did for the rest of his life, he did it inconspicuously. His wife, Katherine, would leave him and they never had children. He would die, in 1964, in Kings County Hospital on the day before Halloween—ten days after being hit by an automobile while crossing a Brooklyn boulevard.

"Weary of looking for heaven and hell; Weary of reading the lies that I tell. Give us a sitting; 'twill change things aright; Walter—Come back to us; just for one night." Without Walter, there was considerably less scientific interest in psychic phenomena. The answer to the age-old mystery would have to be deferred, Bird had presumed, to future generations. Séance research was now as antiquated as the notion of the ether. Yet there was something abiding, they had all felt, in the interplay of mind and spirit. What Plato once believed—that forms and thoughts were of a higher, eternal reality—had been eschewed long ago by his student Aristotle, who held to only what was concrete and perceptible to the physical senses. Who was to say that the student was right; it was much like trying to settle, forever, the case for Spiritualism. Bird recalled Sir Arthur telling him, when they had sailed back to America together on the *Olympic*, that whenever physical science advanced too far and fast, there would be a revival of supernaturalism.

Hereward Carrington had said much the same thing to him. The last of the great ghost hunters, Carrington—who had always looked as though he were in the final stages of a terminal illness—would live forever, Bird felt, on his rabbitlike diet and exotic juices.* He had heard that Carrington went to Los Angeles and found a more receptive audience there for his yoga practice, crankish food, and belief in psychic magic. Bird, on the contrary, had concluded that spirit mediumship, with its legacy of false materializations, could not withstand the scrutiny of a generation whose reference had shifted from the auditory to the visual. Whoever thought séances were quaint and quiet, though, had never sat with Margery, who manifested to the wailing of the saxophone and burst of drums. When one séance was over and she was awakened from her trance, he could remember her smiling at him, as if to say, *Was that not magic?*

◆

The First World War had been a ghostly war. The next great conflict, which Bird had followed from afar and Margery had not lived to see the end of, featured no similar celestial lore or manifestations. Often it had struck him that while the scientists he knew had made it their mission to substantiate eternal life, the new physicists he read about in the *Scientific American* were employed in the development of technology that might destroy intelligent life altogether. Sir Oliver had been right when he predicted how awesome and world-altering was the power of the atom, but evidently wrong, Bird suspected, about Summerland.

For Margery there was no walking away from the spirit world as Bird had—or, like Prospero, relinquishing her occult power. Often she had seemed on the verge of a crack-up, only to recover before the next investigation. The dignitaries still visited her in the 1930s—especially those from Europe, where her work and reputation were less maligned. Early in the new decade a friend of Sir Oliver Lodge's—"a distinguished literary man"—came to stay with the Crandons. Margery acted so strangely around him that he soon decided to cut short his visit—but unfortunately, his psychic influence lingered. At a séance just after his departure, Margery was possessed by a sinister spirit calling itself Lila Lee and claiming to be

---

* In fact, Carrington would die in 1958, six years before Bird.

the deceased lover of the recent visitor. Lila Lee said that after an unhappy love affair with the European writer she killed herself by jumping from an omnibus. A chill descended on the circle when she vowed that Mrs. Crandon would suffer the same fate. Without warning, while Drs. Richardson and Crandon attempted to calm the troubled spirit, Margery arose and rushed from the room. With the sitters in pursuit, she retreated down the hallway and climbed a ladder to the roof of the house. There she stood, close to the parapet, gazing at the street four stories below—while ignoring Mrs. Richardson's frantic pleas to come down. Then she shut her eyes, as if listening for the voice to tell her when to leap.

I Ain't Pretty Anymore

*O*ver time Mark Richardson came to understand Margery's hysteria, the aborted impulse to jump; for "her life became an almost routine existence of trance and uncomfortable control by picture wire, surgeon's tape, locked cabinets and a manifold variety of apparatus. It was a species of slavery, in fact, and Dr. Crandon was, in a certain sense, a slave-driver. But in this connection I now know well that we were all guilty—even Walter." During the 1920s, visitors had often commented that Margery looked younger than her years. By the 1930s at least one reporter observed that she seemed older than her age, though men still had eyes for her and she for them. James Wobensmith, the Great Thurston's lawyer, claimed that at one séance she took his hand and guided it between her legs.

One night, in December of 1932, Margery entertained Prince's secretary, Eleanor Hoffman, who promised not to tell him that they socialized. After dinner and one too many drinks, Margery began to make admissions—not about her mediumship but concerning other things. She was aware of her reputation for seducing the investigators, she said, but she wanted to be clear that the rumors were wrong about her and Bird. He was "disgusting looking," she snorted, "the kind you want to sweep the house out after." Recalling the night he'd picked up a loose girl and took her to a hotel bar, she said—"the girl sat on Bird's lap and wet all over him, that's the kind of girl she was." Margery had only repugnance for the investigator who had tried to bring his floozy back to her house.

Her eyes became softer when she spoke of "Carrie," remembering how good-looking he was and the fun the two of them had. Her mood darkened, though, when she mentioned the rumors concerning Roy. She knew what was said about him and the orphaned boys.

During another confessional with Eleanor, she spoke further about one of the children who came to Lime Street. "The poor little fellow had adenoids," she recalled, "and had to be circumcised." After the operation, which Roy had performed at home, "the little fellow sat up in bed and looked at himself and said, 'I ain't pretty anymore,' and John told him that was all right, he looked that way too."

After the boy was sent back to England, "people were asking his whereabouts and the Prime Minister of England cabled to ask where he was and demanded cable reply," Margery confided. "Why, people even said Dr. Crandon committed illegal operations on little children and murdered them."

Later the conversation turned to Walter's latest manifestations, which included both the fingerprints of beings who had left this world and those about to be born into it. Having shown Eleanor casts of the evidence, Margery put them in a closet and returned with photographs of a "whole rack of pictures of little children—most of them really lovely."

"Those are Dr. Crandon's caesareans," Margery explained, "aren't they sweet? All caesareans."

There were dozens of photographs of young girls and boys.

Another of Margery's confidantes was Eileen Garrett, the most gifted medium with whom the Crandons were associated. A visiting Irish psychic, Eileen didn't produce physical phenomena like Margery. Instead she channeled messages and information. She was to the study of ESP what the Boston medium was to ectoplasmic phenomena—and the two had sat for many of the same scientists and investigators.

In November of 1931, upon hearing that Eileen was coming to New York, Margery had rushed there to meet her for the first time. Arriving at Hyslop House, the ASPR offices, she arranged a sitting while keeping her identity from the Irish clairvoyant. During the séance, Eileen nevertheless identified her as a "powerful medium." She then brought through "a very vital young man," who Margery knew was Walter—for he called her "*Kid*" and identified the name of their childhood dog, "*Victor.*" Through the lips of Eileen Garrett, Walter said: "*Kid you certainly are an old fraud, but I am in on it.*"

The message in effect relayed what Eileen thought of Margery. Years later she remarked that Mrs. Crandon was "probably the most utterly charming woman I have ever known" and that there was an "indefinite something in her presence and eye that made one think she was a medium." Eileen also divulged that Margery, in her desperation, proposed they work together in fraud. "That is why I always think it is a great danger for a medium to seek publicity, because the Crandon mediumship was wrecked on publicity—she didn't need money, she had plenty of money, her husband was a surgeon. She became a great physical medium, the whole of America went mad about her, and she began, of course, having to turn it on; she had her raps and her knocks, she was a sensitive . . . A very very beautiful girl, she certainly had the whole of the psychic world on its toes. But, again, fraud stepped in. There was not money, there was the power of the press and power of her personality, she could do no wrong. Dingwall, all of them, were all at her feet. Price, Carrington . . . all of them."

In truth, not *all* of them.

In 1934 Walter Prince obtained a report proving that the supposed fingerprints of dead Walter—which Margery had been manifesting since 1926—were an exact match to a living member of the ABC Club. Years earlier her friend and dentist, Dr. Frederick Caldwell, had suggested that dental wax might make the perfect cast to absorb Walter's spectral hand impressions. He had given her a sample with his own prints, and she had apparently kept them and presented them on countless occasions as Walter's. Even some of her most devoted supporters could not tolerate this final revelation—one brought to Prince by E. E. Dudley, a former ASPR officer and Margery admirer. "Some of the rats show symptoms of leaving the ship," Prince commented after publishing the exposé that finally and incontrovertibly ruined Margery.

Soon thereafter, he too left his body.

Although Dr. Crandon had warned ten years earlier that Prince was dying of heart disease, the dogged investigator may have wanted to outlive, if not the youthful Mrs. Crandon, then at least her mediumship. Two days after his journal published the exposé, Prince finally succumbed to his many ailments. "Not one day and not one hour did I think Margery's phenomena genuine," Prince had said. And yet, given the influence of her patrons, Margery had remained the jewel of the ASPR for a decade. Her current champion was William Button, a prosperous New York lawyer, who in 1931 became president of the society. A fifty-nine-year-old married man, Button had an intense romantic affair with Margery. They were living at the Plaza together. In what some saw as the pot calling the kettle black, Hereward Carrington said that "Button is so emotionally involved with Margery that he has lost all sense of perspective and even of decency. . . . For the first time in history an S.P.R. is being run by a medium!"

Occasionally, Margery received wider notoriety. Curious as to whether the psychic channel might be a viable method of communication, the engineers at Bell Labs conducted a brief study of her mediumship. They determined that "it will probably not replace the telephone in the foreseeable future." And then, in January 1934, she became the first medium to manifest a ghost heard on the radio, when Station WBZ broadcast the voice of dead Walter singing "Roaming in the Gloaming" with a Scottish accent. *"I must be going. G'by,"* he whispered as he finished the song. The final time Margery's effects received national attention was in February 1938, when *Time* reported that—in an attempt to match the telepathy tests Joseph Rhine was conducting on Eileen Garrett and other psychics—Margery guessed the right suit and number of nineteen out of twenty playing cards drawn from a deck purportedly hidden from her physical vision.

◆

Some had predicted that the Crandons' marriage would end with the crash of the mediumship. Yet while leading independent lives they maintained a frayed bond until the end of the decade. Margery was gravely concerned when, on December 22, 1939, Roy fell in front of their home and fractured his pelvis. She never seemed to recover from his death five days later, at the age of sixty-six, of bronchial pneumonia. In a service that bore none of the vibrancy of Sir Arthur's send-off, the doctor's cremated remains were buried in Woodlawn Cemetery.

What was once a center for the most unusual medley of gaiety and spirit communion, reporters now found to be "a hushed and darkened" place and

Margery "visibly grieved." At 10 Lime Street, she told them Roy's health had been declining for two years, and in that period the couple had abandoned their endeavors in psychic research. More surprisingly she stated, "I do not contemplate making any efforts to communicate with him in after life."

Dr. Crandon died without the attention he had craved as the Galileo of psychic science. As a surgeon-in-chief until the last year of his life, he earned admiration and affection from some of his medical colleagues. A few in his family, particularly his sister Laura, revered him. Spiritualist researchers, like Mark Richardson, eulogized him as a "valiant warrior." However, even before he became interested in psychic phenomena, Dr. Crandon bore a certain stigma. His first two marriages had been disasters and Margery, the third wife, was suspected of being a gold-digger who wanted her son to attend Harvard and have all the opportunities of a Beacon Hill gentleman.

After Andover, John Crandon became a Harvard-educated physician like his stepfather. Again like Roy, he did his surgical residency at Boston City Hospital, where he took part in dangerous and exacting studies. As both subject and scientist, he lacerated himself and endured scurvy ailments for months in order to demonstrate the curative power of vitamin C. His achievements in medicine notwithstanding, John Crandon was a chronically anxious and unhappy man. He married and had two children, but even within the family he almost never spoke of the phenomena that had haunted him since childhood. Nor did John discuss Margery—except to say that some of her work was "genuine particularly in the early years." Roy he called "a great benefactor and a good father"; he insisted that he "never thought about the possibility of his being a scoundrel," though he said that "there's a bit of the psychopath in everyone."

♦

For all of Roy's agnosticism and scientific training, he developed into an inspired dissident who spoke against materialism even as he lived affluently, and against religion even as he became a leader of the Spiritualist faith. "Psychic Research has about as much to do with religion as golf," he once remarked, while at the same time advocating it as the remedy for agnosticism. He, like those researchers who sought proofs of eternal life, were filled with contradictions, as if none of them could really decide whether they were mystics or scientists.

The Harvard psychologists had speculated that Roy took up Spiritualism as a reaction against his puritanical upbringing. But his extremism and experiments with the supernatural showed that he absorbed more of his heritage than he threw out. He never reconciled his rational bent with the mystical strain in his bloodline—his father the Ethical minister, his grandfather the spiritist healer, and his Pilgrim ancestors who had sought a place unspoiled by immorality and materialism. When those Pilgrims arrived to build their shining city on a hill, they brought their superstitions. And when the beatific vision failed to materialize, the New World was seen from their plagued and besieged settlements as a land where occult forces reigned.

Ah, Sweet Mystery of Life!

*F*ollowing the death of her husband, Margery began to retreat from the friends—the members of the ABC Club—who had been in her circle since the early days of her mediumship. After a while, the worst was conjectured. "The poor woman ended up drunk in a degenerate state in New York, in a cheap hotel," Hudson Hoagland remembered. Actually, what saved Margery from the abject fate of the Fox sisters was that even after her last exposure, she had not lost her patrons. Though he spent as much time at his Maine home as she did in New York, Dr. Crandon had never left her. When he died she had his estate as well as the continued support of Button and Richardson. And yet, few were certain of what became of her.

In the second autumn of the Second World War, Francis Russell, a Canadian journalist and historian, decided to find out. His interest had first been piqued eight years earlier when a colleague at Harvard sat with Margery for a series of convincing séances. So impressed was Russell's friend that he had given the medium a copy of his first novel, *River's End,* and had inscribed within it a tribute to her: *"I have seen, and I have believed."* Later, however, he came to disbelieve. At a subsequent sitting Walter produced an ectoplasmic hand that the novelist, upon feeling it, was certain was that of a corpse— probably a child's. He later theorized that the doctor was sneaking body parts out of the hospital, and warned Russell that it was all a "weird business."

By 1940, no one else was reporting on the case. With all of Europe in flames and America beginning to mobilize, the controversy Margery had caused a decade and a half earlier seemed distant and unreal to Russell. Partially for that reason, he wanted to meet and write about her.* Upon con-

---

* Russell's article would not be published until 1959, in *Horizon.*

tacting Mark Richardson, he was surprised to hear that she still conducted séances. And he was soon invited to one. On a stormy evening Richardson accompanied him to Lime Street for a sitting scheduled for eight o'clock. Guests there were no longer fawned over by servants. Mrs. Crandon herself greeted them. Russell did not see the faintest resemblance, though, to the ravishing medium he had read about. "She was an overdressed, dumpy little woman," he noted, "amiable, yet with a faint elusive coarseness about her that one sensed as soon as she spoke." The social preamble was also a thing of the past. Margery led her guests directly to the séance room, a homely studio with chintz curtains, leather armchairs, imitation Chippendales, and a brick fireplace. There were about ten people standing around. Margery showed them a cup Sir Arthur had given her in recognition of her "heroic struggle" and a photograph Sir Oliver had signed.

"Everybody ready?" she asked. In response the circle gathered around the legendary table. "Let's have a little music," she said. Richardson cranked the Victrola and "Ah, Sweet Mystery of Life" crackled from the horn. The lights went out. The song ended. For minutes nothing happened and Russell felt an unbearable tension. Margery sighed, then began to groan like some dying animal. There was a rush of air, a shrill whistle. Then came the voice that seemed to emanate from above the head of the medium. Walter had arrived for his last recorded visit.

The goal of the sitting had been to contact Dr. Crandon and get wax impressions of his fingerprints. Nothing like that happened. There was much banter between the ghost and guests, but Roy didn't come through when Richardson asked for him. *"Not tonight, Doc,"* said Walter. *"Next time, maybe."* Silence ensued, like a dying wireless broadcast.

Margery asked for light, she yawned and smiled, stretched her fleshy arms—and made no apologies for her diminished powers. As her visitors left, she shook hands with each at the top of the stairway. "You must all come to tea next Sunday," she insisted. "I have a feeling it's going to be important. All of you, next Sunday—but not before five o'clock. I have to see about Roy's grave earlier," she chortled. "The landscape gardeners have made an awful mess of it, planted hydrangeas. Roy hates hydrangeas. Now don't forget—next Sunday at five."

Russell, who never saw her again, was not unaffected by the demonstration. He found Walter's personality and presence to be so tangible—"a kind of poolroom johnny from the other world"—that he speculated, as many had previously, that Big Brother was a secondary personality that emerged when Margery was unconscious; for no one, the journalist surmised, could be that good an actress.

◆

In the last years of her life, Margery spent part of her time with William Button in an apartment on the Upper West Side of Manhattan, just three blocks from where Houdini had resided. Around the time that her relationship with the ASPR president ended, she also had a falling-out with Mark Richardson. Her most enduring supporter, the scientist whom Walter affectionately called *"Doc,"* had become too interfering in his efforts to get her to stop drinking. They became "bitterly estranged," and by 1941 she was often alone at 10 Lime Street. The séances were over. The spirit once known throughout the country was now, like Banquo's ghost, only evident to one person. Many evenings Margery sat with a pad in hand, scratching out messages from Walter. By then she realized something that had been reinforced with every loss or defection: only the dead were there for her. In October, when she knew she was dying, an investigator named Nandor Fodor tried to get her to explain her methods and admit her deceit. Her voice was so weak, many degrees fainter than Walter's whisper, that Fodor couldn't at first hear her response. After asking her to repeat herself, she said "sure," more audibly, then, according to him, "I said you could go to hell. All you psychic researchers can go to hell." With a flicker of her old humor, she smiled, attempted to laugh, and told him, "Why don't you guess? You'll all be guessing . . . for the rest of your lives."

Margery, like Houdini, appeared ready to leave her body on Halloween, but she hung on until 1:30 the following afternoon, when she died at home of liver cirrhosis. That evening Mark Richardson claimed to hear a series of inexplicable raps at his house on Marlboro Street. Four years later, Francis Russell also reported a strange occurrence—which he would use to conclude his story on Margery. It was a stifling August afternoon just after the war and he was walking along Cornhill behind Boston City Hall when he stopped under the shade of the awning of a secondhand bookstand. Browsing through the outdoor rack, he came across a copy of his old friend's novel, *River's End,* among the twenty-five-cent throwaways and opened it. There on the flyleaf was the unblemished inscription: *"I have seen, and I have believed."*

When the Rain Stopped

*M*argery had spoken affectionately of her old rival in her final days. And in addition to the lighthearted, almost amorous, pictures of her and Houdini, she had retained this memory. During the magician's last visit to Lime Street the two of them sat briefly alone in her son's room, where she had suggested that he, clearly exhausted, could take a nap prior to their final Charlesgate séance. While reclining on John's bed, Houdini told her about his most wondrous effect. It had occurred, he recalled, on the Fourth of July at Seacliffe, Long Island—when rain began to fall just as his nephew and other children were preparing to set off fireworks. As the heavens tore loose, the boy turned to Houdini and asked him to make it stop.

"Rain and Storm, I command you to stop," the wizard had ordered, raising his hands in supplication to the rain gods. Moments later the storm ended. When his nephew said it would have stopped anyway, Houdini reversed the hocus-pocus, this time ordering the "great Commander of the rain" to make it pour again. As if willed by Houdini, more rain fell. The children urged him to end it as he had before, but he felt he had pushed his luck far enough. At least, that was what he told Margery.

Proceeding downstairs, Margery could hear the murmuring of Roy, Prince, and Munn—voices had always carried well at Lime Street. After joining them she mentioned Houdini's feat to the dubious men in her parlor. They thought it a coincidence, of course, or a story—only in myth could magicians control the forces of nature. Margery was not so skeptical. Many of her best effects, she said, had come during storms. The more electricity in the air, the better her performance.

Sources

A complete list of sources would encompass an entire book in itself. This is so because the primary source material for *The Witch of Lime Street* was collected from newspaper articles spanning well over a decade, journals and magazines, and extensive correspondences. All incidents depicted and everything in quotations are taken from the record. There are a few passages where conversations are described speculatively: examples of this are Houdini's meeting with Sir Arthur Conan Doyle at Windlesham and his conversation with Margery in her son's bedroom. The dialogue in those scenes is not taken from the mind of the author, but rather from the mouths of the characters—as they expressed these specific thoughts and words on other occasions.

As far as primary source material, the Library of Congress, Washington, DC, has the largest collection of Houdini material in the world—including his personal scrapbooks, newspaper articles, and other material on Margery, as well as much of his correspondence with Sir Arthur Conan Doyle. The transcript of Houdini's appearance before Congress, the Anti–Fortune Telling Bill, can be found in the National Archives. The Georgetown University Library has important material on the assault that killed Houdini, which can be found in Fulton Oursler's papers.

Most of the letters between Le Roi Crandon and Doyle are housed at the Harry Hansom Humanities Research Center, University of Texas, Austin. Transcriptions of correspondences between the *Scientific American* judges and officials can be found in the Kenneth Silverman archive at the Houdini Historical Center at the Outagamie Museum in Appleton, Wisconsin. While in Appleton I met a helpful private collector, Tom Boldt, who had more letters between these individuals, including Houdini's correspondence with Stewart Griscom. Many of the letters between the scientists, ASPR investigators, and the Crandons can be obtained at the

British SPR Archive at the Cambridge University Library—where I had some seven hundred pages of documents copied. Also in England, at the University of London, are the letters of Harry Price, who communicated with virtually all of the characters in *The Witch of Lime Street*.

Many of the newspaper and magazine articles I quote from can be found at the New York Public Library. At the Boston Public Library, I was fortunate enough to cross paths with the librarian Henry Scannell, who has a keen knowledge of how to navigate the many Boston newspapers of the day, and also happens to be the grandson of Dr. Crandon's best friend, David Scannell. In addition, the BPL has the letters between Houdini and Quincy Kilby, among others, and material pertaining to Dr. Crandon's dismissal from Boston City Hospital. Boston University has an archive of old *Boston Herald* articles and many Margery stories can be obtained there. The Harvard Theatre Collection has yet more of Houdini's letters. The A. A. Roback papers can be found in Harvard's Houghton archives.

Invaluable to my research was Mark Richardson's unpublished biography of Margery, *Truth and the Margery Mediumship*, which was located in the Maine basement of one of Richardson's grandsons. Some of the material that Richardson's daughter, Marian Nestor, was preparing for her own book on Margery is held at the Duke University Library; the papers of Joseph Rhine and William McDougall are also among Duke's holdings. Hereward Carrington's papers can be found at the Princeton University Library and Walter Prince's at the University of Maine. Houdini's correspondence with Walter Lippmann can be viewed at the Yale University Library. Here in New York, Lisette Coly, granddaughter of the psychic Eileen Garrett, was generous in providing material on Margery, including newly discovered transcripts. The New York Public Library for the Performing Arts has a copy of Houdini's famous Margery pamphlet. The Conjuring Arts Research Center in Manhattan has a vast collection of digitized Houdini material, including some of his scrapbooks. Finally, there is a nice trove of Margery material at the University of Manitoba in Canada.

The following books were useful in researching *The Witch of Lime Street:*

Houdini

Bell, Don. *The Man Who Killed Houdini.* Montreal: Véhicule Press, 2004.

Christopher, Milbourne. *Houdini: The Untold Story.* New York: Simon & Schuster, 1970.

Gibson, Walter and Morris N. Young, ed. *Houdini on Magic.* New York: Dover Publications, Inc., 1953.

Gresham, William Lindsay. *Houdini: The Man Who Walked Through Walls.* New York: Holt, Rinehart and Winston, 1959.

Houdini, Harry. *The Right Way to Do Wrong: An Exposé of Successful Criminals.* Boston, 1906.

Houdini, Harry. *Miracle Mongers and Their Methods.* New York: E. P. Dutton & Company, 1920.

Kalush, William, and Larry Sloman. *The Secret Life of Houdini.* New York: Atria Books, 2006.*

Kasson, John. *Houdini, Tarzan, and the Perfect Man.* New York: Hill and Wang, 2001.

Kellock, Harold. *Houdini, His Life Story from the Recollections and Documents of Beatrice Houdini.* New York: Harcourt, Brace and Co., 1928.

Meyer, Bernard C. *Houdini: A Mind in Chains.* New York, E. P. Dutton & Co., Inc., 1976.

Silverman, Kenneth. *Houdini!!!* New York: HarperCollins, 1996.

Margery

Bird, Malcolm J. *"Margery" the Medium.* Boston: Small, Maynard & Company, 1925.

Bird, Malcolm J., ed. *The Margery Mediumship: Proceedings of the American Society for Psychical Research.* 2 vols. XX–XXI 1926–1927. ASPR, 1933.

Richardson, Mark. W. *Truth and the Margery Mediumship.* Unpublished.

Richardson, Mark W., and Charles S. Hill. *Margery, Harvard, Veritas: A Study in Psychics.* Boston: Blanchard Printing Co., 1925.

Tietze, Thomas R. *Margery: An Entertaining and Intriguing Story of One of the Most Controversial Psychics of the Century.* New York: Harper & Row, 1973.

---

* Specific secondary source for a few of the letters between Dr. Le Roi Crandon and Sir Arthur Conan Doyle.

The Medicine Show, Dime Museum, and Vaudeville Circuit

Bogdan, Robert. *Freak Show: Presenting Human Oddities for Amusement and Profit*. Chicago: University of Chicago Press, 1988.

Hartzman, Marc. *American Sideshow: An Encyclopedia of History's Most Wondrous and Curiously Strange Performers*. New York: Tarcher, 2006.

McNamara, Brooks. *Step Right Up: An Illustrated History of the American Medicine Show*. New York: Doubleday & Company, Inc., 1976.

Nadis, Fred. *Wonder Shows: Performing Science, Magic, and Religion in America*. New Brunswick, NJ: Rutgers University Press, 2005.

Psychic Debunking

Brandon, Ruth. *The Spiritualists*. New York: Alfred A. Knopf, 1983.

Christopher, Milbourne. *Mediums, Mystics & The Occult*. New York: Thomas Y. Crowell Company, 1975.

Houdini, Harry. *A Magician Among the Spirits*. New York: Harper & Brothers, 1924.

Oursler, Fulton. *Behold This Dreamer!: An Autobiography*. Boston: Little, Brown, 1964.

Proskauer, Julien J. *Spook Crooks*. New York: A. L. Burt Company, 1932.

Proskauer, Julien J. *The Dead Do Not Talk*. New York: Harper & Brothers, 1946.

Rinn, Joseph F. *Sixty Years of Psychical Research*. New York: The Truth Seeker Company, 1950.

Roach, Mary. *Spook: Science Tackles the Afterlife*. New York: W. W. Norton & Company, 2005.

Sir Arthur Conan Doyle

MEMOIRS: *The Wanderings of a Spiritualist* (1921), *Our American Adventure* (1923), *Memories and Adventures* (1924), *Our American Adventure* (1923), *Our Second American Adventure* (1923).

DOYLE ON SPIRITUALISM: *The New Revelation* (1918), *The Vital Message* (1919), *The Coming of the Fairies* (1921), *The Case for Spirit Photography* (1925), *The History of Spiritualism* (1926), *The Edge of the Unknown* (1930), *Pheneas Speaks: Direct Spirit in the Family Circle,* reported by Conan Doyle (1927).

Baker, Michael. *The Doyle Diary: The Last Great Conan Doyle Mystery*. London: Paddington Press (UK), 1978.

Carr, John Dickson. *The Life of Sir Arthur Conan Doyle.* 1949. Reprint. New York, Carroll & Graf, n.d.

Ernst, Bernard M. L., and Hereward Carrington. *Houdini and Conan Doyle: The Story of a Strange Friendship.* New York: Albert and Charles Boni, Inc., 1933.

Green, Richard Lancelyn, and John Michael Gibson. *Letters to the Press: The Unknown Conan Doyle.* Iowa City: University of Iowa Press, 1986.

Lellenberg, Jon, Daniel Stashower, and Charles Foley. *Arthur Conan Doyle: A Life in Letters.* The Penguin Press: New York, 2007.

Lycett, Andrew. *The Man Who Created Sherlock Holmes: The Life and Times of Sir Arthur Conan Doyle.* New York: Free Press, 2007.

Orel, Harold, ed. *Critical Essays on Sir Arthur Conan Doyle.* New York: G. K. Hall, 1992.

Pearson, Hesketh. *Conan Doyle: His Life and Art.* London: Methuen, 1943.

Stashower, Daniel. *Teller of Tales: The Life of Arthur Conan Doyle.* New York: Penguin Books, 2000.

Sir Oliver Lodge

Jolly, W. P. *Sir Oliver Lodge: Psychical Researcher and Scientist.* Associated University Presses, Inc., 1975.

Lodge, Sir Oliver. *Raymond, or Life and Death.* London: Methuen, 1916.

Lodge, Sir Oliver. *Past Years: An Autobiography.* New York: Charles Scribner's Sons, 1932.

Spiritualism and Psychic Research

Aykroyd, Peter H. *History of Ghosts: The True Story of Séances, Mediums, Ghosts, and Ghostbusters.* New York: Rodale Books, 2009.

Berger, Arthur S., and Joyce Berger. *The Encyclopedia of Parapsychology and Psychical Research.* New York: Paragon House, 1991.

Besterman, Theodore. *Some Modern Mediums.* London: Methuen & Co., 1930.

Bird, Malcolm J. *My Psychic Adventures.* New York: Scientific American Publishing Co., Munn & Co., 1924.

Blum, Deborah, *Ghost Hunters: William James and the Search for Scientific Proof of Life After Death.* New York: Penguin Books, 2007.

Bradley, Dennis H. *Towards the Stars, The Wisdom of the Gods.* London: T. Werner Laurie Limited, 1924.

Brian, Denis. *The Enchanted Voyager: The Life of J. B. Rhine, an Authorized Biography.* Englewood Cliffs: Prentice-Hall, 1982.

Carrington, Hereward. *The Physical Phenomena of Spiritualism.* Boston: H. B. Turner & Co., 1907.

Carrington, Hereward. *Eusapia Palladino and Her Phenomena.* New York: B. W. Dodge & Co., 1909.

Carrington, Hereward. *Psychical Phenomena and the War.* New York: Dodd, Mead, 1918.

Carrington, Hereward. *Modern Psychical Phenomena.* New York: Dodd, Mead, 1929.

Carrington, Hereward. *The Story of Psychic Science.* London: Rider and Company, 1930.

Carrington, Hereward. *Psychic Oddities: Fantastic and Bizarre Events in the Life of a Psychical Researcher.* London: Rider and Company, 1952.

Dingwall, Eric. *Revelations of a Spirit Medium.* Arno Press, 1922.

Ebon, Martin. *They Knew the Unknown: Fascinating Case-Studies of Famous Men and Women in History Who Explored the Reality Beyond Our Senses.* New York: The World Publishing Company, 1971.

Estabrooks, G. H. *Spiritism.* New York: E. P. Dutton, 1947.

Garland, Hamlin. *Forty Years of Psychic Research: A Plain Narrative of Fact.* New York: Macmillan, 1936.

Garrett, Eileen. *Adventures in the Supernormal: A Personal Memoir.* 1949. Reprint, Parapsychology Foundation Inc., 2006.

Harlow, S. Ralph. *A Life after Death: Twenty Years of Research on Death, Near-Death Experiences and Survival of the Personality.* Garden City, NY: Doubleday, 1961.

Inglis, Brian. *Natural and Supernatural: A History of the Paranormal.* London: Hodder & Stoughton, 1977.

Jung, C. G. *Memories, Dreams, Reflections.* New York: Random House, 1965.

Lawton, George. *The Drama of Life after Death: A Study of the Spiritualist Religion.* New York: Henry Holt, 1932.

Leonard, Todd. *Talking to the Other Side. A History of Modern Spiritualism and Mediumship.* New York, iUniverse, Inc., 2005.

Machen, Arthur. *The Bowmen and Other Legends of the War.* New York: G. P. Putnam's Sons, 1915.

McComas, Henry Clay. *Ghosts I Have Talked With.* Baltimore: Williams and Wilkins, 1935.

McConnell, R. A., ed. *Encounters with Parapsychology.* 1982.

Moore, Robert Laurence. *In Search of White Crows: Spiritualism, Parapsychology, and American Culture.* Oxford: Oxford University Press, 1977.

Murchison, Carl, ed. *The Case for and Against Psychical Belief.* Worcester, Mass.: Clark University Press, 1927.

Murphy, Gardner, and Robert O. Ballou, eds. *William James on Psychical Research.* New York: Viking Press, 1960.

Oppenheim, Janet. *The Other World: Spiritualism and Psychical Research in England, 1850–1914.* Cambridge, England: Cambridge University Press, 1985.

Owen, Alex. *The Darkened Room: Women, Power, and Spiritualism in Late Victorian England.* Virago, 1989.

Podmore, Frank. *Modern Spiritualism: A History and a Criticism.* London: Methuen & Co., 1902.

Price, Harry. *Confessions of a Ghost Hunter.* New York: Putnam & Co., 1936.

Prince, Walter Franklin. *The Enchanted Boundary: Being a Survey of Negative Reactions to Claims of Psychic Phenomena, 1820–1930.* Boston: Boston Society for Psychical Research, 1930.

Richet, Charles. *Thirty Years of Psychical Research: Being a Treatise on Metaphysics.* W. Collins Sons, 1923.

Shepard, Leslie A., ed. *Encyclopedia of Occultism and Parapsychology.* New York: Gale Research/Avon Books, 1978.

Sinclair, Upton. *Mental Radio.* 1930.

Stuart, Rosa. *Dreams and Visions of the War.* London: C. Arthur Pearson, Ltd., 1917.

Tabori, Paul. *Pioneers of the Unseen.* London: Souvenir Press Ltd., 1972.

Tanner, Amy. *Studies in Spiritism.* New York: Appleton, 1910.

Weisberg, Barbara. *Talking to the Dead: Katie and Maggie Fox and the Rise of Spiritualism.* New York: HarperOne, 2005.

Westwood, John Haynes. *There Is a Psychic World.* New York: Crown Publishers, 1949.

The Times

Allen, Frederick Lewis. *Only Yesterday: An Informal History of the 1920s.* New York: Harper & Row, 1931.

Blom, Philipp. *The Vertigo Years: Europe, 1900–1914.* New York: Basic Books, 2008.

Brittain, Vera. *Testament of Youth: An Autobiographical Study of the Years 1900–1925.* London: Victor Gollancz Limited, 1933.

Dos Passos, John. *U.S.A.* New York: Harcourt Brace, 1938.

Edison, Thomas. *The Diary and Sundry Observations of Thomas Alva Edison.* New York: Greenwood Press, 1968.

Fitzgerald, F. Scott. *Tales of the Jazz Age.* 1922. Reprint. New York: New Directions, 1996.

Leuchtenburg, William E. *The Perils of Prosperity: 1914–1932.* Chicago: University of Chicago Press, 1993.

Mencken, H. L. *A Mencken Chrestomathy: His Own Selection of His Choicest Writings.* New York: Vintage, 1982.

Millard, Candice. *The River of Doubt: Theodore Roosevelt's Darkest Journey.* New York: Anchor, 2006.

Rischin, Moses. *The Promised City: New York's Jews, 1870–1914.* Cambridge, Mass: Harvard University, 1977.

Steel, Ronald. *Walter Lippmann and the American Century.* New York: Little, Brown and Company, 1980.

Sullivan, Mark. *Our Times: The United States, 1900–1925.* 6 vols. New York: Charles Scribner's Sons, 1926–35.

Acknowledgments

I would like to thank the following people who helped me in a long and labyrinthine research pursuit: Tom Ruffles at the Society for Psychical Research, Ellen Berlin at the Boston University Medical Campus, Emily Beattie at the Boston University School of Medicine, Joan Smeltzer at the Department of Psychology at Harvard, Tess Hines at the Mary Evans Picture Library, and Jim Matlock, for providing information on the ASPR. There were a number of professors who shared their knowledge with me, among them: Mark Leff and Carol Symes at the University of Illinois at Urbana-Champaign; Leonard Dinnerstein, an emeritus professor at the University of Arizona; and especially my séance companion, Erika Dyson, at Harvey Mudd College, who generously shared her unparalleled knowledge of and research into the history of Spiritualism. The historian Kirk Davis Swinehart was a most valued friend and colleague. Walter Meyer Zu Erpen was kind enough to provide his information on J. Malcolm Bird. And the psychic researcher Lawrence Leshan shared his time and memories. Some writers on psychic phenomena who were also particularly helpful include Stacy Horn, Mary Roach, and Peter Aykroyd, with whom I had a long and enlightening conversation. On magic, William Kalush at the Conjuring Arts Research Center was of great assistance. And Kenneth Silverman graciously steered me toward all the right places for research material. Houdini collectors who shared their material include Mark Willoughby, John Hinson, Larry Weeks, and Sid Radner. John Cox was also a great friend to the book.

I am extremely grateful to Tom Boldt for providing amazing material from his personal Houdini collection, and for ushering me into the Houdini séance circle. Mark Biscoe offered a very important helping hand and manifested a research gem on Margery. Susan Hunsdon was a tireless proofreader. And, above all, my father, Frederic C. Jaher, contributed in myriad ways to the conception and development of *The Witch of Lime Street*.

Like many authors of history, I have a deep appreciation for the librarians and archivists who have assisted me in obtaining material for this book. In particular, I would like to thank Virginia Appuzo and Lynda Unchern at the Cambridge University Library, Tansy Barton at the Senate House Library at the University of London, Clark Evans and Margaret Keickhefer at the Library of Congress, Elizabeth Dunn at the David M. Rubenstein Rare Book and Manuscript Library at Duke University, Emilie Hardman at the Houghton Library at Harvard University, Jessica Murphy at the Center for the History of Medicine at Harvard Medical School, AnnaLee Pauls at the Princeton University Library, Margaret Sullivan with the Boston Police Department, Elizabeth Bouvier at the Massachusetts Supreme Judicial Court, Randy Roberts at Pittsburg State University, Reina Williams and Julia Gardner at the University of Chicago Library, Gail Fithian, Megan Fleming, and particularly Henry Scannell, at the Boston Public Library, Alan Thibeault at the *Boston Herald,* Alexandra Solodkaya at the Pickering Educational Resources Library at Boston University, Matt Carpenter at the Houdini Historical Center in Appleton, Wisconsin, Jean Cannon, Helen Adair, Rick Watson, and Richard Workman at the Harry Ransom Center at the University of Texas at Austin, Elaine Smith and Desiree Butterfield-Nagy at the Raymond Fogler Library at the University of Maine, Jeanette Mockford, Andrea Martin, and Shelley Sweeney, at the University of Manitoba Archives and Special Collections, Nicholas Scheetz at the Georgetown University Library, and Gina Halkias-Seugling and Anne Garner at the New York Public Library. Finally, on the research front, my deep appreciation goes out to David Smith, formerly of the NYPL, for all his effusive help and for opening up so many literary doors to me. And I am forever indebted to Dr. Warren Platt, the NYPL's former expert on religious studies, for his friendship and invaluable and voluntary service as the research assistant on *The Witch of Lime Street*.

At Crown, I would like to thank Tina Constable, my former publisher, for her zealous interest in the book and supreme effort in acquiring it. My former editor and current friend, Rick Horgan, made a tremendous contribution to *The Witch of Lime Street,* beginning with bringing the book to Crown and continuing to this day. I am deeply grateful to him for his remarkable eye and pen, valued suggestions, and for his unwavering belief in both the material and the author. I would also like to thank my publicist, Dyana Messina, for her sage advice, intense dedication, and prodigious campaign, and the extraordinary marketing team of Danielle Crabtree and Jay Sones for bringing their zest, creativity, and unique talents to the project. Erica Melnichok has also been outstanding in her marketing role. Claire Potter has been thoroughly involved with the book and I am grateful to her for her warm support, keen responsiveness, and superb skills. Robert Siek has been masterful in keeping the project on track. Rachelle Mandik's copy edits were extremely helpful as were Nathan Roberson's editorial suggestions. I would like to thank Derek Gullino and Annsley Rosner as well, and David Drake and Maya Mavjee for their overall leadership. And I am deeply indebted to Molly Stern, my publisher, for her trust and strong direction, for making all the right decisions, and for enthusiastically supporting the project at a critical time. I have been lucky enough to work with not one, but two outstanding editors. Domenica Alioto has been a godsend, and I would be lost without her insight, passionate engagement, friendship, efficiency, and sustaining spirit. She is everything a writer could possibly hope for in an editor and a champion of books.

At Janklow and Nesbit I would like to thank Stephanie Koven, Lynn Nesbit, Cullen Stanley, Dimitri Chitov, Michael Steger, and Lenore Hoffman. At William Morris Endeavor I have come to depend on the wise, reliable, and always good-natured Svetlana Katz. Eve Attermann, Erin Conroy, and Ashley Fox have been of tremendous help. And finally I would like to thank my brilliant and incomparable agent, Tina Bennett, for discovering and developing the project and for bolstering it at every stage with her wonderful energy. Tina had the magical ability to turn an obscure film idea into a valuable literary property and I have no doubt that were it not for her, I would still be reading natal charts, rather than writing books, for a living.

Index

ABOUT THE AUTHOR

DAVID JAHER received a BA from Brandeis University and an MFA in film production from New York University. At NYU, he was the recipient of the WTC Johnson Fellowship for directing. A New York native and resident, this is his first book.